THE BOTTOM WORKER IN EAST ASIA

Studies in Critical Social Sciences Book Series

Haymarket Books is proud to be working with Brill Academic Publishers (www.brill.nl) to republish the *Studies in Critical Social Sciences* book series in paperback editions. This peer-reviewed book series offers insights into our current reality by exploring the content and consequences of power relationships under capitalism, and by considering the spaces of opposition and resistance to these changes that have been defining our new age. Our full catalog of *SCSS* volumes can be viewed at https://www.haymarketbooks .org/series_collections/4-studies-in-critical-social-sciences.

THE BOTTOM WORKER IN EAST ASIA

Composition and Transformation under Neoliberal Globalization

EDITED BY

HIDEO AOKI AND TOMONORI ISHIOKA

Haymarket Books
Chicago, IL

First published in 2023 by Brill Academic Publishers, The Netherlands
© 2023 Koninklijke Brill NV, Leiden, The Netherlands

Published in paperback in 2024 by
Haymarket Books
P.O. Box 180165
Chicago, IL 60618
773-583-7884
www.haymarketbooks.org

ISBN: 979-8-888-90245-5

Distributed to the trade in the US through Consortium Book Sales and
Distribution (www.cbsd.com) and internationally through Ingram Publisher
Services International (www.ingramcontent.com).

This book was published with the generous support of Lannan Foundation,
Wallace Action Fund, and the Marguerite Casey Foundation.

Special discounts are available for bulk purchases by organizations and
institutions. Please call 773-583-7884 or email info@haymarketbooks.org for more
information.

Cover design by Jamie Kerry and Ragina Johnson.

Printed in the United States.

Library of Congress Cataloging-in-Publication data is available.

Contents

Acknowledgements

We would like to sincerely thank Dr. David Fasenfest, scss Series Editor, and Dr. Heidi Gottfried, Wayne State University, for their kind, polite, and patient support commenting on and advising about our contributions for this book.

This book features the works of ten sociologists at the Institute of Social Theory and Dynamics. It took almost three years from the initial concept through planning and deciding on the contributors until final publication. From the beginning, especially once the first manuscripts were drafted, David and Heidi provided invaluable opinions on how to refine the chapters, making a significant contribution as they did so. Finally, in September 2022, we welcomed David and Heidi to Tokyo for a forum to finalize the submissions.

David and Heidi provided comments and advice on two parts of this book in particular. The first is the book's keywords and hypotheses. I, as one of the editors, set a new hierarchical concept – bottom workers – as a keyword of this book. Who are the bottom workers? And why are they now called bottom workers? I clarified the contribution of the bottom worker concept to the study of contemporary labor stratification – and established it as a social science concept – by clarifying how it differs in scope from similar concepts such as lumpenproletariat, the urban poor, underclass, working poor, precariat, and industrial reserve army. To this end, I analyzed the various workers that are undergoing significant transformation in the Global North and the Global South under neoliberal globalization and discussed the necessity and importance of conceptualizing them as bottom workers.

David and Heidi were extremely generous with their time, engaging in detailed discussions during this process. They provided important comments and advice on the formation of the bottom worker concept as a useful tool for labor stratification analysis. Without their comments and advice, the bottom worker concept could not have been established as a keyword of this book, and thus this book would not have been possible.

Secondly, David and Heidi provided comments and advice on the overall composition and flow of the book. In particular, they inspired us not to make this book simply a collection of papers, but to clarify the story of bottom workers in each chapter and the overall story of bottom workers across the ten chapters. Critically, they recommended keeping in mind the same points in question between chapters, setting the keyword "bottom workers" as the basis for the book, and clarifying the relationship between chapters as much as possible. This advice enabled us to organize the entire book as a single work of research in which the ten chapters relate to each other organically.

As such, this book could not have been completed without David and Heidi's invaluable contribution. We would like to again express our gratitude to them. We hope that this book will be an important step forward in this field of study, in that the bottom worker concept will serve as an analytical tool for labor transformation in the contemporary world, and become an established, widely used, and increasingly richly refined concept of social science in labor studies.

We would also like to express our gratitude to the bottom worker informants in five cities and surrounding areas in four East Asian countries. It is their cooperation that made the case studies in this book possible. We would also like to thank Mr. Glen MacCabe for proofreading the text of several manuscripts and for his thoughtful and critical comments and corrections as a translator, and Ms. Josiane O'Brien and the entire team at Brill Publishers involved for their support throughout the process of planning and publishing this book.

Finally, the editors would like to express our respect and appreciation for the efforts of the contributors to this book, Keiko Yamaguchi, Ilju Kim, Jah-Hon Koo, Ashita Matsumiya, Shinji Sakamoto, Tatsuto Asakawa, Keishiro Tsutsumi, and Tsubasa Yuki, for their tenacity and persistence over three years to write and complete their chapters.

Thank you very much to you all.

Tables

Illustrations

Figures

Photographs

Notes on Contributors

Hideo Aoki
is the director-general of the Institute of Social Theory and Dynamics. His research interest includes urban issues such as the urban bottom, yoseba, day laborer, homelessness, squatter, state and informality in Japan and the Philippines. His works related to this interest are *Japan's Underclass: Day Laborers and the Homeless*, (Trans Pacific Press, 2000), "Urban Space of Exception and Urban Homo Sacer: Toward Embodying Critical Informality Theory," *Social Theory and Dynamics* 4 (2023), "Marxism and the Debate on the Transition to Capitalism in Prewar Japan," *Critical Sociology* (2020), "The Global City Hypothesis: Focusing on the New Labor, New Poverty, and Urban Bottom," *Social Theory and Dynamics* 1 (2016).

Tatsuto Asakawa
is professor of Sociology at the Faculty of Human Sciences at Waseda University. His research interests span socio-spatial structures of megacities in East Asia, food deserts problems, and method of social research. His works include "Seoul, Tokyo and Shanghai: An Overview," In: Dukjin Chang, Daishiro Nomiya, Haidong Zhang (eds.) *Urban Development and Social Change in Megacities in East Asia* (Chuo University Press, 2021), *Urban Food Deserts in Japan,* Nobuyuki Iwama, Tatsuto Asakawa, Koichi Tanaka, Midori Sasaki, Nobuyuki Komaki, Masashi Ikeda (eds.) (Springer, 2021), "Changes in the Socio-Spatial Structure in the Tokyo Metropolitan Area: Social Area Analysis of Changes from 1990 to 2010," *Development and Society* 45 (2016).

Tomonori Ishioka
is professor of Sociology at the College of Humanities and Sciences at Nihon University. His research interests span urban marginality, embodiment, and method of ethnography. His works include "Training under Uncertainty: Tempography of Underdog Filipino Pugilists," In: Rinehart R, Kidd J, and Garcia Quiroga, Antonio (eds.) *Southern Hemisphere Ethnographies of Space, Place, and Time* (Peter Lang, 2018), "The Habitus without Habitat: the Disconnect Caused by Uprooting during Gentrification in Metro Manila," *Social Theory and Dynamics* 1 (2016).

Ilju Kim
is assistant professor at the School of International Studies at Utsunomiya University. Her research interests include migration, citizenship, gender, and

immigrant labor market participation. She has written journal articles on marriage immigrants' civic engagement, naturalization, and dual citizenship practices in South Korea. Her current project compares the citizenship acquisition of marriage migrants in Japan and South Korea.

Jah-Hon Koo

currently teaches social welfare policy as a sessional lecturer at Dongguk University in South Korea. Having earned degrees in Social Welfare at Yonsei University and McGill University, he worked as a community social worker at a migrant workers center and a community welfare council in South Korea. His research interests include labor and migration policies, and he has conducted research on the power relations and labor process within the workplace of migrant domestic workers in Canada.

Ashita Matsumiya

is professor of Sociology at the School of Education and Welfare at Aichi Prefectural University. His research interests include immigration, social welfare, social work, and community organization.

Yuko Matsusono

is visiting researcher at the Asian Research Institute of International Social Work (ARIISW), Shukutoku University, Japan. Her field is the urban sociology, focused on community and migration in South-East Asia, especially Thailand. She also conducts research on the process of re-integration of families and community after the nuclear disaster in Japan.

Shinji Sakamoto

is associate professor of International Relations at the Faculty of Intercultural Japanese Studies at Otemae University. His research interests span NGOs in the Global South, empowerment, Japanese rural society, and life history study. His works include "Rivalry and Superiority in Village Woman's Life: A Case Study on Living Improvement in Postwar Japan," *Social Theory and Dynamics* 4 (2023), "The Irony of Facilitation in Participatory Development: A Case Study of a Local NGO in Bangladesh," *Social Theory and Dynamics* 2 (2018).

Keishiro Tsutsumi

is professor of Sociology in the Faculty of Human Studies and Social Sciences at Fukuoka Prefectural University. His research interests include urban poverty issues, multiple debt problems, and community issues. His works include "Facility for the Poor and Community: Facility Conflict and 'Good

Relationships," *Social Theory and Dynamics* 12 (2019), "The Homeless Issue and Citizens: What was Shown and What was Hidden in the Course of an Incident, the Case of Nagai Park Problem," *Shidai Shakaigaku* (*Osaka City University Journal of Sociology*) 5 (2004).

Keiko Yamaguchi

is professor at the Faculty of Education at Tokyo Gakugei University. Her research interests span urban sociology, poverty, and social exclusion. Her works include *Urban Poverty in Globalisation: International Comparison of Homelessness in Big Cities,* Keiko Yamaguchi and Hideo Aoki (eds.) (*Minervasyobou,* 2020), "The Spatial Spread of Poverty in the Megalopolis and the State of Segregation, 1975–2000," In: Masami Iwata and Akihiko Nishizawa (eds.), *Poverty and Social Welfare in Japan* (Trans Pacific Press, 2008).

Tsubasa Yuki

is a PhD student at Tokyo Metropolitan University and also a member of Moyai Support Centre for Independent Living which supports people in homelessness in Tokyo. His research interests include gentrification, urban informality, and social exclusion. He has long been engaging in community activism by and for homeless people in San'ya, Tokyo. His works in Japanese and English can be found at https://researchmap.jp/t-yuki.

Introduction

Bottom Workers in Asia: Japan, South Korea, Thailand, and Bangladesh

Hideo Aoki

Abstract

I address three issues in this chapter. First, I analyze the process by which all workers descend the job hierarchy under downward pressure in neoliberal globalization using the labor informality theory. I criticize the traditional informality theory that thinks of formality/informality as the fixed dichotomy and explain the fluid and complex relationship of formality/informality. Second, I propose a concept of the bottom worker, which is the keyword throughout this book, defining the bottom worker and explaining why it is needed now. To this end, I analyze the changing job hierarchy amidst the increasing downward pressure, and on the other hand, compare bottom worker with related concepts: lumpenproletariat, the urban poor, the underclass, the working poor, and the precariat, and explain again the need of bottom worker concept. Third, I analyze the process of workers' housing deterioration due to urban development using the spatial informality theory. I overview the main points of criticism of traditional informality theory through Ananya Roy's critical informality theory. She emphasizes the supreme role of the state in deciding which space is formal or informal. Finally, I reinforce some scholars' weaknesses when regarding the state as an informal entity negotiating with other stakeholders.

Help! It's lockdown! I cannot peddle because passengers disappeared from the streets. My family is dying of starvation before dying of the pandemic.

A homeless vendor in Manila, Philippines (March 24, 2021)

∴

1   Subject and Methodology

This book examines the growing hardships that contemporary capitalism imposes on people working at the bottom of society, *bottom workers*.[1] To do so, it takes up eight case studies from four Asian countries: Tokyo, Osaka, and Aichi in Japan, Seoul in South Korea (hereafter Korea), Bangkok in Thailand, and Chittagong in Bangladesh. In neoliberal globalization, capital moves across borders, and workers follow it. The state, as needed for capital, mobilizes workers and, at the same time, tightens borders to protect national interests. It controls migrant workers' entry to the country and locks them in dormitories, etc. In this circumstance, what specific hardships do home/foreign workers suffer? How do they manage their hardships and find ways to survive? This book examines their labor, housing, lives, networks, lifeworld, etc., and analyzes their hierarchical changes and those human meanings. As an entry into the subject matters of this book, I overview the macroscopic background of work and lives of bottom workers and propose some theoretical ideas to analyze key issues of this book.

Before going to the main argument, I keep in mind methodological issues in understanding bottom workers and the capitalism that produces them. Marx, concerned with the method of capitalist analysis, writes:

> From the imagined concrete (chaotic real population consisting of various subgroups) one would move to more and more tenuous abstractions until one arrived at the simplest determinations. From there it would be necessary to make a return journey until one finally arrived once more at the population, which this time would be not a chaotic conception of a whole, but a rich totality of many determinations and relations.
>
> MARX, 1857=1986: 37

For Marx, there are two paths to analyzing capitalism. The first is a path of the *upward development* of capitalist description. It is a process that goes from concrete to abstract, that is, from the analysis of chaotic concrete capitalism in reality to the general laws of capitalism (Aoki, 2021: 39). The second is a path of the *downward analysis* of capitalist analysis. It is a process that goes from abstract to concrete, that is, applying the general laws of capitalism to

---

1   The word *bottom* does not have any negative meaning. Rather, I give it a positive meaning: bottom workers who support the whole of society economically from the bottom. Apart from any valued meaning, the bottom is an academic concept that specifies both the bottom rank in the labor hierarchy and the bottom place in the living space.

individual capitalist countries. In this way, Marx was fully aware of how to analyze capitalism.

Kōzō Uno, a Japanese economist, inherited Marx's methodological idea and proposed the *Three-Stage Theory* consisting of three abstracting levels of capitalist analysis: *Pure Theory* which is the highest level of abstraction of the analysis of capitalism (Level A: *Generality*), *Stage Theory* which is an analysis of various types of capitalism in its developmental stage (Level B: *Variegation*), and *Empirical Analysis* which is an analysis of particular forms of capitalism in each country (Uno, 1969). Taking over Uno's theory, I further divided *Empirical Analysis* into two levels of abstraction: theoretical construction of each country's particular capitalism (Level C: *Particularity*) and data analysis of the conditions of each country (Level D: *Factuality*) (Aoki, 2021: 27–28).

Following this scheme, in this Introduction I analyze the historical and geopolitical background of the four country cases (Section 2 of the Introduction), corresponding to Level B of the analysis of capitalism. Next, I analyze the historical and structural uniqueness of each country (Section 3 of the Introduction), corresponding to Level C of the analysis of capitalism. Finally, I analyze the current economic conditions in each country and introduce a summary of the eight chapters of this book (Sections 4 and 5 of the Introduction), corresponding to Levels C and D of the analysis of capitalism.

In Chapter 1, Ishioka outlines key concepts for analyzing the lifeworld of bottom workers. How do bottom workers survive hard work, housing, and life? In Chapter 2, I explore the concepts of the bottom worker and informality. Why do bottom workers appear now? How does the state regulate formal/informal spaces? These two chapters correspond to Level B of capitalist analysis. Finally, keeping in mind this methodology, the contributors of this book examine eight cases of bottom workers in Chapters 3 to 10, corresponding to Levels C and D of the analysis of capitalism. They reveal the hardships that contemporary capitalism imposes on bottom workers and suggest many important findings for urban bottom studies.

In the 2000s, there arose a debate on the analysis of capitalism and the state: *methodological nationalism* and *methodological cosmopolitanism* (Wimmer and Schiller, 2002) (Chernilo, 2006a; 2006b; 2007) (Beck, 2007) (Selchow, 2019). In neoliberal globalization, capitalism in each country is increasingly being affected by global and regional economic and geopolitical conditions. Taking this environment into account, criticisms of methodological nationalism, which view capitalism as an economic system completed within a single country, have arisen and advocated the superiority of methodological cosmopolitanism. In this book, the bottom workers in each country are not only a product of the economic and political conditions inside their country but also reflect global and regional conditions surrounding the country. Any analysis that focuses solely on one country's capitalism runs the risk of overlooking important aspects of the development of capitalism in that country.

However, the same can be said about methodological cosmopolitanism. If one country's capitalism is viewed only in relationships between countries, there is a risk that the uniqueness of the internal reproduction of its capitalism is overlooked. In a word, this is an issue of how to think of the relationship between individualism and universalism in the development of capitalism within one country. I take a balanced perspective and apply a methodology that falls between the two to grasp *both* the particularity and the universality of one country's capitalism. The same is true for the analysis of bottom workers in those countries.

2   Historical and Geopolitical Background: Asian Developmentalism

After the Second World War, the Asian economy achieved remarkable development in a wild-goose chase between Japan, the Newly Industrializing Economies (NIES), the Association of South-East Asian Nations (ASEAN), and China. They received major investments from abroad, carried out state-led industrial development, advanced from import-substitution industrialization to export-oriented industrialization, and earned foreign currency through export expansion to grow their economies. In particular, East Asian countries rapidly industrialized and formed an emerging market zone. East Asia became the 'world's factory.' East Asian economic growth remained unchanged through the global economic downturn of the 2000s (Baker and Gadgil, 2017: 10). By 2015, two-fifths of the world's economic growth was achieved in East Asia.

How has this economic development in East Asia been possible? There are many studies on the background of economic development in East Asia, with a particular focus on the role of the state, broadly under *developmentalism theory*. I focus on this theory and look at the overall development of East Asian capitalism.

Wallerstein supplemented the *dependency theory* that explained world capitalism from two poles of core versus periphery, inserted the intermediate stage of *semi-periphery*, and proposed a *World-System Theory* (Wallerstein, 1974; 1979). He especially focused on semi-peripheral countries that achieved economic development through the state's initiative.[2] The tripolar structure

---

2   Johnson argued that the economic development of postwar Japan was led by the state and
     called the Japanese state a developmental state system (Johnson, 1982: 310). Hayashi argues

TABLE 0.1   Model of state-economy-society

	periphery	semi-periphery	core
Wallerstein's world system theory	dependency theory	developmentalism theory	development theory
type of country	dependent country	developmentalist country	developmentist country
degree of development	under-development	undevelopment	development
market	parasitic	controlled strongly	free competition
role of state	puppet	interveing strongly	retrenched
main policy	subordinate	consolidation autonomy	neo-liberal economy
poverty alleviation	not goal	economic growth first	growth and welfare
civil society	external authoritarian	internal authoritarian	liberal and democracy
mutual relationship	external control	subordinate alignment	independent alignment
main region	Global South in general	East Asia Latin America	US, European Union, Japan

of world capitalism (core, semi-periphery, and periphery) was modeled extensively (see Johnson, 1982; Lall, 1996; Katzebstein, 1997; Nelson and Pac, 1999; Kim, 1999; Kelly, 2008; Stubbs, 2009; Boltho and Weber, 2009; Hayashi, 2010; Dent, 2017). See Table 0.1 for a summary of these efforts.[3]

The core countries consist of industrial capitalist countries, whose markets reflect the free competition of capital. The state's intervention in the market is minimized and neoliberal policies are implemented to encourage free competition among capital and between capital and labor. Based on the economic growth achieved, poverty is alleviated through social welfare. Civil society matures, and freedom and democracy become the central principles of society.

---

that the developmental state will not recede with globalization, which reduces the role of the state, and that the state-led model of economic growth is appropriate for Southeast Asia and China too (Hayashi, 2010: 49).

3   Table 0.1 modified Kelly (2008: 329).

At the opposite end are the countries in the periphery, consisting of former colonies, many of which are located in the Global South. These are colony-like countries, where the core country rules both the market and the state and expropriates resources and labor. A market is a place for the increase in the capital of the core country, and the state acts like a puppet of the core country. Most people are poor, and the peripheral state cannot implement poverty alleviation policies. Thus, these countries in the periphery are permanently deprived of the opportunity for economic development and are left in a state of underdevelopment.

However, after the Second World War, some periphery countries achieved a degree of economic development and moved up to the semi-periphery. In those countries, although there were various deviations, governments were generally characterized by military and authoritarian systems, and state-led economic policies were strongly implemented. The state created national corporations, transferred them to privileged business groups (like *zaibatsu* in Japan), intervened in the market, and regulated domestic *and* foreign capital. Its supreme goal was economic growth backed by military power and political independence. Most people remained in poverty, but poverty was supposed to be alleviated by growth as the economy develops. However, the authoritarian regime prevented civil society from maturing and oppressed civil movements challenging state policies. In Asia, Japan achieved rapid economic growth by establishing an authoritarian political system (the Emperor System) with the slogan Rich Country, Strong Army. Japan was regarded as a successful model for escaping underdevelopment.

In keeping this tripolar model of core, semi-periphery, and periphery, I examine the economic relationships between Japan, Korea, Thailand, and Bangladesh. Two conditions were necessary for a peripheral country to step up into the semi-periphery. First, there were historically and geopolitically advantageous conditions in the world system in which the country was located. Those conditions made possible the coercive economic development *from above*. Second, the world capitalist system that was divided into regional economic zones and the economic growth of one country was a product not only of its domestic economy but also of the regional economic zone in which it existed, based on its historical and geopolitical conditions.

3   East Asian Countries

Developmentalism theory emerged out of an analysis of East Asian economic development. After the Second World War, Japan quickly recovered from the industrial devastation caused by its war defeat, and through rapid economic growth, it became a core country. It was followed by Korea, Taiwan, Hong Kong, and Singapore. Korea started as a peripheral country after two wars (the Second World War and the Korean War) and then became a developed country. How could Japan and Korea achieve such astonishing economic growth? Both countries had common historically and geopolitically advantageous conditions (see Cumings, 1984; Gottfried, 2018; Doucette and Park, 2018).[4]

3.1   *Japan*

By the end of the Edo era (1603–1868), that is, before the Meiji Restoration (1868–89), rural industry, especially the cotton industry, had developed, cities had developed, and a commodity economy had permeated the whole of Japan. *Samurai* had studied at clan schools and common people had learned reading and writing at temple schools, accumulating human resources. These established the conditions for the development of capitalism in Japan. After the Meiji Restoration, the state established state-run corporations and privatized them to form big business groups (*zaibatsu*) which then mobilized a high-quality workforce. These processes were made possible by authoritarian state control and strong military force. Japan extended its power overseas, occupied colonies in East Asia, and formed a monopoly economic zone. These prewar experiences became a prerequisite for rapid economic recovery after the Second World War. After Japan's defeat, it was included in the military, political, and economic spheres of the United States, and was made as a frontline bulwark against communist aggression in the Cold War. In particular, the special economic demand associated with the Korean War became a springboard for economic recovery (Gottfried, 2018).[5] In this way, Japan achieved

---

4 Doucette and others analyzed the state-led urban gentrification in East Asia and found it to be a product of economic growth that was a function of historical and geopolitical conditions (Doucette and Park, 2018). On the other hand, Shin asserted that it is important to look at the shadow side of the state-led urban formation, such as forced exclusion through gentrification (Shin, 2019: 8–9). State-led forced economic development has resulted in a distorted society such as wealth imbalance among citizens, traffic, environmental issues such as pollution, etc. Doucette and Shin are referring to different aspects of developmentalism.

5 Gottfried argued that Japan's economic growth was the product of the historical and geopolitical conditions that Japan had, more than due to the Confucian collectivist ethos and feudal status structure (Gottfried, 2018: 426), consistent from the perspective of regionalism. At the same time, the *spirit* of Japanese capitalism, that is, the ethos of the human that led the historical and geopolitical conditions to economic growth is another important condition that made economic growth possible. 'Economy and ethos' are the key factors that unravel the reproductive structure of capitalism, and so seem to be an unavoidable theme to study. But it has to be analyzed along with the analysis of historical and geopolitical conditions. In

rapid economic growth and by 1968 its gross national product surpassed that of Germany to become the second-largest in the world, making it one of the core countries.[6] Japan's economic development was called 'Japan's Miracle' after Japan had been devastated when losing the war in 1945.[7]

3.2   Korea

Developmentalism theory explained how Korea followed Japan and ceased being an underdeveloped country. Korea followed a trajectory of economic growth surprisingly similar to that of Japan (Cumings, 1984: 4). Korea had distinct historical and geopolitical conditions that gave them advantages in economic development. First of all, Korea was under the influence of one powerful nation, Japan before the war and the United States right after the war. Korea comprised the entire Korean Peninsula at that time. Before the war, Japan transferred powerful colonial capitalism to Korea (and Manchuria) (Cumings, 1984; Kohli, 1994). Japan brought steel, chemical, and hydroelectric power to Korea creating a large industrial infrastructure in Korea. An economic zone was established in prewar East Asia, with Japan at the core, Korea at the semi-periphery, and Manchuria at the periphery (Cumings, 1984: 13). Japan's policy in Korea was to increase agricultural production and foster light and heavy industry.[8] Almost all products were taken by Japan and exported to Japan's zone of economic control and beyond. In this way, Japanese rule differed from the colonial management of Western countries, which exclusively expropriated agricultural products. As a late-imperialist country without large colonies, Japan could only compete with the big economic and military powers of Western countries by transplanting industries to its colonies and expropriating their products.

Japan also transferred its military and political governance to Korea to manage its colonies as an imperialist ruler. These historical experiences formed

---

postwar Japan, there was a big debate between Marxists and Weberians over the 'economy and ethos' of Japanese capitalism.

6   Japan's GDP was overtaken by China in GDP in 2010 and has remained in the third rank in the world since then (World Bank, 1960).

7   This understanding of Japan's economic development is an orthodox one. It is not easy to understand the development of Japanese capitalism in the postwar economic growth in the same way as the prewar capitalist debate among Marxist economists and historians (Aoki, 2021). Marxist, Weberian, and modernization theorists mixed in a debate over the economic development of prewar and postwar Japan.

8   In Korea, large-scale heavy industry was transplanted and the formation of conglomerates. But this was not the case in Taiwan, where the economic system was mainly micro- and medium-scale, centered on light industry (Lall, 1996: 126).

the basis for the postwar economic development of Korea as it inherited the colonial residues of the light and heavy industrial bases, economic structure (*Chaebol* of Korea, etc.), and management systems (e.g., corporate familism). Therefore, the postwar economic development of Korea did not start from zero.[9] Korea achieved rapid economic growth under authoritarian state-led economic policies. The Korean people's strong desire to learn and their entrepreneurial spirit supported this rapid growth (see Nelson and Pac, 1999; Boltho and Weber, 2009). This state of mind and the ideology of developmentalism (Kim, 1999: 10) were a legacy of prewar colonial capitalism.

After the war, Korea, like Japan, received enormous economic assistance from the United States as a bulwark against communist aggression in the Cold War. And just as Japan's economy grew by leaps and bounds due to the special demand for Korean War, the Korean economy grew by leaps and bounds due to the special demand for Vietnam War (Stubbs, 2009: 7). Korea promoted state-led economic policies (developmental dictatorship) under strong state leadership. The collaboration between the state and conglomerates (*chaebol*) became the basic condition for economic development. The Korean economy was devastated during Korean War, but it recovered quickly and started to grow rapidly once again after the Vietnam War. It was only after economic growth was achieved that the authoritarian system collapsed that the political system began to be democratized in 1987.

Developmentalism theory has been controversial with regard to Korea. While developmentalism theory emphasizes the role of colonial experiences in economic development in postwar Korea. However, there has been criticism that Japan took all the fruits of Korea's modernization and industrialization, and they were not a product of Korea and its people. Alternatively, an influential theory emphasizes the endogenous and nationalistic development of Korean postwar capitalism as a revival of the native and national capitalism that had already developed *before* the colonial period and that has developed again *after* the oppressive and deviant development of the colonial period (see Chang, 1973; Pak, 1988; Eckert, 1991; Haggard et al., 1997). These theories view the colonial economy negatively, as an abnormally biased economy that hindered the sound modernization and industrialization of the Korean

---

9   There is historical revisionism in Japan, which justifies colonial rule in Korea on the ground that Japanese colonial rule helped to modernize and industrialize Korea after the war. Developmentalism Theory has nothing to do with such ideological conservatism. Developmentalism theorists are, contrary to revisionists, critical of Japanese imperialism that expropriated all the wealth from colonial Korea and the postwar authoritarian state system of oppression of human rights in Korea.

economy. I explain the development of Korean capitalism by looking at both external, cosmopolitan factors which developmentalism theory emphasizes, *and* internal and particularistic factors which endogenous development theory emphasizes.

3.3   *Thailand*

Thailand in Southeast Asia was an underdeveloped country with no colonial experience. After the war, Thailand had a state-led economic system that fostered state-owned corporations with economic assistance from the United States and Japan.[10] However, from the 1970s onward, Thailand turned to an open economic system and has since achieved steady economic development, stepping up to become the fifth *Asian Tiger* following Korea, Taiwan, Hong Kong, and Singapore.

Thailand, a historic kingdom, has not been interrupted by its open-door policy even after several military coups. In 1967, Thailand became a member of ASEAN and promoted the industrialization of agriculture (agribusiness), positively introducing foreign capital, inviting multinational corporations with its cheap labor, fostering industrial and service industries, and achieving long-term stability. In the past, Thailand was a country with a 'triumvirate' consisting of the military, bureaucracy, and Chinese capital, and its economic policies were centered on state-owned corporations.[11]

With the transition to an open economy, the state put in place a soft ruling system that promoted economic policies. And it actively adapted to the global economic environment which promoted such an open economic system. As a member of ASEAN, Thailand, along with Malaysia and Indonesia, achieved economic development and deepened regionalism with trade relations throughout Asia. Despite the kingdom's historical bureaucracy and its military's power in local affairs, Thailand implemented an open economy and a soft political system indirectly supported by the state. In this way, Thailand achieved stable economic growth over a long period and became a developed country under a different model of economic development compared to other East Asian countries, known as the 'Thai Miracle.'

---

10   Information on the capitalism of Thailand was based on the work of Donner, (1991; 2009), Krongkaew (1995), Dixon (1999; 2001), and Warr (2009).

11   The Vietnam War's special demand in the 1960s and 1970s (military and economic aid from the US) and capital investment from Japan and Korea triggered the growth of the economy of Thailand. Afterward, Vietnam opened up to trade in 1986 and began to compete with Thailand for low-wage labor. It promoted Thailand to shift to capital-intensive industries (Dixon, 1999: xi).

3.4   *Bangladesh*

Bangladesh in South Asia finally gained independence in 1971 after being colonized by the Mughals, the United Kingdom, and Pakistan. Today, it remains still one of the poorest peripheral countries in the world and its poverty incidence is said to be higher than in Nepal.[12] The historical fetters of the former colony weigh heavily on Bangladesh's economic development. Its capitalist class base includes landowners, national capitalists, and neo-colonial foreign corporations. Its economic policies are implemented by the military and bureaucratic dictatorship of elites who coordinate interests and the politics of beneficence and patronage.

Bangladesh's economic growth began with aid from the United Kingdom, which was the formerly suzerain state, the United States, and the European Union. Bangladesh has seen gradual reforms in agricultural technology and foreign capital investment aimed at exploiting its cheap labor. In the 1990s, more than 5 million people migrated to the United Kingdom, the United States, and the Middle East, and their overseas remittances became one of the foundations of the building of the national economy. As a result, the economy has grown and the incidence of poverty has been reduced to some degree. The state actively modernized the domestic system, and when economic donors adopted neoliberal policies, the state responded by deregulating the system, allowing foreign capital to invest and multinational corporations to enter the country. This, in turn, improved agricultural technology, created an industrial base and expanded imports and exports.

In this way, Bangladesh is no longer a stagnant peripheral country, but still remained an underdeveloped country. At present, Bangladesh is facing the challenge of how to survive in cooperation with India and China of the BRICS (Brazil, Russia, India, and China), which are rivaling the United States position of political and economic power in South Asia. However, Bangladesh's political structure and bureaucracy have not been easily modernized, with rampant bribery of politicians and bureaucrats and their monopolization of profits, preventing the return of the fruits of economic growth to people and stifling a flexible response to changes in the international environment. Will Bangladesh remain family capitalism and pseudo-democracy, or expand into a fair and equal civil society? Will Bangladesh remain on the periphery, or follow Thai's trajectory and become another Asian tiger in the future? Bangladesh is a laboratory for a peripheral country to get rid of colonial fetters, democratize

---

12   Information on Bangladesh capitalism was based on Robinson and Griffin (1974); Bhuiyan et al. (2005); Lewis (2011), and Khan (2015).

politics and achieve economic growth, and it is a model for state-led nation-building that is different from Japan, Korea, and Thailand.

4   Current Economic Conditions

What is the state of capitalism today in each of these countries, given the historical and geopolitical backgrounds? Here I consider Japan, Korea, Thailand, and Bangladesh in the context of Wallerstein's *World System*. However, even if Japan is one of the core countries and Bangladesh is one of the peripheral countries, it is not easy to decide where Korea and Thailand lie between the core and semi-periphery. After the Second World War, Japan was the first country to achieve economic development, followed by Korea, Thailand, and Bangladesh at present. Then, how can I confirm that those countries achieved economic development? Table 0.2 sketches out the major indicators of the population and economy of these four countries.

While Japan's population declined from 2005–2020, Bangladesh's population growth rate is staggering. Demographics reflect the economic situation of the population. If I take GDP as an indicator of economic growth more generally, the size of GDP is inversely proportional to the growth rate of the population, and the growth rate of GDP is directly proportional to that of the population. The same is true for GDP and the actual urbanization of the population. The ratio of urban population to the total population is highest in Japan, followed by Korea, Thailand, and Bangladesh; the contrast between the high ratio in Japan and the low ratio in Bangladesh is striking.

Every country's population is becoming more globalized. The number of foreign immigrants is on the rise in all countries. There are several causes for the increase in the number of foreigners, but the main cause seems to be the increase in the number of foreign workers coming into the country looking for work. The countries of origin of these foreigners vary. The top three immigrants in Japan are from China, Korea, and Viet Nam while they come from China, Viet Nam, and Thailand for Korea, Myanmar, Laos, and Cambodia for Thailand, and Myanmar, Malaysia, and China for Bangladesh. All four countries have received many immigrants from neighboring countries. It is a historical pattern that has been further reinforced to form immigration blocs in East and Southeast Asia.

Behind the increase in immigrants is a shortage of labor in the host countries. Japan accepted workers from Asian countries in the 1980s, then Nikkei (immigrants of Japanese descent) from Brazil and Peru in the 1990s and has been increasing the number of workers from Asia ever since. Korea had sent

TABLE 0.2   Main indexes of population and economics of four countries

		Japan	Korea	Thailand	Bangladesh
Total population	2005	128.3	48.7	65.4	139.0
(millions)	2020	126.5	51.3	69.8	164.7
Growth rate (2005–2020)		-1.4	5.3	6.7	18.5
Urban population (%)	2005	86.0	81.3	37.4	26.8
	2018	91.6	81.5	49.9	36.6
International migrants	2005	2.01 / 1.6	0.49 / 0.8	2.16 / 3.2	1.17 / 0.8
living in (millions / %)	2019	2.50 / 2.0	1.16 / 2.0	3.64 / 5.2	2.19 / 1.3
GDP per capita (US	1985	11,477/5.2	2,521/ 7.7	775 / 4.6	211 / 3.0
dollars) / growth rate	2018	39,082/0.8	33,622/2.7	7,274 / 4.1	1,671 / 7.9
Trade volume (billions of	1995	779.1	260.2	127.2	8.8
US dollars)	2019	1,426.5	1,045.5	450.5	100.3
Major trading partner	partner 1	China 41.5	China 41.9	Japan 31.3	US 24.3
(export + import, 2010)	partner 2	US 25.6	US 20.2	China 24.3	China 17.5
	partner 3	Korea 8.1	Japan 15.1	US 16.3	Germany 13.8
Major trading partner	partner 1	China 42.6	China 46.4	China 33.1	China 30.5
(export + import, 2019)	partner 2	US 31.2	US 25.9	Japan 23.9	US 14.9
	partner 3	Korea 6.6	Japan 9.5	US 20.1	Germany 14.4
Employment by	Agriculture	4.5 / 3.4	7.9 / 4.8	38.7 / 31.2	51.1 / 37.7
economic activity 2005	Industry	28.0 / 24.1	26.9 / 25.0	22.4 / 22.5	13.9 / 21.6
/ 2020	Service	67.6 / 72.6	65.2 / 70.2	38.9 / 46.3	35.0 / 40.6
Toulist visitor arrivals	1995	3,345	3,753	6,952	156
(1,000)	2018	31,192	15,347	38,178	1,026 (2017)
Internet usage rate of	2000	30.0	44.7	3.7	0.1
population	2018	91.3	96.0	56.8	15.0

The author made a table from the following:
United Nations, 2020, *Statistical Yearbook*, 63rd issue
United Nations, 2018, *Statistical Yearbook*, 61st issue

labor to the former West Germany, the Middle East, and Japan from the 1960s to the mid-1980s, but later became a receiving country accepting workers from Asian countries (Haruki, 2010: 93). Japan and Korea mobilized foreign workers for high-value-added manufacturing such as electronics or auto assembly. This allowed capital to accumulate at a higher level and many foreign workers to send their earnings back to their families.

Thailand has sent many workers to the Middle East since the 1980s and approximately one million workers to the Middle East and Asian countries ever since (Japan Institute for Labor Policy and Training, 2004). On the other hand, Thailand has accepted many workers from neighboring countries, especially Myanmar. "Large numbers of Burmese have been migrating to Thailand for work, from the tens of thousands in the early 1990s to some three million today" (Arnold, 2019: 85). Immigrants in Thailand work in low value-added industries such as garment, shoe manufacturing, and bicycle assembly, especially in Special Economic Zones along the border with Myanmar. Not only informal workers but even regular workers are underpaid and without social security coverage, so work is not a means of escape from poverty.

The Bangladesh government has a policy of encouraging overseas migration as a major source of foreign currency, with a cumulative total of 13 million migrant workers by 2020, who have migrated to the Middle East such as Saudi Arabia, United Arab Emirates, and Oman, with the rest going to Asian countries such as Malaysia and Japan (JETRO, 2022). Migrants to the Middle East are often unskilled workers in the service, manufacturing, and construction industries under poor working conditions and low wages. The number of migrants and the remittance amount sent home fell as the economic environment in the Middle East deteriorated due to lower oil prices and the coronavirus, in addition to rising unemployment among overseas migrant workers and the suspension of the dispatch of new migrant workers. As a result, the destination of migrant workers has been gradually shifting from the Middle East to Asian countries.

GDP per capita is an important indicator that informs the economic power of any country. It is highest in Japan, followed by Korea, Thailand, and Bangladesh. In 2018, Japan is 23.4 times larger than Bangladesh. Conversely, the GDP growth rate order is reversed, higher in Bangladesh, followed by Thailand, Korea, and Japan. Since the mid-1980s, there has been a significant decline in the growth rates of Japan and Korea. By contrast, Bangladesh has maintained a growth rate in the 7% range, and Thailand's has been somewhere in between. While the disparity in GDP growth ratios has been narrowing among the four countries, the real disparity in GDP per capita has been widening. Compared to Japan, the real gap went from $8,956 in 1985 to $5,460 in 2018 in Korea (only

Korea is shrinking), from \$10,702 to \$31,808 in Thailand, and \$11,266 to \$37,411 in Bangladesh even though the growth rate of Japan's GDP is low.

Considering exports and its partners, Japan and Korea export industrial products (IT-related products, etc.), Thailand exports industrial product parts and agricultural products, and Bangladesh exports mainly clothing and agricultural products to China, Europe, and the United States. Regarding the imports and their partners, all four countries tend to import industrial product parts, mineral resources, and agricultural products from Asian countries such as China, India, and Japan. Moreover, in measures of trade value (the totality of export and import), China was either the first or second-largest trading partner for all four countries in 2010. Yet, by 2019, China was the largest trading partner for all, with a larger share of trade value, followed by the United States. While the share of the United States is not small, the tilt toward the Asian trade bloc, led by China, is evident. Both Japan and Bangladesh are increasing China's role as major trading partners. On the other hand, beyond trading with each other, the countries are further connected through supply chains. Japanese and Korean capital has moved and extended supply chain networks to neighboring countries. Thailand and Bangladesh are destination countries for foreign capital. Japanese and Korean orientation of capital investment pivoted east to facilitate the business climate conducive to capital's search for low-wage opportunities in the location of low valued-added manufacturing *supply chains* reaching into poorer neighboring countries.

Behind the movement of people (migrants) and goods (trade) across national borders, the supply chain is developing into a new global production system of capital. It organizes the flow of capital across national borders, from the procurement of raw materials for production to the sale of products. Unlike the unilateral relocation of factories by capital to developing countries, this is a combination of the capital of industrial countries of A (e.g. Japan) and B (e.g. Korea) in their production activities. Bottom workers become incorporated into a transnational production system and become more systematically deprived. Capital expands supply chains to manufacture low-value-added products and expropriates low-wage labor in developing countries. In this way, capital reorganizes the world as 'one factory.' This changes the meaning of national borders, which greatly affects the movement of people and goods across those borders.

Changes in the structure of the labor market are instructive; from 2005 to 2020 the ratio of the population working in agriculture decreased in all four countries, but it still accounted for more than 30% of the population working in agriculture in Bangladesh and Thailand. In the manufacturing sector, the ratio in Japan and Korea has decreased, in Thailand, it has remained at the same level over time and in Bangladesh, which has begun industrializing, it has increased. The service industry has been increasing in weight overall (a general shift to the service economy); in Japan and Korea, it accounts for about 70% of the working population, while in Thailand and Bangladesh, it remains at about 40%. The tendency of the labor market in these countries roughly corresponds to the rate of urbanization of the population as seen above.[13]

The number of foreign tourists has increased in all four countries, especially in Thailand. However, tourism development in Bangladesh seems to be in its infancy. Attracting tourists is one of the important pillars of economic development for these four countries. The ratio of Internet users per capita measures the growth of the technological infrastructure. Korea's users increased remarkably, followed by Japan, and with a marked gap compared to Bangladesh while Thailand falls in the middle. IT products such as the Internet reflect the economic power of Japan and Korea.

In conclusion, the population and economic figures reveal the following trends. First, the measures of both the population and economy are moving in the same direction for all four countries as the economy is growing in each country: there is increasing urbanization of the population, more international migration, GDP and trade growth, increased employment in the service sector, and more tourists and Internet users.

Second, nevertheless, the economic gap between Japan, Thailand, and Bangladesh remains unchanged even as Korea grows does not change the pace of the real GDP and the size of the trade. This lets us know that each country's economic rank and relative position in the regional economy is becoming more fixed and shows that Wallerstein's framework is still valid.

Third, trade partners are shifting from the United States to China and other Asian countries. According to another source, this corresponds to the tendency of cross-border labor migration. As with the tendency of immigration in each country, the same is true for out-migration. In the past, Asian countries mainly sent their labor force to the Middle East, the European Union, and the United States. But now, the destination has shifted to those countries in East Asia facing a shortage of labor (RTWG, 2008: v). Five of the top 10 destinations where East Asian countries send workers are other East Asian countries (Managing

---

13   Capital and labor are becoming concentrated in cities (Baker and Gadgil, 2017: 18). Second
      and third generations of immigrants are born in cities, which have few ties with the rural
      areas, but many remain bottom workers like their first generations having ties with rural
      areas. And now, this phenomenon has spread from central cities to local cities. The pov-
      erty issue also is spreading from central to local areas of the countries.

and Ahsan, 2014: iii). Asian countries are becoming increasingly interdependent within the region, both in terms of capital and labor.[14]

5   Content of This Book

The purpose of this book is to analyze the hardships that neoliberal globalization imposes on the bottom workers in Asian four countries that hold the current/historical and geopolitical conditions. The following chapters analyze eight cases of bottom workers. Those bottom workers are the product of capitalism in four countries with historical and geopolitical backgrounds. I will outline the structure of this book and a short explanation of each chapter. This book has three parts: Part One consists of Chapters 1 and 2 in which key concepts and frameworks for bottom worker analyses are presented focusing on their jobs, housing, and lifeworld, which the following chapters analytically refer to. Part Two, consisting of Chapters 3 to 7, focuses on case studies from these countries. Finally, Part Three, Chapters 8 to 10, focuses on bottom people and the problems of homelessness.

In Chapter 1, "The Lifeworld of Bottom Workers: Dormitory Labor, Households, and Interpretive Labor," Ishioka sketches out three analytical themes impacting bottom workers: (i) jobs for those who work for companies living in dormitories provided by those companies, (ii) households in which bottom workers live within interconnected units, rather than as individuals, and (iii) interpretive labor as a constant and often subtle work of interpretation, of endlessly imagining others' points of view. These are frames for analyzing the lifeworld of bottom workers in Japan, Korea, Thailand, and Bangladesh. Corresponding to the macro-structural analysis of the working conditions of bottom workers, residences, and lives in the next chapter, he points out the importance of the micro-analysis of subjective meanings of living conditions of bottom workers such as values, perspectives, and lifeworld by developing

---

14   There have been some movements to deepen interdependence as the capital and trade of Asian countries shift to the regional market. Those movements have appeared and disappeared all the time. However, "whatever the reason, the difference, in the early years of integration, between a Europe that was backing off from integration and an Asia growing closer is a striking demonstration of the institutional weakness of Asian regionalism. It is thus symptomatic that, in the words of Andrew Pollack, APEC's name does not end with 'organization,' 'association' or a similar noun this attests to the reluctance of its founders to make it an institution (like EU)" (Katzebstein, 1997: 22).

these three themes, and proposing the perspective, framework, and methodology for the whole of the book.

In Chapter 2, "Labor-Spatial Informality of Bottom Worker," Aoki examines the processes of the downward pressure on working people and the constant pressure on their living spaces under neoliberal globalization using critical informality theory and compares the concept of the bottom worker with five often-used concepts that capture people who work at the bottom of society: lumpenproletariat, the urban poor, underclass, working people and precariat. Aoki explains why the bottom worker is now necessary in place of those concepts, as the term captures those workers strongly affected by downward pressure. Finally, he examines spatial informality theory in the context of Roy's critical informality theory and clarifies the role of the state in creating spatial informality.

Part Two consists of five case studies of the bottom workers in Tokyo (Metropolitan Area), Aichi and Osaka in Japan, Seoul in Korea, Bangkok in Thailand, and Chittagong in Bangladesh. They analyze the various aspects of the labor and spatial precariousness or informality of bottom workers. They are classified into four subparts focusing on each chapter's *main* theme.

Subpart One is *Informality of Labor* consisting of Chapters 3 and 4. In Chapter 3, "Transformation of Bottom Workers in the Hotel Industry: Reproduction Structures in Dormitory Labors," Yamaguchi explores the case of a Japanese-style hotel (ryokan) in a hot spring resort near Tokyo. She focuses on the composition of the workforce, the working content/conditions, and the conditions of residence (living-in dormitory), analyzes the transformative process of work quality from multi-skilled service workers regarded as semi-care labor to single-skilled work and general service labor, and change of worker from middle-aged and elderly women from the domestic regions to young dispatch workers and recently young foreign students/trainees from Asian countries in the rationalization of the hotel management under globalization and the transition to an increasing service economy.

In Chapter 4, "Stuck in Bottom Work: Filipina Marriage Migrants' Work Lives in South Korea," Kim and Koo examine the downward occupational mobility of college-educated Filipino marriage migrants in Seoul (and two cities in the southern part of Korea), whose jobs are closed circuits of precarious labor: deskilling factory work, informal economy of survival entrepreneurship and invisible work, and reskilling English teaching. They examine the process by which marriage migrant women are inter-sectionalized in social positions based on gender, ethnicity/nationality, and class, and trapped in the low-skilled and precarious job circuit of the labor market without the possibility of upward mobility.

Subpart Two is *Informality of Space* consisting of Chapters 5, 6 and 7. In Chapter 5, "Exclusion and Inclusion of Japanese Latin Americans: a Case Study on Public Housing in Aichi Prefecture," Matsumiya examines a case of Japanese Latin Americans who were massively laid off from the factories due to the COVID-19 disaster and have lived together with Japanese residents in the public housing estate in Aichi where a car company has employed most Japanese Latin Americans living in Japan. He examines the process by which foreign workers were included in the communities by participating in community activities with the support of inclusive community practices and building mutually supportive relationships with Japanese residents and concludes that the local community can become a resource not only for living their daily lives with Japanese residents without problems but also for assisting them regarding labor and education.

In Chapter 6, "Changes in Asian Cities and Bottom People: the Case of Participatory Community Development in Thai Slums," Matsusono examines cases of slum development policies and their implementation in Bangkok and determines the effectiveness of each slum policy. For that, she focuses especially on participatory community development as a bottom-up approach with which the slum residents participate in organizing communities and solving problems, especially regarding the residence rights and conditions and community discourse (endogenous development, self-help, and populist democratization), examining their effectiveness. Finally, she questions the feasibility of participatory community development to prevent the exclusion of the poor by stabilizing land leasing in the changing economic environment in which many gentrifications are going on.

In Chapter 7, "Microcredit Enhances Informalization: the Outcome of Governmentality in Chittagong Fisher Society," Sakamoto takes a case of fishermen/women living in Chittagong and being caught in a trap of microcredit. He examines the paradox that although microcredit was supposed to help the destitute, it became a trap of deprivation and further poverty of the destitute due to the practices facilitating microcredit operation with the repayment responsibility for collecting debt strictly and the mobilization of neoliberal ideology incompatible with fishermen/women's non-capitalist morals. And he examines key theories such as subsistence ethic, governmentality, capitalocentrism, and poverty capital associated with the microcredit issue, and critically discusses the implications of the paradox of microcredit in contemporary capitalism.

Part Three focuses on the living conditions of homeless bottom people. In Chapter 8, "The Spatial Distribution of Bottom Workers in Tokyo," Asakawa examines the spatial/geographical distribution of bottom people as the poor consisting of foreign population, temporary workers, part-time workers, unemployed workers, single-person and elderly households, and those whose last education was a high school graduate living in the Tokyo Metropolitan Area (TMA), whose income is less than half of the median household income in Japan. He examines their time-series variation in demographic trends such as urbanization using administrative macroscopic statistical data drawing social atlases and the causes of their spatial/geographical distribution. This chapter includes a wide range of poor/bottom people in TMA, and so those findings are useful as a background understanding of the subsequent analyses of homelessness in Tokyo, especially in Chapter 9.

In Chapter 9, "The Past and Present Homeless Issues in Japan," Tsutsumi overviews the development of the homelessness issue in Japan since the 1990s using data from surveys in Osaka with the highest number of rough sleepers in Japan. In this chapter, he clarifies that the labor market forcing workers to become homeless has changed, that this change has resulted in the diversification of homelessness from elderly single men who were construction day workers to include middle-aged, young workers who are unemployed and engaged in precarious jobs and even women, and that it accordingly has become necessary to expand the concept of homelessness from rough sleepers to homeless people in Japan. Finally, he emphasizes that the concept of the bottom worker is needed as a concept that includes these diverse workers from day workers, working poor, and precariat as seen from the history and spread of the homelessness issue in Japan.

In Chapter 10, "Displacement and Entrapment of Bottom People in Tokyo: Urban Regeneration and Slow Violence," Yuki examines the process in which homeless people are displaced from the streets to the low-rent housing in the suburbs of Tokyo and entrapped to San'ya, a *yoseba* which is a district of day workers in Tokyo's inner city. Gentrification of low-rent housing has resulted in its suburbanization. The government has implemented policies of providing homeless people with welfare and housing them to keep them off the streets. Homeless people are given priority to move into low-rent housing in the suburbs of Tokyo. However, social services and employment opportunities are insufficient there. They leave low-rent housing and move to San'ya because it has flophouses, social services, and employment opportunities. Yuki examines such a process of displacement (forced mobility to the suburbs of Tokyo) and entrapment (forced immobility in San'ya) of homeless people.

References

Aoki H (2021) Marxism and the debate on the transition to capitalism in prewar Japan. *Critical Sociology* 47(1): 17–36.

Arnold D (2019) Migrants, mobilizations, and selective hegemony in Mekong Asia's special economic zones. In: Breman J, Harris K, Lee C K. and van der Linden M(eds) *The Social Question in the Twenty-first Century: A Global View.* Berkeley: University of California Press: 77–97.

Baker J and Gadgil G (eds) (2017) *East Asia and Pacific Cities: Expanding Opportunities for the Urban Poor.* The World Bank.

Beck U (2007) The cosmopolitan condition: why methodological nationalism fails. *Theory, Culture and Society* 24(7–8): 286–290.

Bhuiyan A H A, Faraizi A H and McAllister J (2005) Developmentalism as a disciplinary strategy in Bangladesh. *Modern Asian Studies* 39(2): 349–368.

Boltho A and Weber M (2009) Did China follow the East Asian development model? *The European Journal of Comparative Economics* 6(2): 267–286.

Chang K S (1973) Kankoku no kindaikakatei niokeru syomondai [Various problems of economic development in Korea: problems in the modernization process of Korea]. *Kansai Daigaku Shogaku Ronshu* 1: 41–60.

Chernilo D (2006a) Social theory's methodological nationalism: myth and reality. *European Journal of Social Theory* 9(1): 5–22.

Chernilo D (2006b) Methodological nationalism and its critique. In: erard D and Krishan K (eds) *The SAGE Handbook of Nations and Nationalism*: Chap.11.

Chernilo D (2007) *A Social Theory of Nation-state: The Political Forms of Modernity beyond Methodological Nationalism.* London: Routledge.

Cumings B (1984) The origins and development of the Northeast Asian political economy: industrial sectors, product cycles, and political consequences. *International Organization* 38(1): 1–40.

Dent C (2017) East Asia's new developmentalism: state capacity, climate change and low carbon development. *Third World Quarterly* 39(6): 1191–1210.

Dixon C (1999) *The Thai Economy: Uneven development and internationalization.* London: Routledge.

Dixon C (2001) The causes of Thai economic crisis: the internal perspective. *Geoforum* 32: 47–60.

Donner R (1991) Approaches to the politics of economic growth in Southeast Asia. *Journal of Asian Studies* 50(4): 818–849.

Donner R (2009) *The Politics of Uneven Development Thailand's Economic Growth in Comparative Perspective*, Cambridge: Cambridge University Press.

Doucette J and Park B G (2018) Urban developmentalism in East Asia: geopolitical economies, spaces of exception, and networks of expertise. *Critical Sociology* 44(3): 395–403.

Eckert C (1991) *Offspring of Empire: The Kocnang Kims and the Colonial Origins of Korean Capitalism, 1876–1945.* Washington D.C.: University of Washington Press.

Gottfried H (2018) The phoenix rises: Tokyo's origins as a global city. *Critical Sociology* 44(3): 421–435.

Haggard S, Kang D and Moon C (1997) Japanese colonialism and Korean development: a critique. *World Development* 25(6): 867–881.

Haruki I (2010) The development of foreign worker policy in Korea and its background (Kankoku no gaikokujin-rodosha seisaku no tenkai), *Journal of Humanities and Social Sciences* (Jinbun-Shekaikagaku Ronshu) Tokyo: Toyo Eiwa Jogakuin University 28: 93–104.

Hayashi S (2010) The developmental state in the era of globalization: beyond the Northeast Asian model of political economy. *The Pacific Review* 23(1): 45–69.

Japan Institute for Labor Polocy and Training (2004) *Tai niokeru kaigai dekasegi to gaikokujin ukeire no genzho* [Current Situation of Overseas Migration and Acceptance of Foreign Workers in Thailand] https://www.jil.go.jp/foreign/jihou/2004_11/thailand_01.html (referred to on September 2022).

JETRO, Japan External Trade Organization (2022) *Overseas Business Information,* https://www.jetro.go.jp/biznews/2020/07/25daf7f71b7a8e9b.html (referred to on September 2022).

Johnson C (1982) *MITI and the Japanese Miracle.* Redwood City: Stanford University Press.

Katzebstein P (1997) Introduction: Asian Regionalism in Comparative Perspective. In: Katzenstein P J and Shiraishi T(eds) *Network Power: Japan and Asia.* Ithaca: Cornell University Press: 1–44.

Kelly R (2008) No 'return to the state': dependency and developmentalism against neoliberalism. *Development in Practice* 18(3): 319–332.

Khan A R (2015) *The Economy of Bangladesh: A Quarter Century of Development,* London: Palgrave Macmillian.

Kim W B (1999) Developmentalism and beyond: reflections on Korean cities. *Korea Journal* 39(3): 5–34.

Kohli A (1994) Where do high-growth political economies come from? The Japanese lineage of Korea's 'developmental state.' *World Development* 22(9): 1269–1293.

Krongkaew M (eds) (1995) *Thailand's Industrialization and Its Consequences.* London: Macmillan Press Ltd.

Lall S (1996) Paradigms of development: the East Asian debate. *Oxford Development Studies* 24(2): 111–131.

Lewis D (2011) *Bangladesh: Politics, Economy and Civil Society.* Cambridge: Cambridge University Press.

Managing R and Ahsan A (2014) *International Migration for Development in East Asia.* The World Bank.

Marx K (1857=1986) "Introduction to Criticism of Economics," *Marx & Engels Collected Works*, vol. 28th, translated and edited by the Editorial Commissions of Marx & Engels Collected Works, prepared jointly by Lawrence & Wishart Ltd., International Publishers Co. Inc., and Progress Publishers, Moscow.

Nelson R and Pac H (1999) The asian miracle and modern growth theory. *The Economic Journal.* Royal Economic Society 109: 416–436.

Pak I (1988) Gendaikankokusyakai no seikaku to hattendankai nikansuru kenkyu [Research on the character of contemporary Korean society and developmental stage]. *Shakaikagak*: 41: 90–138.

Robinson E A G and Griffin K (eds) (1974) *The Economic Development of Bangladesh within a Socialist Framework.* London: Macmillan Press Ltd.

RTWG, Regional Thematic Working Group on International Migration including Human Trafficking (2008) *Situation Report on International Migration in East and South-East Asia, International Organization for Migration.* Regional Office for Southeast Asia.

Selchow S (2019) Starting somewhere different: methodological cosmopolitanism and the study of world politics. *Global Networks* o(o): 1–20. https://onlinelibrary.wiley .com/doi/abs/10.1111/glob.12262.

Shin H B (2019) Asian urbanism In: Anthony O (eds) *The Wiley Blackwell Encyclopedia of Urban and Regional Studies* Wiley-Blackwell Encyclopedias in Social Sciences Wiley: 1–19.

Stubbs R (2009) Whatever happened to the East Asian developmental state? The unfolding debate. *The Pacific Review* 22(1): 1–22.

United Nations, Department of Economic and Social Affairs (2020) *Statistical Yearbook, 63rd Issue.*

Uno K (1969) Shakaikagaku toshiteno keizaigaku [Economics as a Social Science]. Tokyo: Chikuma Shobo.

Wallerstein I (1974) *The Modern World-System: Capitalist Agriculture and the Origins of the European World-economy in the Sixteenth Century.* Amsterdam: Academic Press.

Wallerstein I (1979) *The Capitalist World-economy: Essays.* Cambridge: Cambridge University Press.

Warr P (2009) Poverty reduction through long-term growth: the Thai experience. *Asian Economic Papers* 8(2): 51–76.

Wimmer A and Schiller N (2002) Methodological nationalism and beyond: nation-state building, migration and the social sciences. *Global Network* 2–4: 301–334.

World Bank, *Historical GDP by Country*, Statistics from the World Bank, 1960. https://en .wikipedia.org/wiki/World_Bank_historical_list_of_ten_largest_countries_by_GDP (referred to in August 2022).

PART 1

Understanding Bottom Workers

∵

CHAPTER 1

The Lifeworld of Bottom Workers

Dormitory Labor, Households, and Interpretive Labor

Tomonori Ishioka

Abstract

This chapter sketches out three analytical themes – *dormitory labor, households*, and *interpretive labor* – that are useful while studying the lifeworld of bottom workers in East Asia. Dormitory labor is a form of work and living wherein bottom workers live in a company dormitory. The provision of a company dormitory is a way for the company to control and contain the worker. This form takes freedom away from workers' lives and leaves them vulnerable. The concept of household is designed to emphasize that bottom workers live with their families or roommates rather than as individuals. Households can survive by multiplying the incomes of several members and coordinating everyone's work schedules to share childcare and care for the elderly. The precarious work and care schedules create inequality and disadvantage. Interpretive labor illustrates the 'lopsided structure of the imagination' (Graeber 2013) but this chapter uses this concept more subversively: minorities could 'notice' the hidden social code for domination through their everyday interpretive labor what the majority could 'see but unnoticed'. The point allows us to get in touch with the bottom worker's skill and insight to survive in the situation.

This chapter sketches out three analytical themes – *dormitory labor, households*, and *interpretive labor* – that are useful while studying the lifeworld of bottom workers in East Asia. Besides the structural aspects discussed in the next chapter, the study of bottom workers requires an approach that is conscious of the lived experience of people in this situation. The chapter discusses why such a micro-qualitative approach to their lifeworld is essential if we are to properly study such workers.

This book is the collective work of members of the Institute of Social Theory and Dynamics (ISTAD). The Institute, of which I am also a member, has for many years been committed to the study of bottom workers like homeless people, day laborers, and migrant precarious workers. Our aim is not merely to shed light on the poverty and precarious existences steadily emerging behind the façade of today's "affluent society" (Latouche, 1993) and "economic miracle" (Johnson, 1982). Instead, ISTAD is concerned with finding ways to expand the concept of 'work' to encompass the reality these people face; the homeless picking up empty cans to scrape out a living, day laborers lining up in front of job agencies early in the morning in the hope of finding a job for that day, jobless people cooking and selling food at street stalls. All of this labor is an important component of work. In Japanese academia, the literature on work has focused on workers in formal employment relationships with capitalists. From this orthodox perspective, when the homeless collect discarded cans, this is not considered work but a miserable activity. Such a perspective regards bottom workers' labor as something lying outside of the production, circulation, and exchange process of commodities in market capitalism. However, the contributors to this book adopt a theoretical position that views the picking up of empty cans as meaningful legitimate work, at least in terms of how "humans as social beings are said to produce their own life, their own consciousness, their own world" (Lefebvre, 1991 68).

As the young Marx wrote in 1844, "although the working class cannot gain so much as can the class of property owners in a prosperous state of society, no one suffers so cruelly from its decline as the working class" (Marx, 1959). Even more than the working class, the work and living conditions of the homeless and day laborers – i.e., of some bottom workers – have seen a significant transformation during periods of economic decline. In Japan, for example, some of those worst affected by the Global Financial Crisis in 2008 were migrant worker communities (Vogt, 2014). Another example of bottom workers suffering in 2008 is the homeless who gathered at the Tent City for the Jobless organized in Tokyo as part of the 'winter struggle.' When capitalists lose money, workers also lose money, and yet in reality it is the bottom workers and their households who lose out the most. The same scenario can be observed during the ongoing COVID-19 pandemic. Focused on the reality faced by the underprivileged, ISTAD scholars have made considerable effort to study how the economic changes in East Asia have also added to the misery of bottom workers.

This chapter expands on the themes used in this study of the lifeworld of bottom workers: *dormitory labor, households*, and *interpretive labor. Dormitory labor* is labor for a company in which workers stay (and are confined) in dormitories provided by the company. Since capitalists find it difficult to keep labor obedient, the technique of regulating workers by providing them with dormitory has long been in use in Japan. Alongside wages and working hours, many job advertisements mention the availability of company dormitories. Bottom workers, including dispatched workers and single mothers raising children, often respond positively to such recruitment methods. For them, finding an apartment in a major city near their workplace is very problematic, making company dormitories an appealing solution. However, these dormitories are a way for companies to confine their workers. The company has control over their lives during both their work and 'free' time. This practice is not simply a 'welfare' initiative but also forms part of the labor management strategy (Andrijasevic, Pun and Sacchetto 2022). The dormitories represent a "spatial fix" (Harvey 2003) for colonizing workers' life world. Moreover, if a company goes bankrupt workers lose their jobs and housing all at once. Improving the situation faced by bottom workers requires this shelter–job–poverty link to be broken.

Household focuses on the fact that bottom workers live within an interconnected unit rather than as individuals (Wallerstein, 1983). Bottom workers survive by bringing together the formal and informal labor of the household members and coordinating everyone's work schedules so as to share the care associated with the elderly and children. In Chapter 5 of this book, Matsumiya presents a detailed life record of Latin American communities in Japan. These are the communities in Japan that have suffered the most during the global financial crisis and the COVID-19 pandemic. Faced with strong downward pressures, residents of Japan who are Latin American have managed to survive by drawing on the communal nature of their households and communities. Yet, at the same time, those incapable of forming a household, for instance homeless elderly men, have become more marginalized. Working-class households can generally be divided into three categories: 1) those with the labor and income of a breadwinner; 2) those which bring together the labor and incomes of multiple household members; and 3) people who are unable to form a household due to labor and family problems and are thus even more disadvantaged. This last group drift away from dormitory labor and become nomads, as illustrated by the elderly Japanese female dormitory labors in *ryokan* (Japanese inns) that Yamaguchi discusses in Chapter 3, and the male day laborers considered by Tsutsumi in Chapter 9.

Wallerstein argues that the capitalist system encourages the endless accumulation of capital by supporting the formation of households, and one can find vast literature on unpaid and informal work in these households (Ueno, 2009; Osawa 2002). Still, research on how household life impacts precarious schedules has only recently emerged (Kalleberg, 2009). New research themes have arisen with respect to not only the household economy, but also household temporality. In Japan and other East Asian countries, as well as the Western context, work schedules create inequality and disadvantage (Gerstel and Clawson, 2014; Rubery et al., 2005). Precarious schedules affect households' daily rhythm. The requirement for husbands to work overtime calls for a readjustment concerning management of the household, with the burden carried by wives who often must work at night, creating difficulties with preparing dinner for the children or taking care of a bedridden older adult. The precariousness of work schedules thereby creates unpredictability in household life. The "flexploitation" (Gray, 2004) of employment makes the scheduling of household life unstable and uncertain. Household members, especially wives, are forced to accept "the normal unpredictability" (Gerstel and Clawson, 2014 35).

Thus, bottom workers are oppressed in the modern world, suffering from work and life patterns which are unsure and with unanticipated schedules. Yet, bottom workers are not passive beings but active selves, possessing the agency to change their situation. *Interpretive labor* is a concept elaborated by David Graeber (Graeber, 2012), which illustrates that "while those on the bottom of a social ladder spend a great deal of time imagining the perspectives of, and genuinely caring about, those on the top, it almost never happens the other way around" (ibid: 119). For instance, in the workplace, a person in a tenured position does not have to worry about a nonpermanent assistant, nor understand they have particular priorities and struggles. However, the assistant must constantly seek to understand what the tenured staff member is thinking about at any given moment and wondering what the situation requires. Graeber argues that this interpretive labor (re)produces a "lopsided structure of the imagination," although I prefer to use the concept more subversively: those on the bottom of a social ladder can notice through their everyday interpretive labor what those at the top can see but do not notice. Methodologically, ISTAD members specialize in intensive ethnographic research and in-depth interviews. These methods allow us to obtain deep insights into the attitudes of bottom worker form in oppressive situations.

In what follows I explore these three concepts in greater detail to provide a blueprint for reading the case studies presented in the rest of this book. It covers a wide range of subjects, and while seemingly fragmented, the topics in these chapters form a coherent whole providing a perspective of the lives of bottom workers and people. Through the analysis provided in this book, we show the importance of these three concepts for understanding and interpreting the difficult conditions and barriers often faced by bottom workers.

1   Dormitory Labor

There are three major phases in the development of dormitory labor in Japan, and its impact on bottom workers: the developmental state, postindustrialization and globalization, and the shelter-job-poverty link that keeps workers in the bottom of society. Each will be discussed in turn.

1.1   *Developmental State*

The developmental state (or developmentalism) has been a frequent topic of sociological debate in the East Asian context (Hayashi, 2020; Gottfried, 2018). Issues like Japan's rapid economic growth, the rise of Asia's newly industrialized economies through export-oriented industrialization, and the formation of megacities and large-scale transport networks (e.g., the bullet train in Japan) have been examined in terms of the developmental state. When considering post-war economic development, the East Asian context differs significantly from the European context in that the labor required for development has been sourced domestically rather than from abroad. In East Asian states and societies with relatively large domestic populations, the developmental states have exploited domestic labor from remote areas.

The phenomenon of dormitory labor emerged amid the reliance on domestic migration of the developmental state. Young workers (especially men) from peripheral regions often found 'group employment', where all the young residents from a provincial village went to work together in the same metropolitan factory after completing secondary education (Kase, 1997). These workers could not afford to rent apartments and the company thus solved the workers' housing precarity by providing dormitories. These dormitories guaranteed housing, but also became a place where total control was exercised over their daily routines. Dormitory labor is a dual system of welfare protection and labor mobilization. Companies monitored young workers and disciplined them, not only in the factory but also back in the dormitories. Work and housing are hence deeply intertwined for dormitory labors.

The 1964 Tokyo Olympics can also be interpreted from the perspective of dormitory labor. The Olympics was a symbol of the Japanese developmentalist nation (Ogasawara and Yamamoto, 2016; Ogasawara and Yamamoto, 2022). The stadiums, railways, and highways for hosting the Olympics were built by workers recruited by factories and construction companies that provided dormitories. Each morning, employers bussed their workers from the dormitories to the work sites.

The young men who live in dormitories are not expected to live there for the rest of their lives; ideally, after living there for a few years, they marry and build their own house in a metropolis. The term "my home" is emblematic of Japan's period of rapid economic development and strongly associated with the typical story of success: a poor man from a remote area who works, saves money, gets married, builds a house, and brings up his children in a city (Mita 2010). The dormitory is therefore considered a place for young workers to *temporarily* stay. A life fitting this story is socially considered to be 'normal' while a life outside of it is seen as having 'failed' or 'abnormal'.

Labelling one's life as 'abnormal' is heavily gendered. Men who are economically deprived and cannot form families tend to become day laborers. As
Tsutsumi shows in Chapter 9, day laborers are used as a disposable labor force
in the Japanese construction industry that, in part, provides special dormitory
districts called "Hanba" for male construction workers. Female day laborers
are often single mothers who work part-time while receiving state subsistence
payments. Some of them work in hotels on a dormitory labor basis while raising their children there (see Chapter 3). The Japanese developmental state has
in this way functioned by recruiting young workers from outlying areas using
the dormitory labor system. The state and society then exclude from the mainstream those workers who are single and economically deprived, despite being
at an age (in their 30s and 40s) when they can support themselves and others
by labeling them as 'abnormal.'

Dormitory labor has also been used for recruitment to remote areas. In particular, in Japan's coal-producing regions like Hokkaido and Kyushu, mining
companies provided dormitories, schools, community centers, and even local
currency for domestic migrant workers. In contrast to factories and construction companies in cities that demand young single workers, coal mines in outlying areas encouraged family migration. Single workers often abandoned the
coalfields once they saw how harsh the work was. However, if a family had
migrated together, the children would go to the local schools and the wife
would join local mothers' networks. This embeddedness made it difficult for
a worker to simply quit their job and move to another area. Here again, we
see that the dormitory labor arrangement was used to secure workers. Finally,
the idea of migrating together with one's family was also promoted in industrial towns. Not only companies, but also local governments built many public housing units in which families who had migrated from the countryside
took up residence. The most representative case of large-scale public housing
is found at Aichi Prefecture where the Toyota Motor Corporation is located
(Matsumiya discusses the public housing situation in Aichi in Chapter 5).
Toyota, a 'private' company nurtured by the Japanese state, has supported the
building of vast public housing estates in Aichi Prefecture.

1.2   *Post-industrialization and Globalization*
The arrangement of dormitory labor has been transformed in post-industrial
society and as a result of the subsequent globalization of the economy. Three
significant changes are evident. The first is the importation of immigrant
workers. Like other East Asian countries, for decades Japan did not rely on
unskilled international migrant labor. Yet, ever since the 1990s and due to the
impact of economic globalization, the immigration of unskilled Brazilians and

Peruvians of Japanese descent has been accepted (where the limitation on accepting only ethnically Japanese people is a sign of Japanese nationalism). These people work and live in public housing estates in industrial regions like Aichi Prefecture. As Toyota shifted the focus of its production to the Global South, the number of Japanese workers decreased. This led to more vacancies in public housing estates that were gradually filled by Japanese Latin American workers. The growing share of immigrant residents in public housing is the first change in Japan's post-industrial society.

Second, aging of the domestic population saw "welfare" not "labor" become the key word in social policy, leading to a profound change in day labor. Whereas day laborers used to work and live in certain districts of large cities, such areas have since become residential spots for welfare recipients. In the past, labor movements flourished in the day labor districts where such workers lived, at times leading to unrest and riots. These were movements of resistance against exploitation by the state, capitalists, and *yakuza* (mafia), all greedy for profit (Yang et al., 2014). Today, in these same areas, the unemployed elderly – mostly single men – live on welfare benefits. The day labor districts that emerged based on dormitory labor have been transformed into areas dominated by a living-without-a-job situation (see Chapter 10).

Third, individualization and social exclusion have fostered further deterioration in the lives of bottom people. Bottom workers have become characterized by a common form of dormitory labor, which results in a spatial concentration of people in similar situations. In Chapter 10, Yuki uses the 'entrapment' concept to examine this phenomenon of bottom workers congregating in districts. Simultaneously, modern information technology means that all job vacancies are now advertised online and accessed using mobile phones, with recruitment and hiring being conducted on an individual basis. In the past, prospective workers were recruited by referrals from those already working, forming social networks and communities that enabled solidarity as bottom workers. Now, the spread of mobile phones means these communities and networks are unnecessary, exacerbating the bottom worker's isolation and individualization. This trend towards atomization has led to weaker relationships with peers and the loss of a community on which they could rely should they become impoverished. Their survival strategies were once based on communities and social networks, yet today these workers are confined to institutionalized frameworks like the welfare provided by local governments and NGOs. The individualization of bottom workers is a major issue and how to empower them is a crucial social priority.

The individualization of the bottom worker is creating a "pinpoint migration path" (Tanno, 2013). In a world where community and social networks have been lost, living in a company-owned dormitory means spending every working day shuttling back and forth between the dormitory and the work site, but without having any access to broader information about the city in which the dormitory is located. Bottom workers do not know much about the city they are living in and, if out of work, they wander from one company dormitory to another. Importantly, they do not move from one *city* to another (e.g., Tokyo to Kanagawa), but in a 'pinpoint' fashion from one *specific address* to another, e.g., from Minami-Senju, Arakawa Ward, Tokyo to Tsurumi Ward, Yokohama, or Kanagawa, where many dormitories can be found. The world of such workers is entirely formed by their company and life around the dormitory; they have no social contact with the wider urban area.

1.3   The 'Shelter–Job–Poverty' Link

The arrangement of dormitory labor has supported the Japanese developmental state 'from below.' This method of labor management enabled young single domestic workers to become housed in metropolitan and regional industrial towns such as in the coalfields. In remote industrial areas, local currency was even issued to restrict the exodus of workers (Ikeda, 2012).

The arrangement of social life produced by dormitory labor differs from what constitutes the basis of modern society. As Goffman notes, people in modern societies separate the places in which they sleep, play, and work. In so doing, without an overall rational plan, people create a social life that crosses multiple domains. At work a woman is a teacher, at home a mother, at the community center she is a member of a music club. We all play multiple roles within a single day, and we place ourselves under different kinds of authority. This woman relies on mobility and transportation to connect these three spheres. It is precisely the physical division of these spheres that makes commuting by train or car necessary. Total institutions are those in which the barriers separating such spheres are removed and people spend 24 hours a day in one place under a single authority (Goffman, 1961.

Dormitory labor has structured the social lives of bottom workers by way of arrangements akin to total institutions. When workers live in a company dormitory, the barriers between sleep, play, and work disappear, with every facet of life being under company control. Moreover, if a person's work contract is terminated, they lose not only their job but also their shelter. Companies have leveraged this fear of eviction to retain workers, even if these workers are dissatisfied with their pay and conditions. The following chapters in this book draw on a range of examples to illustrate the implications of the 'shelter–job–poverty' nexus.

2 Households

The economic and social conditions of bottom workers means that they must live within an interconnected household rather than sustain themselves as individuals, which both sustains them but also reflects serious challenges. Households reflect important interconnected aspects of social life, but also require individuals in the household to manage precarious working schedules. When bottom people cannot form households they remain more vulnerable and have a more difficult time sustaining themselves. Bottom people maintain an informal relationship to the public sector leading to unclear arrangements regarding social supports and tax obligations. Finally, due to recent changes in immigration law, many bottom households depend on and reflect international connections.

2.1 *An Interconnected Unit of Social Life*

Bottom workers tend to survive as households rather than as individuals. They often have two or three jobs per working day (Chapter 4). A typical example is a bottom worker in Osaka who is a construction worker during the day and a part-time worker at a 7-Eleven in the evening. Another is a female worker in Tokyo who works several jobs to survive: a hotel cleaner in the morning, a supermarket cashier in the afternoon, and a hostess in the evening. By forming a 'household' comprised of husbands, wives, and other housemates, individual workers living on the margins make life possible by combining their income and managing unpaid care work in support of each other.

Wallerstein's series of studies (1983) on the household is instructive. He is focus is directed on not with the question of how proletarianization has progressed in many parts of the world, but how it has been deliberately prevented from occurring. His answer is that capital can procure cheaper labor by keeping many people in the Global South semi-proletarianized, enabling further capital accumulation. This insight is also useful in the East Asian context. Semi-proletarian drudgery and domestic work by homemakers have been quickly actualized in this region with a population that is much larger than for countries in Western Europe.

The bottom worker's lifeworld is closely entwined with such semi-proletarian labor (day labor, migrant labor, apprentice labor). Since they cannot survive on their own wages, they can only make living possible by forming households of various combinations of family and friends. Matsumiya (Chapter 5) examines the formation of a mutual support community among Japanese Latin Americans living in a public housing complex (small lodgings ranging from 50–60 m² or 538–645 ft² in floor area), where they live as households. The husbands are workers holding a contract with a Toyota subcontractor's factory, while the wives work part-time and take care of the children. Then, when the husband loses his job, the family joins another household and lives together for a while. Such flexible changes in the composition of households are developing in the lifeworld of bottom workers.

However, the household is also the unit where bottom workers demonstration how they manage by applying their survival strategies (Matsuda, 1998). People can make a life for themselves in this unit even if their income and livelihoods are unstable and unpredictable. Therefore, single people who cannot form households, such as the homeless and day laborers, constitute an even more vulnerable population among bottom workers. This issue further exacerbates the individualization and social exclusion described in the previous section to the point that they can only rely on the government for support in times of need. The fact that they have access only to institutionalized support underlines their isolation from society in general. Moreover, receiving government support entails extensive paperwork and being constantly monitored by government officials. People who do not want their autonomy to be violated often refuse to accept such support. They must necessarily survive by working informally on the streets, with no one to depend on. Thus, a distinction arises between bottom workers who can form a household and those who find that step particularly challenging. The former has the capacity, by depending on others, to survive in the event of illness or unemployment. The latter do not, and hence their survival is directly threatened when jobs disappear during a recession or pandemic.

2.2   Precarious Schedules

The neo-liberalization of East Asian societies has considerably impacted bottom-worker households. In particular, "the web of time" (Gerstel and Clawson, 2018) in household life has become disrupted. Household life not only requires earning enough income to cover expenditures but keeping up with the pace of daily life. The confusion in the organization of time created by neo-liberalization has seen household life become vulnerable.

One example comes from literature on work schedules (Kalleberg, 2009; Gerstel and Clawson, 2018). Similar examples can be found in many East Asian bottom-worker households. Suppose that a doctor employed at a medical care provider decides to work overtime to attend to a patient. This decision also changes the time that the nurses and other staff can go home resulting in impacts on households who make careful decisions on work schedules. Others in their household now must adjust their own web of time as a result. Doctors often live in households with homemakers or housekeepers who easily cope with sudden changes to working hours. However, nurses and other staff must prepare meals for their children and care for the elderly who may live with them in the extended household. Bottom-worker households share their income and manage their daily life by coordinating time. This impact on a bottom worker household's web of time has become standard, a situation known as "normal unpredictability" (Gerstel and Clawson, 2018).

This leads to a discussion of the fundamental aspects of "flexploitation" (Gray, 2004). There is a vast amount of research on the precariousness of employment born out of neo-liberalization (Bourdieu, 1999; Schram, 2015; McRobbie 2020). This literature has problematized the exploitative nature of allocating work to flexible hours, highlighting the destabilizing effect on individual workers' incomes and attitudes. Flexploitation not only affects individuals but households too, forcing a readjustment of the household's "web of time." This relational aspect helps in explaining how flexploitation creates unpredictability in a household. The complex distribution and timing of roles within the household – who cooks the food and when, puts the children to bed, who does the shopping and takes care of the elderly – all must be readjusted; in the example above, the doctor's simple decision to work overtime creates a cascading impact on the overall household's time management. Bottom workers with limited household resources are thus forced to manage their day-to-day lives in uncertain and unpredictable circumstances. In Chapter 4, Kim and Koo analyse how Filipino women who have immigrated to Korea upon marriage are forced to work amid insecure conditions in the Korean labor market, and demonstrates how the uncertainty of the household's "web of time" forms a key aspect of the lives of these women.

2.3   *Informality and Households*

While discussed more fully in the next chapter, informality is a helpful concept that captures the governmental relationship between the state and bottom workers. In particular, the 'grey operation' of the tax system is closely linked to the household formation of bottom workers. For instance, in Japan, whether the income tax (at a rate of 10%) is collected from the earnings of bottom workers – such as the hotel workers in Chapter 3 or day laborers in Chapter 9 – was a grey area and unclear. This also applied to night work (e.g., cabaret club workers), which is a major industry in Japan's large cities. In many instances, the work undertaken, mainly by bottom workers, was implicitly exempt from income tax; instead, such work was deeply connected to informal and non-state groups like the yakuza and fixers. The state tacitly allowed the yakuza to profit from these industries while mobilizing them (as well as formal security forces such as the police) to suppress any attempts by bottom workers and local people to challenge the state's authority. This state grey-area policy of not collecting income tax from bottom workers led to a collaborative relationship between the state and the Japanese mafia.

To ensure they could carry on with their daily lives, bottom worker households sought protection from the local bosses (yakuza), rather than the police. Yet, this informal arrangement changed following neo-liberalization and shift to digital-based government functions in Japan. The introduction of the "My Number Card" and the subsequent digital management of an individual workers' tax payments, all of the income made by bottom workers – previously tacitly treated as a grey area – became subject to income tax. The result is that bottom workers are now subject to the state's strict levy of income tax, and consequently the influence of the yakuza and fixers – who had previously acted patrons and protectors – has weakened. This situation evokes the concept of "poverty capital" (Roy, 2010) which, based on studies in India and elsewhere, sees those at the bottom as the new revenue frontier of tax collection and public finance. With digitalization, 'transparent' tax obligations apply to the household economy of bottom workers. The following chapters discuss the downward pressure on bottom workers caused by neo-liberalization and digital government operations.

2.4   *Households and International Aid*
Through the case studies of Japanese society, this book applies the concept of bottom worker to a broader East Asian context. In this way, the case studies from Korea (Chapter 4), Thailand (Chapter 6), and Bangladesh (Chapter 7) provide a broader geographic analysis. These cases address two intriguing situations on how they impact and define bottom workers: transnational households (marriage migrants) and households that rely on aid.

In Chapter 4 Kim and Koo outline transnational households by describing the narratives of women from the Philippines who migrate to Korea for marriage. There is sociological literature about marriage migration (see, for example, Beck and Beck-Gernsheim, 2014), while in East Asia more generally domestic and migrants are often women leading to the "feminization of migration" (Ogaya, 2015). Within this body of literature, the chapter is emphasizes marriage migrants, those people who work both in the home *and* the labor market outside the home. Kim and Koo document the reality of marriage migrants who, having subsequently divorced their Korean husbands, work two or three jobs while raising children as single mothers. As they carefully point out, marriage migrant women on spousal visas in Korea do not experience any restrictions in the labor market by their visa status. Nonetheless, they are forced to be bottom workers. Marriage migrants suffer downward pressure due to sorting into categories of gender, ethnicity/nationality, and class in the labor market rather than because of their legal status. Traditionally, studies of bottom workers in Japan and East Asia have presumed that they are citizens of the country, focusing instead on the class aspects of their situation. Still, since the beginning of the twenty-first century, the link between bottom workers and migrant workers has become a crucial research topic. In addition, there is a rising number of cases where the bottom worker's household is transnational (e.g., Japanese-Filipino couples), meriting research on the specific challenges these households face (Ogaya, 2015; 2020; Parreñas, 2015).

Households that are lifted up by international aid is addressed in Chapter 6, focusing on slum improvement projects in Bangkok, and in Chapter 7, with a discussion of microcredit in Chittagong. The World Bank and international NGOs (Non-Governmental Organizations) intervene in the lives of bottom workers in a variety of ways. A critical part of these interventions is to assist in the restructuring of households. Participatory development has hitherto functioned to discipline the household life of program participants (e.g., regular program attendance, self-discipline in the form of planned monthly debt repayments), classifying those bottom workers who can as 'good citizen' and those unable to do so as 'evil people.' The paradox of 'participatory development from below' that in effect is being realized 'from above' by the World Bank and large NGOs is most apparent in the households of bottom workers. These are the households lifted by international aid that then become the people most affected by changes due to neo-liberalization policies.

The slum dwellers of the Global South – the preferred term used by the international development elite to describe the Bottom of the Pyramid (BOP) – have become the target of many new financial programs of neoliberalism. Microfinance, for example, promotes the financialization of people at the bottom. The new poverty management apparatus, chanting the mantras of emancipating women in BOP households, also incorporates those engaged in domestic labor at the bottom into the new market for capital. This financialization of bottom people is the topic of Roy's (2010) concept of "poverty capital," which critically analyzes the emergence of a new bureaucracy to manage poverty, is also discussed by Sakamoto in Chapter 7.

3   Interpretive Labor

Finally, we have the third analytical theme for studying the lifeworld of bottom workers: interpretive labor. Many of the chapters that follow employ qualitative research techniques like interviews and ethnographies. Why are such research methods needed to study bottom workers? By amplifying the voices of workers engaged in such interpretive labor, we aim to tackle the dominant values and doxa (Bourdieu, 1990).

The literature on developmentalism and economic growth in East Asia has tended to discuss East Asian geopolitics and international relations, but has ignored the poverty, pollution, and social movements that are produced behind the scenes (Gottfried and Fasenfest, 2020). ISTAD has used the reality faced by homeless people, day laborers, and migrant workers to critique literature that discusses developmentalism and economic growth 'from above' and to view in a holistic manner how developmental states are based on the exploitation of bottom workers. We don't write about the misery of the bottom worker as humanists; humanism is the mother of capitalism, colonialism, and patriarchy (Santos, 2015). Instead, we use reality as seen through a bottom worker's eyes as a strategic point of reference for illuminating the doxa (Bourdieu, 1990), that is, as an epistemology of critical reasoning.

For instance, ISTAD member Mai Yoshida analyzes the details of the Technical Intern Training Program (TITP), Japan's new method of importing migrant workers (Yoshida, 2020). After years of not permitting migrant workers into the labor market, in the 21st Century Japan began to accept migrant workers under the label "intern" rather than "worker." Yoshida's careful research depicts the structure through which exploitation of these intern workers is normalized. In 2013, a Chinese intern working at an oyster-processing factory in Kure, Hiroshima, murdered two people – a Japanese manager and a female employee. Similar murders by Chinese interns took place in Chiba in 2006 and Kumamoto in 2009. Yoshida points to super-exploitation and pseudo-familial control as the drivers of these extreme acts (Yoshida, 2020). In this daily routine of harassment, the intern workers engage in interpretive labor to please the boss, leading to relentless exhaustion. Yoshida elucidates the reality of interpretive labor in which an intern worker who survives in an exploitative structure is constantly observing the faces of Japanese bosses. A Japanese boss does not need to imagine where the intern worker is coming from, or what they are thinking and feeling. Yet, the intern workers must constantly interpret what the boss is thinking about and feeling. If they do not obey and please the boss, they might be summarily dismissed. These "lopsided structures of the imagination" (Graeber, 2012) can cause undue mental distress to the vulnerable. As Graeber points out:

> [E]veryone knows that servants tend to know a great deal about their employers' families, but the opposite almost never occurs.
>
> 2012: 118–119

Those at the top of the pyramid do not need to interpret what those at the bottom are thinking. If those at the bottom say something superfluous, those at the top "[h]it them over the head hard enough and all of this becomes irrelevant" (Graeber, 2012: 116). In other words, the situation can be easily resolved by abandoning cumbersome interpretations and relying on violence. Having the option of violence makes any interpretation about the other person unnecessary, and it therefore makes those at the top of the pyramid stupid ignorant (Mathews, 2005).

Graeber developed the concept of "interpretive labor" with this in mind. It means "a constant and often subtle work of interpretation, of endlessly imagining others' points of view" (Graeber, 2012: 96). A servant cannot live there without constantly interpreting the circumstances of their master. The sound of the master's footsteps coming down the stairs, the way he responds to the morning greeting, the tone of the conversation between him and his family – these are things the servant must pay close attention to in order to determine the master's mood in the morning. The servant, in the first place, is often forbidden to speak to his master. The servant engages in constant interpretive labor with regard to the master's every action, word, and deed. It is this engagement, however, that enables the servant to 'to know a great deal about their employer's families.'

This interpretive labor is closely linked to what Graeber calls the "labor of self-effacement." Using the example of work performed mainly by women, Graeber expounds that much of this work has been arranged in such a way that men do not even notice that women are doing it (Graeber, 2009). For example, behind the scenes at academic symposiums all over the world, women are always taking care to ensure the clean plates are used at afternoon teas and receptions, labor which the mostly male participants are not aware of. Interpretive labor is thus also gendered.

Interpretive labor has a dual quality. On the one hand, the powerless suffer "slow violence" (Chapter 10), exhausted by the endless interpretative labor. Still, on the other hand, they could notice what the powerful could see but unnoticed. They could develop a "skilled vision" (Grasseni 2004) that perceives the situation differently. We will discuss the double quality of interpretive labor further in the Epilogue.

4   Conclusion

This chapter is designed to be a connecting piece to link the macro-structural debate on bottom workers examined in the next chapter with the various case studies that appear from Chapter 3 onwards. I have also emphasized the significance ISTAD, with which the contributors to this volume are affiliated, attaches to micro-empirical research (for example, deep interviews, ethnography) and have argued that researchers need to learn 'from' bottom workers, not simply analyze their conditions. To this end, this chapter introduces the concept of interpretive labor, arguing that it is vital to follow the "professional vision" (Goodwin, 1994) of bottom workers as they forge a path forward amid harsh working and living conditions.

Three concepts – *dormitory labor, households, and interpretive labor* –capture the social conditions that make up the lived experience of bottom workers in contrast to merely describing their experiences. The goal is to develop a toolkit for capturing not the subjectivity of bottom workers themselves, but the conditions from which that subjectivity emerges.

The lifeworld of bottom workers in Japan and other East Asian countries is characterized by a lack of separation between work, home, and play, especially because workplace and home exist as a unity. The dormitory labor arrangement, and the fact that bottom workers survive by bringing formal and informal labor together to form households, are the two main axes of the discussion in this chapter. With dormitory labor, the loss of work leads directly to the loss of shelter. Single bottom workers who cannot afford to form households become the most socially excluded and vulnerable persons, becoming cast-offs from society. The following chapters illustrate this lifeworld, its difficulties, and possibilities through a range of case studies of bottom workers in East Asia. Finally, there are four propositions that guide the vision this book offers: migration policy, uneven development, the transformation of the meaning of labor, and the method of critical ethnography. In the case studies presented in the rest of this book, we shall examine these critical questions in detail.

References

Andrijasevic R, Pun N and Sacchetto D (2022) Transnational corporations and the making of global labor markets. In: Boris E, Gottfried H, Greene J and Tham J C (eds) *Global Labor Migration: New Directions*. Champaign, IL: University of Illinois Press.

Beck U and Beck-Gernsheim E (2014) *Distant Love: Personal Life in the Global Age*. Cambridge: Polity Press.

Bourdieu P (1990) *The Logic of Practice*. Cambridge: Polity Press.

Bourdieu P (1999) *Acts of Resistance: Against the Tyranny of the Market*. New York: The New Press.

Goffman E (1961) *Asylums: Essays on the Social Situation of Mental Patients and Other Inmates*. New York: Anchor.

Gerstel N and Clawson D (2014) Class advantage and the gender divide: Flexibility on the job and at home. *American Journal of Sociology* 120(2): 395–431.

Gerstel N and Clawson D (2018) Control over time: employers, workers, and families shaping work schedules. *Annual Review of Sociology* 44: 77–97.

Goodwin C (1994) Professional vision. *American Anthropologist* 96(3): 606–633.

Gottfried H (2018) The phoenix rises: Tokyo's origins as a global city. *Critical Sociology* 44(3): 421–435.

Gottfried H and Fasenfest D (2020) Understanding the trajectory of Japanese capitalism. *Critical Sociology* 47(1): 149–161.

Graeber D (2009) *Shihonshugi no ato no sekai no tame ni: atarashii anāchizumu no Shiza* [For a Post-Capitalist World: Perspectives on New Anarchism]. Tokyo: Ibunsya.

Graeber D (2012) Dead zones of the imagination: on violence, bureaucracy, and interpretive labor. *HAU: Journal of Ethnographic Theory* 2(2): 105–128.

Grasseni C (2004) Skilled vision: an apprenticeship in breeding aesthetics. *Social Anthropology* 12(1): 41–55.

Gray A (2004) *Unsocial Europe. Social Protection or Flexiploitation*. London: Pluto Press.

Harvey D (2003) *The New Imperialism*. New York, NY: Oxford University Press.

Hayashi M (2020) Democracy against labor movement: Japan's anti-labor developmental state and aftermaths. *Critical Sociology* 47(1): 37–58.

Ikeda H (2012) *Sekitan no bungakushi* [A Literary History of Coal as a Subject]. Tokyo: Impact Publisher.

Johnson C (1982) *MITI and the Japanese Miracle: The Growth of Industrial Policy, 1925–1975*. Stanford, CA: Stanford University Press.

Kalleberg A L (2009) Precarious work, insecure workers: employment relations in transition. *American Sociological Review* 74(1): 1–22.

Kase K (1997) *Shūdan shūshoku no jidai* [The Era of Group Employment]. Tokyo: Aoki Syoten.

Latouche S (1993) *In the Wake of the Affluent Society: An Exploration of Post-development*. London: Zed Books Ltd.

Lefebvre H (1991) *The Production of Space*. Oxford: Blackwell.

Marx K (1959) *Economic and Philosophic Manuscripts of 1844*. Moscow: Progress Publishers.

Mathews A S (2005) Power/knowledge, power/ignorance: forest fires and the state in Mexico. *Human Ecology* 33 (6): 795–820.

Matsuda M (1998) *Urbanisation from Below: Creativity and Soft Resistence in the Everyday Life of Maragoli Migrants in Nirobi*. Kyoto: Kyoto University Press.

McRobbie A (2020) *Feminism and the Politics of Resilience: Essays on Gender, Media and the End of Welfare*. Cambridge: Polity Press.

Mita M (2010) *Social Psychology of Modern Japan*. New York, NY: Routledge.

Ogasawara H and Yamamoto A (eds) (2016) *Han Tokyo Orinpikku Sengen* [The Anti-Olympic Manifesto]. Tokyo: Koushisya.

Ogasawara H and Yamamoto A (2022) *Tokyo Orinpikku Shimatsuki* [The Cleanup of Tokyo Olympics]. Tokyo: Iwanami Syoten.

Ogaya C (2015) When mobile motherhoods and mobile childhoods converge: the case of Filipino youth and their transmigrant mothers in Toronto, Canada. In: Nagasaka I and Fresnoza-Flot A (eds) *Mobile Childhoods in Filipino Transnational Families*. London: Palgrave Macmillan.

Ogaya C (2020) Intergenerational exploitation of Filipino women and their Japanese Filipino children: "born out of place" babies as new cheap labor in Japan. *Critical Sociology* 47(1): 59–71.

Osawa M (2002) Twelve million full-time housewives: the gender consequences of Japan's postwar social contract. In: Zunz O, Schoppa L and Hiwatari N (eds) *Social Contracts Under Stress: The Middle Classes of America, Europe, and Japan at the Turn of the Century*. New York, NY: Russell Sage Foundation: 255–278.

Parreñas R S (2015) *Servants of Globalization: Migration and Domestic Work* (*Second Edition*). Stanford, CA: Stanford University Press.

Roy A (2010) *Poverty Capital: Microfinance and the Making of Development*. New York, NY: Routledge.

Rubery J, Ward K, Grimshaw D and Beynon H. (2005) Working Time, Industrial Relations and the Employment Relationship. *Time & Society* 14(1):89–111.

Santos B d S (2015) *Epistemologies of the South: Justice Against Epistemicide*. Abington: Routledge.

Schram S F (2015) *The Return of Ordinary Capitalism: Neoliberalism, Precarity, Occupy*. New York: Oxford University Press.

Tanno K (2013) *Migrant Workers in Contemporary Japan: An Institutional Perspective on Transnational Employment*. Melbourne: Trans Pacific Press.

Ueno C (2009) *The Modern Family in Japan: Its Rise and Fall*. Melbourne: TransPacific Press.

Vogt G (2014) Friend and foe: juxtaposing Japan's migration discourses. In: Vosse W., R Drifte and V Blechinger-Talcott (eds) *Governing Insecurity in Japan: The Domestic Discourse and Policy Response*. London: Routledge: 68–88.

Wallerstein I (1983) *Historical Capitalism*. London: Verso.

Yang M, Haraguchi T and Sakurada K (2014) The urban working-class culture of riot in Osaka and Los Angeles: toward a comparative history. In: Fraser B (eds) *Marxism and Urban Culture*. Maryland: Lexington: 213–238.

Yoshida M (2020) The indebted and silent worker: paternalistic labor management in foreign labor policy in Japan. *Critical Sociology* 47(1): 73–89.

CHAPTER 2

Labor-Spatial Informality of Bottom Workers

Hideo Aoki

Abstract

This chapter examines the economic informality of labor and the political informality of space from the perspective of critical informality theory. Theories of labor and spatial informality provide perspectives for grasping the conditions faced by laborers, their residences and living conditions, and the overall lifeworld of bottom workers. Neoliberal globalization has imposed hierarchical downward pressure on bottom workers. *Who are the bottom workers? How do they appear now?* Through eight case studies, this book answers these questions. This chapter proposes frameworks for analyzing diverse bottom workers, with these analyses converging on the relationship between and impact of informality on bottom workers and the state. In the final analysis, the material in this volume weaves an understanding of the conditions faced by the bottom worker.

1 Labor Informality

1.1 *Downward Pressure*

This chapter argues that we need to categorize contemporarily employed and self-employed workers as bottom workers. In this way, it lays the groundwork for several of the cases that follow in this volume. Chapter 3 examines dormitory labor (live-in jobs) in which female workers live in dormitories and work in Japanese-style hotels. Chapter 4 explores how female marriage migrants become trapped in a cyclical circuit of precarious, irregular, and low-paid jobs. Chapter 10 reveals the processes by which day laborers, the precariat, the working poor, and others are pushed out into the streets. Taken together they present the stories of vulnerable people who are entrapped in the circuit of bottom jobs to become bottom workers experiencing downward pressure.

There are three issues related to the economic informality of labor based on critical informality theory. First, under neoliberal globalization, there is increasing downward pressure on working people, and informalization of labor is a characteristic of all formal and informal jobs. The labor market becomes restructured, and as a result, various precarious jobs emerge. People increasingly work under poor working conditions and for low wages. Second, in these circumstances, the existing concepts of workers (lumpenproletariat, the urban poor, underclass, working poor, precariat, etc.) are no longer sufficient to reflect the conditions facing people working at the bottom of society, and so the concept of the bottom worker becomes necessary. The bottom worker is a strategic concept that grasps the restructuring of the labor hierarchy. Third, restructuring of the working class is ongoing in countries both in the Global North (hereafter the North) and the Global South (hereafter the South). As capital and labor move across borders, workgroups of migrants coming from the South emerge in cities in the North, while the financial centers emerge in cities in the South.

1.2   *Informalization of Labor*

In neoliberal globalization, the competition among capital has intensified and extended beyond borders. To survive the competition, capital reduces production costs in two ways. First, by increasing productivity through innovation of machinery and equipment. Second, by reducing labor costs. The working conditions become deteriorated, and workers have become more exploited. The International Labour Organization (ILO) called the lack of decent work *informality of employment* (ILO, 2003: 2). I call the deterioration of working conditions the *informalization of labor*. Workers no longer earn a decent living even if they work full-time.

Informalization of labor emerges through three paths. First, the labor in the formal sector becomes informalized, especially when the employment is non-regularized.[1] Their working conditions are irregular with long working hours, provide no compensation for work-related injuries, enjoy precarious employment status, and received low wages such as piece rates and hourly wages. The increase in non-regular employment puts pressure on regular workers who are exposed to the risk of being replaced by non-regular workers.

Second, new informal jobs have emerged in the heretofore formal sector. Toshio Iyotani (1999) identified the jobs that have emerged in global cities. His list includes:

1.   simple service work which supports head office functions, from building management and security to data input,

---

1   Non-regular employment covers various forms of work: contract, probationary, casual, project-based, day laboring, weekly laboring, seasonal, apprentice, etc. Among them, contract employment is the main of non-regular employment.

2. urban service work in response to cities being active 24 hours and the expansion of new urban lifestyles, such as high-end restaurants and boutiques as well as nail services,

3. in-home work such as babysitters and people doing housework,[2]

4. work in urban manufacturing industries with harsh conditions known as sweatshops, which typically subcontract work to the fashion industry and

5. work supplying services requiring large amounts of low-wage workers such as in convenience stores or restaurants (Iyotani, 1999: 195–196).

Those are service jobs for businesses and individuals, and working conditions are substantially no different than jobs in the informal sector. Niitsu called this the sector one that is directly dependent on the formal sector (Niitsu, 1989: 53–57). Most of these jobs come about through subcontracting and outsourcing arrangements. In this way, the formal sector creates many informal jobs.

Third, the traditional informal sector has expanded. Those jobs mostly overlap with new service jobs in the formal sector. They consist of sweatshop jobs (paid and unpaid jobs in factories and households), personal service jobs (housemaids, babysitters, drivers, etc.), and the micro self-employed jobs of street workers (vendors, cleaners, scavengers, etc.). They are substantially underemployed.[3] Therefore, it is more common for households to have multiple working members, and where many of the members in that household have multiple jobs or share the same job.

1.3   *Collapse of a Dichotomy*

Informalization of labor has dismantled the dichotomy of formal and informal. In the past, the formal sector provided *a group of jobs where decent working conditions are guaranteed under modern employment relations*, while the informal sector represented *a group of jobs where employment is left to the arbitrary discretion of the employer, are under micro self-employment, and in which working and management conditions, wages and income are inferior.*[4] However,

---

2   In-home work accounts for one of the fastest-growing job categories, as domestic works such as childcare, cleaning, cooking, and eldercare are outsourced to low-wage workers. The commodification of intimacy and care creates an increasing demand for low-wage workers to perform unpaid jobs. More and more of social life is turned into a transaction for profit.

3   Underemployment refers to a situation where a person is working but wants more work and income. There is visible and invisible underemployment. In the Philippines, visible underemployment refers to working less than 40 hours per week, while invisible underemployment refers to working more than 40 hours per week (Balangue 2013: 2–3). Even if they work long hours, they are in a semi-employed state due to low wages.

4   The ILO firstly characterized the informal sector as follows in the 1970s: easy entry, uncontrolled competition, use of own resources, family ownership, small-scale management,

this dichotomy has collapsed. Neoliberal globalization puts pressure on the working conditions of formal jobs. Some jobs become inferior and are no better than informal jobs. Some people from the formal sector enter the informal sector. Other people, mostly women, enter the informal sector as a sideline. The household crosses both sectors by having its members employed in multiple jobs. Thus, the informal sector becomes reorganized. Its upper part grows as a business with income-earning power as workers (mostly men) in the formal sector enter the upper rank of the informal sector. The bottom part stays in survival-sustaining jobs in the transformed informal sector, which squeezes those workers (mostly females) into its lowest ranks. Originally marginalized workers are pushed out of the informal sector, and the result is an increase in homelessness (those who are no longer housed).

Those stories are the same for workers in the South. Take the case of the street vendor. Urban development has led to increased regulation of spaces in which street vendors do business. Vendors are at the mercy of urban policies and stratified within themselves. Yoshida analyzed the hierarchy of vendors in Manila (Yoshida, 2020: 70). At the top of the hierarchy are business-owned stalls, where vendors have capital and set up full-fledged stores in downtown areas and markets without fear of being evicted. Large corporations (like Unilever) enter the market and produce items previously made and sold by vendors. Little packages of sticky rice are sold in bulk at lower prices to make it hard for street vendors to survive. As a result, there is the following hierarchy of the remaining vendors: semi-fixed vendors who sell the products in pre-fitted shops, welfare-backed vendors who sell the products in temporary stores, sidewalk vendors who sell the products in movable or tatami-mat stores, hawkers (with fixed sales territory) who sell the products sitting on the street or walking in a small area, and hawkers (with unfixed sales territory) who sell the products on foot from street to street. Downward pressure is strong among the vendors, competition is fierce, and those with capital can exclude those without. In this way, within the informal sector informalization of labor progressed. Bottom workers have been pushed down this stratified structure until they are finally kicked out altogether with no option but to join the rough sleepers.[5]

As job hierarchy has become further stratified, the boundary between formal and informal has collapsed. The informal sector is now not only the source of a miscellaneous and diverse labor force but also is strengthening the employment adjustment function for the whole of the labor market.

---

labor-intensive, self-directed acquisition of skills. This triggered an ensuing debate on the definition of the informal sector (Mtero 2011: Chap. 2).

5   Rough sleepers, or *Nojukusha,* is a term used to describe the homeless in Japan.

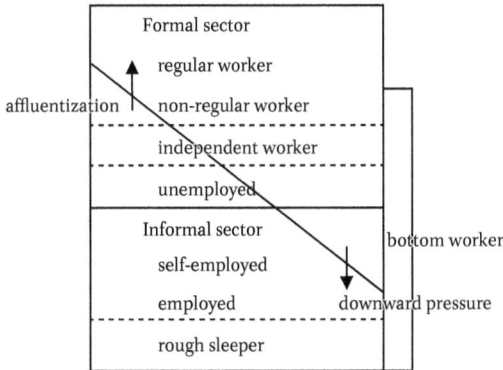

FIGURE 2.1   Downward pressure on workers

In the past, the informal sector was *the informal sector of hope*, a springboard for the rural poor to start their lives in the cities. Now, it has become the *informal sector of despair* where the poor finally arrive due to downward pressure.

This book rejects the fixed dichotomy of formal and informal following many studies (Rakowski 1994; Joshi 1997; Chaudhuri and Mukhopadhyay 2010; Mtero 2011). The boundary between formal and informal has blurred. One flows continuously into the other. I recognize this but do not fully abandon the division of formal and informal labor. I use them as a tool to describe the flow and segmentation of the labor hierarchy. Formal and informal gradations are summarized in Figure 2.1. Informalization of labor means the process of verticalization of the shaded line. Accordingly, the formal sector is stratified upward and some workers become wealthy. In contrast, the informal sector is stratified downward, and finally, some become rough sleepers. *All workers, from non-regular workers to rough sleepers, make up the bottom workers.*[6]

1.4   *Labor Hierarchy*

Who are bottom workers, the focus of this book? To answer this question, I consider the overall labor hierarchy consisting of some combination of indicators such as job status, nature of work, income (wages), and job evaluation.

---

6   Currently, the pandemic has hit the world. It forbids human mobility and activity, forces people to refrain from work, and many businesses close, especially those who work in customer businesses and on the streets. Many are those who make a living at the urban bottom. It is imperative to analyze the serious impact of the pandemic on those workers. In times of disaster, capitalism turns its cruel teeth of deprivation against the bottom workers. The theory of *disaster capitalism* has revealed the story of its cruel deprivation (Klein, 2007).

Referring to previous labor studies and the United States Census, I construct a model of labor hierarchy as shown in Table 2.1. The actual hierarchy is much more complex, with fluid boundaries, and constantly reordered ranking, and any single worker or family member can straddle two or more strata.

TABLE 2.1   Composition of the labor hierarchy

A. Formal sector
1. Corporate worker
   Regular worker
   Non-regular worker
      dispatched worker, contract worker, part-time worker
      short-time regular worker, corporate home worker, day worker
2. Independent worker
   Business contractor
      contract worker who constitutes a business entity
   Micro-individual business
      regular or occasional self-funded small contracter
3. Unemployed
   Cyclical and temporay unemployed
      due to the employment and labor supply-demand relationship
   Structural and chronic unemployed
      when worker's skill or physical ability does not meet the needs of the
      market
4. Economically inactive person
   Persons outside of the labor force
B. Informal sector
1. Miscellaneous job worker in the street or home
   Worker in outsourced job
   Self-employed
   Employed including domestic worker
2. Rough sleeper
   Working rough sleeper
      people who work on miscellaneous jobs in the street
   Non-working rough sleeper
      people who beg in the street and depend on soup kitchen

All workers are exposed to downward pressure and slipping down the hierarchy as a result of neoliberal globalization. Even regular employees are threatened by the risk of being replaced by non-regular employees. The status of casual workers is unstable, especially day workers, who quickly may become rough sleepers when they lose jobs and run out of savings. The temporarily unemployed try to get rehired, but it is becoming difficult to get jobs (Krueger, Cramer, and Cho, 2014). Chronically unemployed have few opportunities for reemployment even as they have not given up on finding employment. They are still job seekers in the labor market.

Economically inactive people are out of the labor market. They are often counted as *non-labor forces* in labor statistics. But their composition is complex. They consist of the following (ILOSTAT, 2019): 1) workers out of the labor market such as workers who are engaged in household or family duties full time; 2) available potential job-seekers who can work but have given up seeking jobs after being repeatedly unsuccessful; 3) the unavailable job seekers who cannot work for a range of reasons. Here I face an issue of how to define a job: *what is a job* and *what it means to work*. Not all but many inactive persons are bottom workers. They are potential workers. The boundary between inactive and chronically unemployed is fluid.

Advancing the organic composition of capital results in excess labor in response to the desire to increase average capital. Marx called this outcome the creation of a *relative surplus population* that consists of three forms (Marx, 1996 [1867]: 635–637): 1) fluid surplus population as the temporarily unemployed in the vicinity of modern industry; 2) latent surplus population waiting for job opportunities in rural areas, that is, the rural underemployed; 3) stagnant surplus population in irregular work conditions such as daily employment. Within these unemployed are the absolute needy. Marx called all of them the *industrial reserve army* necessary for the development of capital-based production. Bottom workers exist in all of these categories. It should be noted that the industrial reserve army is a concept relating to employment by capital. Marx understood informal jobs in this context. The number of self-employed increases in informal jobs: those who are outsourced by employer arrangements and those with little capital. They work in diverse and miscellaneous jobs and are constantly exposed to the loss of customers and variations in the demand for their labor.

The last segment is those working and not working are rough sleepers. They work to survive while living on the streets. They are stratified based on work status and the level of their survival resources. They earn their livings by working on miscellaneous jobs such as peddling, waste collection, parking lot monitoring, a sandwich man, lining up in a soup kitchen, and begging under the scorching sun or on a snowy day. All these activities are contributing to wealth redistribution and circulation in society. *The concept of labor should be expanded to include these activities*. We should regard them as an integral part of working people at the bottom of the labor market.

In summary, this book targets the following workers: *the non-regularly employed, independent workers, the unemployed, economically inactive people,* that is, *the industrial reserve army,* and *informal job workers, rough sleepers, in a word, bottom workers*. Most of them are in poverty or at risk of being in poverty and quickly fall into welfare recipients or go to the streets if the economy turns sour, or if they suffer a workplace accident or become ill. This book regards the increase of bottom workers as *an indication of the whole of the workers' downward mobility* in neoliberal globalization.

Downward pressure leads to a decline in the job status of working people and the impoverishment of their lives. Impoverishment is not only due to lower or interrupted wages and income but also to debt. The poor borrow money to finance their businesses, make ends meet, etc. Today, there is a variety of microenterprises through which the poor borrow money, from traditional moneylenders and mutual financing associations to pawnshops, banks, local microfinance such as *Grameen Bank*, and global finance companies (Roy, 2010). However, the poor debtors often cannot pay the interest and repay their debts, so they borrow from other moneylenders or finance companies, offering their houses and land as collateral. Repeating it, they finally become penniless and multi-borrowers. Their poverty deepens. They are forced into overwork to pay off their debts. This is another difficulty that bottom workers face at present. They are trapped in a vicious cycle of poverty, debt, and overwork, become debt slaves who work to pay off their debts, and finally become suicide bombers (ibid.: 147). Chapter 7 examines the tragedy of poor fishermen who were trapped in a vicious cycle due to microcredit debt.

2   Defining the Bottom Worker

2.1   *Related Concepts*
The bottom worker is a concept that squarely grasps the transformation of the labor hierarchy under neoliberal globalization. So far, people at the bottom of society have been referred to by various concepts. Why is this new concept of bottom workers needed now? It is necessary to clarify the overlap and difference between the bottom worker and the related concepts. How do the bottom worker and those concepts overlap and differ from each other? I examine five concepts in greater detail: lumpenproletariat, the urban poor,

the underclass, the working poor, and the precariat. Those concepts have been used in common parlance to refer to people struggling to work and live, mainly in the cities of the North. Here I return to the *original meanings* of those concepts when they first emerged and relative to the bottom worker (see Table 2.2). Workers do not only move down the rank, but perform multiple jobs across the ranks, sometimes move up the rank, and some workers circulate between the ranks. In today's pandemic of COVID-19, many workers have plummeted down the rank from regular employment to rough sleepers (Ruffini and Wozniak, 2021). Given this complex hierarchical reality, I examine into which part of the labor rank each concept of working people corresponds and explain the overlap and differences between each concept and the bottom worker.

2.1.1 Lumpenproletariat

Lumpenproletariat is coined word by Marx. He distinguished the working class from the lowest sediment of the relative surplus population who struggle with pauperism, and listed those falling into the lumpenproletariat (Marx,1996: 637): vagabonds, discharged soldiers, discharged jailbirds, escaped galley slaves, rogues, mountebanks, lazzarone [declassed proletarians], pickpockets, tricksters, gamblers, maquereaux [pimps], brothel keepers, porters, literati, organ-grinders, rag-pickers, knife grinders, tinkers, beggars — in short, the whole of the indefinite, disintegrated mass (Marx,1979: 149). It is not easy to compare the lumpenproletariat with the bottom worker because the concept of lumpenproletariat has two problems. First, it is a concept consisting of a mixture of various people *outside and inside* the class hierarchy in early industrial capitalism. Second, the lumpenproletariat was the victim of the rapid and forcible emergence of industrial capitalism. However, Marx and Engels did not sufficiently analyze the economic process of lumpenproletariat emergence and emphasized their politically reactionary and counter-revolutionary role. "The 'dangerous class' (lumpenproletariat-quoter), the social scum, that passively rotting mass thrown off by the lowest layers of old society may, here and there, be swept into the movement by a proletarian revolution; its conditions of life, however, prepare it far more for the part of a bribed tool of reactionary intrigue" (Marx and Engels, 1848: 494). As an economic class, the lumpenproletariat, if not always, overlap with bottom workers as the victim of capitalism. As noted previously, even rough sleepers are people engaged in a variety of economic activities. If the concept of lumpenproletariat is to be used, its composition should be demarcated, and the economic provision of each subgroup should be clarified.

TABLE 2.2   Range of each concept and bottom worker

Type and rank of worker		Lumpen-proletariat	Urban poor	Under-class	Working poor	Precariat	Bottom worker
Corporate worker	unstable regular worker	×	×	×	·	·	×
	non-regular worker	×	×	×	·	·	×
	day worker	×	×	·	·	·	·
Independent worker	business contractor	×	×	×	·	·	×
	micro-business	×	×	×	·	·	·
Unemployed	cyclical unemployed	×	·	·	·	·	·
	structural unemployed	·	·	·	×	·	·
Economically inactive person		·	×	·	×	×	·
Informal job worker	outsourced worker	×	·	×	×	×	·
	self-emplopyed	×	·	×	×	×	·
	employed	·	·	×	×	×	·
Rough sleeper	working RS	·	×	×	×	×	·
	non-working RS	·	×	×	×	×	·
Whereabout worker	worker in the North	·	×	·	·	·	·
	worker in the South	×	·	×	×	×	·

·: including ×: not including

2.1.2   Urban Poor

Urban poor is a concept that has been widely used to refer to the poor living in the cities, which corresponds to the rural poor. The concept of the urban poor has been especially used in studying urban poor in the South. It emerged as a result of the over-urbanization in developing countries in the 1950s, before neoliberal globalization (Kitahara and Takai, 1989: 56). Rural poor migrated to the cities, engaged in informal jobs, and lived in informal settlements. Those people were subsequently called the urban poor.

The urban poor and bottom workers existed and worked at different times. Urban poor were mainly ex-rural poor who migrated to the cities with strong rural ties. Bottom workers refer to those city-born poor not having many rural ties. The poverty of the urban poor is rural poverty that is transferred to the cities, while the poverty of the bottom worker is (re)produced in the cities. Urban poor refers to the informal job workers, while the bottom worker includes non-regular, unemployed, informal, and rough sleepers. Urban poor refers exclusively to those who live illegally in informal settlements, while bottom workers include those living in informal settlements, those having legal rights to land and houses, and those on the streets who do not have even illegal living space. Finally, bottom workers are at first urban workers, but it also includes workers in agricultural and fishing villages. Chapter 7 examines fishermen/women's villages in the Chittagong suburbs.

2.1.3   Underclass

The underclass is a concept used to describe people who emerged in the urban slums of the United States under early neoliberal globalization. Underclass refers to those who were chronically unemployed and dependent on welfare and crime to survive, especially young African-American males. They lost jobs because they could not keep up with the innovative production technology in the factories and could not move to rural areas or developing countries following the relocated factories from cities (Wilson, 1987). At first, mass media portrayed them negatively, as social outcasts, welfare-dependent, lazy, and dangerous people who commit crimes. Then, Wilson analyzed the historical background of their emergence and reconstructed the underclass as a scientific concept to analyze people living in the slums. Such an underclass differs from the bottom worker as follows. Underclass originally referred to the poor in slums in the US, but bottom workers include slum people, those who live in ordinary areas or informal settlements, as well as rough sleepers on the streets. While the underclass has an ethnic connotation of African-American *as its original usage* was, bottom workers include all those who struggle to work and live, regardless of ethnicity. The underclass has a connotation of those who are outside of the class structure and excluded from society, but bottom workers include people who are inside and outside the class structure.

2.1.4   Working Poor

Working poor is a concept referring to those in need, whose income does not allow them to earn a decent living even if they work hard every day. The working poor is those who relate to capital employment. It includes those in full-time and non-regular employment, and the temporarily unemployed. The core of the working poor is a variety of non-regular workers. There is no strict definition of the working poor. I think of it tentatively as the following. In the United States, the working poor is officially understood as those whose earnings from formal employment are insufficient to avoid poverty (Bureau of Labor Statistics, 2013). In Japan, the working poor include mainly females who work to supplement the family income, single mothers, *freeters* (free-Arbeiters which means non-regular workers, especially those with short-term contracts jumping from job to job), NEET (Not in Education, Employment or Training) young people and low-waged elder workers (Takano, 2012). The working poor is those who are kept in poverty no matter how hard they work. The more they work, the more they are kept in poverty. In contrast, bottom workers include the working poor, as well as the unemployed, informal job workers, and rough sleepers.

2.1.5   Precariat

The precariat is a compound word of precarious and proletariat, which grasps the whole of people in precarious work affected by downward pressure as a result of neoliberal globalization. According to Guy Standing, the coiner of the precariat, the precariat consists of the following: undocumented workers, temporary and contract workers, women, the elderly, the disabled, immigrants, and minorities in precarious employment and wage/income status (Standing, 2011: 2013a: 2013b: 2014).[7] The precariat is those who are not covered by labor welfare such as benefits, insurance, and pensions. They move from job to job, have no career, no firm identity as a worker, are finally abandoned by their families, and are excluded from the communities. They are not fixed as a class, but are in the process of class-in-making, repeatedly getting fired, and getting jobs. Therefore, the precariat is a dangerous class that is dissatisfied with and hates society.[8]

---

7 Standing situated migrants as a central group in the precariat. "The migrant becomes a central figure in both the understanding of precarity and processes of precarization" (Jørgensen, 2015: 2).

8 Standing called those who are excluded from society the *denizens* distinguishing from the citizens (Standing, 2011: 15).

Like this, Standing emphasized the job instability of the precariat. It includes the whole of employed people exposed to downward pressure. Hence, it overlaps greatly with the bottom people. And it is a concept that encompasses all work, life, lifeworld, and identity. It also is the same as the bottom worker.

On the other hand, the precariat and bottom workers differ in the concept's scope. The precariat is a concept that covers the employed and the unemployed *relating to employment by capital*. Bottom workers cover those who are cut the tie with capital employment: self-employed workers and workers in miscellaneous informal jobs and rough sleepers.

The precariat is a concept that refers to working people exclusively in the North. It does not refer to working people in the South.[9] In contrast, bottom workers refer to the whole of those at the bottom *both in the North and the South*. Capital from the North flowed to the South. The North-like cities of multinational companies emerged in the city of the South. The poor from the South migrated to the North. The South-like world emerged in the cities of the North. Bottom workers are also intertwined with each other. There is no reason for separating the North and the South.

Standing claimed that the precariat is different from the traditional working class. According to him, the working class is those who enjoyed stable employment in the industrialization era and could expect to be reemployed even if they lost their jobs. In contrast, the precariat is those who have unstable jobs and have no prospect of reemployment if they lose jobs in the post-industrialization era. However, it does not make sense to distinguish the precariat from the working class. The precariat is the contemporary working class. Both stable and precarious workers belong to proletariats who have no means of production and whose fate is left to the arbitrary capitalist will and at its mercy:

> free in the double sense, that as a free man he can dispose of his labour power as his own commodity, and that on the other hand he has no other commodity for sale, is short of everything necessary for the realization of his labour power.
>
> MARX, 1996: 179

---

9 Siegmann and Schiphorst claimed "The precariat in industrial countries should include informal workers in underdeveloped countries. Given ongoing changes in the world of work affecting both underdeveloped and industrialized countries, it is time to bring the notions of informality and labour precarity together" (Siegmann and Schiphorst, 2016: 119)

Standing did not define rigorously what class is. Rather than class, the precariat is a social category that includes various working people who have suffered labor precarity. The precariat is "a particularly vulnerable segment of the working class, it is not a class in its own right" (Wright, 2015: 1).

2.2   *Bottom Worker*
With comparisons to those concepts in mind, the bottom worker is characterized as follows. It is a wide concept that includes all people working in precarious and poor conditions due to downward pressure in neoliberal globalization: the precariat, the working poor, the underclass, the urban poor, parts of the lumpenproletariat, and parts of economically inactive persons, in a word, the contemporary working class.

The bottom worker is both a hierarchically relational concept and an ontological concept conditioned by precarity and inferiority. And it is a comprehensive concept. *Comprehensive* has four meanings. First, labor precarity and inferiority lead to income precarity and scarcity (poverty). The latter leads to residential precarity and inferiority. Bottom workers are people living in bottom spaces, which I discuss the detail in the next section.

Second, the bottom worker is a concept referring to wide space: people working in urban and rural areas and the North and the South. Urban/rural and the North/South are not dichotomous but continuous as mentioned above.

Third, bottom workers from the South move to the neighboring countries (South to South), the North (South to North), and vice versa (North to North and North to South). See Table 2.2. Except for the urban poor, other concepts have been not much concerned with bottom workers in the South. Bottom workers shoot for the whole move of workers between the South and the North.

Forth, bottom workers recognize and evaluate their living environments: work, income, residence, and life. And they act according to or against them. In doing so, they reproduce, transform or escape their environments. The bottom worker is a concept that includes a lifeworld such as values, recognition, and activities.

3   Spatial Informality

3.1   *Political Informality*
This section examines spatial informalization, i.e., residential destabilization led by labor precarity. Bottom workers lose residence with eviction by the state (central/local governments) and/or acquire residence through negotiation

with the state. Chapter 5 examines the process by which Japanese-Brazilians lost their jobs, moved into public housing, and formed a community with Japanese residents. Chapter 6 examines the process by which slum residents got housing and improved the environmental conditions by joining participatory community development projects. Chapter 9 examines the process by which people with diverse work backgrounds lost housing and became homeless. Chapter 10 examines the displacement of ex-homeless welfare recipients to low-rent housing in the suburbs and the return to low-rent flophouses in the city center. In these processes, the residential poor such as migrants, slum dwellers, and the homeless lose housing (informalization of residence) and/or get housing (formalization of residence). They are the results of negotiation, cooperation, and resistance with/against the state and stakeholders: administrative departments, property developers, landowners, corporations, consumers, residents, ordinary citizens, etc.

I examine four issues about spatial informality. First, the understanding of informal space has changed. So far, informal space exclusively referred to the poor and those not subject to the state's regulation. Now it becomes a space defined through negotiations among various stakeholders including the wealthy. The formal/informal boundary of space has become interchangeable. Second, although informal spaces are made through negotiations among stakeholders, the strongest of which is the state that sorts spaces into formal and informal zones. Third, even when there are differences of opinion or interest conflicts within the state, it always resolves into a single measure: either to allow people to live or to banish them. Fourth, the state excludes informal space. But exclusion does not mean mere oppression. The state regulates, *de*-regulates, and *un*-regulates informal space within its permissible limits. It excludes *and* includes informal space. The determinability of space is the base of the state's sovereignty.

3.1.1   Space War

Neoliberal globalization has informalized labor *and* residence of bottom workers. How does it affect their living spaces? Where do bottom workers live? Bottom workers are the first victim of spatial transformation. A metaphor of the 19th century fits well with the 21st century's description of spatial warfare.

> Every large town may be looked upon as a place of human sacrifice, a shrine where thousands pass yearly through the fire as offerings to the moloch of avarice.
>
> LAING, 1844: 150

The city is the most important place for the accumulation of capital. The state invites capital to cities preparing the place for capital growth (laws and institutions). Capital multiplies itself and develops a new place for increases in capital. This is done in two ways. First, by regenerating existing places (internal expansion of the city). Second, exploring new places for investment (external expansion of the city). In this way, urban spaces are reorganized. However, bottom workers work and live in those spaces. Capital (and the state) confronts negotiate, and struggle for profit, and bottom workers confront, negotiate, and struggle for survival. The result is clear. Capital mostly wins. Spaces, where humans live, turn into business districts. Agents representing capital monitor space, select who comes and goes, and exclude people who do not have money. Andres Hansen called this a struggle over *space war*. "The nation-state, geopolitically, with its patent on the means of violence, has traditionally played an important role in the praxis of space wars and imperialism" (Hansen, 2006: 21). The main battlefield of space war is the global city with high capital concentration. The results of the spatial war are clear. Bottom workers cannot compete with the wealthy, capital, and state. Davis vividly depicted the devastation in global cities of the South (Davis, 2006). People's misery doesn't stop in the South. Marx's words, referring to the primitive accumulation of capital in the 19th century, come back to life in the 21st century.

> "Improvements" of towns, accompanying the increase of wealth, by the demolition of badly built quarters, the erection of palaces for banks, warehouses, &c, the widening of streets for business traffic, for the carriages of luxury, and for the introduction of tramways, &c, drive away the poor into even worse and more crowded hiding places.
>
> MARX, 1996: 651

3.1.2   Formality and Informality

The theory of over-urbanization has regarded informality as a key concept in the studies of the informal settlement in developing countries. Informality has been characterized by the following. 1) Informal space is a place that is formed accidentally, unintentionally, and non-politically. The poor from rural areas have nowhere to live in the cities, so build houses on public or private lands without the owners' consent. These are informal settlements. It was thought of as a natural phenomenon, and land occupation as having no political significance. 2) It is a non-legitimate space. People live in the settlements without the landowner's consent. They have no legal right to live there. 3) It is a space beyond the state's regulation. Hence, people do not pay taxes. 4) It is an unofficial space. Hence, they have no official address and neighborhood association which is the endpoint organization of the local government. 5) It is a space that is segregated politically and socially. At the boundary of the space, there is an invisible wall that divides people's lives. People who live there have been entirely hidden and shut up in the closed spaces of the city (Porta and Shleifer, 2014). On the contrary, formal spaces are those that are deliberately formed, politically controlled, and legally authorized. They are legally owned, predictable, and regulatable by the state and capable of tax collection.

Cities in developing countries have been presented in the context of a rivalry between informality and formality. Informal space should be integrated into the formal space, and spatial integration was an essential condition for urban modernization. However, in neoliberal globalization, the city changed. Its economic and social structure became fluid and complex. Who creates informal space? how do they create it? Here a reversal of understanding of informality occurred. A. Roy answered these questions with an alternative theory, the critical informality theory (Roy, 2004: 2005: 2009). She overturned the traditional informality theory. The points are organized as follows.

3.1.3 Continuous Informality

The boundary between formality and informality is fluid and changes through the negotiation among the stakeholders. The state finally decides the boundary. And while informal spaces are legally unauthorized, they are permitted by custom. Drummond calls public spaces where – although illegal – residence is permitted by custom *pseudo-public spaces* (Drummond, 2000: 2377). Raco calls spaces where the boundary between public and private space is vague *hybrid spaces* (Raco, 2003: 1871). Hence, formality and informality are not distinctly divided. It is *a question of degree*, and on a 'continuum in which the two form the poles' (Mcfarlane and Waibel, 2012: 2). Informal practice functions in a formal space, and formal rule functions in an informal space. And finally which space is informal or not is decided by the state.

3.1.4 The Wealthy's Informality

Informality has so far referred to the living spaces of the poor – but it relates to the whole of the city including the wealthy (Arabindoo, 2012; Varley, 2013; Roy, 2005: 2009; Schindler, 2016). The wealthy are also deeply involved in informality (Roy, 2009: 83). The wealthy sometimes illegally monopolize public land and develop subdivisions and gated communities. They create informality through the commercialization of public space. They have financial and political influence, paying bribes to win over government officials, and engaging attorneys to manipulate the law. Thus, their informality is easily formalized.

On the contrary, the poor have neither financial nor political influence, so their informality remains unchanged.

4   State and Spatial Informality

4.1   *Spatial Regulation*
Informality is, first of all, a legal concept and by definition illegal. It is the state that adjudicates matters of law. The state places itself above the law, enforces and adjudicates the laws, and creates informal space as a *space of exception* (Agamben, 1995: 25). Informality is the same. The decision of informality is in the hand of the state. The state then takes precedence over the law.

The state draws a line between formal and informal spaces. *Formality and informality are functional products of state regulation* (Lombard and Rakodi, 2016; Roy, 2005: 2009; Silvia and Shaw, 2012). The state considers circumstances and divides spaces at its discretion. When, where, and how is space decided as formal or informal? The ability of arbitrary decisions is the basis of state sovereignty. The state frequently permits deviation from the law, leaves legitimate practice as it is, crowds out the illegitimate, and creates informality – but by doing so, the state makes its existence sustainable. Informal settlements are not unnecessary eyesores – they are spaces that complement the state's housing policies. Without informal settlements, the state cannot regulate formal settlements too.[10] These circumstances lead us to recognize that informality is a *dependent variable of the state* and a *tool of governance*. It is in flux due to arbitrary state actions. The boundary between formality and informality also is in flux.

4.2   *Selective Spatial Informality*
The state creates informality *selectively* (Crossa, 2014; Roy, 2009). Certain spaces are approved and formalized, but others are not approved and are consequently informalized. Spaces that are not approved are excluded, marginalized, and strictly regulated by the law. For example, vendors with established brick-and-mortar stores often are permitted to sell the products on the street. The informality of a formal subject is permitted. However, street vendors are

---

10   "Brazilian cities are marked by an 'unstable relationship between the legal and illegal.' While it may seem obvious and apparent that the urban poor is engaged in informal and illegal occupation of land, much of the city itself is occupied through the 'misrule of law'"(Roy, 2009: 80). The state cannot regulate an unknown and uncanny population without authorizing illegal land occupation (favelas).

not permitted, and their activities are restricted. The informality of an informal subject is not permitted. Vendors with strong finances can pay fines or bribes to the police, and their trading is permitted. Vendors without money are driven off the streets. Like this, informality is further divided into formality and informality, and the decisive factors of division are financial and negotiating power. Finally, when the state requires – such as when the government hosts an international conference – all the vendors with and without finance are driven off the streets for beautifying them. The state tolerates informal settlements and illegal activities on the streets but suddenly cracks down on them in case of emergencies such as big events, pandemic lockdowns, etc.

4.3   *Unregulated Regulation*

Informality was so far referred to spaces that are beyond the regulation of the state, that is, *un*regulated spaces (AlSayyad, 2004; Kurtūst, 2012; Mcfarlane and Waibel, 2012; Roy, 2009). Such space was unfettered, unstructured, and difficult to predict what happened there. Hence, the state was frightened by the bottom people. However, the fact is different from it. *Informality does not mean an absence of regulation but is one form of regulation.* Informality is not a product of the failure of urban planning, but a premeditated and planned product of the state. The state sometimes *intentionally* does not regulate spaces and leaves them as *de-regulated* in a state where regulation is unnecessary. Like this, informality is not beyond regulation but *within* a framework of state regulation.

4.4   *Informal State*

The state maintains the highest position among various stakeholders engaged in negotiations. However, the state itself is not a unitary entity. It is an aggregation of actors from separate administrative departments. Values and interests are always not agreed upon among them. They negotiate, coordinate, and squeeze a single decision. *The state is an informalized entity.* This is a constructionist understanding of the state (Kreibich, 2012; Cuvi, 2016; Schindler, 2016). It emphasizes interactions among departments. It holds a dynamic and flexible perspective. However, it has a risk to miss the *will of power* that binds the wills of the departments. No matter how conflicting and divided the departments are, the state is *a* power that binds them together. It means four things. First, the state creates informality externally. Second, the state includes informality within it. Third, internal informality is a continuation of external informality. Fourth, the state then brings together different wills to a unity of purpose. Thus, the state is a united entity and a *formal subject* of governance.

What follows is a common story. The Environmental Health Bureau Department oversees urban beautification and environmental improvement.

It prioritizes the clearance of informal settlements. On the contrary, Welfare Support Bureau Department is in charge of social security. It prioritizes the welfare of residents. However, no matter how policy conflicts between them might be resolved, the state finally must take *one* decision: either clearing informal settlements or allowing informal settlers to stay. If environmental improvement takes precedence, informal settlements are removed. If the welfare of residents takes precedence, informal settlers are permitted to stay. In the end, residents are not consulted and have only two choices: to leave or to stay.

4.5   *Negotiated Informality*

How about the negotiation itself, by the way? Informality is a product of negotiation between the various land stakeholders (Villamizar, 2015: 2,24; Gandhi, 2012; Keck, 2012; Mcfarlane and Waibel, 2012). The state formulates urban plans, first by negotiating internally and then externally with various actors. Some studies understand informality as a micro-actional process, analyze actions (negotiations) of various actors in detail, and hold the dynamic and flexible constructionist view (Altrock, 2012: 188). Various stakeholders participate in urban planning and establish their respective roles and rights through multiple layers of negotiations. Negotiations are implemented formally and informally with the practices of bribes and patronage. Urban planning is a process of tension and bargaining between legal/illegal, public/secret, and orthodox/ unorthodox, that is, formality/informality. In this process, the wealthy with financial and political influence begin negotiations with the upper management of state organizations (top-down). Bottom people, lacking financial and political influence, negotiate with the lower levels of state organizations and go up the hierarchy (bottom-up). For the wealthy, lobbying is a tool for solving problems: for the bottom people, it is the final tool. For them, negotiation is a 'weapon of the weak' (Scott, 1987) as the last resort.

Even if this understanding of negotiations itself is correct, finally, the following have to be confirmed. Constructionist understanding has a risk that macroscopic spatial analysis is reduced to microscopic analysis of action. By doing so, it overlooks the supreme power of the state. The state always leads the negotiations among stakeholders and always decides the final measure. The state is not an informal entity. The poor are forced to confront the state in the end.

5   Informality Theory Afterwards

This section considered spatial informality based on critical informality theory. The key Points are four. 1) Formality and informality are citywide phenomena that include the wealthy as well as the poor. 2) Formality and informality are products of the political process of negotiation among various stakeholders. 3) Formality and informality are on a continuum. Informality appears in the formal space, and formality appears in the informal space. 4) The state leads negotiations and decides the final measure. It is a willful entity before the residents (bottom workers).

Later, Roy developed her critical informality theory by combining G. Agamben's theory of the state of exception and *homo sacer* and G. Spivak's *subaltern* theory (Spivak. 1988; Agamben, 2005; Roy, 2011). She focused on the state's governance, proposed a politico-philosophical perspective to understand the governance of the whole of the city using some keywords: peripheries, zone of exception, urban *homo sacer*, subaltern urbanism, etc., and clarified the supreme position of the state around formality and informality. Her perspective on urban governance is important. However, she was not out of a critical interpretation of the whole of the city. To empirically analyze bottom workers in cities, it is necessary to lower the epistemological perspective to the ontological level and face the realities of the city. Roy's urban theory needs to be bridged to this chapter. This is the next task.

References

Agamben G (1995=1998) *Homo Sacer: Sovereign Power and Bare Life.* trans. by Daniel Heller-Roazen, Board of Trustees of the Leland Stanford Junior University.

Agamben G (2003=2005) *State of Exception.* trans. by Attell K, Chicago: University of Chicago Press.

AlSayyad N (2004) Urban informality as a 'New' way of life. In: Roy A and AlSayaad N (eds) *Urban informality: transnational perspectives from the Middle East, Latin America, and South Asia*: 7–30.

Altrock U (2012) Conceptualisation informality: some thoughts on the way towards generalisation. In: Mcfarlane C and Waibel M (eds) *Urban Informalities*: 171–193.

Arabindoo P (2012) Bajji on the beach: middle-class food practices in Chennai's new beach. In: Mcfarlane C and Waibel M (eds) *Urban Informalities*: 67–88.

Balangue G (2013) "Jobless growth," IBON Facts and Figures, Manila: IBON.

Bureau of Labor Statistics (2013) A profile of the working poor, 2011 (BLS Report # 1041). Washington, DC: US Bureau of Labor Statistics.

Chaudhuri S and Mukhopadhyay U (2010) *Revisiting the Informa Sector: A General Equilibrium Approach.* London: Springer.

Crossa V (2014) Reading for difference on the street: de-homogenising street vending in Mexico City. *Urban Studies* 53(2): 287–301.

Cuvi J (2016) The politics of field destruction and the survival of Sao Paulo's street vendors. *Social Problems* 63: 395–412.

Davis M (2006) *Planet of Slums*. verso.

Drummond L B W (2000) Street scenes: practices of public and private space in 13
urban Vietnam. *Urban Studies* 37(12): 2377–2391.

Gandhi A (2012) Informal Moral Economies' and Urban Governance in India in
Context. In: Mcfarlane C and Waibel M (eds) *Urban Informalities*: 51–65.

Hansen A (2006) *Space Wars and the New Urban Imperialism*. Lund: Lund University.

ILO, International Labour Organization (2003) Decent Work and the Informal
Economy, International Labour Conference, 90th Session, 2002.

ILOSTAT, International Labour Organization (2019) Persons outside the labour
force: How inactive are? By Rosina Gammarano.

Iyotani T (1999) Translator's Interpretation for the Japanese version of Sassen S
(1996) *Losing Control? Sovereignty in An Age of Globalization*. New York: Columbia
University Press.

Jørgensen M B (2015) Precariat – what it is and isn't: towards an understanding of what
it does. *Critical Sociology* 40(7–8): 1–16.

Joshi G (1997) Urban Informal Sector in Metro Manila: A Problem or Solution?
International Labour Organization of the Philippines, Manila.

Keck M (2012) Informality as borrowed security: contested food markets in Dhaka,
Bangladesh. In: Mcfarlane C and Waibel M (eds) *Urban Informalities*: 111–127.

Kitahara A and Takai Y (1989) Urban Society and Urbanization in Southeast Asia.
Sociology of Southeast Asia: Family, Village, and City, edited by Kitahara, Sakai-
Shisosha, 53–73.

Klein N (2007) *Shock Doctrine: The Rise of Disaster Capitalism*. Metropolitan Books
Henry Holt and Company.

Kreibich V (2012) The mode of informal urbanization: reconciling social and statutory
regulation in urban land management. In: Mcfarlane C and Waibel M (eds) *Urban
Informalities*: 149–170.

Krueger A, Cramer J and Cho D (2014) Are the long-term unemployed on the margins of the labor market? *Brookings Papers on Economic Activities* Profect Muse
Mission: 229–299.

Kurtŭst S (2012) Informality as a strategy: streer traders in Hanoi facing constant insecurity. Mcfarlane C and Waibel M (eds) *Urban Informalities*: 89–110.

Laing S (1844) National Distress, London (from Marx, 1867=1996: 651).

Lombard M and Rakodi C (2016) Urban land conflict in the Global South: towards an
analytical framework. *Urban Studies* 53(13): 2683–2699.

Marx K (1852=1979) *The Eighteenth Brumaire of Louis Bonaparte, Marx-Engels Collected
Works*. Moscow: Progress Publishers.

Marx K (1996) *Capital: A Critique of Political Economy, vol.1, Marx-Engels Collected Works.* Moscow: Progress Publishers.

Marx K and Engels F (1848) *Manifesto of the Communist Party, Marx-Engels Collected Works.* Moscow: Progress Publishers.

Mcfarlane C and Waibel M (eds) (2012) *Urban Informalities: Reflections on the Formal and Informal.* Farnham: Ashgate Publishing Ltd.

Mtero F (2011) *The Informal Sector, Micro-Enterprise Activities and Livelihoods in Makana Municipality, South Africa.* London: LAP LAMBERT Academic Publishing.

Niitsu K (1989) *Gendai Ajia no suramu: Hettentozhōkoku toshi no keny* [Slum in Contemporary Asia: Study of Cities if Developing Countries] Tokyo: Akashi Shoten.

Porta R L and Shleifer A (2014) Informality and development. *Journal of Economic Perspectives* 28(3): 109–126.

Raco M (2003) Remaking place and securitising space: urban regeneration and the strategies, tactics and practices of policing in the UK. *Urban Studies* 40(9): 1869–1887.

Rakowski C (1994) *Contrapunto: The Informal Sector Debate in Latin America.* New York: State University of New York Press.

Roy A and AlSayyad N (2004) *Urban Informality: Transnational Perspectives from the Middle East, South Asia, and Latin America.* Lanham: Lexington Books.

Roy A (2005) Urban informality: toward an epistemology of planning. *Journal of the American Planning Association* 71(2): 147–158.

Roy A (2009) Why India cannot plan its cities: informality, insurgence and the idiom of urbanization. *Planning Theory* 8(1): 76–87.

Roy A (2010) *Poverty Capital: Microfinance and the Making of Development* London: Routledge.

Roy A (2011) Slumdog cities: rethinking subaltern urbanism. *International Journal of Urban and Regional Research* 35(2): 223–238.

Ruffini K and Wozniak A (Spring 2021) Supporting workers and families in the pandemic recession: results in 2020 and suggestions for 2021. *Brookings Papers on Economic Activity* (Reading on April 2022).

Schindler S (2016) Producing and contesting the formal/informal divide: regulating street hawking in Delhi, India. *Urban Studies* 51(2): 2596–2612.

Scott J (1987) *Weapons of the Weak: Everyday Forms of Peasant Resistance.* New Haven: Yale University Press.

Siegmann K and Schiphorst F (2016) Understanding the globalizing precariat: from informal sector to precarious. *Progress in Development Studies* 16(2): 111–123.

Silvia R and Shaw K (2012) Hip-hop and Sociality in a Brazilian Favela. In: Mcfarlane and Waibel (eds) *Urban Informalities*: 129–147.

Spivak G (1988) Can the Subaltern speak? In: Nelson C and Grossberg L (eds) *Marxism and the Interpretation of Culture.* Chicago: University of Ilinois Press.

Standing G (2011) *The Precariat: The New Dangerous Class.* London: Bloomsbury.

Standing G (2013a) Defining the precariat: A class in the making. *Eurozine.*

Standing G (2013b) the precariat, jargon: *Key Concepts in Social Research.* American Sociological Association 13(4): 10–12.

Standing G (2014) *A Precariat Charter: From Denizens to Citizens.* London: Bloomsbury.

Takano A (2012) Working poor and poor labor environment: redefinition incorporating reservoir. *Kumamoto-gakuen Journal of Commerce,* Kumamoto Gakuen University 17(1): 105–128.

Varley A (2013) Postcolonialising informality? Environment and Planning D: Society and Space, Network-Association of European Researchers on Urbanisation in the South (N-AERUS) 31(1): 4–22.

Villamizar-Duarte N (2015) Informalization as a processes: theorizing informality as a lens to rethink planning theory and practice in Bogota, Colombia. RC21 Conference, The Ideal City: between myth and reality: 1–27.

Wilson W (1987) *The Truly Disadvantaged: The Inner City, The Underclass, and Public Policy.* Chicago: University of Chicago Press.

Wright E (2015) Is the precariat a class? *Global Labor Journal.* 7(2): 123–135.

Yoshida M (2020) Informality saikō [Reconsideration of informality]. *Annals of Japan Association for Urban Sociology* Japan Association for Urban Sociology 38: 65–81.

PART 2

International Case Studies

..

CHAPTER 3

Transformation of Bottom Workers in the Hotel Industry

Reproduction Structures in Dormitory Labors

Keiko Yamaguchi

Abstract

In this chapter, the reproductive structure of bottom workers in the hotel industry is examined by clarifying the process and background of how the organization and labor composition are transformed in Japanese-style hotels located in hot spring tourist areas by means of qualitative research methods. The newer management of the case study hotel promoted the rationalization of hotel operations and control of labor. The profiles of those engaged in low-paid labor at the hotel have changed from middle-aged and elderly women from the countryside to young international students from outside Japan. In addition, aesthetic labor, focused on maintaining the proper look and attitudes, has been reified and strengthened. Although intersectional management is evident in the allocation of workers in these hotels, in the long term, the composition of the labor force has been influenced considerably by policy trends, resulting in a patchwork mobilization of the labor force. In this transformation, the primary aspect that supports the structure of labor reproduction of workers at the bottom is the existence of a live-in system involving employee dormitories in which work and housing are combined and daily life is linked to the company. Although times have changed and the layers of those who live-in dormitories and perform live-in jobs have been transformed, they have not been interrupted and are used as a bottom-line and flexible labor force.

Globalization is advancing worldwide, and the service economy is growing to match it. Following this, the industrial structure of developed countries is shifting from secondary to tertiary industries. The global tourism and hospitality sectors witnessed exponential growth in recent decades, and together, they now form the world's largest service sector (Ottenbacher et al. 2009; Tisdell 2001). The accommodation industry occupies an important position in the tourism and hospitality industry because of the varied types of employment it offers. However, it has been noted that the industry often has poor working conditions and a large number of bottom workers. Japanese hotels are no exception.

This chapter examines reproduction structures among bottom workers in the hotel industry by exploring the transformation process and background of the organization and workforce composition in Japanese-style hotels (called *ryokan* in Japanese) located in an area of hot spring tourism in Japan. This chapter is organized as follows. First, the characteristics of Japan's tourism and hotel industry are summarized. Second, the purpose and methodology of this study are presented in light of previous work on working conditions, labor force composition, and inequality among hotel workers. Third, an overview of the *ryokan* and hotel industry is presented by considering its industrial and labor characteristics. Fourth, by employing one specific hotel as a case study, the transformation of the organization and labor force composition is described. Fifth, the policy context that influenced this transformation is summarized. Finally, the inequality structure that reproduces the bottom in the Japanese hotel industry is discussed.

1   Tourism and the Hotel Industry in Japan

Tourism is an important industry in Japan, and it has been strongly promoted by the Japanese government. In 2003, the government established the Tourism Nation Council and launched the Visit Japan Project. In 2006, the former Basic Law on Tourism, which had been enacted in 1963, was completely revised, and the Basic Law for the Promotion of Tourism Nation was enacted. This new law states that "it is extremely important to realize a tourism-oriented nation for the development of our country's economy and society in the 21st century"; therefore, the provisions of the law are positioned an important policy pillar. In recent years, the policy Tourism Vision for the Japan of Tomorrow was formulated in 2016 as part of a new national development to become an advanced tourism country. A key issue in this vision was to enhance the attractiveness of Japan's tourism resources and make them a cornerstone of regional development, positioning tourism as an important industry that would be combined positioned together with regional revitalization. Since that time, the number of inbound tourists from Asian countries increased significantly. The number of inbound travelers to Japan has increased dramatically due to various collaborative efforts undertaken by the Japan National Tourism Organization and other inbound stakeholders. The number of foreign visitors to Japan was 5.21 million in 2003, exceeded 10 million in 2013, and peaked at 31.88 million in

2019 (Japan Tourism Agency ed. 2019). Furthermore, with international events such as the Olympics approaching, high expectations exist for the industry.[1]

The accommodation industry occupies an important position in the tourism and hospitality industry, due to the large amount and varied types of employment it offers. However, the low level of working conditions in this sector has often been noted. As a whole, the service industry primarily offers unskilled or low-skilled employment opportunities (Crang 1997; Shaw and Williams 1994; Wood 1997). In particular, hospitality and tourism are often low-paid, low-skilled, tourism negatively, exposed to poor management, limited to part-time and seasonal employment, and devoid of a clear career structure (Partington 2016; Walmsley 2004). In particular, the accommodation industry is characterized by frequent turnover (Iverson and Deery 1997; Duncan et al. 2013), low wages even when working full time (Knox 2011), increased work intensity (Seifert and Messing 2006), and precarious and seasonal employment (Lundberg et al. 2009). According to Linda McDowell, "labor economists, geographers, and sociologists who are interested in exploring both hyper-exploitation and labor segregation in new service-based economies have turned to the hotel as an ideal site" (McDowell et al. 2007: 2).

The labor situation in Japan's accommodation industry is no exception. However, despite the popularity of hot springs and the large number of hotels serving them throughout the country, little research exists on labor in the accommodations industry in Japan. This study provides a case study of the changing state of bottom work in hotels in Japan. The characteristics of hotel labor in Japan are unique among developed countries, and it is worth taking its specificity into account as follows.

First, the employment of foreign nationals is restricted by Japanese laws and regulations. The immigration system in Japan is one of the most rigid and unequal in the world. The system has never officially accepted unskilled migrant workers for hotel or other labor. However, as mentioned in the section 4 of the chapter, due to the labor shortage under the bubble economy in the late 1980s, the Immigration Control and Refugee Recognition Law was amended in 1990, thereby allowing the immigration of foreign nationals of Japanese descent. Japanese Latin Americans have often worked as part-time workers in the manufacturing industry. Thus, who has been working in hotels in the service industry?

---

1   Similar to other countries, the COVID-19 pandemic has transformed trends in the tourism and hospitality industries radically. Trends post 2020 require further investigation.

Second, the Japanese spirit of hospitality, *omotenashi*, exhibits a strong normalizing effect on the Japanese service industry. Traditional *ryokan* hotels are particularly insistent on following this norm. Sylvie Guichard-Anguis highlighted that in the *ryokan*, one can encounter nature and that the *ryokan* shelters the culture of hospitality, a fundamental aspect of human relations in Japan (Sylvie 2009). *Ryokan* hotels have marketed themselves as providing high quality and attentive service, known as home-like hospitality. It is important to produce such performances, which they do by wearing kimonos that evoke a sense of tradition and nostalgia. Workers have been expected to possess attributes, words and deeds that are appropriate for good hospitality. Hence, many women have been mobilized. Hotels are characterized by a type of labor that provides quality and close care, termed home-style hospitality. For this, a large female labor force has been mobilized. How has this gender-intersecting inequality changed?

Third, hot spring resorts were like hot spring pools with a constant flow of diverse people (Takeda and Moon 2010: 179). Japanese hot springs attract a specialized type of service industry providers that rely on a marginalized reproductive labor force. Hot springs have long been linked to poverty and the mobilization of disadvantaged people, including single mothers, welfare recipients, and fluid workers. What is the background for this? This chapter identified the importance that dormitory labors (working while living in a company-supplied dormitory) demonstrate for Japan as a means of mobilizing the labor force at the bottom and depositing poverty. Thus, this chapter is also a detailed case study of "dormitory labor," a focal point in Chapter 1.

Fourth, also related to the third point, studies have investigated hotel labor, even within the same Asian region. For example, Ellen Otis identified labor practices in a 300-room luxury hotel in Beijing that opened in the late 1990s. Unmarried, urban-born young female workers aged 17–28 were employed at the front desk of this hotel and trained in self-presentation and aesthetic labor with an awareness of elite male guests (Otis 2006, 2008, 2016). Conversely, rural-born female workers did not have urban household registration and were forced to work in the informal sector under poor conditions (Otis 2012). The number of new luxury hotels is increasing in Japan; thus, it is possible that these labor practices can be observed in Japan. However, the hotel industry is divided into different tiers, ranging from low-priced hotels to five-star luxury hotels. Furthermore, their labor practices differ (Otis 2012). By contrast, this study focuses on traditional, large, affordable *ryokan* in Japan. In these places, although the number of individual guests has been increasing, many group guests hold large banquets. Therefore, these *ryokans* require many workers and tend to have high labor mobility because of their ease of entry and poor working conditions. In other words, the clientele and employees differ from those in Otis's modern foreign luxury hotels. Therefore, the dormitory system has been preserved in Japanese *ryokan*, which employs female bottom workers. Japanese *ryokan* is an appropriate subject for a discussion on the transformation of Japan's bottom workers and is the focus of this book.

2 Labor Force Segmentation and Inequality in the Hotel Industry

Since 2000, as globalization and the service economy developed, the research identified various challenges for hotel-related labor. For example, hotel labor tends feature frequent turnover (Iverson and Deery, 1997; Duncan et al. 2013), low wages for room attendants (Knox 2011; Kensbock et al. 2017), precarious or seasonal employment in general (Lundberg et al. 2009), changes in working conditions due to business consolidation and outsourcing (Cañada 2018; Knox 2010; Seifert and Messing 2006), the impact of emotional labor in hotels on turnover intention (Lv et al. 2012), and the tendency to emphasize aesthetic labor in hotels and its burden on workers (Otis 2016; Tsaura and Hsieha 2020) have been noted. Who are the people working in these employment situations, and under what inequalities do they labor? Many studies of hotel labor have examined the question, focusing on the characteristics of class, gender, ethnicity, and age. Patricia Adler and Peter Adler explore the typology of the occupational culture and lifestyles of laborers at luxury Hawaiian resorts. Four categories were identified: new immigrants, locals, managers, and seekers, with each group being identified as having unique characteristics and career paths (Adler and Adler 1999).

Immigrant workers from abroad received have particular focus. As globalization progressed, research exploring the impact of migrant labor expanded. Some attention has been paid to migrant tourist workers (Bianchi 2010), most work has been done on newcomer immigrants with little education or skills. Numerous studies exist on the tendency of this group to take jobs at the bottom of the low-wage sector of the labor market, their working conditions, and their survival strategies (Alberti 2014; Baum et al. 2016; Knox 2011 et al.; Markova et al. 2013). In recent years, it has also been noted that hotels rely heavily on migrant workers to fill both management and lower-level positions (McDowell et al. 2009).

However, the approach of developing specific classifications in advance has been criticized, and work is now being conducted on the fluidity of classifications. Increasingly, studies of diversity and organizational inequality focus on the fluid forms of social differences and approach them through the lens of intersectionality. Much of this research examines the generation of social inequality by empirically presenting how gender, ethnicity, class, age, and other subdivisions intersect. Furthermore, various actors, including workers, managers, customers, and labor intermediaries, are treated as contested areas that play an important role in mobilizing social differences among workers.

Linda McDowell and colleagues explore how a divided and segmented migrant labor force is assembled to serve guests in a hotel. They argue that a dual process of interpellation operates within service sector workplaces that are reinforced and resisted in daily social practices and relationships among managers, workers, and guests in a hotel (McDowell et al. 2007). Sarah Dyer and colleagues argue that migration status should be understood to intersect with gender in the production of a gendered performance at work. They demonstrate that migration status operates in similar ways to gender as a basis for labor market discrimination and segmentation, through the naturalization of skills in particular bodies (Dyer et al. 2010).

The addition of intersections with physical age and other factors should also be considered. To examine privilege and penalty, Shelagh Mooney and colleagues discuss the intersections of gender with age and ethnicity in hotel careers. They point out that hotel class processes are based on gendered, body-age, and ethnicity stereotypes, and class penalties are indicators of women's differences (Mooney et al. 2017). More recently, Gabriella Alberti and Francesco E. Iannuzzi showed that intersectional management is used to capture fluid forms of valorization of social difference, influenced by workers' practices of embodied intersectionality through the selective performance of entrenched stereotypes and their everyday encounters with an internationalizing clientele (Alberti and Iannuzzi 2020).

To examine the segmentation and inequality of hotel workers, research that takes this intersectionality perspective demonstrates advantages for unraveling the complex generation of inequality and placing both the limitations and capabilities of workers' agency in diverse settings in perspective. However, the Japanese case, which features extreme control over labor mobilization, is more structurally prescriptive, and immigration itself is policy restricted. In this context, how does intersectional management, combining gender, ethnicity, class, and age, function, and what are the structures that govern it? This study examines structures of inequality among bottom workers in Japan, in a way that sets up older-style categories while also taking a perspective on intersectionality.

This chapter examines the reproductive structure of bottom workers in the hotel industry by clarifying the process and background of how the organization and labor composition are transformed in those *ryokan* located in hot spring tourist areas. Particular attention should be paid to changes in the composition of gender, race, age, and ethnicity in bottom labor, and the background of their mobilization will be discussed. Reproductive structures include economic aspects, such as income and status, and micro aspects, such as motivation and consciousness. The latter is an important sociological perspective. However, this chapter focuses on the chronological changes in the economic aspects and their context.

This chapter's results also form a contribution to research related to inequality dealing with hotels in Japan. As noted earlier, academic work that dealt with bottom workers in Japanese hotels was limited. In this context, Chris McMorran describes the complex ways in which different scales and regimes of mobility interact with the bodies, personal lives, careers, and aspirations of *ryokan* employees through fieldwork at a local hot spring in rural Japan. He draws attention to aspects of the reproduction of immobilization, which he calls the "production of fixities," and points out that mobility and immobility should not be viewed as opposites but as conditions that intersect in subtle ways in the daily lives of individuals (McMorran 2015). Here, focusing on inequalities that intersect with gender by capturing the characteristics of highly mobile hotel workers is important. However, his approach does not explain why such conditions emerge, identify the reproductive structure of bottom-line labor, or determine the changes that are taking place in this structure. This chapter will contribute to the advancement of hotel labor studies in Japan by filling in these gaps.

Hotel workers are stratified according to their occupations and positions. However, hotel labor, which inevitably includes kitchen, restaurant, and cleaning operations, requires a vastly underpaid service workforce. Our target is those service workers who have nonregular employment and receive nearly minimum wages. However, in the hierarchy of bottom workers mentioned in Chapter 2, the key term of this book, this group is higher than workers who are unemployed or who work in the informal sector. The category of hotel workers as bottom workers overlaps in many ways with the categories of the working poor and the precariat. However, the low level of working conditions, the mobility requirement due to the need to move from one area to another in search of work, and the precariousness of living in employee dormitories make hotel workers work together to impede an easy life. Some hotel workers are to be placed in the bottom class and will not be mismatched as targets here.

In this investigation, I conducted a case study using qualitative research methods. This study has begun in 2006 at a large-scale *ryokan* at a hot spring resort in the Tokyo metropolitan area. The hotel was originally a small inn, but it expanded, as it accepted increasing numbers of tourists from the Tokyo metropolitan area during Japan's economic boom period, from 1955 to 1975. This

PHOTO 3.1   Exterior of a *ryokan*
             PHOTO BY THE AUTHOR

ryokan is a typical large Japanese-style hotel. The research involved more than 10 visits to the *ryokan* since 2006, with a minimum stay of 2 days and a maximum stay of 3 weeks. The research participants included 30 former and current hotel employees, 6 hotel managers, 4 self-employed workers, 8 employees of three affiliated companies, 7 temp agency employees, 8 social welfare and employment managers, and a *geisha* girl. In addition, several other informal interviews were conducted.

3   Trends in the Japanese Hotel Industry

First, we summarized the labor market and economic characteristics of *ryokan* hotels using statistical data. The Japanese Hotel Business Act identifies the following types of hotels: general hotels, *ryokan*, inexpensive rooming houses, and boarding houses. This chapter focuses on large *ryokan* that provide food and accommodation packages at hot spring resorts.

As shown in Figure 3.1, since 1970, the number of hotels and guest rooms in Japan has changed significantly. While the number of *ryokans* significantly

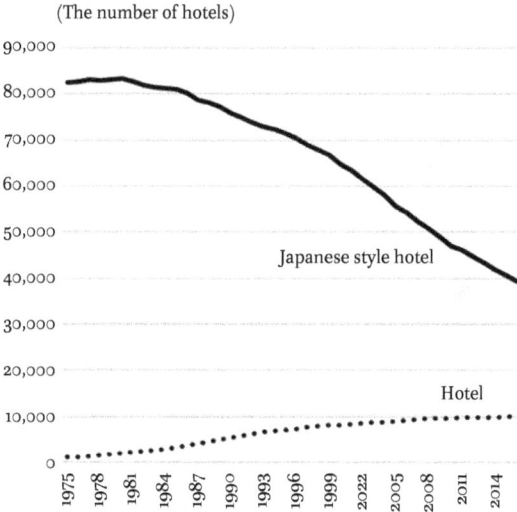

FIGURE 3.1   Trends in the number of hotels
SOURCE: DATA FROM THE NUMBER OF
ENVIRONMENTAL HEALTH FACILITIES
FROM THE MINISTRY OF HEALTH, LABOR,
AND WELFARE

decreased, the number of general hotels continued to increase, from 2,039 in 1980 to 10,101 in 2016. Figure 3.2 shows trends in the number of guest rooms per hotel. The number of rooms in general hotels has increased rapidly and surpassed that of *ryokan* hotels. In 2016, the number of guest rooms in regular hotels was 869,810 (Ministry of Health, Labor and Welfare 2017).

Changes in the demand for hotels demonstrated a substantial impact on the hotel industry. Approaches to tourism, such as in the provision of group tours for employees, had sharply increased during the economic boom period. Hotel owners invested in facilities such as large banquet halls and entertainment centers and increased the number of guest rooms to meet this demand. Furthermore, business hotels, which provide a simplified service specializing in accommodation, also had expanded after the mid-1960s. However, in the late 1980s, individuals and small groups became the primary users of hotels. Many hotels encountered difficulties, including substantial debt, the need to secure additional funding, aging facilities, and low occupancy rates. Many hotels were caught in a downward spiral (Ministry of Land, Infrastructure, Transport, and Tourism ed. 2006: 140–1). Since 2000, even well-known and established hotels filed for bankruptcy. The Great Tohoku Earthquake in 2011 exacerbated these difficulties. To survive, many Japanese hotels have begun offering additional

(The number of rooms)

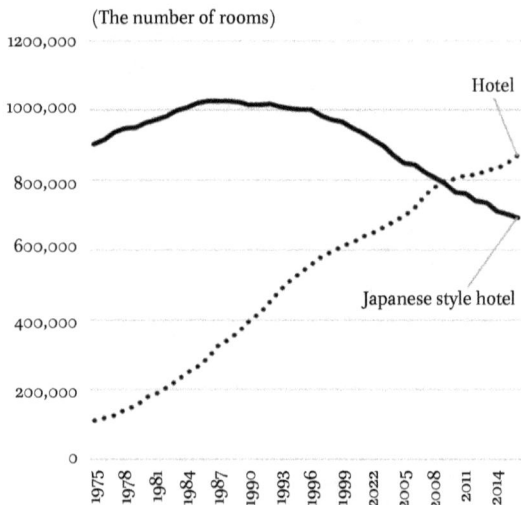

FIGURE 3.2   Trends in the number of guest rooms in hotels
SOURCE: DATA FROM THE NUMBER OF
ENVIRONMENTAL HEALTH FACILITIES
FROM THE MINISTRY OF HEALTH, LABOR,
AND WELFARE

incentives, such as open-air spas, reserved baths, and discounted room prices. They also provided joint sponsorship of events with regional partners.

Currently, however, the number of inbound hotel guests from Asia is increasing. Furthermore, given the government's strong promotion of tourism, since the 2000s, some districts and facilities in large cities have been redeveloped. The number of luxury hotels owned by foreign capitals has also increased, especially in large urban areas. Some large hotels are vying for these expanding groups, and small- and medium-sized hotels have been adding new value. For example, the restaurant Auberge, which targets middle-class guests, also offers accommodation. Before the beginning of the COVID-19 pandemic, the hotel industry was expected to continue to perform well ahead of the 2020 Tokyo Olympics.

4   Labor Market Characteristics and Labor Conditions of Hotels

The accommodation industry is among the largest parts of the service industry by employment and has historically been one of the few spheres of the economy where women can easily find work. Japan had witnessed a decrease in hotel employment from 649,934 in 2009 to 635,038 in 2014. In 2014, women accounted for 56.2% (356,905) and men for 43.8% (277,444) of employees in the accommodation industry. Of female employees, 26.6% were full-time regular employees, 55.7% were full-time nonregular employees, 10.8% were temporary workers, and 6.9% were classified as other employees, including the self-employed and family employees. Of male employees, 50.6%, 31.2%, 6.4%, and 11.8% were full-time regular employees, full-time nonregular employees, temporary workers, and other employees, respectively (The Statistics Bureau 2018). Thus, women accounted for a higher proportion of nonregular and temporary employees than men.

In the following, the characteristics of a gendered and stratified industry and labor are demonstrated through the case studies of three women (one of whom is a married) who worked at inns, hotels, and resort facilities. It should be noted that these three women demonstrate challenges that approach homelessness and are not representative of women working in the hotel industry as a whole. However, their cases indicate the characteristics of bottom workers in the hotel industry and will be discussed here to outline the characteristics of their industry and labor.

Michiyo (6os)

Born in the Tohoku region of Japan, Michiyo worked in a restaurant after graduating from high school, founded her own restaurant in her 30s, and she ran it until she was in her early 50s. However, one of her brothers became seriously ill, and closing her business to take care of him was necessary. That brother passed away, as did their parents. She sought work through local employment agencies, but her age made finding work a challenge, and she could not survive on short-time employment. In the 2000s, when she was in her 50s, she began to work at a large *ryokan* in the Kanto area through the employment security office. She works mainly as a room attendant and banquet attendant, in part-time shifts with long breaks in between. She did not understand the job well at first and found it hard and physically demanding. She is paid by the hour. She began as a seasonal migrant, so she still has her handbook for migrants issued by the local employment security office, but now, she works year round.

Michiyo quit her job to care for her family, which is often expected of women. She then began working at *ryokan* in large metropolitan areas as a migrant worker because the number of jobs in rural areas was insufficient. In this case, a woman worked at one *ryokan* for a long time on a part-time basis.

Nao (40s)

After graduating from high school, Nao worked for a temporary employ-ment agency for about 10 years. After getting married, she and her hus-band worked as front-desk clerks, cleaners, and cooks, while living in company dormitories at various Kanto branches of well-known hotels. However, they were laid off, and were required to leave the company housing. They looked for work for a long time but could not find a posi-tion, so they rented a Leo Palace (a nationwide chain of furnished rental apartments) and lived in it, draining their savings. They continued to look for work, but in the end, their savings ran out, and they were required to leave their rooms. Later, they saw an advertisement on TV about Haken Mura (Tent City for the Jobless; emergency winter support for the jobless for the winter of 2008, organized in Tokyo), and came to Tokyo, hoping to find a soup kitchen.

Nao and her husband worked for various group company hotels and lived in company dormitories. However, when they lost their jobs, they also lost their residence. Subsequently, they were unable to find other jobs and had to spend their savings.

Megumi (30s)

Megumi is from the northern region of Japan. Her father was a strict and violent man, and she did not want to spend much time at home with him. After finishing school, she stayed home to help with the household chores, but in the 1990s, when she was a teenager, she left home to live and work at a food processing and manufacturing plant elsewhere in the same prefecture. However, the factory where she worked was dam-aged in the Great East Japan Earthquake, and she lost her job and had no guarantee of future employment. After that, she began working at a hot spring hotel in the metropolitan areas in search of a dormitory labor. She worked at several hotels, but the work was so demanding that she could not keep up. Then, thinking "Tokyo is the only place for me," she came to Tokyo, using the last of her money on the trip.

In Megumi's case, because of family relationship problems, she had to move out of her home. She had been seeking dormitory labor since she was a teen-ager and secured a job at a hot spring hotel. However, the work at the hotel was difficult for her.

The cases of these three individuals who came to work in the study hotel, albeit temporarily, show the intersection of gender inequality and class and represent their disparate working conditions. First, the fact that Nao and her husband worked at the front desk, doing cleaning, and as cooking staff indicates that diverse occupations and places exist for men to work in hotels that provide both lodging and food and beverage functions. Many women work part-time serving food, cooking, and cleaning, including waitress work, all of which involve providing services that involve closer interactions with clients. In the past, many *geisha* houses were found in large hot spring resorts, and women were dispatched to hotels in this role. Also, many women worked in the various restaurants and retail stores clustered in the hot spring resort area. Hot spring tourist areas were gendered, and diverse "areas dedicated to service industry workers" (Takeda 2006) exhibited concentrations of reproductive labor.

Second, as Michiyo and Megumi report, hotel work is hard work. Hotel work tends to be irregular and require working long hours. The demand for labor varies weekly and throughout the year, in response to the seasons and holidays. In addition, for some employees, the number of working hours per day can also be irregular. In particular, room attendants (*nakai* in Japanese) tend to work irregular hours, including long lunch breaks and nighttime overtime, to facilitate the rhythms of the guests. Recent years have seen a changing awareness of the need for privacy among hotel guests, and *ryokans* moved toward simplifying the necessary work by reducing interfering services. However, irregular working hours are all but unavoidable. Moreover, the significant demand for both emotional (Hochschild 1983; Shani et al. 2014) and physical labor is similar to what several previous studies have highlighted.

Also, to ensure the continuation of the hotel's hospitality services, employees are strongly encouraged to perform emotional labor. As noted, hospitality and employee subordination are strong norms in the Japanese service industry. In addition, employee training and management now tend to be more focused on enhancing hospitality. Managers require employees to smile, be well-groomed, and be sensitive to guests at all times. In the hotel observed in this chapter, to improve the quality of the emotional labor involved in personal services, feedback from guest questionnaires is provided to employees during meetings. Emotional labor is now more routinized and controlled. Although the work is physically and emotionally demanding, many positions pay only minimum wage.

Third, the hotel industry in Japan, as in other countries, is labor-intensive, suffers from chronic understaffing, and exhibits a high turnover rate. Previously, hotel work was considered not to require a resume because the positions were regarded as unskilled, and high turnover was expected. In addition, the hot spring resort areas, in particular, were characterized by a high degree of independence of individual *ryokan* and the spatial characteristics of the limited space in which rival lodging facilities were clustered together. This meant that employees were often recruited, and they could quickly move to a neighboring hotel and work there.

The labor shortage is a serious problem), especially for hotels in peripheral and regional cities with small populations. It should be noted that local hotels are less well staffed than urban hotels (Kantani 1995). In the interviews conducted for the research, the dispatching companies noted similar difficulties. Therefore, hotel owners seek to recruit workers in a variety of ways, including through public employment agencies, job posting magazines, web advertisements, newspaper flyers, word-of-mouth, and the use of dispatching companies (temp agencies). Some major hotels offer welfare support, such as the provision of childcare facilities, to attract female workers. Also, some hotels enter into partnerships with daycare centers, vocational schools, and universities (Takeda and Moon 2010).

Fourth, the three women worked in various roles for different lengths of time. Michiyo, for example, had her own restaurant. After being unable to find

PHOTO 3.2   Restaurant in a hotel
PHOTO BY THE AUTHOR

work in her hometown, she looked for work in hospitality. After, like Michiyo, being required to abandon a different line of work, Megumi looked for a dormitory labor, worked at a manufacturing plant, and then was hired at an inn. Both were single and had few people to rely on. The hotel industry exhibits a long history of attracting women (and couples) who are in need of a place to live and work.

Hotels, especially those located at hot spring resorts, are often equipped with employee dormitories. A survey of 940 Japanese hotels conducted by the Japan Labor Research Organization in 1993 found that 76.4% of *ryokan* hotels in hot spring areas, 63.0% of *ryokan* hotels at resorts, 59.5% of resort hotels, and 55.8% of hotels at resorts provide company dormitories or housing for employees (Japan Institute of Labor 1994: 59–60).[2] The report related to the provision of employee dormitories to the scale of the business. Providing company housing is an important means of securing workers and dealing with irregular working patterns mentioned in Chapter 1. In addition, the provision of accommodation is considered a benefit to laborers who earn low wages. The significance of the company housing for bottom workers will be discussed in detail at the end of this section.

Jeong-sil Moon examined these characteristics of hotel labor in relation to gender inequality. She highlighted that the gendered nature of service work ("extension of domestic work") allows for workers with no experience to enter hotel work, as well as noting that dormitory labors attract divorced women and single-mother households by screening female workers according to anticipated differences (e.g., "family circumstances" such as single, divorced, or with children, and "family norms" such as women being in charge of housework and childcare in the family) (Moon 2012: 38). Hotel work is regarded as an extension of housework for housewives and exists in a system in which the gender inequality of familial difference is embedded.

The industrial and labor characteristics of Japanese hotels themselves demonstrate much in common with those of other countries. During the major economic and social changes of the recent years, some aspects changed, but others did not. In the following, we discuss the changes in the composition of the labor force and the background, particularly those at the bottom of the labor force who work for minimum wage, using one hotel as a case study.

---

2   The respondents decided whether hotels were "resort hotels" or "hotels at resorts," and the difference was unclear (Japan Institute of Labor 1994).

5   Transition in Laborer Composition: from a Case Study of One Hotel

This section clarifies the kind of labor mobilized at an understaffed hotel and changes in the composition of the hotel's labor force. The business models of a range of hotel types are dependent on sales strategies and location. The case study below was conducted in Wakanoki Hotel (a pseudonym), located in a metropolitan area.

The Hot Springs resort, which includes Wakanoki Hotel, is located in the Kanto region, approximately 150 kilometers from central Tokyo. Many years ago, Hot Springs was a rustic post town at the foot of a famous mountain. Following the completion of a railway line from Tokyo, a large number of hotels were established there. In the mid-1950s, a string of large new hotels was opened to meet the demands of the increasing number of tourist groups and construction workers who required accommodation in the area while building dams and highways. Hot Springs became a thriving area with many hotels, souvenir shops, restaurants, amusement facilities, and staffing agencies for *geisha* girls.

The Wakanoki Hotel is the largest in the area. It opened in the mid-1950s and was subsequently expanded later. In the 1970s, at the height of its popularity, the hotel accepted 900 guests per day and provided invited tours sponsored by manufacturers, tour groups sponsored by companies, senior citizen's associations, and agricultural cooperative associations. However, in the 2000s, it filed for the Civil Rehabilitation Law and then reopened under new management. The new management invested in new services and events and built private baths. After this transition, customers have gradually returned to the facility, and in recent years, the number of tourists from China and Korea have increased. At present, accommodation costs approximately 11,000 yen per day, including breakfast and an evening buffet. Wakanoki Hotel is considered a large-scale hotel, known for the reasonableness of its rates, taking into consideration the facilities on offer. The labor force working at the hotel changed over the course of its 50-year history.

Focusing primarily on the low-wage hospitality sector, changes in the workforce related to employment patterns and the division of labor can be divided into three periods: a peak in the 1970s, new management in 2000, and the mid-2010s and after.

5.1   *The Peak*

During the 1970s, the hotel employed many room attendants, who wore traditional Japanese clothing and were assigned to particular rooms to look after guests with great care. The room attendants began work at 6:00, serving tea, helping guests check out, and removing tea sets from the guests' rooms (Figure 3.3). They rested for 5 hours during the day and then greeted new customers and changed tea sets at approximately 15:00. If required, they assisted at drinking parties as well. Although their shifts were scheduled to end at 21:00, they often worked late to accommodate the guests. Of the approximately 40 people employed in this department in the case hotel, half were migrants from Aomori prefecture in northern Japan (*dekasegi* in Japanese). In Aomori, where places of employment are limited and there is heavy snowfall in winter, there has long been a labor practice of seasonal *dekasegi*, mainly among farmers. The duration of *dekasegi* in Aomori has existed since longer than in other regions and changed form over time.[3] Room attendants were classified as either main workers, who wore traditional Japanese clothing, or apprentice workers, who wore simple uniforms. Migrant workers started their tenure as apprentice workers.

Male all-around workers (*banto* in Japanese) began work at 8:00, putting away the bedding. After resting for 2 hours, they began to serve food, lay out bedding in the rooms, and clear tables at approximately 15:00. Approximately 20 men worked in this section. Meanwhile, women living nearby were hired as part-time cleaners. After the guests departed, these women cleaned the rooms and all common spaces by vacuuming the floors and wiping down desks, windows, TVs, and so on with damp cloths. They worked from 9:00 to 15:00. From the late 1970s on, members of the C association, an informal temporary employment agency, helped with the breakfast buffet and sometimes assisted at drinking parties in the evening. The local association was owned by the former owner of a staffing agency for *geisha* girls. As many as 30 workers, including former *geisha* girls, worked at the association at that time.

Also, the hotel employed dishwashers, cooks, drivers, drinking-party staff, and front-desk clerks. Many *geisha* girls were dispatched to assist at drinking parties. The migrant workers from Aomori were primarily as cleaners,

---

3   Migrant laborers were commonly hired in hot spring areas during Japan's high economic growth period. Between 1958 and 1997 in the hot spring resort of Hakone and between 1958 and 2003 in the hot spring resort of Atami, migrant labor continued to be indispensable, with a peak in the early 1970s (Takeda and Moon 2010: 83–4). Both resorts are in the Tokyo metropolitan area. A number of factors have been identified as contributing to the development of Japan's high-growth economy in the post-war period, which has been referred to as the "Japanese miracle." Amongst these, Sassen (2001: 314) highlighted that a key factor underlying them included the mobilization of substantial numbers of migrant laborers from rural areas. This occurrence is in contrast with the development of some advanced economies. This study revealed that such labor force mobilization from rural to urban areas is found in Japan's hospitality industry, wherein many women are employed.

Time	Front-desk clerk	Cleaner	Room attendant	Drinking party staff	C association	All-around workers (Banto)
1 2 3 4 5 6 7 8 9 10 11 12 13 14 15 16 17 18 19 20 21 22 23 24	Check in and out, helping guests	Cleaning rooms and public space	Serving tea and helping check out / Greet customers and serving parties	Serving drinking parties	Serving breakfast / Helping with parties	Putting away *futons* / Serving parties, put out *futons* and clear tables

* ┆┄┄┆ Outsourcing
   ▭   Shift

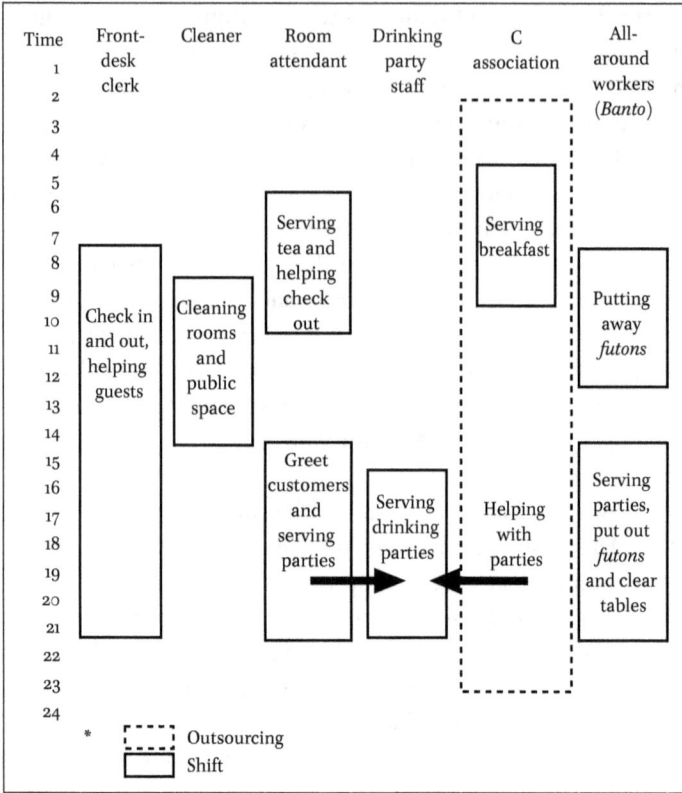

FIGURE 3.3   Laborer composition and duties in the 1970s
SOURCE: CREATED BY THE AUTHOR

dishwashers, room attendants, and male all-around workers. Many seasonal migrant workers from rural areas were employed in this way during this era. Japanese Brazilians were also employed, but none worked at the hotel for long.

Immediately before the reopening of the hotel, the labor force was made up of 85 regular workers (including 30 women), 40 part-time workers (37 women), and 70 migrant workers (40 women). A total of 150 of the 230 workers at the hotel came from Aomori. However, as the availability of seasonal work decreased, an increasing number of laborers worked throughout the year or did not return to Aomori.

5.2   After Reopening

The division of labor at the hotel changed after its reopening in the 2000s (Figure 3.4). Room attendants no longer wore traditional Japanese clothing and

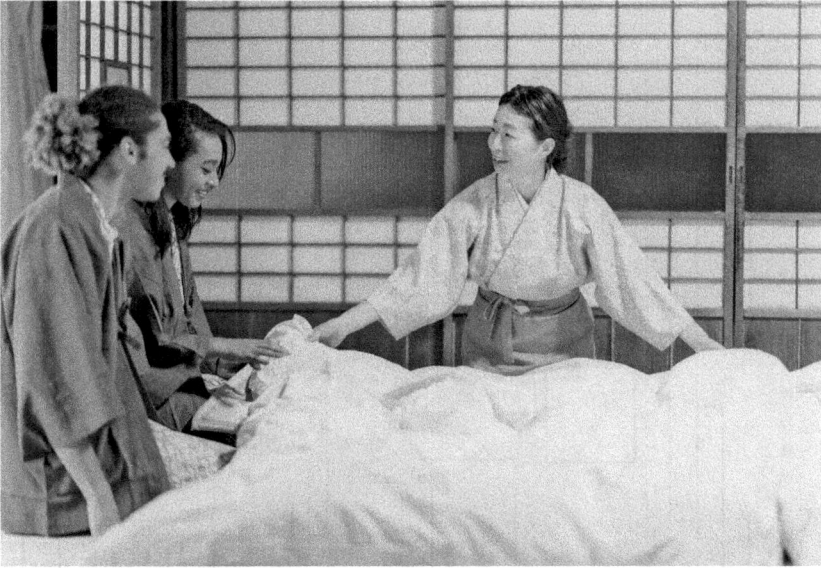

PHOTO 3.3   Room attendant's work at a *ryokan*
SOURCE: PHOTO BY RECEP-BG/ GETTY IMAGES

were no longer assigned to specific rooms. Rather, they worked at a breakfast buffet from 6:00 to 10:00, rested for 5 hours, and began the dinner shift at 15:00. Many middle-aged and elderly women from rural areas were employed part-time in these positions. After the hotel made migrant employees from Aomori redundant, they rehired fewer than 10 skilled workers. In addition, five female Chinese trainees in their 20s worked as room attendants. They were recruited for one year through a trainee program managed by a major travel agency. Another 10 or so Japanese youth were hired part-time through a nationwide dispatch company for one month during the busy season.

Cleaning was outsourced to a cleaning company based in a neighboring prefecture. That company had a branch office inside the hotel and employed three full-time and 80 part-time workers. These workers were middle-aged and elderly women from the local area, including the area near the city. Many exhibited extensive experiences working at other hotels. The kitchen staff worked in two shifts. Dishwashers began work at 8:00 and returned to work at 19:00 or 20:00. Front-desk staff, who were largely young regular workers, worked three shifts. *Geisha* girls were rarely sent to the hotel. Because of management policies, 50 full-time employees were hired after reopening, and the hotel recruited 10 new graduates.

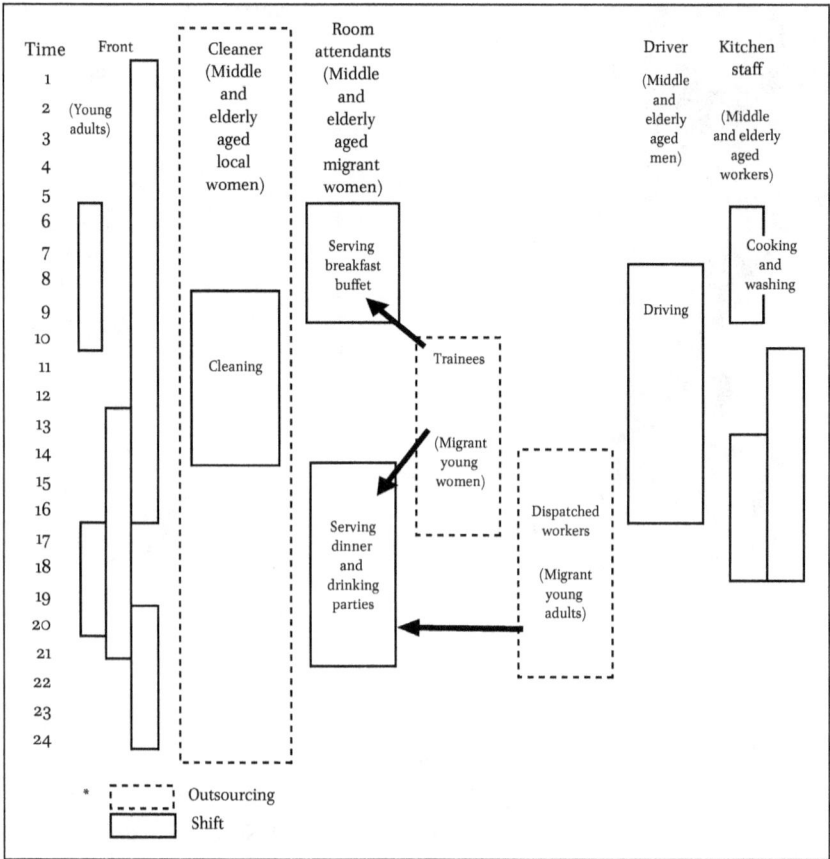

FIGURE 3.4   Laborer composition and duties after 2000
SOURCE: CREATED BY THE AUTHOR

The hotel invested in employee training in areas such as basic business etiquette and behavior, including how to greet guests. Regular meetings were held, with lectures given by the company president. In addition, the management carefully checked the use of cooking ingredients and beverages.

5.3   Since the Mid-2010s

The composition of the labor force has dramatically changed since the mid-2010s. Some recent college graduates were hired for full-time employment because of the company's desire to hire key employees. However, retaining these employees over a long period has proven difficult.

The hotel now employs more than 10 in-house workers, who perform the accounting and guest booking, as well as approximately 10 employed at the front desk, in the lounges, and as drivers, with more than 10 in customer services. The kitchen has a staff of 10 chefs and about 5 assistants. About 5 employees are engaged in washing in the kitchen, and a further 10 work part-time in the kitchen. In the 2010s, cleaning that was outsourced to an external company was returned to part-time employees. However, the total cost of cleaning has not changed. The cleaning department includes approximately 20 part-time employees and several casual staff.

In addition, the hotel now employs many foreign laborers, including 10 trainees from China and about 10 regular and 10 irregular employees who are international students at a local language school. Another five language school students work at the hotel year-round, while the others work only on weekends. Many of such international students are from countries in Southeast Asia. On the weekends, the hotel provides transport for these employees between their place of residence and the hotel but, and during longer holidays, they live at the hotel's dormitory. Many male students serve food in the restaurant, and many female students work in the kitchen. Because they wear burkas that cover their heads, female Muslim students do not work as waitresses.

A general manager said, "at first, we were worried that foreigners would not be able to serve at a *ryokan*, but there haven't been any problems." International employees make up most of the hotel's labor force. However, an employee admitted that labor shortages remain serious.

In essence, migrant workers from Aomori, who were brought back to work after the hotel reopened, have become part-time workers and, since the mid-2010s, Japanese workers in the low-paying hospitality sector have largely been replaced by international students and trainees. The hotel owner targeted young international students as a stable and inexpensive workforce that attracts guests by creating a fresh and lively atmosphere. These employees are expected to be able to speak Chinese to meet the demand of the growing numbers of Chinese tourists in recent years.

6   Changing and Unchanging Ethnic, Gender, Age, and Aesthetic Disparities

This chapter highlights several changes in the gender, ethnic, and age composition of workers as the rationalization of hotel management progresses. These changes are summarized as follows (Table 3.1).

In the first term, the workforce mainly consisted of migrant workers from Aomori, fluid workers who moved from one hotel to another, and local residents. The work style required close customer service and tended to involve

TABLE 3.1   Changes in hotel workforce composition

	First term	Second term	Third term
Worker attributes	Migrant workers from Aomori (*dekasegi*)	Migrant workers from Aomori (*dekasegi*)	Foreign students
	Fluid workers	Trainees	Trainees
	Local residents	Dispatched workers	Fluid workers
		Fluid workers	Local residents
		Local residents	
Work style	Close contact and long working hours	Transition to simplification	Simplification and work shifts

SOURCE: CREATED BY THE AUTHOR

long hours. In the second term, workers from Aomori began to decline but trainees from China and dispatched workers were newly hired. The work style was a transitional period wherein close services are gradually simplified. Finally, the third term was when the number of international students and trainees clearly increased. Customer service was simplified, and shift work patterns were introduced.

The largest recent change is the sharp increase in the number of international trainees and students employed at the hotel. The core employees continue to be Japanese, and they are assisted in their roles by nonregular international workers. Furthermore, since 2010, the previous disparity between Japanese and international workers in nonregular positions diminished. This is due to both a shortage of labor and a rationalization of dining provision. The communication between staff and guests is less important when meals are served buffet-style instead of according to the traditional private dining pattern in the guests' rooms. Furthermore, the reduction in human costs is not a top priority for labor restructuring. The hotel owner observed "manpower is so important in the hotel business; it is central to the business. Yes, the business cannot be established without human resources. Wanting to hire good workers while lowering pay is just a self-serving story." The hotel manager expressed a strong desire for a stable and good-quality workforce by employing workers from abroad instead of using laborers from rural areas of Japan.

Second, the gender order remained stable over the past 50 years. Women are still most of the employees working in food preparation, food service, and cleaning roles, and drivers are invariably men. However, some changes have occurred. International male laborers have begun to work as waiters in restaurants, while Muslim women who wear burkas work as kitchen cooking assistants where they do not come into contact with hotel guests. In other words, the appearance is considered more important than the sex of the employee. The number of workers from rural areas is aging and unsteady. This is partly due to the declining and aging population in rural areas, but it is also a reality that working conditions in such inns are poor and not chosen by workers.

Third, in connection with this, beyond the emotional labor that has long been a strong element in the Japanese service industry, aesthetic labor (Nickson et al. 2003; Nickson et al. 2005; Warhurst et al. 2000; Warhurst et al. 2007), as discussed previously elsewhere, has become a more important aspect part of the business of large and affordable hotels, such as the one examined in this case study. Employees are expected to follow detailed manuals that present the right look and attitude to appeal to hotel guests. This staging that satisfies customers and adherence to the rules in the manual is strictly enforced by management. Also, job placement by age may be related to aesthetic labor. Customer-facing positions, such as working at the front desk and on the restaurant floor, where there is a strong aspect of "interactive service work" (Leidner 1991), are staffed by young adults. Conversely, room attendants, cleaners, and dishwashers tend to be middle-aged or elderly. Because the hotel industry is a customer-facing business that produces unusual, wonderful spaces, youthfulness is emphasized. In general, hotel employees are not required to perform high levels of aesthetic labor, such as the level of expression of beauty and style seen among models in the garment industry, and an intensification of aesthetic labor occurred in the hotel sector by means of the reification of proper appearance and attitude in the employee manual.[4]

Kiyoto Tanno notes that the principle of globalization principle that causes these changes is the reintroduction of disparities (Tanno 2007). In the *ryokan* examined in this case, in addition to the introduction of novel ethnic differences, the way that employees are seen and experienced by customers and the way that aesthetic labor-oriented differences were introduced are important.

---

4   Otis noted that the hotel company "trains" frontline workforce in the art of deference, using instructional manuals that choreograph feminized embodiment. In addition, in the process of self-transformation, workers develop an acutely feminized bodily awareness and a hyper-consciousness of customer preferences (Otis 2007: 102). In the light of this, Heidi Gottfried (2013: 248) noted that "service requirements for physical performance elaborate and induce modes of gender interaction and domination." How workers perceived the intensification of aesthetic labor is beyond the scope of this chapter. However, it is an important perspective for examining modes of domination and it is recommended that it be the subject of future research.

While jobs have been streamlined and simplified and the immigration hurdle has been lowered, aesthetic labor increased in importance.

Gabriella Alberti and Francesco E. Iannuzzi highlight that because hotel labor is fundamentally customer-oriented, both the organizational context and also the employer's strategies and assumptions regarding customer preferences are important (Alberti and Iannuzzi 2020). For the context of this hotel, the employer's assumption that the appearance of a person wearing a burka will alarm customers more than gender issues fits this description. An aspect of intersectionality appears here as well, which could be called the factor of intersectional management in hotel labor.

7   Patchwork Routes to Mobilize Labor

When viewed over the long term, it is clear that the transformation of the composition of the workers has been strongly influenced by Japan's own labor force mobilization policies. As noted earlier, the Wakanoki Hotel sought to secure labor through a variety of channels in the face of chronic labor shortages. The background policies regarding and routes for the hotel's main labor are as follows. Table 3.2 shows the main labor-related laws and policies in Japan.

First is the route of *dekasegi* labor from rural areas of Japan, including Aomori, under the *dekasegi* policy set during from Period I. Migrant labor itself has been practiced since ancient times, but during Japan's period of rapid economic growth after World War II, policy researchers realized that a large amount of labor would be needed to enable the development of urban and industrial infrastructure and respond to housing demand, especially in the major cities. The great economic disparities in the country allowed migrant farm laborers from rural areas to be mobilized. The government institutionalized the *dekasegi* system by establishing organizations such as the *dekasegi* task force and issuing *dekasegi* handbooks, which could double as identification cards, at employment security offices. Most of these migrant workers were male construction workers, but some also included female workers in hotels. The hot spring resort where the case *ryokan* is located also began accepting migrant workers in the mid-1960s through a Job Offering Council. Over time, the hotel created a more stable route to recruiting workers by hiring women living in Aomori directly through the Aomori employment security office. Initially, laborers from Aomori only worked during certain seasons but, as time went on, they began to work year-round. In the 2000s, domestic *dekasegi* labor, as recorded in government statistics, was very limited.

TABLE 3.2   Major changes in laws and policies related to labor in Japan

1946	Enactment of Constitution of Japan
1947	Enactment of Labor Standard Law
	Enactment of Employment Security Law
1951	Enactment of Immigration Control and Refugee Recognition Law
1959	Enactment of Minimum Wage Act
1966	*Notice of "Outline of Measures for Dekasegi Workers" from the Director-General of the Employment Security Bureau*
	Enactment of Employment Measures Act
1974	Enactment of Employment Insurance Act
1985	*Enactment of Law for Securing the Proper Operation of Worker Dispatching Undertakings and Protection of Dispatched Workers*
	Enactment of Equal Employment Opportunity Law
1990	*Major revision of Immigration Control Law (The establishment of "Spouse or Child of Japanese National" or "Permanent Resident" status allow foreigners of "Japanese descent" to stay in Japan, and the status of residence of "trainee" was established)*
1993	Enactment of Regulation for Enforcement of the Act on Improvement of Personnel Management and Conversion of Employment Status for Part-Time Workers and Fixed-Term Workers
1999	Major revision of Worker Dispatch Law (Liberalization of target tasks; negative listing)
2003	Implementation of many youth support measures
2007	Enactment of Labor Contract Act
2008	*300,000 Foreign Students Plan by the Ministry of Education, Culture, Sports, Science and Technology*
2009	*Major revision of Immigration Control Law (Abolition of Alien Registration System and creation of new residency management system)*
2015	Enactment of Act on the Promotion of Female Participation and Career Advancement in the Workplace (10-year time-limited legislation)
2018	*Major revision of Immigration Control Law (Creation of a visa for "Specified Skilled Worker")*
	Enactment of Act on the Arrangement of Related Acts to Promote Work Style Reform

Note: Italicized text indicates laws and policies referenced in this section

SOURCE: CREATED BY THE AUTHOR

Second, the background to the appearance of dispatch workers (mainly Japanese) in Phase II was the enactment of new laws and the expansion of mobilization routes through dispatch agencies. In 1985, as the earlier migrant routes from rural areas tapered off, the Law for Securing Proper Operation of Worker Dispatching Undertakings and Protection of Dispatched Workers (commonly known as the Worker Dispatching Law) was enacted. Until that point, officially, much dispatch work was prohibited in Japan, but this was later deregulated. The scope of work for which dispatch labor can be used gradually expanded and now goes largely unregulated. Many agencies sprung up that dispatch personnel primarily to hotels, inns, and resort facilities. The largest companies focus their efforts on securing young college students and freelance workers with a focus on a placement service for young workers called *risoba* (temporary work in resort areas). Interviews with representatives of major temp staffing agencies indicate that the majority of registrants continue to be in their 20s and 30s, but the number of middle-aged and older registrants in their 50s and 60s has been increasing, as has that of international workers. The agency is putting efforts into internet marketing, including web advertising, and it is working in partnership with holiday agencies and language schools to keep young workers in the market.[5]

Also, this is the route taken by international training programs that appeared around the time of Phase II. Japan's foreign trainee programs changed significantly over time, but a program in effect from 2006 to 2010 was used by this hotel, the China Traveling Trainee Acceptance Program. This program was led by the Japan National Tourism Organization, an independent administrative agency, to provide training in Japan related to developing the tourism industry between Japan and China (Japan International Tourism Organization 2006). According to interviews with former project officials, the actual overall sending and receiving operations were commissioned by a major private-sector travel agency and were fully handled by a staffing agency specializing in the travel and hotel industry. The project was conducted within the group-supervised acceptance program. The target participants were students over the age of 18 from 13 China Travel and Tourism Schools throughout China, who were required to

---

5   There are various types of temporary staffing agencies. For instance, it is reported that multinational temporary-help firms have tailored business practices (Gottfried 2015). Temporary firms have created a new labor market niche in Japan by recruiting "house-wives" for part-time temporary employment. Packaging two housewives as a full-time equivalent was a tempting option for employment workers alike in the light of legal exemptions built into the tax code (Gottfried 2015: 53). Either way, they are mobilized as a cheap cost and easily calculable labor force.

have studied Japanese for 2 years. The trainees underwent one year of training at hotels throughout Japan. The project accepted a total of 870 trainees over the past 5 years, 85% of whom were women. This program was closed in 2010 by a 2009 amendment to the Immigration Control and Refugee Recognition Act that limited the content of the training program. Students like trainees are a transient labor force without the expectation of long-term employment.

Fourth, the route of hiring foreign students through language schools appeared in Period III, backed by a government policy intended to increase the number of international students. In 2008, the Japanese government announced its plan to admit 300,000 international students into the country by 2020. The number of international students had increased dramatically, from 51,000 in 1998 to 300,000 in 2018. Although international students come with the ostensible purpose of studying at Japanese language schools and universities, many studies and reports identified that for man, the purpose of arriving in Japan is to work. Due to Japan's strict immigration control system, international students are only allowed to work for limited hours. However, the government tacitly acknowledged that many international students have become a valuable labor force. In all aspects, the lives and status of international students are restricted, and they exhibit inferior worker's rights to those enjoyed by Japanese workers. In addition, many of these students live in dormitories at language schools, and if they cease to study, they cannot remain in the dormitories or renew their visas. Language schools have become a starting point for recruiting and introducing students to find part-time jobs, and in effect, the schools seem to have become labor brokers. Thus, language schools are sites for pooling and mobilizing a flexible labor force.

Fifth, in recent years, major developments concerning international workers also have occurred. In 2018, the Diet passed a bill to overhaul Japan's immigration control law. The changes were adopted to provide the aging nation with a supply of blue-collar workers from abroad. The revised law marked a drastic policy shift, paving the way for an influx of an estimated 340,000 workers from abroad, enabled to work across 14 industrial sectors, including the hotel industry, for the 5 years following the creation of the new visa system in 2019. This major reform of immigration control will certainly encourage the continued reorganization of labor in the hotel industry. However, the Japanese government does not assume that international workers will remain permanently in the country. Furthermore, with the exception of some skilled workers, international workers are not eligible for Japanese social security. As mentioned in Chapter 5, the inadequacies of Japan's immigration policy are responsible for its negative externalities. For example, foreign nationals of Japanese descent who were admitted as immigrants experienced significant difficulties with the immigration process and with settling in Japanese communities.

The above routes represent only the major ones directly related to this hotel (including those that will be discussed in the future). In her work on the feminization of migration, Saskia Sassen identifies a number of routes that are used by the sending state (the government in the society of origin) and private agents (including illegal ones). She identifies the organization of multiple circuits that are being transnational and globalized by the workers themselves (women seeking work). Then, these multiple levels of layering and circuitry of chains are identified as global survival circuits (Sassen 2002). Although this chapter does not represent the entirety of such a circuit, nevertheless, a patchwork of circuits becomes visible at the national and international levels, where new migration infrastructures are being formed.

8   Conclusion

This chapter examines the reproduction structure of bottom workers in the hotel industry by exploring the transformation and background of the organization and workforce composition of a Japanese-style hotel. Among the findings of this study are the following.

The newer management of the case study hotel promoted the rationalization of hotel operations and the control of labor. The profiles of those engaged in low-paid labor at the hotel changed from middle-aged and elderly women from Aomori to young international students from outside Japan. The quality of work changed from multi-skilled service work regarded as semi-care labor to single-skilled work and general service labor. Along with these organizational and labor changes, the roles played by gender and ethnicity also changed. Next, the gendering of labor that characterized the service industry historically has been overshadowed to some extent by ethnic and aesthetic roles. In particular, aesthetic labor, focused on maintaining the proper look and attitudes, have been reified and strengthened. Intersectional management can be seen in the allocation of workers in these hotels, but over the long run, the composition of the labor force has been strongly influenced by policy trends, resulting in a patchwork mobilization of the labor force.

In this transformation, the main thing that supports the structure of labor reproduction of workers at the bottom is the existence of a live-in system involving employee dormitories, whereby work and housing are combined, and daily life is tied to the company. As noted earlier, the hotel workforce features a diverse range of occupations and positions, but many bottom workers use company dormitories. Although times changed and the layers of those who live-in dormitories and perform live-in jobs have been transformed, they have not been interrupted, and they are used as a bottom-line and flexible labor force.

Needless to say, not all of those who use the company dormitories are in the bottom class, as some are college students working part-time as temporary workers, while others use the dormitories for very short periods. However, some workers living in the dormitories have precarious living conditions and these workers had low-paying jobs and long hours performing physically and emotionally difficult work. The dormitories are located close to the hotels that employ these workers; in daily life, their relationships and consciousness are inseparable from the workplace mentioned in Chapter 1. In addition, they are living precariously and in near poverty because if they lose their jobs, they lose their housing.

In addition, as they come to live-in company dormitories for longer periods, their living conditions may become more difficult. Most of the migrant workers from Aomori employed during the time of the hotel's renewal in Phase II were middle-aged or older, and while some returned to their places of origin, some exhibited no subsequent destination. When these hotel workers lost their jobs, they could have begun working at hotels at other hot spring resorts if they were still young enough, physically able, and exhibited the networks to enable them to work. However, as management is streamlined and outsourced in many hotels, opportunities for middle-aged and elderly workers to find work are becoming limited. As individuals age or become unable to work, they might become increasingly impoverished and settle in a hot spring resort, sometimes availing the social welfare or public housing services for which they qualify. For example, according to a social welfare officer in the hot spring resort where the Wakanoki Hotel is located, approximately 200 elderly individuals live alone in their households in the central area of the resort. Thirty of these individuals qualify for and receive welfare services and are referred to as "people from elsewhere." They are entitled to receive priority welfare because they have no relatives or property. The officer also mentioned that the lives of the elderly who are not on welfare are very difficult.

Masami Iwata noted that work housing, the housing provided by companies to their workers, exists for two reasons: one is as a welfare program for workers, and the other is as a convenience for companies to carry out their business. She identified three risks: the end of employment is directly linked to the loss of housing, workers' freedom is easily restricted, and the social function of housing goods, which serve as a starting point for belonging to society, is threatened (Iwata 2009: 170–3). In Japan, one's home is extremely important for social life.

Strong prejudices and disadvantages attached to having an irregular residence exist, and once one loses one's home address, various restrictions arise for one's life. Workers' lives are entirely enclosed in their workplaces, and their freedom is easily restricted, emotionally and physically. In addition, Akihiko Nishizawa notes that working in the hotel or in the sex industry and living in company dormitories is an important point of entry into the Japanese urban under-class, characterized by disorganized and unstable conditions and precarious employment situations (Nishizawa 1995; 2000). Hot spring areas are specific spaces in which gender-biased and marginalized workforces are concentrated.

The problems associated with such dormitory labors place an additional burden on international migrant workers. As noted earlier, international stu-dents, especially at language schools, use the school dormitories. If they leave their school, they cannot remain in the dormitory or renew their visa unless they find a new school or job. Thus, they face more restrictions on their lives while working low-wage jobs than the Japanese do. This situation leads to schools becoming part of the apparatus for pooling workers with integrated jobs and residences.

Due to the new visa system's revisions implemented in 2019, the number of foreign workers will increase, and company dormitories will likely continue to be used. The disadvantaged lifestyle based on company dormitories is not likely to change anytime soon. The case of hotel labor in Japan directs our attention again to the need to observe structural and prescriptive aspects of labor.

References

Adler P A and Adler P (1999) *Paradise Laborers: Hotel Work in the Global Economy.* New York: Cornell University Press.

Alberti G (2014) Mobility strategies, 'mobility differentials' and 'transnational exit': the experiences of precarious migrants in London's hospitality jobs. *Work, Employment & Society* 28: 865–881.

Alberti G and Iannuzzi F E (2020) Embodied intersectionality and the intersectional management of hotel labour: the everyday experiences of social differentiation in customer-oriented work. *Work, Employment & Society* 27(6):1165–1180.

Baum T, Cheung C, Kong H, Kralj A, Mooney S, Thanh H N T, Ramachandran S, Ružić M D and Siow M L (2016) Sustainability and the tourism and hospitality workforce: a thematic analysis. *Sustainability* 8(8): 1–21.

Bianchi R V (2010) Migrant tourist-workers: exploring the 'Contact Zones' of post-industrial tourism. *Current Issues in Tourism* 3(2): 107–137.

Cañada E (2018) Too precarious to be inclusive? Hotel maid employment in Spain. *Tourism Geographies* 20(4): 653–674.

Crang P (1997) Performing the tourist product. In: Rojek C and Urry J (eds) *Touring Cultures: Transformations of Travel and Theory*. London: Routledge, 137–154.

Duncan T, Scott D and Baum T (2013) The mobilities of hospitality work: an exploration of issues and debates. *Annals of Tourism Research* 41: 1–19.

Dyer S, McDowell L and Batnitzky A (2010) The impact of migration on the gendering of service work: the case of a West London hotel. *Gender, Work and Organization* 17(6): 635–657.

Gottfried H (2013) *Gender, Work, and Economy: Unpacking the Global Economy*. Cambridge: Polity Press.

Gottfried H (2015) *The Reproductive Bargain: Deciphering the Enigma of Japanese Capitalism*. Leiden: Brill.

Hochschild A (1983) *The Managed Heart: Commercialization of Human Feeling*. Berkeley: University of California Press.

Iverson R D and Deery M (1997) Turnover culture in the hospitality industry. *Human Resource Management Journal* 7(4): 71–82.

Iwata M (2009) Naze hakenroudousya wa 'ryou' ni irunoka?: Koyou ni shibarareru nihon no 'zyu' [Why dispatched workers are living in 'Company Dormitories': Japanese 'Habitation' bounded by employment]. *World* 788: 168–177.

Japan Institute of Labor (1994) *Hoteru ryokan gyoukai no roudouzizyou* [Current Labor Conditions in the Hotel Industry]. Tokyo: Japan Institute of Labor.

Japan International Tourism Organization (JNTO) (2006) *Chugoku ryoyukennsyuusei ukeire puroguramu goteiansyo* [Proposal for a program to receive trainees from China].

Japan Tourism Agency at Ministry of Land, Infrastructure, Transport and Tourism ed. (2019) Kanko hakusyo (The White Paper for Tourism), 2019 version. Tokyo: Nikeiinsatu kabushikigaisya.

Kantani T (1995) Hoteru ryokan no roudouzizyou [Detailed Information on jobs in hotels]. *The Japanese Journal of Labour Studies* 425: 21–31.

Kensbock S, Patiar A and Jennings G (2017) Hotel room attendants' delivery of quality service. *Tourism and Hospitality Research* 19(3): 382–393.

Knox A (2010) 'Lost in translation': An analysis of temporary work agency, employment in hotels. *Work Employment & Society* 24(3): 449–467.

Knox A (2011) 'Upstairs, Downstairs': an analysis of low paid work in Australian hotels. *Labour and Industry* 21(3): 573–594.

Leidner R (1991) Serving hamburgers and selling insurance: gender, work, and identity in interactive service jobs. *Gender & Society* 5(2): 154–177.

Lundberg C, Gudmundson A and Andersson T (2009) Herzberg's Two-Factor Theory of work motivation tested empirically on seasonal workers in hospitality and tourism. *Tourism Management* 30(6): 890–899.

Lv Q, Xu S and Ji H (2012) Emotional labor strategies, emotional exhaustion, and turnover intention: an empirical study of Chinese hotel employees. *Journal of Human Resources in Hospitality and Tourism* 11(2): 87–105.

Markova E, Anna P, Williams A M and Shaw G (2013) Migrant workers in small London hotels: employment, recruitment and distribution. *European Urban and Regional Studies* 23(3): 406–442.

McDowell L, Batnitzky A and Dyer S (2007) Division, segmentation, and interpellation: the embodied labors of migrant workers in a Greater London hotel. *Economic Geography* 83: 1–25.

McDowell L, Batnitzky A and Dyer S (2009) Precarious work and economic migration: emerging immigrant divisions of labour in Greater London's service sector. *International Journal of Urban and Regional Research* 33(1): 3–25.

McMorran C (2015) Mobilities amid the production of fixities: labor in a Japanese inn. *Mobilities* 10(1): 83–99.

Ministry of Health, Labour and Welfare The number of Environmental Health Facilities (accessed 1 November 2017) at: https://www.e-stat.go.jp/stat-search/files?page=1&toukei=00450027&tstat=000001031469.

Ministry of Land, Infrastructure, Transport and Tourism (ed.) (2006) *Kanko hakusyo* [The White Paper for Tourism]. Tokyo: Kokuritu Insatukyoku.

Moon J (2012) Roudoushijou no saihen to zyoseiroudousya: onsenrizotochiki no roudousizyou wo jireini [Labor market restructuring and women workers: a case study of the labor market in a hot springs resort area]. *The Annals of Japan Association for Urban Sociology* 30: 29–41.

Mooney S, Ryan I and Harris C (2017) The intersections of gender with age and ethnicity in hotel careers: still the same old privileges? *Gender, Work and Organization* 24(4): 360–375.

Nickson D, Warhurst C, Cullen A M and Watt A (2003) Bringing in the excluded?: aesthetic labour, skills and training in the "new" economy. *Journal of Education and Work* 16(2): 185–203.

Nickson D, Warhurst C and Dutton E (2005) The importance of attitude and appearance in the service encounter in retail and hospitality. *Managing Service Quality* 15(2): 195–208.

Nishizawa A (1995) *Inpei sareta gaibu: toshikasou no esunogurafi* [Hidden Outside World: Ethnography of the Urban Underclass]. Tokyo: Sairyusya.

Nishizawa A (2000) Toshikasou no kashika to henyou [Visualization and Transformation of the Urban Underclass]. *Yoseba* 13: 27–37.

Otis E (2006) Virtual personalism in Beijing learning deference and femininity at a global luxury hotel. In: Lee C K (ed.) *Working in China Ethnographies of Labor and Workplace Transformation.* London: Routledge, 101–123.

Otis E (2008) Beyond the industrial paradigm: market-embedded labor and the gender organization of global service work in China. *American Sociological Review* 73(1): 15–36.

Otis E (2012) *Markets and Bodies: Women, Service Work and the Making of Inequality in China.* Palo Alto: Stanford University Press.

Otis E (2016) Bridgework: globalization, gender, and service labor at a luxury hotel. *Gender & Society* 30(6): 912–934.

Ottenbacher M, Harrington R and Parsa H G (2009) Defining the hospitality discipline: a discussion of pedagogical and research implications. *Journal of Hospitality and Tourism Research* 33 (3): 263–283.

Partington S N (2016) Hospitality employment: the good, the bad, and the ugly. In: Lashley C (ed.) *The Routledge Handbook of Hospitality Studies.* London: Routledge: 207–219.

Sassen S (2001) *The Global City: New York, London, Tokyo.* Princeton: Princeton University Press.

Sassen S (2002) Global cities and survival circuits. In: Barbara E and Hochschild A-R (eds) *Global Woman: Nannies, Maids, and Sex Workers in the New Economy.* New York: Henry Holt Company: 254–274.

Seifert A M and Messing K (2006) Cleaning up after globalization: an ergonomic analysis of work activity of hotel cleaners. *Antipode* 38(3): 557–578.

Shani A, Uriely N, Reichel A and Ginsburg L (2014) Emotional labor in the hospitality industry: the influence of contextual factors. *International Journal of Hospitality Management* 37: 150–158.

Shaw G and Williams A (1994) *Critical Issues in Tourism: A Geographical Perspective.* Oxford: Blackwell.

Sylvie G A (2009) Japanese inns (Ryokan) as producers of Japanese identity. In: Sylvie G A and Okpyo M (eds) *Japanese Tourism and Travel Culture.* London: Routledge, 76–101.

Takeda N (2006) Sabisugyou syugyousya tokkachiki no keisei: Hakonemachi to Atamishi no zireikara [The formation of concentrated area of the service industry workers: the case of Hakone and Atami]. *The Sociologist; Journal of the Musashi Sociological Society* 8(1): 89–122.

Takeda N and Moon J (2010) *Onsen rizot sutadizu: Hakone Atami noiyasi kukan to sabisu waku* [Studies of Hot Spring Areas: Healing Spaces and Services in Hakone and Atami]. Tokyo: Seikyusya.

Tanno K (2007) *Ekkyo suru koyou sisutemu to gaikokuzin roudousya* [Transnational Employment Systems and Migrant Workers in Japan]. Tokyo: University of Tokyo Press.

The Statistics Bureau [Economic Census 2018]. (accessed 1 September 2020) at: http://www.e-stat.go.jp/ SG1/estat/ List.do?bid=000001030871&cyccyc=0.

Tisdell C (2001) *Tourism Economics, the Environment and Development: Analysis and Policy.* Northampton: Edward Elgar Pub.

Tsaura S H and Hsieha H Y (2020) The influence of aesthetic labor burden on work engagement in the hospitality industry: The moderating roles of employee attributes. *Journal of Hospitality and Tourism Management* 45: 90–98.

Walmsley A (2004) Assessing staff turnover: a view from the English Riviera. *International Journal of Tourism Research* 6: 275–287.

Warhurst C, Nickson D, Witz A and Cullen A M (2000) Aesthetic labour in interactive service work: Some case study evidence from the "new" Glasgow. *Service Industries Journal* 20(3): 1–18.

Warhurst C and Nickson D (2007) Employee experience of aesthetic labour in retail and hospitality. *Work, Employment and Society* 21(1): 103–120.

Wood R C (1997) *Working in Hotels and Catering (2nd ed.).* London: Routledge.

Yamaguchi K (2011) Gurobarizetion to ryokanroudouryoku no saihen [The restructuring of a Japanese-style hotels workforce in a globalized society]. *Social Theory and Dynamics* 4: 59–76.

CHAPTER 4

Stuck in Bottom Work

Filipina Marriage Migrants' Work Lives in South Korea

Ilju Kim and Jah-Hon Koo

Abstract

This chapter examines how Filipina marriage migrants' social location shapes their unique and precarious position in the South Korean labor market. In particular, we draw from theories of intersectionality and social construction of skill to examine how Filipina marriage migrants become bottom workers. Drawing on in-depth interviews with 54 Filipina marriage migrants residing in major metropolitan areas in South Korea, we identify three processes that lead these women to bottom work: *deskilling, channeling into informal work* and *reskilling into the secondary labor market*. The analysis reveals that these mostly college-educated women experience downward occupational mobility without the promise of future upward mobility, being stuck in bottom work. The chapter concludes with policy implications, emphasizing the need to promote both cultural recognition and economic redistribution to improve the working lives of marriage migrant women.

> You accepted us as part of your family. Then accept us 100%, not 50%.

••
•

Mary, a single mother of one and college graduate in her late 30s, was juggling one full-time night shift job and three part-time jobs at the time of her interview. The cycle of working day and night with no days off began when she divorced her husband and started working at a cell phone parts factory in the Seoul metropolitan area around 2004. Dedicating herself to her work to put food on the table and cope with her frustration regarding having a failed marriage, Mary became one of the most favored employees at her factory: 'Koreans, they have limited working time, but me, I worked 24 hours'. Whenever there was a new product introduced to the line, she would sleep for a few hours in the company break room and then get back to work to demonstrate the new process to the other workers. However, when the company decided to relocate to China, her workdays suddenly decreased to three days per week. She then started 'to aim higher' and began taking jobs translating and teaching English. However, this meant that she had to combine three or four part-time jobs to maintain a monthly salary sufficient to ensure her own and her teenage son's survival. Despite working extremely long hours for over a decade, Mary had never been able to obtain a permanent, full-time position. She claimed,

> There are a lot of Filipinas in Korea who are giving so much to society and working hard ... it was not recognized by anybody. Until now, we're working as a contractual. ... You accepted us as part of your family. Then accept us 100%, not 50%.

Mary's claim regarding the economic contribution she and her fellow Filipinas were making and her consequent call for their 'full membership' in Korean society challenge the relative silence of the existing literature on the work lives of marriage migrants (Kim, 2018; Piper and Lee, 2016; Piper and Roces, 2003). Often labeled as 'brides', with reproductive duties in the family (Lee, 2012), marriage migrant women's paid work outside the home – as Mary argues, a full half of their lives – has received relatively scant scholarly and policy attention. Studies show that marriage migrants mostly engage in highly feminized, low-skilled and precarious labor in their destination countries (Piper and Lee, 2016; Suzuki, 2007; Tang and Wang, 2011). South Korea (henceforth Korea) is no exception. According to the National Survey of Multicultural Families, marriage migrants work in precarious situations (MOGEF, 2019). Approximately 27.9% of marriage migrants in Korea work as manual laborers, which is more than twice the percentage observed in the general population (13%). Among employed marriage migrants, only 16.7% work in professional or office jobs – about half the national figure. About 40% of marriage migrants are temporary or day laborers, in contrast to less than one-quarter of the general population (23.5%). Marriage migrants are therefore more likely than the general population to suffer job insecurity. Despite this bleak picture of marriage migrants' employment situation, employment-related aspects of marriage migrants' lives and the challenges they face in this domain remain understudied (Piper and Lee, 2016: 484).

Drawing on in-depth interviews with 54 Filipina marriage migrant women residing in major metropolitan areas in Korea, this chapter examines how these women's intersectional social position based on gender, ethnicity/nationality and class shapes their experience as 'bottom workers' (see Chapter 2). In particular, we draw from theories of intersectionality and social construction of skill to examine how Filipina marriage migrant women become bottom workers. We identify three processes that lead these women to bottom work: *deskilling, channeling into informal work* and *reskilling into the secondary labor market*. The analysis reveals that these mostly college-educated women experience downward occupational mobility without the promise of future upward mobility, being stuck in bottom work. The chapter concludes with policy implications, emphasizing the need to promote both cultural recognition and economic redistribution to improve the working lives of marriage migrant women.

1 The Social Construction of Marriage Migrant Women's Skill

As advanced economies increasingly emphasize the importance of skilled migrants (Boucher 2020), recent studies have critically examined how migrants' skills are acknowledged and utilized in practice. These studies demonstrate that the skills of migrant women and ethnic minorities are often devalued (Creese and Wiebe, 2012; Riano and Baghdadi, 2007; Shan 2013) and that migrants face considerable institutional barriers to getting their foreign credentials recognized (Bauder, 2003). Previous work also points to the socially constructed nature of migrants' skills, as its realization depends heavily on the existing social hierarchy in the host country (Liu-Farrer et al., 2021). More specifically, immigration policies and employment practices in the host country shape migrants' labor market participation by influencing how their skills are recognized, depending on their gender, race/ethnicity, and class.

The notion of the social construction of skill has mostly been discussed in the context of highly skilled labor migration and has rarely been applied to different forms of labor mobility (Liu-Farrer et al., 2021, 2241; but see Zaman, 2006), such as marriage migration. Nevertheless, studies suggest that the migration category plays a role in the construction of migrants' labor market experiences. For example, previous work points out that the dependent visa status of immigrant women often obscures their labor market participation and application of skills in some Western immigrant destinations such as Canada, the US and some EU countries (Kofman and Raghuram, 2005; Raghuram, 2004). In these countries, immigrant women often suffer from occupational downgrading because of their dependent visa status, which limits their access to the labor market, channeling them into low-paid light manufacturing, service and care work (Creese and Wiebe, 2012; Man, 2004; Riaño and Baghdadi, 2007). As a last resort to avoid discrimination in the formal labor market, some turn to self-employment as 'survivalist entrepreneurship' (Banerjee, 2019; Romero and Valdez, 2016).

Unlike the above-mentioned Western immigrant destinations that prohibited full access to the host labor market for those on dependent visas, marriage migrant women are legally granted unrestricted access to the labor market in Korea. However, a few existing studies demonstrate that their participation has largely been limited to precarious jobs (Piper and Lee, 2016; MOGEF, 2019). This means that labor market practices, rather than immigration policies, are the main forces that marginalize marriage migrant women, thereby making them 'bottom workers'. This is different from the situation of trainees or international students in Japan, whose visa statuses generally determine the kind of jobs and industry sectors (see Chapter 3). This unique situation of marriage migrant women's labor market participation in Korea, however, has received little academic attention.

Recent studies analyzing migrant women's work experiences in the host society demonstrate that an intersectional approach is useful in examining how the influence of gender is mediated by ethnicity and race, class, family structure and migration policy, which co-constitute the social construction of minority women's skill (Banerjee, 2019; Romero and Valdez, 2016). Although the non-recognition of foreign credentials and work experience is the major mechanism of devaluing immigrant labor (Bauder, 2003), previous work shows that gender relations are central in shaping migrant women's unique, disadvantaged position. For highly skilled migrant women, for example, their expected primary caregiver role in the family and a lack of government support for childcare hinder their active participation in the labor market (Man, 2004; Riaño and Baghdadi, 2007). Migrant women are also actively channeled into feminized caregiving occupations by government-funded settlement agencies (Creese and Wiebe, 2012) or by their own choice in an attempt to subvert legal restrictions that prohibit them from working (Banerjee, 2019).

As the intersectional approach suggests, however, migrant women's marginalized social position does not mean that they are ever defined exclusively by oppression (Collins, 2010; McCall, 2005). In the labor market context, migrant women may actively cultivate and promote their ethnic and cultural resources to fit the demand in the host country (Erel, 2010; Riaño and Baghdadi, 2007). For example, Erel (2010) demonstrates how some migrants gain access to skilled employment by creating new forms of cultural capital that are valued in the host society. These migrants combine what they bring from their country of origin with new skills acquired in the host society and utilize migrant networks. Whether these attempts result in occupational upward mobility for migrant women or not would, however, still be circumscribed by existing hier-archies in the host labor market with regard to one's gender, race/nationality, and class.

The following section provides a brief history of migration in Korea and the labor market context in which Filipina marriage migrants are integrated, followed by an examination of Filipina marriage migrants' labor market par-ticipation, focusing on how women's skill is (un)recognized. The section also includes a discussion of how women adjust their skills to meet the demands of the local labor market or to avoid discrimination, showing how women's social position, based on their gender, ethnicity/nationality and class, shapes their incorporation into poorly paid and unstable occupational sectors, as well as the informal economy.

2 Marriage Migrant Women's Labor Market Participation in Korea

Since the late 1980s, Korea, once a major labor exporter, has become a labor-importing country because of labor shortages in the small and medium enter-prise sectors (Seol, 2000). Similar to the immigration policies of Japan that have never officially accepted unskilled migrant labor (see Chapters 3 and 5), the Korean government has attempted to manage these shortages by bringing in only temporary migrant labor. Simultaneously, marriage migration has been an important option for female migrants to achieve stable residency status under the rigid immigration and visa policies for low-skilled labor migrants in East Asia (Piper, 2003). In contrast to the limited stay allowed for temporary migrant labor, local governments in Korea have promoted the marriage migra-tion of ethnic Korean women from China since the early 1990s (Lee, 2008). The pool of marriage migrants diversified to include women from other countries as commercial marriage agencies mushroomed around 2000. Facing a record-low birth rate in 2006, the Korean government devised a series of policy plans to actively integrate marriage migrants into Korean society. Data from 2018 show that more than 231,000 marriage migrant women reside in Korea, with women from Vietnam making up the largest share (33%), followed by non-Korean women from China (20%), ethnic Korean women from China (19%) and women from the Philippines (9%) (MOGEF, 2019).

Given that most marriage migrant women enter the labor force as married women with childcare responsibilities, their work lives are similarly subject to the inequality that native Korean married women face in the labor force. For example, Jeon (2014) reports that college-educated marriage migrants' work experiences resemble those of native Korean married women. Studies have documented how the institutional context and gender ideology of the labor market hinder highly educated married women's full-time employment in Korea (Brinton and Oh, 2019; Cho and Cho, 2015). Employment in Korea is characterized by an internal labor market structure and employment protection for core workers, with relatively little inter-firm mobility. This situation has made it difficult for workers to negotiate their work hours. Combined with the tendency for women to be disproportionately responsible for childrearing and household labor, workplace norms emphasizing long work hours obstruct highly skilled married women's participation in full-time employment in Korea (Brinton and Oh, 2019).

In addition to the gendered inequality, studies suggest that marriage migrant women experience ethnicity/nationality-based discrimination in the labor market. Access to professional and white-collar occupations is particularly difficult for marriage migrants, given that their credentials and the work experience they obtained in their home countries are seldom recognized (Yang et al., 2010). Government-run programs that are designed to alleviate such difficulties have largely been unsuccessful. Although government-run institutions such as the Multicultural Family Support Center and Women Resource Development Center[1] provide employment support programs for marriage migrants, previous work shows that they often fall short of providing sufficient job training opportunities to offset the difficulties migrants face in getting their credentials recognized (Jang et al., 2009; Yang et al., 2010). Government institutions tend to provide programs such as information literacy, cooking and baking classes, which do not provide the substantive skills training necessary for employment (Jang et al., 2009). Other programs, such as those providing training to become an interpreter or language instructor, are more successful, but the available positions tend to be part-time or irregular. Participation in such training programs is also limited to a few individuals with a certain level of educational attainment (Jang et al., 2009). Thus, scholars criticize the government programs for tending to channel marriage migrant women into feminized, low-skilled jobs rather than catering to their diverse needs and unique backgrounds, resulting in a very low rate of actual employment for women completing such programs (Jang et al., 2009).

---

1 Multicultural Family Support Center is policy delivery organizations intended to support multicultural families' stable integration and family lives. Based on the Multicultural Families Support Act enacted in 2008, there are currently 218 centers nationwide. Women Resource Development Centers are government-commissioned agencies that provide vocational trainings, counselling and job placement service, especially for women. There are 53 of these Centers nationwide.

3   Methods

This study's analysis is based on in-depth interviews with 54 Filipina marriage migrants residing in urban areas of Korea. These data are part of a larger ethnographic study on the incorporation experiences of Filipina marriage migrants. The interviews were conducted from May 2014 to September 2018 in the Seoul metropolitan area and two additional cities in the southern part of Korea. Women were recruited for participation in the study through a combination of snowball and purposive sampling strategies to seek diversity in terms of length of stay in Korea, marital status and citizenship status. During the interviews, questions were asked to gather information about the women's overall work history (both in the Philippines and in Korea), the process of getting a job and challenges they encountered in the workplace. All interviews were conducted in a mixture of Korean and English.

The mean age of the Filipina marriage migrant participants was 39 (range: 23–63) years. The average length of stay in Korea was 11.5 years. About one-third of the participants were divorced and/or separated at the time of the interview. Most of the participants (87%) had completed at least some college education in the Philippines. Given that only 15.6% of marriage migrants, regardless of their country of origin, finished college or above (MOGEF, 2019), participants in this study tend to be better educated than the overall marriage migrant population in Korea. Thus, they may not be representative of all marriage migrants. However, as we illustrate below, this allowed us to illuminate the processes through which mostly highly educated marriage migrants become bottom workers.

4   The Closed Circuit of Bottom Work

Through the course of their work lives, most women in this study held multiple jobs spanning various sectors and forms of employment. The women usually started working by engaging in manual labor at factories located in their neighborhoods. Some later moved on to English teaching jobs, a trajectory considered to be upward mobility in terms of social status and hourly wages. However, several women explained that factory work and English teaching jobs had many commonalities related to blocked career mobility and job insecurity. Some women also worked in the informal economy through network business/marketing and side jobs, which seldom provided access to stable income or social protection. The following section presents the processes that lead to each of these three prevalent job types, with an eye on how women's skill is devalued through gendered and ethnicized evaluation of their skill. This analysis shows how the interviewed women experienced *deskilling*, channeling *into informal jobs* and *reskilling into the secondary labor market* as they navigated and negotiated their labor market participation. We argue that the processes reveal how these women become bottom workers without the opportunity for upward mobility.

4.1   Deskilling: Factory Work

According to Bauder (2003, 701), deskilling refers to the loss of access to occupations that migrants previously held because their foreign education and credentials are not recognized in the host country. As 'survival employment' to ensure economic survival, the Filipinas in this study were frequently channeled into menial factory jobs and low-skilled service jobs that were often below their qualifications. More than one in four participants began their work life in Korea at a factory in the Seoul metropolitan area. Factory work was the most easily accessible type of employment, both for the participants with a college education upon arrival and for those with less education. Because of a lack of information about the Korean job market, the women usually started their work lives through friends' referrals. Most of the study participants reported engaging in manual labor/manufacturing jobs at small and medium-sized factories. They cut and folded cloth in a garment factory, assembled and inspected the parts of cell phones or cars, and processed and packaged food. The work often did not require a high level of Korean language ability, educational credentials or previous work experience. However, these manual labor jobs rarely offered opportunities for skill development or promotion.

Having worked as a teacher at a public elementary school in the Philippines for three years, Joyce felt frustrated staying at home for three months after her arrival in Seoul after marriage. She recalled, 'Before, in the Philippines, I worked from seven o'clock until nine o'clock. And then suddenly I came here [to Korea], and then there's nothing to do. I wanted to work'. Knowing that her teacher's certificate was of no use in Korea, she asked a handful of friends she knew for help and was told about a small garment factory in her neighborhood. Joyce worked at the factory for six months before leaving when she got pregnant. After giving birth to her son, however, she never returned to the factory. Joyce always told her friends, 'If you keep working at the factory, you cannot go anywhere else. If you can't speak [Korean], then you have to work at the factory until you die. You should study Korean'.

Joyce was among the few who were able to look for and try out other jobs thanks to her husband's stable employment, but others, especially those without a college education and/or those in unstable economic and familial situations, found it difficult to leave the factory. A little less than one in three women were separated or divorced at the time of the interview. For those who have not acquired Korean citizenship upon their divorce or separation, the dissolution of marriages meant unstable legal status and limited job opportunities. Two women were working at a factory as undocumented workers. Divorce or separation also led to precarious housing situation as it was often the women who leave the house. The instability influenced the kind of work participants took on because it was difficult for these women to build mid to long-term career plans which may involve further education and training.

Judy, a 37-year-old high school graduate and a divorcee, worked at a garment factory for eight years until she recently had to quit because of chronic back pain. When Judy left her Korean husband after having years of strained relationship with her in-laws, she wandered around acquaintances' homes and *jjimjilbang*, the Korean dry sauna where one can stay overnight, before she began to share a studio with a Filipina she met in her neighborhood. When the Filipina got married, Judy moved to the studio right next to her married friend's house. This householding strategy (see Chapter 1) enabled Judy to have at least some sense of stability to continue working at the factory as she went through divorce. Judy's factory, which was located in a satellite city of the Seoul metropolitan area, was a small garment factory with about 30 workers. In her time there, Judy only once received a raise in her monthly salary, which was below the minimum wage. She often worked on holidays without receiving holiday pay. She and the other workers continued to work in this factory only because they were paid on time, whereas other garment factories in the city were always behind schedule. After eight years, she finally quit because of a herniated cervical disc she developed from years of sedentary work, having rarely had a chance to learn new skills or be promoted:

> My supervisor asked me to practice using the sewing machine one day, but [the] other workers were jealous because they didn't want me to do sewing. My hands were so fast, and it was easier for them if I remained in the assistant position. I just gave up the sewing position.

Becoming a seamstress would have earned Judy a better wage, but the busy schedule of the factory did not allow non-skilled workers like Judy to learn advanced skills. Thus, still unskilled, Judy then moved to a plastic injection factory after a month of resting at home. She was still in pain but had no other way of surviving: 'My [plastic injection] machine is very heavy. You use all your strength [to work the machine]. That's why I have muscle pain all the time'.

As most women soon realized that working in a factory was not a good long-term strategy for economic independence and survival, they turned to an alternative. Those with a college education looked for English teaching jobs and sometimes succeeded in landing a part-time position. Joyce's determination not to go back to the garment factory again motivated her to apply for an English teaching job. However, although the English teaching job may seem better in terms of hourly pay, as will be detailed later in the chapter, some women ultimately chose to return to or start work in a factory. In this sense, factory work was both the beginning and the end of many of the interviewed Filipinas' work lives in Korea. It provided these women with a relatively structured work arrangement and stable full-time employment, both of which were rarely found in English teaching jobs or in the informal economy, as discussed below.

Women's appearance and nationality of origin sometimes posed a challenge in securing factory jobs, leading them to engage with the informal economy. Some women reported that they faced discrimination in the process of hiring because of their 'foreign face'. Nina, a 43-year-old college graduate, was referred to a bag packaging factory in her neighborhood by a local Women Resource Development Center. When she went to the factory with Corazon, a 40-year-old college graduate, she was told that they could not hire them because 'there are so many good-quality Koreans applying for the position'. Nina recalled that she was struck by the comment because Nina and Corazon were both naturalized Korean citizens who had lived in the neighborhood for more than 10 years. The task of packaging bags did not require more than basic conversation-level Korean, with which Nina and Corazon had no problem. Nina tried another garment factory and got hired, whereas Corazon gave up on searching for factory positions altogether after this disappointing experience. Instead, she started a small-scale business buying and selling Philippine products as a last resort, like many other women in this study who experienced discrimination in the formal labor market.

4.2 Channeling into Informal Jobs: Survival Entrepreneurship and Invisible Work

The informal economy refers to 'all economic activities by workers and economic units that are not covered or insufficiently covered by formal arrangements' (ILO, 2015, 53). Because it is relatively easy to engage in such informal activities without formal credentials, skills or financial capital, most of the participants had engaged in informal economic activities to earn enough to take care of themselves in the absence of sufficient formal options because of a language barrier and various other obstacles (see also Chapter 2). As Corazon's story illustrates, self-employment often became a way of resisting racism and discrimination in paid employment.

Approximately one in five of the Filipina participants had experience working or currently worked in the informal economy in various capacities. Many were involved in the informal economy created within the Philippine ethnic communities in Korea. Unlike ethnic communities that are usually located in specific geographical areas of traditional immigrant destinations, Philippine ethnic communities in Korea are networks of co-ethnic organizations that are geographically dispersed, but often registered under the Embassy of the Philippines or Multicultural Family Support Center (Kim and Kim 2021). Within these communities, participants bought and sold Philippine products and engaged in network business/marketing for various products and services, such as telecommunication services and Philippine health products and insurance plans. Some were domestic workers, especially at the US Army base in Seoul. In addition, the women took on various side jobs with informal arrangements. Although the women felt it was easy to take on such jobs in the informal economy, they often resulted in irregular incomes and/or long working hours, with little financial return. As this kind of work was not covered by the law, these jobs also lacked social protection and security.

In the eyes of her Korean neighbors, Elvie, a certified electronic engineer in the Philippines and single mother of one son, had no job. Her Korean neighbors often commented to her, 'You don't have any job. You should ask for some help'. However, Elvie was considered 'one of the success stories' among Filipinas making a living in Korea by buying and selling Philippine products in urban Filipino communities. Her primary customers were undocumented Filipino migrant workers. She sold various Philippine products out of her home and at a Filipino street market held each Sunday after the Catholic mass in Hyewha.[2] Her business was particularly busy following crackdowns on undocumented migrant workers in her neighborhood, when she would send packages containing daily necessities by parcel post to workers who were hiding in their homes. Elvie's case represented the rare successful experience – being able to make a stable living solely from informal buying and selling. For the rest of the participants, engaging in the informal economy often meant an unstable and almost invisible income. And while Elvie was lucky enough to secure a living through informal business, it is worth noting that her option was severely limited when she first decided to sell used cell phones on the street market. She

---

2 The street market near Hyewha Catholic Church in Seoul emerged in the late 1990s, when the Catholic Archdiocese of Seoul Office began to offer mass in Tagalog. Every Sunday around more than dozens of street vendors sell Philippine products such as food and sundries.

was running away from home, from a quick-tempered and oftentimes violent husband who was having an affair at the time. With only a box of jewellery she received from her husband during her seven years of marriage and a brief work experience at a factory before marriage, she chose to do what "most of the Filipinos do," that is, buying and selling to the Philippine communities.

As most participants got pregnant within their first year of marriage, they faced the daunting task of adapting to a new country while taking care of a newborn baby. Further, most of the women wanted to work because of the economic needs of both their Korean family and their natal family in the Philippines. Many mentioned financially supporting their family members in the Philippines whenever the needs arise (e.g., college tuition for relatives), which motivated them to take on low-quality jobs that are available or multiple jobs. Jobs in the informal economy tended to allow flexible work arrangements, and many participants said they turned to such jobs because they had to take care of their infant and toddler children. Christine, a 35-year-old mother of three and a two-year college graduate, assembled auto parts at home for five years after she quit her factory job upon the birth of her first child. Her side job, which provided compensation on a piece-rate basis, did not pay well considering the hours she put in; it also isolated her from the outside world. However, with her husband working only occasionally, she thought she had little choice:

> It was so difficult to find work because of the baby ... We lived in a small room, and I only did side jobs and stayed home. I assembled car headlights by hand. I did it day and night, staying up all night. What I earned was only 300,000 won [approximately US$260] per month at best, but my husband had no [stable] job, so I did my best ... [Back then] we had to borrow money from a friend to buy baby's milk, and [we] lived without any heat during the winter. I was obsessed with the thought of earning money quickly to get through the winter with more heat, but I couldn't work outside because the baby was too small.

Confining herself to her home to increase her output, Christine gradually found herself doing strange things. One day, she put the television remote control in the freezer. On another day, she found toilet paper soaking in water in the washing machine. When she was eventually diagnosed with depression, she cut back on her work hours and joined a Korean class and other community activities, following her doctor's advice. Christine's case may seem extreme, but the women who were involved in the informal economy usually lacked social support, tending to work alone or in small groups.

Other women did domestic work for well-off families through informal arrangements. In particular, performing domestic labor for families living on US military bases was not uncommon among the study participants. Because access to these military bases was restricted to authorized personnel, these jobs were acquired through referrals from those who already worked on the bases. Joan, a 49-year-old high school graduate, first gained access to this kind of work through a friend, who was working for a US military family as a domestic worker. Joan quit her job in a garment factory, where she had worked since moving to Seoul with her son after divorcing her husband. She liked the transition because she was able to 'own [her] time'. Luckily, Joan was very good at finding new employers to sponsor her access to the base before her current sponsorship expired. She had worked as a housekeeper and a babysitter for the past decade:

> I felt very comfortable because I'm the owner of my time. Especially for housekeeping – mostly, my housekeeping job is for a single military [personnel]. They give me [the] security number [to enter the house], and if I enter, the money is already here (tapping on the table) ... I like cleaning [more] than babysitting. If I babysit, sometimes for five kids, we have to go everywhere ... running and fleeing. I become very tired.

Despite her sense of 'owning' her time, Joan's description of her work sounded far from her having control. When asked about her income, she said, 'It depends on your employers. If [you have] so many employers, more income. No employer, no work, no income ... It depends on the blessings ... Maybe monthly, 2,000 dollars, 1,000 dollars, 80 dollars, because my job is part-time, daily pay'. With her income fluctuating every month and even every day, Joan strived to make the most of her 'blessings'. She began her day with housekeeping for a family in the morning and then continued with babysitting for another family in the evening, which would occasionally end at 3 o'clock in the morning. Since this work was based on a private employment arrangement, Joan, who was almost 50, was not entitled to severance pay or a pension, much less worker's compensation, insurance, or annual leave.

Networking business/marketing jobs were popular among those who were relatively well off in terms of their economic situation. Many women were attracted to this type of work because it did not require formal credentials, skills or a formal commitment of time in an office. Instead, this work relied on the women's co-ethnic network. The women in this type of business explained their work as 'working while you're chatting with your friends and making new friends'. The promise of multilevel marketing systems was that, after a woman invited many of her friends as customers under her account, she would be rewarded with commissions. However, to join the business, they first had to be customers themselves and buy expensive products. After becoming a representative, it was unclear to what extent the women would be compensated for the time and effort they dedicated to marketing the products. Ella, a 34-year-old part-time English teacher, had recently joined a multilevel marketing network based in the Philippines that sold nutritional supplements and other daily items. Her friends had constantly asked her to join: 'They said it's easy to earn money. You can just meet a lot of people, they said, like communicating with them ... I paid 167,000 won [US$150] to join. Where's my money now? They said, "You'll be having [it] soon" (laughs)'. As shown in Ella's case, network business/marketing could easily become an unnecessary expense rather than a source of additional easy income.

Although the women usually chose to engage in the informal economy as a strategy to avoid discriminatory experiences in the formal labor market and to capitalize on their ethnic social network, such pursuits rarely provided stable income that guaranteed their economic survival or upward mobility. Therefore, most of the interviewed college-educated women turned to the English teaching labor market to negotiate their skills and enter into what they considered a white-collar job.

4.3 Reskilling into the Secondary Labor Market: English Teaching

English teaching jobs were the most accessible type of office job for urban Filipina marriage migrants with a college education. Half of the participants were working as English teachers when they were interviewed. Most of the women first gained experience teaching English in less institutionalized settings, such as home-schooling or private tutorials, and then moved into private academies and after-school classes at public schools. It may seem that these women successfully reskilled, applying their language ability and college degree to fit the needs of Korean society. However, most of these positions resembled the secondary labor market, which is characterized by underemployment and instability (Park, 2011). Most participants who worked in English teaching jobs lamented the characteristics of their nonstandard employment, such as the work being part-time, temporary and on an independent contract basis, which did not guarantee their job security. The work also tended to be within the larger framework of care work, as the women mostly took on day-care or kindergarten positions, teaching pre-schoolers part-time or on contractual terms. Part-time teaching at elementary schools and private academies was also common.

The women's experiences in the English teaching labor market illustrated how their English language ability and teaching skills were often judged based on their ethnicity/ nationality and gender. Although coming from the Philippines and being female granted these women relatively easy access to part-time daycare and kindergarten positions that focused more on caring than teaching English, they often reported discriminatory practices at private institutions with more advanced curricula. Joyce, a former elementary school teacher in the Philippines who was introduced above, shared her discouraging job search experience:

> I called a lot of them [English language institutes] and [said], 'I'm from the Philippines, and I'd like to work in your company as an English teacher'. Then 'Oh, you're a Filipino? Sorry, but we're only hiring native speakers.' ... The mere fact that I'm a Filipino doesn't mean that I'm not capable, but they didn't even give me a chance. You should at least give me a chance for a demonstration, and, if I'm not good at teaching, then you can fail me ... I think there would be a better opportunity for me in other institutions, but because of that experience, I didn't [seek other opportunities] anymore.

Joyce gave up on looking for better offers and replaced another Filipino part-time teacher at a private academy. Her predecessor did not have legal documentation, and the pay was not good, but Joyce was tired of being turned down. With the pressing need to earn their own money to send occasional remittances to their family members in the Philippines and to cover their own needs, Joyce and other women accepted the available work. Employers' exercise of ethnic boundary marking (Kim 2018) in the two-tiered English teaching labor market was reinforced by ethno-national prejudice prevalent in Korean society. Even after securing a position, discrimination from students' parents could make these women's work difficult. Michelle, a 42-year-old former accountant, was constantly questioned about her ability to teach English, until she finally quit. When the students in her class at a private academy told their parents that their teacher was from the Philippines, the parents complained to the director of her academy that their children were 'not learning anything'.

Disenchanted with the part-time and contractual work arrangements of English teaching jobs, some women looked towards factory jobs after years of teaching. When the first author met Jan in 2014, she seemed quite satisfied with her English teaching job at a private academy. She proudly detailed her journey from working as an English-speaking nanny for a four-year-old to becoming a part-time English teacher for middle school students. Having worked as an elementary school teacher for almost a decade in the Philippines before migrating to Korea, she felt that she had found the right place for her. She aspired to teach in a public school as a regular teacher. When the first author met Jan again four years later, she was working in a food processing factory. When asked about the change, she expressed her frustration over the lack of job security and career development prospects in English teaching jobs:

> Teaching jobs in Korea, there's no assurance, especially for non-native teachers. We couldn't have our four major social insurances [the national pension, national health insurance, employment insurance, and industrial accident compensation insurance] or whatever benefits like that ... I need some benefits or [a] more stable job. In teaching, when I stopped [working at] the academy, I didn't receive anything like separation pay, no bonus, nothing, nothing ... So many teachers are switching from academies and after-school [classes], which do not pay well, to factories, like food processing companies. They're switching. Why? Because of the [social welfare] benefits.

The transition from teaching English to factory work was physically challenging. Jan was working the night shift, from eight in the afternoon until five in the morning, in a factory located on the outskirts of the Seoul metropolitan area. Her one day off each week was dedicated to a part-time teaching position at a community center. She was holding onto a teaching job as a side gig just in case she wanted to return to teaching:

> If only teaching were a kind of *actual job*, which is stable, that would be good. It's a white-collar job. I have the self-esteem [that is] still high, and I didn't totally stop my classes so that I can have the option, for example, if I'm tired of the factory, I'll just start teaching again. Just like that.

For Jan, after eight years of teaching English at a private academy, she realized that it was not an 'actual job', with the four major social insurances, job promotion opportunities and stability. Another Filipina who offered private tutorials while running a small store also commented, 'Teaching English is not for your lifetime. You should think of another option. I have my family. I cannot survive [only by teaching English]'.

As was the case for Jan, many of the Filipinas moved back and forth between teaching English and factory jobs. For these women, there was not much difference between the two types of jobs. Although the hourly pay was higher for teaching English than for factory work, the women pointed out that the remuneration for teaching was not necessarily better given the extra hours they had to put in preparing lesson plans and teaching materials. Because the women usually had to combine multiple part-time jobs that were spread across different cities, they were always on the run. Cindy, a 40-year-old college graduate, recalled her 10 years of working in kindergartens:

> I slept only three hours a day during the first year. [I kept thinking], 'What should I show to the kids? What props should I make?' I went and met the kids every day, so I had to develop new things. For schoolchildren, books are enough, but [for] those kids who are five or six years old, books alone don't work. So I made props, [coming up with] something interesting, prepared songs and dances and all that … I usually skipped meals to meet the class schedule. My lesson in Gimpo started at 10 am and ended at 12:20 pm. But my next class started at 1 pm in Mokdong. I really had to move quickly.

Tired of juggling multiple teaching positions and running around to different places, 48-year-old Frances, who was divorced at the time of her interview, took on a live-in nanny job at a US military base: 'One hour [of lessons] here, and [then] I traveled for one hour to another place, and [then] I traveled to another place. I got tired'. Similarly, Mavi, a 37-year-old former English teacher who had worked as an accountant in the Philippines, ended up choosing to work in a garment factory over teaching English. Compared with her eight years of teaching English, she seemed more satisfied with her current work as a seamstress in the garment factory. For Mavi, English teaching represented 'hard work and small money':

> At night, you must make your lesson plans. We have a lot of things to prepare. But, for garment factory work, you sleep [at night] and be calm [once your work is over]. (laughs) At first, it was very hard for me. 'Oh, I want to go back to teaching'. I felt like a fool: 'I'm a teacher. Why am I doing this?' But after I got my salary, I didn't want to teach [anymore] because it was doubled.

In the secondary labor market that emerged for Filipinas in the English language teaching industry because of their ethnicity/nationality and notions of gendered competence in caring, highly educated Filipinas with varied work experience struggled to mold themselves into English teachers, only to realize the limited upward mobility afforded by these jobs. Some women strived to acquire professional credentials such as Teachers of English to Speakers of Other Languages (TESOL) certification to advance their English teaching careers to the level of native speakers. However, the tuition fee for TESOL certificate courses was often two or three times their monthly income, which made it almost impossible for these women to obtain this certification.

5   Conclusion

We examined how Filipina marriage migrants' intersectional position based on their gender, ethnicity/nationality and class shaped their experiences as bottom workers. We identified processes through which the Filipinas in this study engage in bottom work. As the Filipinas in this study navigated their place in the labor market, they often experienced *deskilling* because the credentials they had earned in the Philippines were rarely recognized. Some had recourse to *informal work* to avoid discriminatory practices in the formal labor market, whereas others engaged in *reskilling*, applying their English language ability and developing teaching skills to take advantage of the high demand for teachers in the English language teaching labor market. Upon coming to Korea, most women initially experienced deskilling and engaged in menial factory labor and low-paid service work, but those with relatively stable socio-economic conditions were able to try their luck in small businesses or the English teaching labor market. However, the jobs available to these women in the secondary labor market of the English language teaching industry revealed the gendered and ethnicized nature of such work: These jobs tended to place more emphasis on caregiving than on language education, and some women reported discriminatory practices towards Filipina teachers. These three processes seldom allowed these women the opportunity to gain skills and pursue upward occupational mobility.

As we have illustrated, it is impossible to disentangle these women's economic hardship from the discrimination and exclusion they experience based on their gender, ethnicity/nationality and class. The intersectional nature of the processes through which women get stuck in bottom work raise an important issue regarding policy decisions. Scholars such as Nancy Fraser (Fraser, 1998; Fraser and Honneth, 2003) have formulated a dilemma in the pursuit of social justice by contrasting the goals of (economic) redistribution and (cultural) recognition. As Fraser acknowledges, this contrast does not mean we must choose one goal and discard the other. Along these lines, the present chapter concludes by addressing the dilemma and discussing how the seemingly contrasting goals can be integrated in terms of policy and practice, in order to improve the employment situations of marriage migrants.

Although the Korean government formally advocates multiculturalism as a policy value, critics have argued that the government applies exclusionary policies to temporary migrant workers by suppressing their labor rights and applies assimilation policies to marriage migrants and their children (Woo et al., 2015; see Berry, 2005 and Castles and Miller, 2003 for a categorization of immigration and social integration policies). In line with the 2008 Multicultural Family Support Act, government-run institutions such as Multicultural Family Support Center provide marriage migrants with various types of support. Counseling services and educational programs that assist in women's general adaptation are offered, and programs for cultural exchange (e.g. intercultural education and festivals focusing on food or traditional dress) are promoted. However, the precarious situations of the Filipina marriage migrants described in this chapter suggest that these approaches do not help these women to become self-sufficient. More specifically, critics note that integration programs for marriage migrant women should specifically aim to develop skills necessary for employment, rather than focusing on general social adaptation (Jang et al., 2009; Yang et al., 2010). In short, the Korean government's integration policy lacks attention to structural inequalities, particularly in the material or economic sense (Park, 2009).

The Korean government has recently emphasized its commitment to supporting marriage migrant women's employment and economic self-sufficiency (MOGEF, 2019). Nonetheless, as shown in this chapter, the jobs these women frequently take on are characterized by gender- and ethnicity-based discrimination. Focusing on employment and skills training alone cannot sufficiently address these problems. The present findings suggest that marriage migrants deserve the recognition of their ethnic and cultural differences, as well as the redistribution of income, fair jobs and other economic opportunities. Therefore, we propose that the government and social organizations approach the issue of marriage migrants in terms of promoting the rights of bottom workers. Acknowledging and raising social awareness of the hidden labor contribution of marriage migrants may be an important first step in this direction.

References

Banerjee P (2019) Subversive self-employment: intersectionality and self-employment among dependent visas holders in the United States. *American Behavioral Scientist* 63(2): 186–207.

Bauder H (2003) 'Brain abuse', or the devaluation of immigrant labour in Canada. *Antipode* 35(4): 699–717.

Berry J W (2005) Acculturation: living successfully in two cultures. *International Journal of Intercultural Relations* 29(6): 697–712.

Boucher A K (2020) How 'skill' definition affects the diversity of skilled immigration policies. *Journal of Ethnic and Migration Studies* 46(12): 2533–2550.

Brinton M C and Oh E (2019) Babies, work, or both? highly educated women's employment and fertility in East Asia. *American Journal of Sociology* 125(1): 105–140.

Castles S and Miller M J (2003) *The Age of Migration: International Population Movements in the Modern World*. New York, NY: The Guilford Press.

Cho D and Cho J (2015) Over-heated education and lower labor market participation of Korean females in other OECD countries. *Women's Studies International Forum* 48: 1–8.

Collins HP (2010) The new politics of community. *American Sociological Review* 75(1): 7–30.

Creese G and Wiebe B (2012) 'Survival employment': gender and deskilling among African immigrants in Canada. *International Migration* 50(5): 56–76.

Erel U (2010) Migrating cultural capital: Bourdieu in migration studies. *Sociology* 44(4): 642–660.

Fraser N (1998) From redistribution to recognition? dilemmas of justice in a 'post-socialist' age. In: Willett C (ed.) *Theorizing Multiculturalism. A Guide to the Current Debate*. By C. Willet. Blackwell Publishers. Malden, MA: Blackwell, pp. 19–49.

Fraser N and Honneth A (2003) *Redistribution or Recognition?: A Political-Philosophical Exchange*. London: Verso.

ILO (International Labour Organization) (2015) *Transition from the Informal to the Formal Economy Recommendation (No. 204)*. International Labour Organisation Geneva.

Jang S-Y, Y-S Kim, Leen R, Jang I-J and Yu J-Y (2009) Basic Research for the Development of Employment Support Program for Female Marriage Immigrants [*Yeoseonggyeoroniminja Chuieupjiwon Purogurem Gaebaleul Uihan Gichoyeongu*]. 2009–08. Policy Study. Seoul: Korea Employment Information Service.

Jeon E H (2014) A narrative study on the job-seeking activities and job experience of well-educated marriage-immigrant women [*Gohangryeok Gyeoronijuyeoseongdurui Gujikhaldonggwa Chuieupgyeongheume Gwanan Nareotibu Yeongu*]. *Journal of Lifelong Education* 20 (3): 233–67.

Kim I and Kim M (2021) Paths to Civic Engagement: Opportunity Structures and Marriage Immigrants' Associational Lives in South Korea. *Journal of Asian Sociology* 50(1): 247–272.

Kim Y-S (2018) Care work and ethnic boundary marking in South Korea. *Critical Sociology* 44(7–8): 1045–1059.

Kofman E and Raghuram P (2005) Gender and skilled migrants: into and beyond the work place. *Geoforum* 36(2): 149–154.

Lee H-K (2008) International marriage and the state in South Korea: focusing on governmental policy. *Citizenship Studies* 12(1): 107–123.

Lee H (2012) Political economy of cross-border marriage: economic development and social reproduction in Korea. *Feminist Economics* 18(2): 177–200.

Liu-Farrer G, Yeoh B S and Baas M (2021) Social construction of skill: an analytical approach toward the question of skill in cross-border labour mobilities. *Journal of Ethnic and Migration Studies* 47(10): 2237–2251.

Man G (2004) Gender, work & migration: deskilling Chinese immigrant women in Canada. *Women's Studies International Forum* 27(2): 135–148.

McCall L (2005) The complexity of intersectionality. *Signs: Journal of Women in Culture and Society* 30(3): 1771–1800.

MOGEF (Ministry of Gender Equality and Family) (2019) 2018 Jeonguk Damunhwagajok Siltaejosa Yeongu [A Study on the National Survey of Multicultural Families 2018]. Ministry of Gender Equality and Family.

Park A C (2011) *A Critical Ethnography of Filipino English-Speaking Teachers (FESTS) in Korea: Contesting the Deliberate and Default and Advocating for Human Capitalization and Glocalization*. Ph.D. Yonsei University, South Korea – Seoul.

Park K-T (2009) *Racism [Injongjuui]*. Seoul: Chaeksesang.(in Korean).

Piper N and Lee S (2016) Marriage migration, migrant precarity, and social reproduction in Asia: an overview. *Critical Asian Studies* 48(4): 473–493.

Piper N and Roces N (eds) (2003) *Wife Or Worker?: Asian Marriage and Migration*. Maryland: Rowman & Littlefield.

Raghuram P (2004) The difference that skills make: gender, family migration strategies and regulated labour markets. *Journal of Ethnic and Migration Studies* 30(2). Routledge: 303–321.

Riaño Y and Baghdadi N (2007) Understanding the labour market participation of skilled immigrant women in Switzerland: the interplay of class, ethnicity, and gender. *Journal of International Migration and Integration / Revue de l'integration et de la migration internationale* 8(2): 163.

Romero M and Valdez Z (2016) Introduction to the special issue: intersectionality and entrepreneurship. *Ethnic and Racial Studies* 39(9): 1553–1565.

Seol D H (2000) Past and present of foreign workers in Korea 1987–2000. *Asia Solidarity Quarterly* 2: 6–31.

Shan H (2013) Skill as a relational construct: hiring practices from the standpoint of Chinese immigrant engineers in Canada. *Work, Employment and Society* 27(6): 915–931.

Suzuki N (2007) Carework and migration: Japanese perspectives on the Japan-Philippines economic partnership agreement. *Asian and Pacific Migration Journal* 16(3): 357–381.

Tang W A and Wang H (2011) From victims of domestic violence to determined independent women: How Vietnamese immigrant spouses negotiate Taiwan's patriarchy family system. *Women's Studies International Forum* 34(5): 430–440.

Woo S-M, K-H Joo and Kim H-J (2015) *Da-Mun-Hwa-Sa-Hoe-Bog-Ji-Gae-Lon* [Introduction to Multicultural Social Welfare]. Paju: Yangseowon.

Yang I, M Min and Kim S-H (2010) *Yeoseonggyeolhoniminjaui gyeongjehwaldong siltaewa jeongchaekgwaje* [Economic activities of women marriage immigrants in Korea and their employment policies]. 10-27–04. *Economic Humanities and Social Research Association Collaborative Research Series*. Seoul: Korean Women's Development Institute.

Zaman H (2006) *Breaking the Iron Wall: Decommodification and Immigrant Women's Labor in Canada*. Oxford: Lexington Books.

CHAPTER 5

Exclusion and Inclusion of Japanese Latin Americans

A Case Study on Public Housing in Aichi Prefecture

Ashita Matsumiya

Abstract

Many Japanese Latin Americans have been indirectly hired by offices that dispatch temporary workers and contractors instead of being directly employed. This shows that they are still considered to be "economic adjustment tools" as bottom workers. The purpose of this chapter is to examine the reality of the exclusion of Japanese Latin Americans as bottom workers, and the process of inclusion through community practice in public housing. In studies of Japanese Latin Americans in Japan, the resources necessary for them to experience upward mobility must be obtained from bridging relationships with Japanese people. This chapter focuses on the formation of social relationships in terms of the labor and life problems associated with Japanese Latin Americans in local communities in Aichi Prefecture in central Japan, where auto-industries affiliated with Toyota Motors are concentrated. Many of them are concentrated in suburban public housing, leaving them excluded from the labor market and residential space. First, I examine these communities in a theoretical sense. Then focus on public housing, which has a notable population of Japanese Latin Americans, analyzing issues related to the settlement of migrant workers. Second, I examine the community responses in such areas, where residents have borne the responsibility of resolving such issues about exclusion.

With the economic downturn caused by the COVID-19 pandemic that began in winter of 2020, the unemployment rate of migrant workers in Japan has dramatically increased. According to a survey conducted in Mie Prefecture in May 2020 (322 immigrant residents in Mie Prefecture), 10.2% were unemployed, and in a survey conducted in Shizuoka Prefecture in June 2020 (317 Brazilians and Filipinos living in Shizuoka), 22.1% were unemployed.[1] Compared to the

---

1   https://www.japanlivingsupport.com/wp-content/uploads/2022/8/1, *The Shizuoka Shimbun* 2020/7/22.

total unemployment rate (2.9%) for Japan in the same time period, it is clear that there is a high unemployment rate among migrant workers. The author's survey of migrant workers in December 2020 confirmed that they are not only unemployed but also increasingly impoverished due to reduced working hours. Unemployed immigrants were forced to help themselves to obtain information about various benefits. The high unemployment rate of migrant workers in Japan shows that they are still considered to be "economic adjustment tools" as bottom workers.

This chapter analyzes the exclusion and inclusion of Japanese Latin Americans in public housing communities in Aichi Prefecture. Many of them are concentrated in suburban public housing, leaving them excluded from the labor market and residential space. The chapter has two aims. First, I will examine these communities theoretically. I will focus on public housing, which has a notable population of Japanese Latin Americans, analyzing issues related to the settlement of immigrant residents in public housing. Second, I will examine the community responses in areas where residents have borne the responsibility of resolving such issues about exclusion.

1   The Socioeconomic Structure of Japanese Latin Americans in Japan

1.1   *Labor Issues of Japanese Latin Americans*
In considering the labor issues of Japanese Latin Americans, we cannot ignore the labor market centered on the manufacturing industry, which has led the Japanese economy, including companies such as Toyota Motor Corporation. With the labor shortage under the bubble economy in the late 1980s, the *Immigration Control and Refugee-Recognition Law* was amended in 1990, allowing the immigration of foreign nationals of Japanese descent (Sharpe, 2010).[2]

As a result, the immigration of Japanese Latin Americans has increased, especially among Brazilians and Peruvians. From the early 1990s, such immigration rapidly increased, recording the highest population in 2007 for Brazilians (316,967) and in late 2008 for Peruvians (59,723) (Figure 5.1).

A major turning point was the economic downturn that began in the fall of 2008. The downturn caused by the credit crisis directly struck Japanese Latin Americans, who mostly worked as precarious workers in the manufacturing

---

2   Sharpe (2010) argues this process was a government initiated *de facto* guestworker program to satisfy demands for cheap labor under the guise of a policy to facilitate "ethnic return" migration.

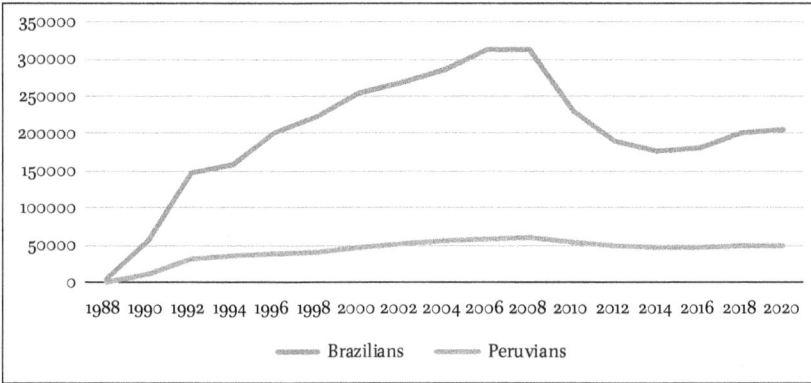

FIGURE 5.1   Population trends of Brazilians and Peruvians in Japan
SOURCE: STATISTICS ON FOREIGN RESIDENTS IN JAPAN (PLOTTED BY THE
AUTHOR)

industry. Many Japanese Latin Americans were indirectly hired by offices that dispatch temporary workers and contractors instead of being directly employed, and this made their employment insecure (Higuchi and Tanno, 2003). The economic downturn of 2008 directly affected Japanese Latin Americans, causing them to suffer drastically higher rates of unemployment compared to Japanese citizens without mixed heritage. According to Higuchi (2014), about half of Latin American workers lost their jobs from September 2008 to March 2009, while the unemployment rate in Japan was below 5% in the same period. Many migrant workers often lost not only their jobs but also their housing, including company dormitories. Many of their residences were located in the suburbs of large cities where automobile-related factories were concentrated, and their livelihoods were threatened by their increasing economic deprivation.

Subsequently, as the economy began to recover from this economic downturn in 2013, the population of Japanese Latin Americans in Japan began to increase. However, their insecure situation in the labor market did not change. According to the annual report, the *Notification of the Employment Status of Foreigners*,[3] 52.6% of Brazilians and 40.2% of Peruvians were temporary and contract workers as of the end of October 2020 (Table 5.1).

Additional issue is that the socioeconomic structures affecting these migrant workers are being passed down to the next generation. The issues associated

---

3   https://www.stat.go.jp/data/roudou/sokuhou/tsuki/index.html,2023/1/1.

TABLE 5.1   Ratio of Brazilians and Peruvians employed to temporary and contract workers

	2010	2011	2012	2013	2014	2015	2016	2017	2018	2019	2020
Brazilian employees	1,16,363	1,16,839	1,01,891	95,505	94,171	96,672	1,06,597	1,17,299	1,27,392	1,35,455	1,31,112
Temporary and contract workers	70,034	68,854	57,035	52,939	51,763	52,671	57,942	64,622	71,379	74,025	69,013
Ratio (%)	60.2	58.9	56.0	55.4	55.0	54.5	54.4	55.1	56.0	54.6	52.6
Peruvian employees	23,360	25,036	23,267	23,189	23,331	24,422	26,072	27,695	28,686	29,554	29,054
Temporary and contract workers	11,848	12,430	11,163	10,997	10,758	11,032	11,651	12,468	13,140	12,966	11,688
Ratio (%)	50.7	49.6	48.0	47.4	46.1	45.2	44.7	45.0	45.8	43.9	40.2

with immigrant children living in Japan include those relating to Japanese language skills, adaptation to school, unenrollment in school, and ethnic identity. Brazilian and Peruvian children specifically have been found to experience low rates of high school enrollment. Analysis of census data shows that the high school enrollment rate of 17-year-old Brazilian young persons who have lived in Japan for more than five years increased from 30% in 2000 to 50% in 2010; yet, compared to young persons of other nationalities, their enrollment rate is noticeably low (Takaya et al., 2015). The education level of individuals aged 19 to 21 based on nationality was "junior high school" for 33.7% of Brazilians and 26.3% of Peruvians; thus, there are a significant number of individuals in this group who have not been educated beyond junior high school. This is considered to be significantly lower than the high school enrollment rate of the Japanese population during the same period. In addition, compared to the rates of the university of those in their 40s (i.e. their parents' generation), the numbers are similar for Brazilians but lower for Peruvians, showing a decrease in the university enrollment rate over time. Looking at these data, it appears unlikely for second-generation Japanese Latin Americans to achieve upward social mobility. Underlying these issues is the point that, "in Japan, people are generally not used to ethnic diversity, which puts second-generation Japanese Latin Americans at a disadvantage." (Higuchi and Inaba, 2018). What we need to think about here is how the educational level and livelihood-related stability of one's parents will have a significant impact on college enrollment. Therefore, when considering issues for second-generation Japanese Latin Americans, it is essential to look at resources that allow them to overcome social disadvantages related to instability in their livelihood, including the employment of their parents.

In response to such challenges surrounding the precariousness of the labor and the lives of migrant workers, the Japan government has introduced virtually no immigration policy. Instead, local communities in smaller cities have been pushed into providing solutions to the various issues associated with Japanese Latin Americans.

1.2   Focus on Community Responses

Since Japan began accepting Japanese Latin Americans of Japanese descent in 1990, there has not been any adequate federal immigration policy (Shiobara, 2020; Takenoshita, 2016). As a result, the social services necessary for Japanese Latin Americans are provided by the private sector instead of the public sector, being dependent on localized responses by local communities where Japanese Latin Americans are concentrated to reside. The formation of mutual help relationships among Japanese Latin Americans in Japan, which is the focus of this chapter, must be considered from such a characteristic point.

The formation of such relationships takes place in the regional cities where the manufacturing industries are concentrated, rather than in the metropolitan areas where the financial industries that have shown growth under globalization are located. Looking at the situation internationally, this is an unusual phenomenon. In most cases outside of Japan, the focus of the discussions on "bottom workers" including immigrants relates to the inner cities of metropolitan areas as discussed in Chapters 8. However, the areas where Japanese Latin Americans live and work are not big cities like Tokyo but smaller cities near Metropolitan areas where the automotive industry is concentrated, especially Toyota Motors, which has led to recent economic growth in Japan (Nibe et al., 2022; Matsumiya, 2022). Thus, we need to focus on communities in these smaller cities around metropolitan areas where the number of Japanese Latin Americans has increased. Therefore, discussed as "suburbanization of poverty" in Chapter 1, this chapter focuses on the formation of social relationships in terms of the structural problems associated with Japanese Latin Americans in local communities in Aichi Prefecture, where auto-industries affiliated with Toyota Motors are concentrated.

2 Public Housing with an Increasing Number of Japanese Latin Americans Accumulation of Immigrants in Public Housing

Since 1990, many Japanese Latin Americans have migrated as workers into the Tokai Region in central Japan to work in its concentrated industrial plants, which mainly serve the auto industry. Aichi Prefecture has more Brazilian residents than any other part of Japan. Its 2019 population of Brazilians was the highest in Japan at 61,435.

In Aichi Prefecture, the 2016 survey of immigrants shows that 70.2% of Brazilians are employed part-time and 20.8% are employed full-time. Economic deprivation is also noticeable, with 15.7% of the population having a monthly household income of fewer than 2 million yen (US$25,000). As such, these workers continue to remain in an insecure situation in which the majority are indirectly hired in the manufacturing industry (Matsumiya, 2022).

Many of these immigrants live in public housing, so in January 2021, of the 49,473 households in 297 public housing estates, 15.4%, or 7,097, were households consisting of immigrants. By nationality, most were Brazilian, followed

TABLE 5.2   Immigrant residents in public housing in Aichi
              Prefecture (ratio)

Year	All public housing in Aichi Prefecture	Homi public housing in Toyota City	Housing Estate x in Nishio City
2005	5,722(10.3%)	471(50.3%)	46(56.2%)
2007	6,383(11.6%)	507(54.4%)	45(56.3%)
2009	6,383(11.6%)	558(58.2%)	34(52.3%)
2011	5,942(11.6%)	501(56.7%)	35(48.6%)
2013	5,941(11.9%)	532(60.1%)	37(52.1%)
2015	6,167(12.5%)	541(61.7%)	35(51.5%)
2017	6,731(13.9%)	557(65.1%)	38(58.9%)
2019	6,842(14.5%)	551(66.6%)	43(62.3%)
2021	7,097(15.4%)	537(67.9%)	48(66.7%)

by Chinese and Peruvian.[4] Housing estates with more than half of their occupants in households with foreign nationality are not rare, and the percentage in some exceeds 60% (Table 5.2).

The number of immigrant households in public housing in Japan has proliferated during the past 30 years, but when the *Public Housing Law* was enacted in 1951, immigrants were not permitted to live in public housing. The national government's basic stance in the 1970s was that "a foreigner could not request the use of public housing as a right." In contrast to this national government policy, in 1980, the Ministry of Construction expanded conditions for occupancy to, in principle, include "persons who have received permission for permanent residency," removing obstacles to approving persons who had obtained alien registration. Later in 1987, limits on the period of residency of registered immigrants were revoked, and in 1992 "persons who have obtained alien registration" were "recognized to have qualifications to apply for occupancy as similar as possible to those of residents."

---

4 Documents provided by Aichi Prefecture Publishing Housing Management Office (Matsumiya 2022).

Thus, with low rent and relatively little discrimination in housing, a rising number of immigrants have selected public housing that they can occupy by satisfying the conditions: only co-resident relatives, income standards, joint surety, and so on (Inaba et al., 2010). As occupancy by immigrants advanced, those who had already moved in brought in their relatives and friends, forming communities in the housing estates where immigrants were concentrated. Since 1990, in the Tokai Region and northern Kanto that have had regional industrial cities with a high concentration of manufacturing industries, the concentration of Japanese Latin Americans has formed communities of immigrants in many housing estates.

It is impossible to ignore that concentrating Japanese Latin Americans in public housing has resulted in social problems such as infractions of garbage disposal rules, illegal parking, noise, difficulty collecting community association fees, and conflict with Japanese residents. It is also indicated that, under the revision of the *Public Housing Law* in 1996 to, "appropriately provide public housing to people who truly have difficulty obtaining housing, such as elderly or disabled people," welfare measures were strengthened by lowering income standards and relaxing obstacles to the admission of elderly people. This resulted in problems such as the increase in the ages and decrease in the incomes of occupants of public housing, transforming public housing into welfare facilities accompanied by their stigmatization, stirring up prejudice and discrimination by their neighbors, and breaking human relationships in housing estates (Mori, 2013). In this sense, it can be viewed as a structure that forces bottom workers, specifically immigrants from South America, into districts with low-class housing (Higuchi, 2010: 159).

Considering a local community, consisting mainly of public housing occupied by many Japanese Latin Americans, the structural problem is cited that the welfare category which includes elderly people, disabled people, and single-parent households increases, concentrating "the locked-in low-income class," which in turn means more elderly people, difficulty operating community associations, the formation of isolated places, and the separations of occupants from the majority of society (Hirayama, 2011: 229). The *Public Housing Law* enacted in 1951 was originally for "low-income earners who have difficulty obtaining a home," but when the law was enacted, it was also assumed that a "latent middle class" would also enter public housing, and the income quantile covered the bottom 80% of incomes. However, the income standard for occupancy has been lowered in steps; until now the coverage rate is 25%. This was accompanied by the toughening of restrictions on high-income earners and the application of rents equal to those in the private sector, resulting in the legal system prohibiting occupancy by middle-income earners and further concentrating on low-income earners. Linked to such trends, occupancy standards for the welfare categories of elderly and disabled people and single-parent households have been relaxed, strengthening the character of public housing as places that gather people in these categories. It has been clearly shown that, consequently, in public housing, there are many households with annual incomes below three million yen, and the turnover rate has fallen, entrenching the residents (Hirayama, 2011: 226–227).

At the same time, Mori (2006) argues that a characteristic of those occupying public housing in Japan is an increase in elderly and immigrant occupants. Both are "housing deprived people" who have difficulty obtaining private housing with only their resources and share economic neediness. Concentrating such needy people in the same space saps the local vitality of housing estates, resulting in institutionalization. Moreover, stigmatization that strengthens negative images of and isolates these spaces appears, and such prejudice is internalized by people of the district, negatively impacting behavior and human relations, further dividing the residents and hampering community creation. Gathering poor people into public housing accelerates the negative spiral, "residents protect their own dignity by differentiating themselves from other residents and maneuver to get out and people with the ability to rise in society aim to escape," (Mori, 2006: 106) increasing destitution. Public housing in Japan became a space for bottom people to gather and live together.

How will the formation of relationships between migrant workers and host society proceed in public housing, where such social exclusion is concentrated? In many catchment areas, serious conflicts and difficulties in living and educational issues are noted (Kajita et al., 2005; Inaba et al., 2010). Next, I would like to discuss a theoretical framework for capturing this issue.

3   Theoretical Framework

3.1   *Theory of Segmented Assimilation in Japan*
Many studies have been accumulated on the exclusion of migrant workers from host societies, especially in the United States. Portes' theoretical framework is one influential approach to considering these issues (Portes, 2005; Portes and Rumbaut, 2006; Hayashi, 2017). It explains the adaptation of immigrants to the host society and social mobility between generations in terms of three points: 1) the conditions of their withdrawal from their home countries; 2) the types of the human capital of immigrants; and 3) the reaction of the government, employers, and native population of the host country, and the presence/absence of ethnic communities.

In Japan, empirical tests based on Portes' theoretical framework have been conducted. In those studies, an important factor that impacts the social mobility of second-generation immigrants is the relationship between ethnic communities and the host society. Hayashi (2016: 116) points out that the segmentation has been related to the host society's reception (state, market, and community), and a large part of it depends on state policies. Nevertheless, he emphasizes the importance of the relationship with host society, which guarantees access not only to cultural capital (language, customs, and values), but also to social capital through which immigrants can obtain numerous privileged information and eventually receive support towards better setting into the host society (Hayashi, 2016: 120–121). Takenoshita (2015) also points to the importance of community and social capital in segmentation. He analyzed a survey on immigrant residents in Shizuoka Prefecture, arguing that "social capital in terms of the social ties of family, relatives, and those from the same country did not contribute to occupational upward mobility among Brazilian workers in Japan" (Takenoshita, 2016). Although Japanese Latin Americans have had significant difficulties in making ties with native Japanese people, "the resources necessary for Brazilians to experience upward mobility must be obtained from outside of their ethnic communities, where bridging relationships with Japanese people plays an important role for Brazilians to go from temporary workers to full-time workers." (Takenoshita, 2018: 164).

3.2   Theories on Community and Exclusion

It has been pointed out that through the social capital held by immigrants, especially through "bonding" social relational capital, they can gain access to useful autonomy in the labor market (Portes, 1998). In contrast, the study of Japanese Brazilians suggests that the relationship with the host society is effective. What is important here is the formation of relationships in the local communities where many Japanese Latin Americans live. In other words, it is important for Japanese Latin Americans to build relationships with Japanese citizens who do not have the mixed heritage in the host society, since the role played by their ethnic communities is limited in terms of facilitating social mobility.

Local communities are counted on to resolve widespread welfare problems that impact everyone from the elderly to children, and various other social problems related to disaster prevention, crime prevention, and so on. Specifically, as shown by the supplementary roles of local communities in social inclusion or initiatives, or by the theory of social inclusion which holds that a community is the only empowerment strategy to oppose exclusion

(Byrne, 2005), local communities are counted on to function as safety nets for people who have been excluded from the labor market.

When considered according to the verifiable knowledge of past community theory, it should be immediately imagined that such a scenario is not simple. Amidst the trends—the falling rate of participation in block or community associations, the liberation of close bonds from local communities, and the weakening of local communities—it is possible to see these as daunting challenges and that too much is expected of existing local communities (Delanty, 2013; Young, 2007).

Another problem is the fact that specified classes are excluded from strengthening the capabilities and improving the performance of local communities. Many previous studies have validated that a community has an exclusionary mechanism. In other words, the strengthening of a local community is accompanied by a process that strengthens identity, resulting in exclusion. This is the dilemma by which strengthening a community is accompanied by exclusion, and presents the aporia that a strong community, or a community that fills some function, is homogenous and is either highly cohesive or that its actions increase cohesiveness, while, inversely, a weak community is highly heterogenous, and its cohesiveness is low.

This aporia seems an essential problem when considering a community. As stated by Delanty, "community" connotes a double meaning, which is to say that as a political concept it has exclusivity premised on regional characteristics and distinctiveness, while conversely it has inclusiveness that aims for universality, but this definition itself prioritizes exclusivity of a community premised on regional characteristics and distinctiveness (Delanty, 2013). Young also defines community as being based on antinomies, and hence an inclusive community cannot exist (Young, 2007).

There has been a criticism of the theory of such a linkage of community with exclusion. That is a criticism concerning the mechanism of exclusion based on the actual state of a local community. This corresponds to the theory of Portes, who detected the danger that the argument surrounding social capital tends to lead to exclusiveness, placing excess demands on group members, constraining the liberty of individuals, and flattening norms at a low level (Portes, 1998; Field, 2003). This point has clearly shown the paradox that in contrast to the inclusion function of a local community that is expected to act as a safety net, a vector of exclusion is included in a strong community with an inclusion function. There will be no expectations of communities acting as safety nets that rise amid the midst of the contraction of the public sphere and private sphere.

Below, to consider the issues of community and exclusion, I examine prefectural housing in Nishio City.[5] Specifically, Housing Estate x where the percentage of immigrant households was highest in Aichi Prefecture by FY2007 (Table 5.2), and Japanese Latin Americans are supported through active participation in the local community, two features that are extremely significant for the concern addressed by this chapter.

4   Local Community and Japanese Latin Americans in Nishio City

4.1   *Japanese Latin Americans in Nishio City*

Nishio City is in Southern Nishimikawa (central Aichi Prefecture), dominated by auto plants related to the Toyota group, and since 1990, consisting mainly of Brazilians had increased to more than 5% of the population in 2007. Since the financial crisis of 2008, their number (mainly Brazilians) has fallen, but in the past few years, the number of technical trainees has risen, mainly from the Philippines, Vietnam, China, Indonesia, and so on. In January 2020, the immigrant population of the region was 10,470, or 3.7% of the total. Of them, the number of Brazilians was still the highest at 38.4% of all Japanese Latin Americans.

These mostly Brazilian Japanese Latin Americans are concentrated in eight prefectural public housing estates in the city, where 26.6% of households are immigrant households. Among these eight housing estates, their percentage is highest in Housing Estate x. In 2020, 48 immigrant households occupied this 69-unit building, for a percentage of 66.7%. Housing Estate x was the estate with the highest percentage of immigrant households in Aichi Prefecture by 2007. Block P where Housing Estate x is located is also the site of a personnel placement agency's dormitory constructed in the 1990s, and in April 2020, of the 956 people residing in Block P, 291 were Japanese Latin Americans. This means that about 30% of its population were Japanese Latin Americans, mainly Brazilians.

As this shows, Block P in which Housing Estate x is located in a district where Japanese Latin Americans are concentrated, but in the early 1990s when the Japanese Latin Americans began to increase, a movement to exclude the increasing number of Japanese Latin Americans appeared there. For example, a movement appeared in opposition to the planned construction of the

5   The author has, since 2001, continued to interview concerned persons and observed participation as a community worker. Later analysis is based on the results of this fieldwork (Matsumiya 2022).

personnel placement agency's dormitory. I remember being told, "men did not care, but among women, almost all those middle-aged and older opposed immigrants and told their grandchildren not to walk in front of Company M's dormitory." A variety of problems occurred as more Japanese Latin Americans were concentrated in public housing, including infractions of garbage disposal rules, illegal parking, noise, truancy by children, and friction between residents.

An authoritative perspective on these problems was provided by the theory of *Invisible Residents* (Kajita et al., 2005; Hayashi, 2017). The results of this research explained that structural problems in Japanese society, which include an employment system that requires migrant workers, problems related to the structure of the industry, and a lack of immigrant policy at the national level, are imposed on regions where high concentrations of immigrants reside. It portrayed a mechanism that, although the concentration of Japanese Latin Americans in such regions continues, they form "divided communities" short on human resources and social capital. This increases the number of "invisible residents" who are not perceived by local society because of their lack of social life, and local society pays for external diseconomies that the market creates (Kajita et al., 2005).

Survey on public housing by Inaba et al. (Inaba et al., 2010: 2402) sets the beginning of the appearance of problems as the time when the percentage of Japanese Latin Americans in a housing estate reached 10%. An opinion survey of Japanese residents conducted in 2004 and 2005 in Nishio City revealed that 60% held negative views of living near Brazilians or Peruvians (Yamamoto and Matsumiya 2010). Below I want first to confirm that similar exclusion movements occur in many other regions in Japan with high concentrations of Japanese Latin Americans.

Considering the state of participation of such Japanese Latin Americans in local communities, a "survey of Japanese Latin Americans of Nishio City" conducted in September 2008[6] shows that, overall, more than half "do not participate." This reveals that, even when limited to the local community, their rate of participation in block associations, community associations, local events, children's associations, local disaster prevention training, and so on is extremely low. In contrast, a survey conducted in the same period in three prefectural housing estates where Japanese Latin Americans are concentrated in Nishio City confirmed a 100% participation rate by Japanese Latin Americans in community associations of housing estates, with 31% having served as association

---

6   This survey was conducted jointly with Nishio City administration. It was done by sampling alien registration registers and sending 1,000 questionnaires by mail and having the respondents return them by mail, achieving a recovery rate of 23.4%.

officers. Examining the composition of officers of community associations in FY2017 in Housing Estate x shows that the community association president was Peruvian, the vice president was Brazilian, and that Brazilians were responsible for parking or electricity and crime prevention. This reveals that, in contrast to a local exclusion trend, Japanese Latin Americans actively participate in their local communities. How has such a trend become possible? Next, I want to consider community practices in Housing Estate x where this trend has progressed.

4.2   *Community Practices That Overcome Exclusion in Housing Estates*
I will begin with scenes of the daily life of Japanese Latin Americans in this housing estate. They concentrate on prefectural housing for the active reason that it is independent of the personnel placement agency's dormitory, and for the passive reason that they select public housing where there is relatively little discrimination because owners of private rental properties still practice discrimination. In either case, when they select the housing estate, they often take advantage of a network of relations or connections with acquaintances in their workplaces, and accordingly, a network of Japanese Latin Americans forms in the housing estate. A network of this kind in the housing estate was not linked to community association activities, but prefectural housing in Nishio City that focused on Housing Estate x is characterized by a community association that takes approaches to facilitate participation by Japanese Latin Americans.

I will now observe this process in the actions of Mr. T[7] who served as community association president in Housing Estate x from 1992 until 2002. Mr. T became president of the community association at the same time Japanese Latin Americans were increasing. When they reached 15 households in 1995, problems related to language appeared in the activities of the association. He aimed to overcome such problems by newly appointing interpreters or translators to assist the community association officers. Garbage separation was a particularly serious problem; therefore, the garbage disposal rules were translated into Portuguese, and the city's environmental department attached foreign language explanations to the waste disposal calendars and garbage bags. In 1997, a further rise in the number of Japanese Latin Americans was accompanied by the selection of Japanese Latin Americans as community association officers and group leaders. When immigrant households occupied more than

---

7   A man in his sixties who has lived in Nishio City since he was 19 years old and is employed as a regular employee of a transport company.

40% of the dwelling units in 1998, Mr. T requested that a Brazilian resident be appointed as vice president of the community association. In 1999, he created a system in which a immigrant resident took over collecting community association membership fees. Beginning that year, a booth selling Brazilian cuisine was opened at festivals held by the block associations, and immigrant resident was appointed to serve as an officer of the children's association. The interpretation and translation members were newly appointed inside the housing estate and to the block association of Block P where the housing estate is located. In this way, beginning in the last half of the 1990s, a series of mechanisms for the participation of Japanese Latin Americans in the local community was established, and then in 2007, a Peruvian was appointed to the post of community association president.[8] Such activities have impacted the participation of Japanese Latin Americans in the self-rule of other prefectural housing estates in the city.

What I want to note here is that Mr. T did not just encourage assimilation in the region; he also reorganized its organizational framework. Important documents are translated into Portuguese, and cleaning activities, meetings of community association officers, and broadcasting in the housing estate are conducted with interpreters providing information in Portuguese. Mr. T, who led this movement, summed up the issue as follows. "This should not be a problem imposed on housing estates or community associations where immigrants live. It is missing the point to say that it was imposed on the people of the region because it was called back by national policy." Nevertheless, he emphasized the role of the local community, stating "the community can only tackle the issue step by step." In other words, although the region did not cause the problem, he demonstrated the region's willingness to tackle it. Moreover, instead of the approach called exclusion, he created a series of procedures to facilitate their participation in the local community.

4.3 Class Factors

By national policy, public housing has a class characteristic; its residents include many low-income blue-collar residents regardless of nationality. Past research on the structure of Japanese people's consciousness of immigrants has shown that blue-collar people hold stronger exclusive attitudes and are more likely to look upon immigrants as negative elements (Hamada, 2010).

---

8   A man in his forties who has lived in Housing Estate x since 2001. He offered himself as a candidate for association president at a 2007 community association meeting where people were being pressed to run. He served as community association president for four terms until 2010 and two terms from 2012 to 2013.

However, there is room to reconsider the character of this culture of blue-collar people. Roth, who conducted fieldwork related to this issue in a Brazilian community in Japan, has shown that blue-collar Japanese have negative awareness of Brazilians because of their role as competition in the labor market on the one hand, but when in a neighborhood, relations and at festivals and so on are positive about forming relationships with Brazilians (Roth, 2002: 127–128). The formation of relationships in a region that Roth has clarified can also be discovered in a community surrounding an apartment building in Nishio City. To cite one example, Mr. T, who was head of the Apartment Building x community association, responded to the author's question, "why do you work hard to conduct such activities?" by answering, "I consider a spirit of moral obligation and humanity to be important because I have always been a truck driver. Therefore, it is not that a person is a Brazilian, but that he is trustworthy." It is possible to see the generous sharing of such culture as a condition permitting coexistence in public housing occupied by many blue-collar workers of Japanese and even foreign nationalities. The author's analysis of a questionnaire survey of Japanese residents of Nishio City did not find any tendency for blue-collar workers to hold negative consciousness, but rather showed that the closer their relationships with immigrants, the more positive they were (Yamamoto and Matsumiya, 2010), a finding that can be said to back up this interpretation.

Although the participation of Japanese Latin Americans as members is ensured and Japanese Latin Americans conduct activities, the participation of Japanese Latin Americans in the activities of the community association is not free of problems. For one thing, foreign officers who interpret and regulate relations between Japanese residents and Japanese Latin Americans had complicated relationships with some of the Japanese Latin Americans, who were harassed by them for scratching their cars etc. or were harshly questioned by Brazilian nationals who demanded to know if they were the allies of the Japanese or people with Japanese ancestry. Therefore, Japanese Latin Americans were appointed as officers very carefully. In one housing estate, the officers were selected through consultations among the Brazilian residents. This was done because of the danger that a designation by a Japanese association president would be met with hostility by Japanese Latin Americans who claim that the person who has been designated as "an ally of the Japanese."

One more problem is continuity in the community association officer organization that changes once a year. In Nishio City, there are housing estates with a policy of not including immigrants in accounting management, and there are community associations that have adopted negative attitudes to the participation of Japanese Latin Americans after a change of officers. It is a fact that claims such as "Japanese understand what they are told," "in a housing estate with only Japanese residents, illegal garbage disposal does not occur," or "we cannot make immigrants understand us," and the feeling that immigrants cause housing estates' problem is deeply rooted.

Of course, amid such exclusion movements, difficulties, and so on, instead of trying to resolve challenges to daily life in the activities of local communities such as garbage problems or language-related problems through exclusion from the local community, it is important to aim to resolve these problems as regional challenges by discovering ways to permit participation by Japanese Latin Americans. It is probably possible to discover one approach that can resolve the dilemma of community strengthening and exclusion.

To spread such local communities, it may be possible to see easier interactions between Japanese and immigrants as a special characteristic of public housing because it is easier to establish "order" and more difficult to segregate in public housing than in private apartment buildings. However, as shown below, aiming to expand community association activities of a housing estate beyond the range of prefectural housing and putting them into practice in a local community, will have ripple effects outside the housing estate.

4.4   Ripple Effects outside of a Local Community

As a ripple effect outside the housing estate, the block association of Block P where Housing Estate x is located approved the establishment of the Committee to Support Interaction with Foreigners as a subordinate organization of the block association in March 2006. This committee is an organization formed by electing one officer from each of the four parts of the Block P block association to undertake local initiatives to support Japanese Latin Americans. The four persons who are elected are all former presidents of a part of the block association, and they are appointed for three years. An officer of the original block association who guided its activities commented as follows: "We felt that if we did not do something, we would turn into a dead-end community. When a problem appears, people critically blame the increase in immigrants. We felt that if we did this, that would not happen." "We thought that because nothing could be done during the one-year tenure of the block association president, we wanted it tackled for three years."[9] Accordingly, the support activities of the housing estate expanded into Block P.

Also, the formation of Committee G to introduce the Japanese Latin American's support activities throughout the entire city with the Housing

---

9   Interview with the former president of Block P block association (sixties, male) in April 2016.

Estate x community association as its parent body has regionally expanded the practice at the housing estate level. Committee G was formed in 2001 under the guidance of Mr. T and had about 40 members in 2020. They included concerned persons in the Block P block association, the community association president, and other officers of the housing estate, concerned members of the local disaster prevention organization, leaders of the Japanese Latin Americans, a manager of the personnel placement agency Company M, and the author and other university-related persons. Two members of the city assembly elected from the district served as advisors. Operating committee meetings that are held in a local community center five or six times a year are attended by the committee members, an employee of the city's regional support and cooperation department, and representatives of local elementary and junior high schools who attend as observers. At each of its two-hour meetings, problems related to Japanese Latin Americans are shared, and specific measures to deal with these are studied. The committee conducts two principal activities, (1) supporting local activities and (2) supporting the education of foreign children, and it aims to meet the needs of diverse Japanese Latin Americans, not only at the housing estate level, but throughout the city. The activities of Committee G can be summed up under the following five categories.

1. As educational support, parents and guardians of foreign children who attend the local public elementary school attend regular discussion meetings. The contents of their discussions are proposed to school officials at operating committee meetings. In August, the foreign parents and guardians, the school principal, assistant principal, and supervising teachers hold a barbecue as a social get-together at a meeting room in Housing Estate x. Building on this foundation, the company has been offering Japanese language classes for foreign children, school career information sessions, and job placement assistance in cooperation with the local government.

2. The foreigner's disaster prevention volunteer group was formed in 2013. It has almost ten members, and its representative is a Peruvian, Mr. D. It holds study meetings to plan and implement disaster prevention activities by Japanese Latin Americans with a Japanese Red Cross volunteer group, the local fire department, and officials of the local disaster prevention organization. Through these activities, a system is created in which immigrants proactively participate in the local community, rather than being on the receiving end of support.

3. At the Block P festival in October and a festival held at the local community center in March, foreign members of Committee G hold social events where they introduce Brazilian and Peruvian cuisine. It is an opportunity

to expand the mutual exchange of activities not only in the complex but also in the community as a whole.

4. Foreign members of Committee G attend meetings of the Nishio City Japanese Latin Americans Council and the Nishio City Multicultural Coexistence Promotion Committee to share problems and offer proposals concerning matters that have been studied by the operating committee.

5. The Aichi Prefectural Housing Community Association Liaison Committee is a federation of community associations of prefectural housing estates primarily concerned with activities of the Nishimikawa Branch formed in 1995. It works to share problems common throughout Aichi Prefecture and promote community association activities. It exchanges views with and inspects community associations at other housing estates in the prefecture.

Such activities by Committee G have ripple effects: the local community in Housing Estate x from Block P block association to the entire city. As city policy, since 2000, multicultural coexistence measures have been promoted, and include completing various translation projects, hiring interpreters, strengthening links between 17 departments concerned with Japanese Latin Americans since 2004, and having the city board of education increase the number of bilingual teaching assistants. Since 2009, three meetings of the Japanese Latin Americans Council and two meetings of the Multicultural Coexistence Promotion Committee have been held, and the "Promotion of the Formation of a Multicultural Coexistence Promotion Society" had been included in the regional welfare plan.

It can be argued that a factor that has played a role in substantially transforming local government policies in this way is the existence of written proposals and requests submitted to the Mayor of Nishio City based on discussions at annual meetings of Committee G dating back to 2001. The written proposals and requests were not only submitted in the name of Committee G but were jointly signed by the block association and community association presidents, and the president of the Local Community Promotion Consultative Committee, while others were submitted based on the formation of a local consensus of a citizens group and the housing estate community association and block association. Therefore, the city which cannot ignore requests by representatives of the residents has also transformed the way it conducts its operations. Also, since 2013, Mr. T has been appointed as the vice-representative of the Multicultural Coexistence Promotion Committee, linking discussions conducted in Committee G to the organizational framework reflected in city policies. These local community practices have led to the development of new measures to support foreign labor and education in the absence of a national immigration policy.

4.5 Effectiveness of Local Community Practices in Supporting Migrant Workers

What impact have the above efforts had on the livelihood stability and educational support of migrant workers? It can be said that the above efforts have had a certain impact on labor and family issues such as unemployment among migrant workers after the collapse of Lehman Brothers.

In a survey conducted in April 2009, 25 of the 39 foreign households in Housing B were found to be unemployed (Matsumiya 2012). In addition, the number of Latin American residents who are not unemployed but are in financial difficulties due to the drastic reduction of working hours has increased, and the community has been weakened by the withdrawal of Brazilian food stores and the reduction of activities led by Brazilian residents. In response to this serious situation, the community of Japanese Latin American residents, the residents' association of the housing complex, and the support organization for foreign residents based on the residents' association strengthened their cooperation and acted.

It is noteworthy that the self-governing community activities of the housing complex play an important role in the practical operation of the emergency employment measures project and the education support system. In April 2009, the Japanese language classes in Apartment B evolved into a support program for foreign children who were not attending school, and a briefing session for foreign residents on the flat-rate benefits was held in the town of S (76 people attended) with the support of the G association.

In fiscal 2009, Nishio City has also been promoting measures such as the establishment of the Council for the Promotion of Multicultural Conviviality, and one of the areas it has been focusing on is educational support. The Nishio City Board of Education has been assigning temporary staff to public nursery schools and promoting the "Multicultural Child Rearing Support Project." Until 2008, this project was the first of its kind in Aichi Prefecture to be carried out independently by the city, then since 2009, with the support of the International Affairs Division of the Regional Development Department of Aichi Prefecture (4.5 million yen budget), the city has been providing consultation and assistance by a coordinator for children from abroad, school enrollment information sessions, initial guidance in Japanese and other languages, preschool, and early adaptation classes.

In addition, we provide consultation and support by a coordinator for foreign children, school guidance sessions for the "Special Support Project for

Children Not Attending School," a survey on the actual situation of children not attending school and "Early Adjustment Classroom" were conducted by using the "Aichi Prefecture Special Fund for Employment Revitalization Project" in 2009, which requires at least the half of the budget to be used for employment of the unemployed. This project was entrusted to Committee G, and the newly hired staff (three regular and two temporary staff who can speak Portuguese and Japanese) provided Japanese language instruction and other learning support to five children who were not attending school (three of whom were unable to attend Brazilian schools due to their parents' unemployment) and five children who were not attending nursery school or kindergarten. Japanese language instruction and other learning support were provided to five children who were not attending preschool or kindergarten. As a result of this project, one child each has started attending nursery school and elementary school, and two children have started attending junior high school. The classes are held in a dormitory room of a temporary staffing company located in the town of S. Cooperation with the local temporary staffing company as well as the local community association, community association-based support organizations, and the government is progressing. These community activities can be seen as having led to policies aimed at improving the labor problems of migrant workers as bottom workers and the educational problems of their children.

4.6   Formation of the Logic Which Resists Exclusion in Local Communities

In what form did the logic that, instead of excluding Japanese Latin Americans, encourage their participation in the local community in Housing Estate x in this way? The author believes that among factors accounting for the advance of local participation by Japanese Latin Americans in this district, an extremely important role was played by the logics of local consensus formation that overcome various confrontations and which was built by a class of Japanese leaders who confronted an increase in Japanese Latin Americans (Matsumiya, 2012). The logic that is shown below is entirely expressing opposition to a movement to exclude Japanese Latin Americans confirmed at a meeting of the operating committee of Committee G.

The following are types of logic that were used most often. One argues that immigrants should not be the objects of exclusion by declaring that positioning "a foreigner as a member of the community association and block association," means that the foreign resident has been accepted as a member of the community association and block association and would pay membership fees, and on this premise, the foreigner has become "a member of the region by paying membership fees." The following comment by Mr. T is an example: "At first some asked why immigrants were at a Shrine festival. As it is a religious ritual, that may be so, but because they live in the district and pay the same block association fees, it is natural for immigrants also to take part. Isn't that appropriate, considering the district as a community of its residents?" Based on this logic, logic based on disaster prevention and children has often been employed. The logic that emphasizes disaster prevention is clearly expressed by the words, "if an earthquake occurs, both Japanese and immigrants face the same problems, so those in the same district should be on good terms." Logic emphasizing children was also used: for example, "measures to coexist are for the sake of the children" or "aside from adults, children can get along well." Both forms of logic dare to avoid the categorization called "immigrants" to appeal for the strengthening of a community which includes immigrants.

Another form of logic often used argues that efforts to enmesh Japanese Latin Americans at the local level are "for the benefit of local self-rule; not for the benefit of the immigrants." This statement can be read as expressing the intention to promote activities without excluding Japanese Latin Americans by going so far as to not push "immigrants" to the front. Recently the following statements have been seen: "Half of the houses are occupied by people 65 years old and older. The members of the block who are reliable are immigrants. Among the 12 buildings, immigrants are group leaders in five, and in the rest, they are women in single-parent households or elderly people. As a result of aging, the only young people are immigrants and members of single-parent households. Whenever possible, I want young immigrants to take the lead." Another is, "we don't want to be in the role of their helpers; rather we want them to be part of our team. When a powerful earthquake or other disaster occurs, the Japanese are no help because they are old. The immigrants will take responsibility. Not only disaster protection, but also cleaning up after. They will take the lead in various activities." These comments show that people are counting on Japanese Latin Americans participating in efforts to deal with challenges facing the residents of public housing where aging and welfare measures have advanced. And these can be thought of as the logic of the community's function for people living in public housing in general. Until now, in prefectural housing in Nishio City, a system in which Japanese Latin Americans serve as officials has been created, the people are counting on young people including foreign children progressing one more step to fill central roles in the conduct of community activities.

5   Conclusion

I conclude by reconsidering the question I posed in the introduction: Under circumstances where local communities are expected to improve the lives of bottom workers, how can a local community that does not lead to exclusion be formed, by studying the practice in a local community centered on prefectural Housing Estate x in Nishio City. With low rent and relatively little discrimination in housing, a rising number of immigrants have selected public housing that they can occupy by satisfying the conditions. It is anticipated that, regardless of the circumstance in which social exclusion is concentrated, the challenge to local communities in public housing has been resolved. And these community practices contributed to the formation of municipal policies for labor and education issues in Japanese Latin Americans.

These findings have focused on how the participation of diverse concerned people in this way has created a mechanism for the participation of Japanese Latin Americans beyond the scope of the community association of Housing Estate x. To state this according to the concern of these findings, it can probably be described as intentionally striving to strengthen the community without doing so through exclusion. These results may seem to be a special case of Nishio City. However, the findings also support this result in Homi Public Housing in Toyota City, the largest Brazilian population center in Japan (Nibe et al. 2022; Hayashi 2017).

Of course, another problem is that it is based on block associations and community associations. The major limitation is that the category "resident" is not applied to technical trainees whose stay is limited to a period of three to five years. Furthermore, the exclusion of "immigrants who do not join the block association" is still legitimate. Even key members who have aggressively promoted the acceptance of Japanese Latin Americans in the region have expressed extremely exclusionary views such as, "I cooperate with people who reside here permanently, but cannot cooperate with people who are only here temporarily," or "I hope that owners of apartment buildings will not admit anyone simply because of strict exit-entry controls of the small and medium-size personnel placement dormitory." This can be described as participation not by all immigrants but only by immigrants who are permanent residents of the district. Thus, the effect may not extend to the category of bottom workers in general such as mobile women workers in Chapter 3 or day laborers in Chapter 10.

However, the activities of Committee G appear to have somewhat overcome this challenge in that they have led to measures covering not only immigrants who are permanent residents but all immigrants in the city. What the analysis of the community activities of Housing Estate x and Committee G has shown is the importance of the process of continuous change in local communities. The method is a transformation that overcomes the limits of a local community with an exclusion function one limit at a time.

While it is true that the issue of exclusion in local communities continues to be a major problem, it is possible to derive pathways to exclusion through community practice. In addition to this, the central theme of this chapter has been the process by which the local community becomes a support resource for the labor and education of migrant workers as bottom workers. In particular, community activities play an important role in resolving livelihood issues in areas where needy people congregate in the suburbs of large cities, in the context of inadequate immigration policies. From this point of view, it can be seen that the community functions to a certain extent in response to the exclusion faced by bottom workers.

References

Byrne D S (2005) *Social Exclusion*. Berkshire: Open University Press.

Delanty G (2013) *Community*. London: Routledge.

Field J (2003) *Social Capital*. London: Routledge.

Hamada K (2010) Gaikokujin syujyu chiiki niokeru nihonjinn-jyuminn no haitasei/kannyousei to sono kitei youinn [Factors of exclusive consciousness in Japanese local areas where have]. *The Annals of Japan Association for Urban Sociology* 28:101–115.

Hayashi B N (2016) Visibility & the capitals of migrants. *The Sociological Review of Nagoya University* 37:113–134.

Hayashi B N (2017) The logic of network formation in Homigaoka. *The Annual Review of the Tokai Sociological Society* 9:120–137.

Higuchi N (2010) Toshi ethnicity kennkyu no saikouchiku ni mukete [Toward a reconstruction of urban ethnic studies]. *The Annual Review of Sociology* 23:152–164.

Higuchi N (2014) Global economic crisis and the fate of Brazilian workers in Japan. *Social Science Research* 28:185–207.

Higuchi N and Inaba N (2018) Kanngeki wo nuu [University enrollment among Japan's second-generation migrants]. *Japanese Sociological Review* 68(4):567–583.

Higuchi N and Tanno K (2003) What's driving Brazil-Japan migration? the making and remaking of the Brazilian niche in Japan. *International Journal of Japanese Sociology* 12(1): 33–47.

Hirayama Y (2011) *Tokyo no hateni* [*Conditions of City*]. Tokyo: NTT Press.

Inaba Y, Ishii Y, Igarashi A, Kasahara H, Kuboota A and Fukumoyo K. (2010) Koueijyuutaku oyobi toshisaiseikikou no chinntai-jyutaku niokeru gaikokujinn kyojyu nikannsuru kennkyu [A study on the residence of foreigners in rental housing of urban renaissance agency and public housing]. *Journal of Architecture and Planning* 75(656):2397–2406.

Kajita T, Tanno K and Higuchi N (2005) *Kao no mienai teijyu-ka.* [Invisible Residents].Nagoya:Nagoya University Press.

Matsumiya A (2012) Chiiki base no kyouseironn wa gaikokujinn no syakaisannka ni todokunoka [The effectiveness of community-based coexistence theory for foreigners' participation in community activities]. *Social Theory and Dynamics* 5:43–59.

Matsumiya A (2022) *Kakawari no junnkann* [The Sociology of Community Practice]. Kyoto: Koyo- syobo.

Mori C (2006) 'Shisetsu-ka' suru kouei dannchi [Institutionalize 'Public Housing']. *Contemporary Thought* 34(14): 100–108.

Mori C (2013) Bunndan sareru kougai [Divided Segmentalized Suburban]. In: Machimura T (eds) *Toshi kukann ni hisomu haijyo to hannkou no chikara* [Exclusion in Urban Space and Power of Resist]. Tokyo: Akashi-syoten.

Nibe N, Nakamura M and Yamaguchi (eds) (2022) *Toyota City in Transition,* Singapore: Springer.

Portes A (1998) Social capital. *Annual Review of Sociology* 21(1): 1–24.

Portes A, Fernández-Kelly P and Haller W (2005) Segmented assimilation on the ground. *Ethnic and Racial Studies* 28:1000–1040.

Portes A and Rumbaut R G (2006) *Immigrant America: A Portrait.* Berkeley: University of California Press.

Roth J H (2002) *Brokered Homeland.* Ithaca: Cornell University Press.

Sharpe M O (2010) When ethnic returnees are *de facto* guestworkers. *Policy and Society* 29(4): 357–369.

Shiobara Y (2020) Genealogy of tabunka kyōsei: a critical analysis of the reformation of the multicultural co-living iscourse in Japan. *International Journal of Japanese Sociology* 29: 22–38.

Takaya S, Oomagari Y, Higuchi N, Kaji I and Inaba N (2015) 2010 nenn kokusei-cyousa nimiru gaikokujinn no kyouiku [Education of Japan's foreign residents viewed from the 1980 and 1985 Census: family background, schooling and marriage of foreign youths]. *Bulletin of Osaka Seikei University* 1:40–62.

Takenoshita H (2015) Social capital and mental health among Brazilian immigrants in Japan. *International Journal of Japanese Sociology* 24(1): 48–64.

Takenoshita H (2016) Roudoshijyou no ryuudouka to Nikkei Brazilian wo meguru hennyuu youshiki [Labor market flexibilization and the incorporation of Japanese-Brazilian immigrants in Japan]. *Journal of Law, Politics, and Sociology* 89(2): 498–520.

Takenoshita H (2018) Iminn ukeire no seido-teki bunnmyaku to ninngenn-kannkei. [The Institutional Context of and Human Relationship of Immigrant]. In Sato Y (eds) *Social capital to kakusa syakai* [Social Capital and Society]. Kyoto: Minerva-syobo.

Yamamoto K and Matsumiya A (2010) Gaikokuseki-jyuminn syujyu-toshi niokeru nihonn-jin jyuminn no ishiki. [Japanese residents' attitudes toward 'new comer' Japanese Latin Americans in three highly concentrated cities of Nikkei Brazilians]. *The Annals of Japan Association for Urban Sociology* 28: 117–134.

Young J (2007) *The Vertigo of Late Modernity.* Los Angeles: Sage.

CHAPTER 6

Changes in Asian Cities and Bottom People

The Case of Participatory Community Development in Thai Slums

Yuko Matsusono

Abstract

In this chapter, changes in the slum community, which are representative places of residence for the bottom people in Thailand, are examined in terms of labor and the dynamics of Asian cities following the 40-year changes in the four cases of participatory community development in Bangkok. Asian cities have undergone major changes since the 1990s. Inequality is widening due to the progress of informalization of a wide range of labor in the globalized labor market. The struggle for urban space is intensifying owing to global urbanization and gentrification. Participatory community development was introduced in the 1980s. Participatory community development in slums introduced a bottom-up development method as a top-down organization by aid agencies, NGOs, the administration, and governmental organizations, resulting in spontaneous development. It was implemented with the background of "community discourse" as the theory of endogenous development. The process of activities for environmental improvement and residential stability provided an opportunity for community strengthening. Looking at the subsequent stages of the projects clarifies that despite the apparent improvements in housing, the difficulties in the livelihoods of slum dwellers have deepened.

From the latter half of the twentieth century, when slum problems were discussed under urbanism in developing countries, to the present day, Asian cities have undergone major changes.[1] Amidst such changes, the slum was a typical place of residence for the bottom people. This chapter examines the change in the slum problem and the effect of the policy, using cases of participatory

---

1 Chapter 5 and this chapter discuss community organizing. Chapter 5 deals with community organization with the increase in the number of foreign bottom workers newly residing in the housing complex. Community organizing of slum dwellers is housing right seeking survival and community organizing seeking stability of residence.

community development in Bangkok slums.[2] Although Thailand continues to grow as a middle-income country, slums have not noticeably decreased. A slum is an urban space in which poverty becomes visible, and slum policies aim to solve poverty and make it invisible.

The chapter addresses three points: First, problems related to slums in Thailand will be reviewed in the context of changes in Asian cities. The slum policies of contemporary Asian cities undergoing globalization have been examined in association with neoliberal policies and the global economy. Second, the background of participatory community development will be shown along with Thailand's development policy during this period, pointing out the background of "community discourse formation" in Thai society. Third, the philosophy, methods, and background of participatory community development in slums will be discussed. Based on the above, cases of participatory community development in Thai slums since the 1980s will be studied.

1   Positioning of Slum Problems in Thailand

1.1   *Slum Problems in the Theory of Over-Urbanization*

In the latter half of the twentieth century, studies on cities in developing countries focused on over-urbanization and the informal sector. The theory of over-urbanization discusses urban poverty relating to rural poverty. Urban slums, which evolved as residential areas for poor migrants, were considered "a filthy, poor, and illegal part of delayed modernization." The shabby slums were "something to be eliminated" to develop a modern city. From this perspective, the development of such poor residential areas has become an urban policy issue.

Asian cities have experienced substantial economic development over the past four decades and are now in globalization and widening disparities, with economic and social changes dramatically altering their appearance. While some slums and illegally occupied areas (informal settlements) are being reclaimed, others are being formed and expanded. Subsequently, the informalization of labor is also increasing. This chapter focuses on slums as urban spaces with visible poverty as well as community development policies.

---

2   In this chapter, Bangkok refers to the Bangkok Metropolitan Administration (BMA).

1.2 *Socioeconomic Changes and Slum Problems in Urban Thailand*

This chapter will use Bangkok, Thailand, to examine changes in the slums surrounding the city since the 1980s.[3] As with many Asian cities, urbanization in Thailand has advanced significantly since the 1980s. The urban population has nearly tripled, and the ratio of urban population to the total population has increased from 26.8% in 1980 to 51.4% in 2018, surpassing the rural population, which has been declining since 2000 (UN 2018) and has been dominant since. The population of the Bangkok Metropolitan Administration (BMA) has increased from 4.7 million to 8.8 million (2020), while the population of the Bangkok Metropolitan Region (BMR: Bangkok and five surrounding provinces) has reached about 14 million, indicating growing urbanization in the suburbs.

Thailand's economic structure has also dramatically changed. Since the 1980s, the country has grown economically through financial liberalization and industrial investment, while shifting progressively toward a heavy chemical industry and service economy, along with industrial decentralization. GDP has grown significantly, and GDP per capita has increased approximately tenfold from $718 (1980) to $7791 (2019), reaching the status of a middle-income country. The minimum wage in Bangkok has increased by approximately six times per day, from 54 Baht ($2.64) in 1980 to 336 Baht ($10.74) in 2020. Bangkok has become a megacity; however, urban and environmental problems such as traffic and air pollution have simultaneously become more serious. The growth of the new middle class since the 1990s has been notable. Urban areas have expanded, and industrial parks and residential areas have developed in the suburbs (Askew 2002).

These changes in the population and economy have resulted in the reorganization of urban spaces, changing the urban landscape of Bangkok dramatically since the beginning of the 2000s, with shopping centers, office buildings, hotels, and condominiums built continuously along with the development of expressways, intracity transportation, and urban redevelopment. Today, there are more than 200 skyscrapers over 100 m in Bangkok. Urban redevelopment and gentrification are ongoing. Apart from the slum policy, urban development has also led to a drastic shrinkage of slums in urban centers. The price of land skyrocketed, intensifying competition for space. Meanwhile, new slums were built in suburbs with unused land.

---

3 Thailand National Statistical Office *Population and Housing Census, Labor Force Survey:* All Relevant Editions (TNSO 2020a; TNSO 2020b).

Moreover, the social characteristics of the population have changed. Compulsory education was extended from six years in 1980 to nine years in 1999 and the rate of advancement to higher education has increased since the 1990s. The university enrollment rate, including open universities, increased from approximately 10% in 1980 to approximately 50% in the 2010s. Modern factory labor requires at least a junior high school or vocational education degree, leading to educational advancement. The demographic structure has also changed dramatically. The most striking phenomenon was the rapid drop in the birthrate. The total fertility rate, which was 5.05 in the early 1970s, dropped to 2.95 in the early 1980s and further to 1.53 by the early 2010s, similar to that in developed countries. This leads to labor shortages, causing labor migration from neighboring countries.

These urbanization and demographic situations have altered the work and mobility structures of slum dwellers. Slums bloated during the over-urbanization stage due to labor migration and relocation caused by wage gaps and economic disparities between urban and rural areas (Todaro 1969), as people without sufficient industrial bases were employed in the volatile informal sector. The low wages and instability of these jobs led to poverty. The employment environment has changed drastically, including changes in industrial structures and locations due to rural and economic development, a shift to a service economy, the advancement of tourism, and economic globalization. The international labor migration pattern has also changed drastically. While Thai residents from both rural areas and urban slums migrated to areas such as the Middle East as workers in the 1980s, Thailand accepted 2.8 million foreign workers (about 10% of the labor market) from neighboring countries (Myanmar, Cambodia, and Laos) in 2019.[4]

As the new middle class grew, information and communication technology progressed rapidly. In the 1990s, cell phones and the Internet spread faster than telephones. Although the data were from 2016, household-based Internet access was 60% nationwide, which is the norm for young metropolitan adults (TNSO 2016). Social media is used daily in cities. Thailand's long-term plan, "Thailand 4.0," which began in 2015, aims to make it a high-income country through future industries, including digitalization.

---

4   This is the number of legal workers. There are also illegal temporary residents. Office of Foreign Workers Administration, Department of Employment, Ministry of Labour, Thailand (August 2019).

Although Thailand continues to grow as a middle-income country, slums have not noticeably decreased. In 1985, Pornchokuchai identified dense areas based on aerial photographs and conducted a quantitative survey. He confirmed that approximately 1 million people live across 1020 slum locations, 20% of Bangkok's population (Pornchokuchai 1985). A subsequent survey found that in 1987, 41% of slum household heads and 65% of residents were born in Bangkok (Pornchokuchai 1992). By the end of the 1980s, slums transitioned from temporary housing for migrants to a period of reproduction for the poor.

In 2016, there were 2,067 slum districts with 2.06 million people, according to statistics from the Bangkok Metropolitan Administration. These slums have been classified as slums by the community committee (described later) and can be said to be the slum population certified by the government. (BMA 2017). Since 2000, both foreigners and residents have occupied new slums. During this period, employment and labor opportunities increased within commuting distance in peri-urban rural areas. Amidst global economic change, the work of bottom people, including slum dwellers, has seen widespread informalization (Matsusono 2006).

Changes in industrial distribution throughout Thailand have decreased the relative dominance of slum dwellers in the urban lower labor market. The informalization of labor extends to all fields. While the working spaces of street vendors are decentralized, new occupations such as delivery and motorcycle taxis are created. Side jobs that can be performed at home have spread to rural areas, whereas manufacturing has spread to suburban industrial parks. For example, waste collection, a typical informal sector occupation in the 1980s, has been transforming into a recycling business, and there has been subcontracting for the same in suburban villages. The survival strategies of slum dwellers remain the same: multiple jobs and rapid changes, but with the added effects of a competitive labor market with foreign labor.

Slum dwellers constitute a large proportion of the urban poor population. As a result of Thailand's overall economic growth, this gap has widened. The changing relationship with rural villages has increased the need for slum dwellers to settle and survive in cities. Economic hardship increased because of the increasing informality of labor. Owing to urbanization and the expansion of metropolitan areas, the location conditions of slums are changing. They are forced to form new slums on land with bad conditions and are forced to leave their residential land close to the jobs of slum dwellers. Bangkok's slums are located on leased public or private land and suffer from tenure instability as urban development progresses.

2   Changes in the Slum Policy and Community Development

2.1   *Changes in the Slum Policy*

Until the early 1970s, the slum policy focused on the removal of slums while constructing housing for low-income families; however, it could not keep up with the increase in slums. Participatory community development began in the late 1970s with NGOs and activists. In 1979, the Asian Institute of Technology (AIT) launched the Building Together Project (BTP), a pilot project for participatory housing construction. After the 1980s, the National Housing Authority (NHA) and the World Bank launched the Slum Improvement Program (SIP) to improve the environment of slum areas. The NHA's responsibility was to develop infrastructure, and the BMA's was to manage the project through regional organizations by establishing residents' committees. These committees were replaced by the institutionalization of community committees by the BMA's Community Development Department in 1986.

Subsequently, the Urban Community Development Office (UCDO), established in 1992, launched a full-scale participatory community development program. The Community Organization Development Institute (CODI), established in 2000 to take it over from the UCDO, launched the Baan Mankong Project (BMP) in 2003 as an urban living environment improvement project using participatory community development methods. Community development has been a priority of social development since the 8th National Development Plan (1997–2001). The background of participatory community development as the core of slum policy lies in the development approach described in the next section.

2.2   *The Background of Slum Policy Implementation: Political and*
Economic Changes, and Development Policies in Thailand

Until the early 1980s, economic development was the theme of Thailand's development plans. The first development plan (1961–1966) and the fifth development plan (1982–1986) set goals for infrastructure, rural, and economic development while reducing gaps. Regional development, including Eastern Seaboard development, was proposed for decentralizing the industry. Although the goal was to solve the problem of over-urbanization and poverty, it also resulted in the expansion of the Bangkok metropolitan area.

Thailand's economic growth accelerated during the late 1980s. Financial liberalization attracted industrial investment, and a bubble economy was created through the shift to the heavy chemical industry and service economy, and the decentralization of industrial estates to regional areas. This bubble burst during the Asian currency crisis of 1997. The seventh socio-economic development plan set sustainable development goals, and the eighth and subsequent plans put more emphasis on social and human development instead of economic growth, setting the goals of "sustainable development" and "balance between economy, people, and environment."

The Asian currency crisis in 1997 reversed the economic boom that began in the early 1980s, leading to an economic crisis with negative growth. What was proposed at that time was the "sufficient economy," which originated from King Bhumibol's statement at the time. He stated that Thailand did not need to develop into a big tiger in terms of GDP; rather, it should seek social stability and people's well-being. It can be said that this is an alternative theory of the development and genealogy of Buddhist philosophy. The "sufficient economy" was included in the 1997 Constitution and has since become a pillar of development plans. The philosophies of the Sufficient Economy include moderation, reasonableness, and self-immunity. While responding to the impact of globalization on material life, culture, society, and the environment, we aim to create harmony, security, and sustainability based on knowledge and ethics. Here, the community (*chumchon* in Thai) rooted in Thai history and culture is emphasized. This has been linked to social development practices in rural areas and slums. It is at the core of many practices and discourse generation of Buddhist monks, intellectuals, and NGO activities, all of which have continued since the 1980s.

By including this idea in the development plan, Thailand's development policy seems to have shifted toward the balanced central human development and emphasized the community. However, in Thailand in the 2000s, there were two development approaches: the progress of economic development in line with the neo-liberal economy by the government and the national development plan that emphasized community-oriented and social development under a sufficient economy. In terms of urban development, green cities and environmental considerations coexist with large-scale urban development.

The Thaksin administration started in 2001 and proposed the Kingdom of Thailand Modernization Framework (KTMF). He attempted to transform Thailand into a strong state in an era of world capitalism and globalization. Thailand 4.0, a policy aimed at making Thailand a high-income country and promoted by the Prayuth administration, is a continuation of Thaksin's policy. He focused on the reduction of gaps and decentralization, including the improvement of community resilience, bottom-up advocacy, and the introduction of universal insurance. Informatization also progressed, including the establishment of a healthcare system and resident registration system. These social policies are not only election-conscious populist policies but also a strategy for community utilization as a more efficient measure against the poor from a neoliberal point of view.

2.3   *Participatory Community Development in Thailand*

The philosophy of participatory community development is "empowering slum dwellers to become the main actors in development." It provides a foundation on which residents can build their abilities and provide funding, organizations (networks), human development, and skill training. NGOs and the government work collaboratively as advisors. Sometimes, the project is carried out with the participation of residents based on the formation of savings associations.

The theoretical basis for this approach is Chambers' idea of self-reliant development (Chambers, 1997). In the field of international development theory, aid agencies such as the United Nations introduced this to rural development in the 1960s. It was also implemented as a part of rural development in Thailand, with the establishment of the Community Development Department by the Ministry of Interior in the 1970s. Pioneering community-based activities, as seen in the Sarvodaya Shramadana Movement in Sri Lanka, were also there. Additionally, Alinsky's community organizing method was shared through NGO networks in the Asian region (Murphy 1990; Shanahan 2014).

Although this approach produced some results in rural development, it was only introduced to slums in large cities until the 1980s. There was a rapid turnover of residents in the slums of large cities; unlike in rural areas, the foundation of communality was weak, and community organization was vague. Participatory community development based on the idea of self-reliant development requires community organization, the study of development, voluntary participation of people, and project continuity. To implement participatory community development, the challenges were the creation of "regionality as space" and "opportunities for communality" in slums as urban communities during the development process. This project requires implementation by combining two issues: improvement of the living environment of the urban poor and community building. The UCDO was established based on several preceding cases, as shown in the case study in Section 4, and CODI was established to replace it. The SIP was established with the support of the World Bank, and CODI was established as a public organization with a national budget. In this process, a collaboration between the UN-Habitat and an Asian network (the Asian Coalition for Housing Rights) was also undertaken. In other words, the development approach and methodology were a bottom-up method introduced overseas under government leadership.

3   "Community" (Chumchon) Discourse and Policy Making

As mentioned in the previous section, a "bottom-up approach" was introduced and advocated in participatory community development in Thailand as an "external and top-down" development policy. On the other hand, "community discourse" prevailed during this period, giving meaning to "participatory community" in urban slums, where the foundations and systems of urban slum communities were unclear. While the "external" organizing method is regarded as a civil society bottom-up approach, the meaning of endogenous development is provided in "community discourse."

This "community discourse" has both theoretical and practical backgrounds. Theoretically, it is "community culture," a historical sociological approach to Thailand by Chatip Natspha. In this theory, the community does not imply an urban but a rural community (*mu baan*) in Thailand, and he posits it as the socio-cultural foundation of the "community culture theory," which is unique to Thailand and based on the economic history grounded in Thai rural society (Natspha 1984). Prawase Wasi, a medical doctor and social activist suggested the "power of community" for practical social development through his experience in community health projects (Wasi 2003) (Wasi 2009). In Thailand, many NGOs have been conducting various activities in rural areas and slums since the late 1970s,[5] thus providing a background.

Shigetomi points out two backgrounds that spread the idea of community through these activities and theoretical discussions, resulting in its incorporation into national development plans (Shigetomi 2009: 45–46). The first was the development of the theory of "community as a culture in Thailand." In other words, ideas such as community culture and community power were broadly interpreted as "Thai culture theory" through the activities of NGOs in the 1980s, strengthening the theory of endogenous development. Second, people involved in social movements resisting the state and the state elite, as well as improved social movements, formed a network in terms of "emphasis on community values," creating "community discourse," which was eventually embodied in constitutions and national development plans as community development (Shigetomi 2006). This discourse was linked to the "sufficient economy," and was reflected in the national development plan and projects.

---

5   The introduction of participatory community development methodologies in slums in Thailand was a late start in Asia. However, since the 1970s, NGOs such as the Prateep Foundation and the Human Settlements Foundation (HSF) have been working on the issue of urban poverty in various ways.

Community discourse restrains both the private and public sectors in a developing society and emphasizes voluntary solidarity, cooperative relationships, and the strengthening of communities. In the context of slum problems and development, "participatory community development" aims to reduce poverty and improve living conditions based on the spontaneity of residents, the discovery of their problems, and empowerment through networks. Community discourse is not theory-focused; the term has been spoken of based on a variety of practices, which became discourse and was incorporated into policies while people began to identify with Natspha's "community culture theory." As a result, participatory community development in slums, initiated earnestly after the 1990s, was carried out for the empowerment and self-help of the poor. This includes the BMA's legislation of community committees and CODI's development projects, such as the BMP and other NGO projects.

4   A Case Study in Bangkok

The author encountered the just-launched BTP and NHA slum improvement programs during investigations conducted in Bangkok in 1980. The AIT staff enthusiastically emphasized the importance of their participation. In slums where the SIP was introduced in the 1980s, the pathways in the areas improved, and in the 1990s, various projects gained momentum. I felt that residents' participation would contribute to solving slum problems. In some slums, leaders worked actively in collaboration with temples and the government's community health services. Many community committee leaders were female. At the meetings held at the ward offices, opinions were eagerly exchanged.

As the economy developed, resident registration, social security, and universal insurance systems were introduced in the 2000s. With the full-scale implementation of the BMP by CODI in the 2000s, "participatory community development" activities seemed to spread widely. The BMP incorporated microfinance into the organizing process. As discussed in this study, participatory community development is now being implemented in projects for informal settlements under the bridge as well as for the homeless, highlighting the benefits of the method.

I continue to follow the cases of slums since the 1980s (Table 6.1). While the organization and improvement of the living environment have been successful, some issues needed to be addressed. In particular, improving employment, the mobility of residents, and the increase in the informality of residential areas owing to urban development are greatly affected by the dynamics of the entire city's surrounding slums.

TABLE 6.1   Overview of case studies

	BTP (Building together project)	SIP (Slum improvement program)/ community committee	BMP (Baan Mankong project)	UBCP (Under bridge community project)
Commencement year	1979	1978 /1986	2003	2002
Implemented by	Asian Institute of Technology (AIT)	National Housing Authority (NHA)/Bangkok Metropolitan Administration(BMA)	Community Organization Development Institute (CODI)	Human Settlement Foundation (HSF)
Description	Self-help resettlement pilot projects	Enviroment improvement/ Formation of the residents' organizations by the BMA	Saving groups and a housing improvement project	Resettlement project for squatter residents
Organizer	Experts at AIT were permanently stationed at community offices	NHA Staff/ Liaison meetings at ward offices. Community workers visiting on site	CODI workers Workshop centered	Staff at HSF Networks among the squatters
Incentive for the residents	Tenure security Housing construction	Improvement of the community / Obtaining budgets	Improvement of housing Acquiring housing stability	Tenure security Housing construction
The number of projects in BKK	1 site	662 slums(BMA) (2017)	194 communities (2018)	3 sites

SOURCE: CREATED BY THE AUTHOR

Case 1: Participatory Housing Construction Project (BTP: Building Together Project)

Professor Angel of the AIT was the theoretical leader of this project (Angel 1983). Two hundred housing units in the form of terraced row houses, with 15–20 units each, were constructed on approximately 1.7 hectares of land in the suburbs of Bangkok (Angel and Phoativongsacharn 1981). The project was characterized by construction, wherein a group of residents worked together to build 15–20 units. Residents were recruited to create groups on the condition that they could commute to the project site, despite being informal settlements and slum dwellers in need of housing. The basic structure of the block-built housing units was constructed jointly by the residents' group who would be living there, while the layout and interior design of each unit were done by the respective residents. The units were allocated after completion. The group worked on the construction with advice from AIT experts. The work was conducted mainly on weekends and at night and was designed to build a network of residents through this process.[6]

This project was planned as a pilot project for participatory housing construction, and AIT staff set up an on-site office for support. Before the joint construction of the units, construction materials such as blocks and bricks were manufactured by residents. The network creation activities included recreational activities, joint wall paintings, and discussions on vacant land utilization. Those involved in the development policy exemplify this as a rare success of community building with resident participation. Each completed house has its unique finish, and commercial activities begin within the district. Through the project, it was found that community and living conditions improved. Architectural experts and organizers, such as the AIT staff, took time and effort to encourage resident participation.

More than 30 years later, this community, which bore the name of the project, is still alive. There has been a considerable turnover of residents, and the overall standard of living has improved. The residents' organization formed during construction later became a community committee institutionalized by the BMA. The on-site office of the AIT was transformed into a meeting place for the community, and a children's playground planned by the residents was built on vacant land. New community activities, such as nursery schools and small businesses, are also underway.

---

6   I visited the AIT and the project site in 1980, just after the project started. I then revisited the site in 2001 and 2014.

However, the surrounding area has changed significantly. When the project began, although they were within the urban area, the areas around the site were mostly unused and difficult to access. Today, these have become new middle-class residential areas with nearby subway lines, restaurants, and Starbucks. However, the existence of poor communities is delicate.

Case 2: Slum Improvement Program (SIP) and Community Committees

The Slum Improvement Program initiated by the NHA in 1977, with the support of the World Bank, was undertaken in conjunction with the organization of residents' committees by the BMA (Sheng 1992). Residents' committees were later institutionalized as community committees by the BMA in 1986. In slums, in collaboration with public institutions and NGOs, these committees served as the foundation for the implementation of activities to improve the living environment, income, community health, education, and welfare of the residents.

In slum T, where the SIP was implemented in 1978, a community committee was formed by the BMA in the late 1980s. Its female leader collaborated with the CODI, ward development workers, and monks of the adjacent temple for project implementation. In addition to running a nursery school and health center, she focused on a project to increase earning opportunities. Small-scale businesses, such as manufacturing products using medicinal herbs grown in slums and massage delivery services, were planned. Using temple facilities, lifelong learning activities were also conducted with the cooperation of the monks.[7]

For slum dwellers, the difference between a residents' committee of the SIP and a community committee under the Bangkok Metropolitan Administration Ordinance is the sense of ownership of development. The residents' committee of the SIP was supposed to maintain an improved living environment, including cleaning drains and managing health centers. After the organization of the community committee, the residents identified their needs, drafted projects on their own, and drafted a budget to implement them. Development workers facilitated activities during the organization, but the residents and their leaders carried out the activities in an embodiment of the practical theory of community organization.

For slum dwellers, participation in community committees and other activities helped clarify area boundaries and membership as a rural community.

---

7   T is a slum where the Slum Improvement Program had been implemented since 1978. The author conducted a quantitative survey in 1981 and has visited the slum every few years since then to conduct further interviews.

Simultaneously, a signboard with the name of the community was put up at the entrance, and the term "community" (chumchon in Thai) became an everyday word. The residents participated in the construction of pathways and children's parks in the slums and undertook projects to improve the living environment while receiving advice from NGOs and governmental developers. With the opening of daycare centers, some people have even obtained commuting jobs. The sense of community has increased through the operation of health centers and entrepreneurial projects. The leader commended the administration. Slum organizations became organizations that collaborated with the government rather than against authority.

However, around 2000, the slum area reduced by half, while the population density increased. The land where the slums are located straddles the land of temples and private land; this is because private land has been replaced by public and commercial land. (cf. photo) Shopping centers and high-rise condominiums were towering in surrounding areas. Another nearby informal settlement was turned into a shopping-center site. There was also a turnover among residents. Community health services and health volunteering were also implemented; since the 1990s, the same lady has served as the slum's leader. The people participating enthusiastically and who are at the center of the activities end up staying in the slum, whereas those who do not end up leaving. Consequently, the livelihood of the remnants did not improve sufficiently. This has also been observed in other districts (Endo 2011). The adjacent temple has become magnificent, but housing-unit improvement has been very slow (Photos 6.1, 6.2 and 6.3). Employment instability continues, and activities have stagnated in recent years.

Case 3: Baan Mankong Project (BMP)
Baan Mankong ("secure house" in Thai) is a microfinance-based living environment improvement project run by the CODI, aimed at organizing residents and networking based on savings groups. The residents initiate project planning and, through the community network, manage projects to improve their living environment, with the goal of self-reliant living.

The slum dwellers first formed a savings group of several dozen households, and the project progression revolved around this group. Subsequently, through savings association activities such as loan repayment, residents' participation in planning, and cooperation with other institutions, a resident network was established. Residents learned about the projects and participation, and CODI workers and building experts were involved in determining the master plan. Through a series of participatory processes starting from the planning stage,

PHOTO 6.1   Bangkok slum in 1980

PHOTO 6.2   Bangkok slum in 1999

PHOTO 6.3   Bangkok slum in 2016

social relations, mutual aid, norms, and the distribution of responsibility were carried out within the community to empower residents. The community organization method was well integrated into the process.[8]

During the implementation phase of housing and infrastructure development, residents also participated in construction work. Even after the houses were built, network activities continued simultaneously with the mortgage repayments. Although the entire process involved the government, CODI workers, and volunteers, they were advisors, with resident groups being the main actors. Kawasumi conducted a participatory observation of the BMP and assessed that, through a series of activities, the residents felt that they were leading the planning process while gaining the ability to solve problems in their daily lives within the community. He pointed out that projects such as the BMP may lead to endogenous development (Kawasumi and Fujii 2007).

---

8   The status of the CODI's project implementation is based on the information on its website, and Boonyabancha was interviewed in 2002 on their philosophy.

In the BMP, savings-group activities played an important role in participatory development, where the organization was gradually reinforced, and people worked collaboratively by building community networks. For residents, the creation of a savings group was a condition for receiving unsecured loans, which in turn led to the acquisition of a stable place to live in a better environment. The objective of this project was not only to improve the living environment and build houses but also to strengthen the community, aiming at social and human development, such as mutual support and collaboration. Furthermore, issues such as land use and ownership are considered important by the BMP. This is different from the BTP, where the construction work process was used for organization, from the SIP, which aimed to achieve organization in the maintenance process after improvement, and from community committees, which coming up with project ideas was considered the process of organization (Boonybancha 2005) (Archer 2010).

Somsook Boonyabancha, the head (now advisor) of the CODI, was a member of the research group led by Professor Angel on housing problems of the poor and the AIT in the 1980s. Professor Angel was the theoretical advisor of the BTP discussed in Case 1, and his experience with participatory housing construction projects was carried over to the BMP. In the CODI project, savings groups were used as the foundation for network formation to address land issues and create organizational opportunities. Boonyabancha stated that networks were the power of the poor. She has since been active in networking activities in Asia (Boonyabancha 2009) (ACCA 2014).

The BMP began as a series of 10 pilot projects in 2003, and by 2011, it had rolled out over 90,000 households in 1546 communities across the country. As of 2018, it was implemented in 194 areas in Bangkok (CODI 2019a). The results reported until 2011 were as follows: 43.6% long-term land lease agreements, 34.8% acquisition of ownership, including land sharing, 8.2% short-term land lease agreements, and 13.4% permission for land use, such as public land. However, its pace has slowed since 2013 (Bhatkal and Lucci 2015). The BMP, a participatory development project, is a time-consuming process. Of those that were started, 45% were completed, 35% were in progress, and 20% were canceled as of 2018 (Boonyabancha and Keer 2018). However, it has been reported that over 500 slums in the country are at a risk of clearance. With the BMP, while slum dwellers—who had been facing problems such as slum clearance and instability of land lease agreements—aimed for stability and better living conditions regarding land use and land contracts, it can be said that its limitations have also been revealed. The BMP method does not address poor bottom people, such as informal settlers and homeless people. Case 4 addresses this issue.

Bangkok has seen rapid urban development and expansion of its urban area since the beginning of the 2000s. The slums spread to the suburbs and were pushed out by highways, office developments, commercial facilities, and residential developments. Land has become a competitive resource.

Case 4: Under-Bridge Community Project (UBCP)

This was a resettlement project by an NGO for informal settlers living under bridges. There are many rivers and canals in the BMA area, and informal settlers are the city's poorest. A 1994 survey by the Human Settlement Foundation (HSF) identified 2163 people in 620 families in 65 locations. Unlike slums, informal settlements are unorganized, with several families living in a scattered manner. The HSF organized these residents and eventually built new communities at the three resettlement sites.[9]

In response to the forced removal planned by the BMA in 1996 and 1997, informal settlers created under-bridge development groups (UBDGs) with the support of the HSF and others to form a network and negotiate with the NHA. Residents were divided into three districts to obtain new relocation sites closer to their original settlements. At this time, the condition of the negotiations was that the land was located within a distance from which residents could continue their current occupation. Community committees were formed in some areas, and the UCDO (later, CODI) also formed savings groups. The NGO staff said that residents learned that they were able to negotiate and acquire land only because they were able to network and organize.

Relocation to resettlement sites began in 2001. Support for organizing new communities continued, including the formation of decision-making mechanisms and savings groups. A 2004 study examining residents' levels of satisfaction reported that, after relocation, 65.5% said that they were satisfied overall, and residents' networks were also active (Khankhang 2004). After visiting in 2007, Shimokawa reported that even in resettlement sites, the recycling and small-scale manufacturing businesses that existed before relocation were able to continue, and there were discussions within the communities about these businesses (Shimokawa 2007).

---

9   The author visited the HSF in 2001 during the course of this project, interviewing them about the networking and negotiation process leading up to the acquisition of the resettlement sites, and visited some under-bridge residents. The HSF workers gave the leader of the informal settlement a prepaid cell phone for the organization. Informal settlers began to form a network by informing each other of the risk of forced removal (Matsusono 2002).

This is similar to community development in slums, where residents identify their own needs, plan and implement projects, and receive support. The UBCP is unique for connecting people not covered by the BMA's community committees, such as informal settlements, and organizing them into a network to obtain a living place.

4.1   Significance of Organization and Institutionalization

The UBCP was a pilot project conducted by an NGO for informal settlements. CODI incorporated this approach (CODI 2019b). Welfare funds and projects dealing with canal residents and homeless people were also initiated. Additionally, CODI is implementing the Strong Communities 20-year Project 2000–2020, which includes rural areas, in line with the Social Development Plan. Participatory community development originally intended to be "resident-led," seems to be gradually evolving into a form fostering local leaders who can collaborate with the government. For urban and poor slums, embracing participatory community development means accepting organization and institutionalization. Applying to serve on a BMA community committee will make members and the scope of the area visible, and they will share the goal of improving the living environment through savings groups. Organizations can also obtain budgets from an urban policy perspective. These efforts are improvements to the living environment, and the government, which is responsible for community development, emphasizes community discourse. Outsiders, such as NGOs and workers who are working on-site, emphasize "organization" and the role of "expert facilitators." The most important aspect of these projects is the "process" and resident empowerment during the process (Matsusono 1998). However, for the poor, such as slum dwellers, the time cost of participation is compensated by the collective outcome of stable land use and improved living conditions for the entire community. While the issues of slum environment and illegality can be addressed, employment, an individual livelihood matter, has not been addressed as a key issue by either community committees or the BMP.

It can be said that the BTP was considered an example, and has the characteristics of a housing project; SIP is environmental improvement and community organizing; BMP is participatory community development; and UBP is participatory community development, including the right to residency movement. However, considering Thailand's development approach during this period and Bangkok's urbanization process, the content of "participatory" may be seen as "collaboration with the government."

5   Conclusion

As seen in these cases, participatory community development in slums, which is said to have been successful to some extent, introduced a bottom-up development method as a top-down organization by aid agencies, NGOs, the administration, and governmental organizations, resulting in spontaneous development. It was implemented with the background of "community discourse" as the theory of endogenous development. It cannot be said to be based on a movement against power or the concept of rights in civil society. Methodologically, "organization," "participation in the process," and "independence" are emphasized. As a result, institutionalization led to its incorporation into policies. Some goals were achieved in terms of fostering collaborative leaders and strengthening communities in the improved areas. Organizers such as the government and NGOs emphasize self-reliant participation, but from the residents' perspective, they collaborate with the government (Castanas et.al. 2016). However, participation in projects will provide stability, for the time being, improving the environment to some extent.

Securing a dwelling from which they cannot be driven away is crucial to the urban lives of the poor. In urban development, slum dwellers strategically choose to participate in community development to obtain more stable places of residence. Selling houses and the right to housing, which they have gained, are also options for the future. This has led to the replacement of residents. In recent years, mutual aid and communities have been reported to be useful in addressing issues common to the local people, such as responses to floods and COVID-19.

Slum clearance was a policy to address "what we want to eliminate" and "the marginalized people in urban areas." In some cases, fences were built to hide them. Participatory community development has similar governmental goals in terms of environmental improvement. Effective improvement was possible by encouraging residents' participation in self-help activities through endogenous development to strengthen the community.

In rural areas, which have been the source of over-urbanization over the past 40 years, families and communities have supported people's livelihoods through economic and social changes. Changes in intergenerational employment and adaptation through education are strategies for family kinship networks (Kitahara 1996). Rural areas are supported by the urban economy, but they also serve as safety nets and places to return to. Slums have proven to be an extension when urban slums are directly connected to rural areas. However, in Bangkok, the slum population is increasing because of the production of the poor, and the bottom people are exposed to global economic competition and gentrification as well as the informalization of labor. This cannot be addressed by using community resilience strategies alone. Looking at the subsequent stages of the projects clarifies that despite the apparent improvements in housing, the difficulties in the livelihoods of slum dwellers have deepened. When established residents leave slums, more unstable people flow in, as employment remains unstable, intensifying competition for urban spaces. Livelihood problems and exclusion from the settlements were unresolved and worsened. However, a slum is a typical place of residence for people at the bottom.

Difficulties in competing for urban spaces are increasing because of the changes in the local environment and land use caused by the expansion and development of urban areas. Since the period of economic development in the late 1980s, land use has shown that slums decreased in urban centers and increased in the suburbs. The slums and project sites of Cases 1 and 2 were on the urban periphery at the time, and these have become new middle-class residential areas with good transportation networks and shopping centers today. Urban development in the BMA has expanded beyond these areas and will continue to expand further. With the construction of highways, railroads, and subways, urban areas are expanding rapidly, and the expansion of residential areas for the new middle class is further marginalizing the living spaces of the poor. The stabilization of land leasing promoted by the BMP has reached its limits, and the number of slums and informal settlements facing removal is increasing. Under these circumstances, will "participatory community development," which includes the homeless and informal settlers, continue as projects to improve living environments for low-income people? The gentrification of cities, which will continue to progress, is expected to further marginalize bottom people, including slum dwellers.

In this study, we provide valuable suggestions by continuously observing cases since the 1980s, taking this background into account. The slum was a typical place of residence for the bottom people with visible poverty. Community development provides the minimum foundation for life for the bottom people. Housing is a fundamental right. Poverty has become invisible, but the problem of poverty has not been solved. Participatory community development in Thailand, a middle-income country, is also related to participatory methods and neoliberal policies. Community utilization, a participatory method, is positioned as an efficient measure against the poor.[10] Quantitative verification and further follow-up are required to generalize the results.

---

10   Participatory methods started in rural areas in developing countries, but are being applied to community welfare for the elderly in developed countries under neoliberalism.

References

ACCA (Asian Coalition Community Action) (2014) *215 Cities in Asia*. Fifth Yearly Report of Asian Coalition for Community Action Program. Available at: http://www.achr .net/upload/files/1%20ACCA%20How%20it%20works%201-4.pdf (accessed 30 August 2021).

Angel S and Phoativongsacharn Z C (1981) *Building Together*. Bangkok: The Human Settlement Division, Asian Institute of Technology.

Angel S (ed.) (1983) *Land for Housing the Poor*. Singapore: Select Books.

Archer D (2010) *Empowering the Urban Poor Through Community-Based Slum Upgrading: A Case of Bangkok*. Thailand ISOCARRP 2010 Congress Report.

Askew M (2002) *Bangkok: Place, Practice and Representation*. New York: Routledge.

BMA (Bangkok Metropolitan Administration) (2017) *Statistical Profile of Bangkok Metropolitan Administration 2016*. Available at http://apps.bangkok.go.th/info_gi dsedbkk/m.info/bkkstat/stat_2559_eng.pdf (accessed 5 May 2023)

Bhatkal T and Lucci P (2015) *Community-Driven Development in the Slums: Thailand's Experience Urban Poverty*. Case Study Report Development progress.org, Overseas Development Institute. Available at: https://www.odi.org/sites/odi.org.uk/files/odi -assets/publications-opinion-files/9668.pdf (accessd 30 August 2021).

Boonyabancha S (2005) Baan mankong: going to scale with "slum" and squatter upgrading in Thailand. *Environment and Urbanization* 17(1): 21–46.

Boonyabancha S (2009) *Community Development Fund in Thailand: a Tool for Poverty Reduction and Affordable Housing*. Nairobi: UN-HABITAT.

Boonyabancha S and Kerr T (2018) Lessons from CODI on co-production. *Environment and Urbanization* 30(2): 444–460.

Castanas N, Yamtree P K, Sonthichai B Y and Batréau Q (2016) Leave no one behind: community-driven urban development in Thailand (Working Paper Dec 2016), International Institute for Environment and Development.

Chambers R (1997) *Whose Reality Counts? Putting the First Last*. London: Intermediate Technology Publications.

CODI (Community Organization Development Institute) (2019a) Baan Mankong Collective Housing. Available at: http://www.codi.or.th (accessed 9 May 2021).

CODI (Community Organization Development Institute) (2019b) News from Thailand's busy Homeless People's Network. Available at: https;//encodi.or.th/wp -content/uploads/2020/01/Homeless-network=Update=May-2019.pdf (accessed 24 September 2021).

Endo T (2011) *Toshi o ikiru hitobito* [Living with the Risks: Risk Response of Urban Low-income Class in Bangkok].Kyoto: Kyoto University Press.

Kawasumi A and Fujii T (2007) Shokibo-juminsosiki wo toshita community kaihatu ni kansuru Kenkyu [Study on community development by neighborhood groups on urban poor in Thailand]. *City Planning Review Special Issue* 42(1): 106–111.

Khankhang S (2004) *Satisfaction of Dwellers toward the Under-bridge Community Housing Project.* MA Thesis (unpublished), Mahidol University, Thailand.

Kitahara A (1996) *The Thai Rural Community Reconsidered: Historical Community Formation and Contemporary Development Movement.* The Political Economy Centre, Faculty of Economics: Chulalongkorn University.

Matsusono H Y (1998) Bannkok no juminsoshiki [The urban resident organizations in Bangkok—from project-cooperative style to self-help development style]. In: Hataya, N (ed.) *The Urban Resident Organizations in Developing Countries.* Chiba: Institute of Developing Economies: 77–96.

Matsusono H Y (2002) Bangkok no jukankyou-kaizen seisaku [The housing environment improvement policy in Bangkok—the attempt of the resident resettlement project], *Ajiken World Trend,* Institute of Developing Economies, 76: 16–20.

Matsusono H Y (2006) Informal sector kenkyu no keihu [Some aspect of informal sector studies: from the theory of over-urbanization to labor informalization under the globalization], *Bulletin of the College of Human and Social Welfare Studies, Shukutoku University* 40: 101–115.

Murphy D (1990) *A Decent Place to Live: Urban Poor in Asia.* Bangkok: Asian Coalition for Housing Rights.

Nartsupha C (1984) *Thai Village Economy in the Past.* Chiang Mai: Silkworm Books.

Pornchokuchai S (1985) *1020,* Bangkok: Japanese Volunteer Center.

Pornchokuchai S (1992) *Bangkok Slums Review and Recommendations.* Bangkok: Agency for Real Estate Affairs.

Shanahan C (2014) *A Theology of Community Organization Power of the People.* London: Routledge.

Sheng Y K (ed.) (1992) *Low Income Housing in Bangkok: A Review of Some Housing Sub-Market.* Division of Human Settlement Development: Asian Institute of Technology.

Shigetomi S (2006) Bringing Non-Governmental Actors into the Policy making Process: The Case of Local Development Policy in Thailand, IDE Discussion Paper 69, Institute of Developing Economies, *Japan External Trade Organization (IDE JETRO).* Available at: http://hdl.handle.net/2344/149 (accessed 30 August 2021).

Shigetomi S (2009) Thai ni okeru community-shugi no tenkai to fukyu [Communitarianism in Thailand: Its development and institutionalization up to 1997 constitution]. *AJIA Keizai* 50(12): 21–54.

Shimokawa M (2007) Activity report of award winners of International Year of Shelter for the Homeless Commemoration in Thailand. *Housing* 1–32. Available at: http://pweb.sophia.ac.jp/shimokawa/poverty/text/somsook&HSF.pdf (accessed 3 May 2021).

TNSO (Thailand National Statistical Office) (2020a) *Population and Housing Census.*

TNSO (Thailand National Statistical Office) (2020b) *Labor Force Survey.*

TNSO (Thailand National Statistical Office) (2016) *The Information and Communication Technology Survey.*

Todaro M P (1969) A model of labour migration and urban unemployment in less developed countries. *The American Economic Review* 59(1): 138–148.

United Nations (2018) *World Urbanization Prospects 2018.* Available at: https://populat ion.un.org/wup/Country-Profiles/ (accessed 3 May 2021).

Wasi P (2003) Overview of political reform issues. In: McCargo D (ed.) *Reforming Thai Politics.* Singapore: ISEAS Publishing. pp.21–27.

Wasi P (2009) His majesty the king and the new development code, *Manusya Journal of Humanities* 12(1): 40–52. Available at http://www.arts.chula.ac.th/~manusya/jour nal/index.php/manusya/article/view/147 (accessed 30 July 2021).

CHAPTER 7

Microcredit Enhances Informalization

The Outcome of Governmentality in Chittagong Fisher Society

Shinji Sakamoto

Abstract

Microcredit is honored as one of the most successful poverty-alleviation programs in economic development among developing countries. Contrarily, this chapter remarks that the program enhances the poverty level of the bottom people. The nature of governmentality in microcredit gives such an ironic outcome. In Bangladeshi coastal areas inside/neighboring Chittagong city, Hindu low-caste fisher people access a local NGO's microcredit program. Not a small number of credit defaulters are seen among the borrower groups. The basis of the default, some cases suggest, is the rule system (interest rate, loan schedule, and repayment responsibility rules) the program has. The borrowers think the rules are unfair to them. The anger toward the system explodes kicking debt demonstrations. As for the reason for such anti-credit wrath, the discussion leads to a view that it is a moral discontent delivered from the fishers' subsistence ethic. And then, about the trigger of the borrowers' moral fury, we focus on the development workers' facilitation practices, which is another face of governmentality in microcredit. Arguing such ironical consequences, this chapter attempts to clarify the issue of the nature of microcredit, namely the practical limitation of the development scheme driven by neoliberalism.

This chapter discusses the physiognomy of governmentality in microcredit. It is well-recounted that microcredit serves to poverty alleviation in developing countries. Contrarily we see here the adverse matters that microcredit program destructively enhances the poverty level of the poor. It means that microcredit does not rescue the destitute from misery but locks them into it. Microcredit is further informalizing the bottom workers.

Microcredit is a kind of development program driven by resident groups. There are millions of borrower groups all over developing countries. Since Grameen Bank was awarded the Nobel Peace Prize in 2006, there have been heightening levels of public interest in the program. At the same time, however, it is shown that default on microcredit has become conspicuous. Many credit defaulters are seen in various areas. Suicide cases of defaulters are reported again and again.

Microcredit is honorably trumpeted as one of the most successful development programs focusing on the poorest of the poor. Exactly, it is a kind of financial service for those who lack any property. The program is dispatched toward the almost penniless people: the bottom. A misfortune, then the program leads, is multiple borrowing. In India, the multiple borrowing from some microcredit institutes causes the default issue consequently. In Bangladesh, this chapter remarks minutely, the two-way borrowing from microcredit institutes as well as local moneylenders happens. Penury people are suffering from pennilessness more severely than before they encountered the microcredit program. This is the informalization microcredit wreaks.

The basis of the default problem is, this chapter suggests, the rigorousness of the microcredit program system. Credit borrowers state the system is unfair to them. The anger toward the credit system explodes and kicking debt demonstrations emerge in various areas. This chapter clarifies the moment when the rage against microcredit breaks out among poor people. The moment consists of three parts.

One is the nature of governmentality (Foucault 2007) in the microcredit program. The program assumes the techno-engineering aspect inside the program's operating system (interest rate, loan schedule, and repayment responsibility rules). The second part is the effect of the subsistence ethic (Scott 1985). Anti-credit wrath of the borrowers originally comes from moral discontent.

As for the second part, then, we focus on the development workers' facilitation practices —it is another face of governmentality in microcredit—as the trigger of the borrowers' moral fury. Workers' communicative approach toward the borrowers makes them believe that the workers should be their patronages (like local bosses). Care work for embedding the manner of self-reliance in the heart and body of the borrowers ironically breeds them heteronomous sense. This is the third part in the moment of anti-microcredit actions. From these parts, finally (but provisionally) an idea comes that the governmentality of the microcredit system reflexively makes "counter conduct of the bottom people" against the governmentality itself.

The discussion proceeds as follows. Section 1 describes the default issue in the microcredit program. It suggests that the loan management system corners the credit borrowers to the edge of debt. Sections 2-4 argue about anti-microcredit movements. Using the cases in the low-caste fisher society of Chittagong Bangladesh, sections 3 and 4 examine the causal logic that the subsistence ethic ignites the borrowers' indignation toward the credit system.[1] Sections 5 and 6 demonstrate the potential for paradox inherent in the facilitation of microcredit. Chittagong fisher cases in section 5 and other case studies in section 6 show the plausibility that facilitation directs people to convince the credit agency to remit the debt. At last, sections 7–9 present two ideas about the relationship between microcredit and capitalism. One is that "capitalocentrism" (Gibson-Graham, 1996) is one of the roots of delivering microcredit. The other is that there occurs farther-informalizing the bottom people where microcredit forces them into the "poverty capital" (Roy 2010).

1   Social Engineering Aspect of Microcredit

Microcredit is collateral-free financing for the poor. It is a service designed to organize the impoverished and provide loans to finance small-scale businesses (they are called "microbusiness"). Borrowers use the loan money for hut shops, street stalls, peddling, cow rearing, seed paddy, and so on. It is said the basic role of microcredit is lending money to the penniless lacking the chance to access any other financial services (commercial bank, local finance, community mutual aid, etc.).

The real significance of microcredit, however, is often said to lie in the empowerment of impoverished people. Microcredit enables people to contribute to household income. Additionally, it can make them share their problems with the organization and work together to arrive at a solution. Microcredit agencies call for the borrowers to make a group and attend group meetings. At the meetings, the group members engage in dialogues about their predicaments. This process is thought to help people develop a sense of agency, gives them the courage to resist the status quo, and heighten their desire to take action. For instance, it is probable that some borrower groups collectively oppose local loan sharks' inducement. From such aspects, as a development program, microcredit is differentiated from commercial finance. It is endowed with the functionality of social movement.

---

1   In this book Chapter 4 (the Filipino marriage female migrants' survival struggle in South Korea) and Chapter 5 (anti-discriminative lifeworlds between the Latin Americans and the Japanese) discuss the ethnic factors impacting the life of the bottom people. Both are approaching the works of "nationality" forming the life of bottom people. Now this chapter remarks on the "caste" of Bangladeshi bottom people as a context manifesting the default issue in microcredit.

Until now, many development experts have repeatedly stressed that micro-credit brings about poor people's empowerment. But at the same time, some researchers and journalists describe problems with microcredit. There are reports on default cases (Bateman, 2010; Sinclair, 2012). And as a serious matter, there are not a small number of defaulters committing suicide. In 2010 news agencies told that more than 80 microcredit defaulters have taken their lives in Andhra Pradesh, India. These suicide cases all happened within a few months inside the state.[2] On the background of such tragedy, press reports suggested three incidents accompanied by the operating system of microcredit service.

The first thing is the interest rate. Microcredit agencies usually demand bor-rowers pay loan interest. The interest rate of microcredit is set less than that of local money lending. The low level of interest rate is a beneficial point where the agencies appeal to the local people. But such lowness leads the borrowers into over-indebtedness from multiple loaning. Reasonability does harm to both the agencies and the borrowers.[3] The second is a rigid repayment schedule. In general, microcredit agencies adopt the term-strict repayment rule. Regularly weekly/biweekly installment cycles are popular, but anyway, program workers never allow the borrowers' payback arrears. The workers wait for the delin-quents to come to group meetings from morning to evening. They sometimes come door to door for debt collection. At last, when the debt failure occurs the workers demand the other group members pay on behalf of the debtor. Grameen Bank and other agencies employ such a group liability system for debt failure. Grameen Bank first applies the system and succeeds in a high-level recovery rate (every year over 90%). Now many other agencies follow this Grameen method.

For the microcredit agencies, these three aspects—they mean relatively moderate interest rate, period-regularly rigid repayment schedule, and default-confining group liability rule—are all useful means to manage the borrower groups. In other words, these are the managemental scheme required for the order in microcredit. But from the author's view, these ruling mechanisms are regarded as the social engineering set of governmentalities that enforces the impoverished to be *homo sacer* (Agamben).

---

2 "India's micro-finance suicide epidemic" https://www.bbc.com/news/world-south-asia-11997 571 (the last access was on 7th January 2023).

3 According to the same news report mentioned in note 2 (above), annual interest rates of microcredit vary from 24–30%. They are low compared to those of usurious money lend-ers charging 36–120% annually. But microcredit "can lead impoverished, ill-educated peo-ple to ruin." Defaults occurred from "multiple lending, over-indebtedness, coercive recovery practices."

The word "governmentality" accounts for the matter Michel Foucault argued concerning the genealogy of political skill/technique of the European Classical Age in his lectures at Collège de France in 1977–78 (Foucault, 2007). According to Foucault, governmentality means

> the ensemble formed by institutions, procedures, analyses and reflections, calculations, and tactics that allow the exercise of this very specific, albeit very complex, power that has the population as its target, political economy as its major form of knowledge, and apparatuses of security as its essential technical instrument.
>
> FOUCAULT, 2007: 108

Governmentality was originally seen in pre-modern Hebrew societies as pastoral power (realistically the power of shepherds controlling the herd of livestock) (Foucault, 2007: 123–4). Such exercise then has been adjusted to popular control. It peculiarly-overtly works in modern European society where public hygiene or social medicine developed for the health policy (for example reducing infant mortality, preventing epidemics, and lowering the rates of endemic diseases) (Foucault, 2007: 367). As available equipment set for social order management, governmentality is, Foucault suggested, the art of population salvation. It means that the *raison d'être* of governmentality is found in its goodness as the pastoral power has been so from the past (Foucault, 2007: 126–7).

We can regard microcredit as a current modern incarnation of governmentality. Development theorists-practitioners (the author calls them "development technocrats") invent the rigid loan system. Development agencies' efforts to enlarge the service area. But as a result, such restless pursuit for poverty alleviation —beneficial good conduct— invites poor people's death. The interest rate is superficially seen as favorable, but its operation has often provoked multiple loaning: namely, it can be a device that makes the debt-laden. The repayment schedule is embodied when the agency workers monitor not only the single borrower but the borrowers' groups so minutely (in a similar vein as the shepherd watches a herd of sheep). The group liability system works as a mutual monitoring system inside the borrowers' group. Development technocrats think that group responsibility rule gives the members sense of discipline. But probably the members suffer from the pressure for repayment and the fear of criticism; extremely that of exclusion.

The case study will suggest one thing, by their governmentality, the microcredit agency not frees the bottom workers from distress but relocates them into it. Probably microcredit would work as a development artifact still-informalizing the bottom. Formerly Spivak (1999) criticized microcredit as one of the development programs rushing those who are exploited by capitalism into further exploitation in the capitalist world. Then, inheriting Spivak's view, Sato (2008; 2016) stated that microcredit is an outcome of the tightening of neoliberalism in the postmodern world. She indicates rigid (namely bureaucratic) management system of microcredit thoroughly reflects the recent neoliberal trends in the global finance world. Referring to their discussions, the last section will give a view that the potential of far-informalizing the bottom workers is delivered from the aspect of neoliberalism in microcredit. The next section will show the cases of the microcredit agency's governmentality and the borrowers' resistance against it in the Bangladeshi fisher society.

2   Anti-credit Movements in Chittagong Coastal Society

CODEC (Community Development Centre) is a Bangladeshi NGO founded in 1985 in Chittagong. The target areas are five coastal districts along the Bay of Bengal. In these areas, CODEC has created residents' groups, called *samity* in Bengali, and has then offered several programs through the groups, including microcredit.[4] But for long years CODEC has faced loan delinquency among samity members in the microcredit program.

CODEC offers a microcredit program in the coastal district inside/outside Chittagong city. There are Hindu fishing communities along the target area. The fishers are the lowest-caste people, called *Jordas*. Jordas residents earn money by catching *Irishi*. Irishi (in English *hilsa*) is the national fish and is very popular among the Bengals. However, the restriction of the fishing season (June-October) makes it difficult for the fisherpeople to earn a stable income. To make matters worse, people have been recently faced with sharp drops in their total catch. This decline stemmed from the invasion of large-scale, high-technology capital-intensive style fisheries and the seawater pollution nearby huge shipyards cause. Although many residents want to change jobs (for example, they hope to become factory workers or service laborers in central Chittagong city), their hope can hardly be realized. In Bangladesh, about 90% of the total population is Muslim. As non-Muslims, they are liable to be blocked from many kinds of job opportunities. Also, Jāti (the rigid hierarchical

---

4   CODEC's samity consists of 30–40 members. The samity members live in the same village. There are adult male samity, adult female samity, and child samity in the areas. The adult samity members access a variety of programs, including literacy classes, mangrove forestation, job training, sanitation and family planning services, group savings, and microcredit. Child samity members attend CODEC's nonformal school.

occupation system based on the caste system) hampers their attempts to transition to different work.[5] The Jordas are thought to be hurt by two forms of exclusion: religious and caste discrimination.

Facing these problems, Jordas fishers are suffering severely in their attempts to manage their livelihoods. Thus, they borrow large amounts of money from the *dadandar*, the local wealthy Muslim moneylenders/fish brokers. Dadandar lends money at excessive interest rates (100–150% per year) in the off-season for Irishi and bargains Irishi at low prices in the fishing season. Repetitive debt and forced sales descend the Jordas fishers into extreme poverty.

CODEC organizes the Jordas people and arranges microcredit services, attempting to rescue them from the debt inferno. The main reason for poverty among the fisher residents is the outrageous interest rate at which moneylenders extort large sums of money from the residents. Therefore, CODEC appeals to the residents to use microcredit to break out of the debt cycle. It also encourages them to begin selling fish using credit.[6] The profits from selling fish help them avoid the compulsive fish bargaining with the dadandar.[7]

3   Default of Samity Members

However, many samity members did not break their connection with the dadandar. They keep connections with the moneylenders in the expectation that they will receive patronage from them. As the minority excluded by both religion and caste, the Jordas people are tormented by strong anxiety about their livelihood. With such deeply rooted anxieties, they seek to make ties with

---

5   Jāti concerns occupational discrimination in Bangladesh. For instance, Dhaka city corporation employs "Bhangi" people as workers in public waste collecting services. The Bhangi is the Hindus positioned in what is called the "outcaste" of the caste system. From interviews with some corporation service workers, the author heard about the emergence of discrimination against them. Many workers are employed as non-regular employees. Low wages, insecure hiring conditions, and city dwellers' harassments pressure them to try to change jobs. But hopelessly their caste position breaks the hope.

6   Interest rate of CODEC's microcredit loan is annually 21% (and that in Grameen Bank is 20% yearly). In the loan repayment rules CODEC sets a "Decline Interest" system. Under the system, borrowers return installments with variable interest prices that add up on each term day (Interest price = [the number of lending days]/365*0.21). Repayments are made in weekly installments when the regular samity meeting opens.

7   The author did field surveys on CODEC's programs at Sitakunda Thana ("Thana" refers to a county in the Bangladeshi division system) neighboring Chittagong city. In 1997, 2001, and 2004, he did participated observation as well as interviews with the samity members during the samity meetings.

the powerful and request patronage from them. But the moneylenders only exploit them. The dadandar stalks to the Jordas and whispers sweet words such as "I will help you," only to turn around and squeeze them for money. As a result, the fisher's debts increase exponentially. Not a small number of microcredit group members have fallen into loan arrears or have defaulted on microcredit.

Case 1: Jordas Male Samity

Thirty members have joined this samity. All members are fishers. They use loans to buy/repair fish nets and boats. This is an extra meeting for discussing the issue of loan default.

A CODEC worker stated the number of defaulters. There were seven defaulters. The vice president of the samity demanded that the defaulters clear the debt. But during his appeal, two members (a defaulter and a non-defaulter) began to quarrel harshly. The workers and other members hastily stopped the fight. Then one of the quarrelers (the defaulter) left the meeting. Nobody prevented him from leaving.

After the fight, another member (non-defaulter) showed his positive feeling toward dadandar. He said the man is a good person "because he sometimes gives me meat." "This is true." "He is good." Other members followed his speech one after another. Finally, the speaker said again that dadandar "always listens to our agony so honestly." (The researcher interprets that the members applaud the moneylenders because they lend money conveniently just when the fisher face a lack of money during the off-season of the hilsa fishery.)

CODEC held meetings with the samity members to solve the problem. At the meetings, field workers demanded that fisher people end their relationship with the moneylenders. The group members voiced strong opposition to these demands. They claimed that the moneylenders are good people and refused to listen to the workers' efforts at persuasion.

Case 2: Jordas Female Samity

Twenty-five members have joined this samity. Many (not all) of them are fish peddlers. The members use loan money for fish peddling or another small business (poultry, small grocery shop, etc.). This samity also had many defaulters.

At this regular meeting, only nine members (of the twenty-five) came to the meeting when thirty minutes passed from the scheduled starting time. A field worker scolded the attendees. One member murmured: "To make money we can't attend the meeting." The worker reacted to the words: "You come to the meeting to make money." All attendees bent their heads. After that, the attendees left one by one and the meeting ended.

The attendees decreased as the groups repeated the meeting. Several groups boycotted the meeting. The strong tension between CODEC workers and samity members hampered subsequent meetings. Some male villagers guarded the entry zone and shut out CODEC field workers not to enter the village.

Case 3: Jordas Female Samity (the Same Group as Case 2)
Every samity must have a weekly regular meeting at a designated place and schedule.

The time was 16:00. The meeting was scheduled to open at 15:00. But only seven members were present. CODEC sets the rule that the samity can open the meeting when the number of attendees exceeds 40% of the members.

The researcher asked attendees some questions: "Why don't the other members come?" The members replied: "Now our husbands come home from fishing. We are busy preparing their meals." "Do you like fish vending?" "No." "No." "I want to work at a jute mill." "CODEC never gives me the chance to work at the factory." To this answer, the worker reacted: "CODEC is an NGO, not a company."

The researcher questioned whether the members evaluate CODEC's programs positively. One member answered that the programs were unfavorable. Some other members agreed to this. The researcher continued: "Are CODEC's programs unfavorable for you all?" One member replied: "CODEC never helped us. It never cared about us." Soon, a worker angrily interrupted: "We gave you the chance to participate in many kinds of development programs." To the worker's rage, the members shouted as follows: "No, no." "You never gave us any help." The worker denied such claims: "No, no, it is not right."

At a later meeting, the researcher directed another question to the members: "Who solves your poverty?" Some members answered promptly. "CODEC." "CODEC solves." Hearing these answers, a worker told them, "Programs are not aid, CODEC's task is to support your self-help." All members became quiet.

After the interview, all attendees went home. The meeting was over.
Case 1 teaches us that the Jordas view the dadandar as their patron. Furthermore, case 3 shows us that samity members regard CODEC as their patron. This can be seen through how members expressed their discontent toward COEDC. The members looked to CODEC as their guardians (problem settlers). So, they expected CODEC to cancel their debt. But CODEC firmly demanded members' repayment. Its coherent attitude triggered the battle at the meetings. Cases 2 and 3 show the samity members' antipathy against CODEC.

4   Background of the Antipathy

In the previous description, three incidents are clarified on the manner and attitudes of microcredit borrowers.

1.   The samity members regard CODEC as their patron in the same way they regard the dadandar.
2.   The members requested debt cancellation (=patronage) from CODEC.
3.   They became angry at CODEC's rejection of debt cancellation.

What allows such a chain of friction? It is important to view that the conflict occurred basically in the local patron-and-client relationship. Carrying this as a framework for consideration, we will examine the mechanism under which the friction was generated. James Scott's "subsistence ethic," as a referential key term, leads us to a reasonable answer.

In *Moral Economy of the Peasants* (1976), Scott uses the concept of subsistence ethic to explain the nature of subsistence strategy among Asian peasantries. The subsistence ethic refers to a norm forcing village farmers to maintain egalitarian distribution of products. Small peasants relying on this norm can expect support, aid, or charity from the local rich during times of emergency (for example after a bad harvest). At times, the rich may decline to support the peasantry, and at these moments the peasants realize the rich are exploiting them. The peasants become furious when the rich deny the patronage because they see this as a breach of the subsistence ethic (Scott, 1976: 29–34).

To the wealthy's betrayal, then, the peasants feign superficial obedience to them. This is pretended modesty that veils wily intentions. Affecting an air of mock dutifulness, the peasants try to obtain the patronage of the wealthy and to prevent thoughts of counter-suppression among the rich (Scott, 1976: 7). But when the peasants can no longer bear their deprivation, they resort to "weapons of the weak" (Scott, 1985). Such weapons consist of donation pilfering, theft, and many kinds of criminal conduct. These weapons assume two kinds of significance. First, they bring some profit or benefit to the peasants. Second, they make the exploiters perceive the anger of the exploited. The weapons are the counter strategy employed to convince the exploiters to change their manners. Small peasants react to the moral violence wrought by the rich with subtle skills that include both politeness and rudeness.

With Scott's argument in mind, we can form an insight about the Jordas fisher folks. Using polite manners, the samity members utilize CODEC's microcredit service. The service itself directs the members to identify CODEC as another patron, akin to the local moneylenders. Therefore, when CODEC rejects requests for debt cancellation, the samity members feel discontent and resort to their weapons, with absenteeism and boycotting of the meeting serving as typical weapons of choice, as are late arrival to the meeting and early slipping out.

Generally, microcredit agencies adopt a group liability system for debt repayment. CODEC set the repayment rule that the other members must compensate for the defaulter's debt in a samity. (In Grameen Bank's credit program, the responsibility unit consists of five borrowers. When one member would go into default, the other four members would be required to repay the money instead of the defaulter.) But when the samity members can't proceed with the loan reimbursement regularly, the workers hold extra meetings to collect money (Case 1 portrays a tumult in the meetings). Occasionally the field workers visit the door-to-door of the samity members to collect money. The pressures these formal/informal rules impose, however, can inflict the borrowers with harsh stress. Though the group members may agree that microcredit programs have value, they may become unsatisfied with the operation of the credit system opposing the logic of the subsistence ethic. In Cases 2 and 3 samity members unintentionally or intentionally release their complaints about the loan system. Making the repayments is not an easy matter, and with the added pressure from these rules must surely bear no small amount of stress among many samity members. Their behavior is polite, but their mentality is by no means gentle. Such annoyance would lead the borrowers to cause intentional delays or other countermeasures in the samity meetings.

Their Jāti "Jordas" confines one's job chances totally into fishing (and related work). It hampers them to access non-fishing work like factory work, shop clerk, farming, and so on. Also, such logic can be embodied in their microbusiness. Most of the Jordas samity members apply the loan money to the fishing gear or fish peddling cost. Few are doing other business (for example poultry, grocery shop, and so on). The members almost unanimously say, "We live in the Jordas area, so we can't do other work." Such a remark evokes a view that caste discrimination narrows their microbusiness into fishery(-related) ones.

Anyway, on the other hand, CODEC finances money for fishery and fish peddling to the samity members. Namely, it helps their work style adherent. The researcher sometimes heard the CODEC workers encourage the members, uttering "bear up," "good catch" or "more sale." It means CODEC rarely hopes the samity members' occupational change. CODEC demands the samity members to lend money repeatedly for fish catch and fish sale. Meanwhile, it orders them not to run to the dadandar. Because the NGO believes, the Jordas people can't get over poverty without breaking off the financial chain with the local moneylenders. In reality, however, the samity members never break the chain with the dadandar. It turned out that they fall into the two-way debt owning to the dadandar and CODEC.

Microcredit is a kind of financial service. That is the entity of it. As a financial institute, CODEC is positively concerned with the samity members' business operations. In the meantime, it hardly commits to the members' living conditions. The rigid (technocratic) governance in microcredit spots such a stance. But the stance enrages the people fiercely.

5   Paradox of Facilitation

So then, what makes samity members place CODEC as their (new) patron? CODEC's facilitation probably relates to their entitlement of patronage to CODEC. This section begins to describe the concept of facilitation in development studies.

Microcredit is a kind of participatory development program. Participatory development is a term that refers to a type of community development in a developing country. After the surge of the aid model, since the 1970s participatory development has been uptaken rapidly, and it is still recognized as the mainstream development paradigm. The reason for such paradigmatic honor lies in its logic asserting community residents' self-help efforts. The phrase "participatory" specifies the stance of those agents. Residents are to create an organization (community-based organization: CBO) of their own volition, then plan and execute initiatives of their own accord. The significance of participatory development, then, is in the fact that it can be realized through peoples' "agency" (the will of self-reliance for social change).

And as for the participants' sense of agency, it is well-referred that the firmness of such a peculiar stance is delivered from the facilitation of development technocrats. According to the development theorists, local people's participation hardly realizes without outsiders' instructive facilitation toward the people. It is believed that local people's agency is only established while there is controlled by development workers. This kind of conceptualization is rooted in the intentionality of the technocrats who contribute to the theory and practice of development. There are few cases where CBOs emerge spontaneously and forge ahead independently across all aspects (Friedmann, 1992: 143). Realistically before CBOs embody, development workers effort to continue dialogues with target people annoyed with poverty. This kind of communicative consultation is part and parcel of the concept of participatory development. Participation, in a sense, can be said as an invention of social engineering.

As Chapter 6 in this book addresses, these ideas regarding facilitation have been discussed by the development Cereb-theorist Robert Chambers (Chambers, 1983, 1997) and others (Cernea, 1991; Friedmann, 1992; Pieterse,

2010). Discussion is based on the following kinds of identified issues. People such as the impoverished or slum dwellers lack the inherent desire for current status reform. At the core of this, a set of values in complete opposition to the will to reform are heavily at work. These can be termed a sense of passivity, fate, misfortune, or the like, but they all are termed as the culture of silence (Freire, 1972). In a culture of silence, people attempt to explain their circumstances by supernatural logic, such as reincarnation, and therefore fail to understand that the current conditions are determined by accepted social structures, such as exploitation by powerful persons.

Scholars and practitioners have worked to design and refine a set of facilitation methods called "participatory tools." CODEC had institutionalized its participatory tool. The tool involves a series of two parts. The first is a baseline survey and the second part is organizing activities. Baseline survey means the phase that CODEC selects the target people in the villages. Selection proceeds under the basic standard that samity members "must be a person living in a family that its total price of the property is less than the local (prefecture level) price of 1-acre cultivate-land." Following this standard, CODEC approaches the poorest of the poor, exactly the bottom people, matching for samity members.

The second phase is organizing. A CODEC officer explained the process as follows. At first, the field worker visits the villages informally and talks with the villagers about their daily life problems. The worker pressures them with questions on the problems and answers to the questions on the prior knowledge CODEC has archived. For example,

Q.   "We can't sell Irishi at a good price at the market."
A.   "Dadandar conspires with market brokers. They operate to keep the fish price anytime very low to let you lend money from the dadandar."

And in such dialogues, CODEC workers attempt to convince the selected villagers to join the program. They say, "When you attend CODEC programs jointly with other samity members, then you and your comrades can raise your income, and send your children to school."

But not a small number of the samity members have become defaulters.[8] Before long, CODEC workers requested that the delinquent members pay back the debt. On the other side, samity members hoped for COEDC's benevolence (debt cancellation). But when the CODEC's kindness was unfulfilled, the members thereupon changed their attitudes from the expectation of benevolence

---

8   According to CODEC officers, the average repayment rate of loans among all groups of the Chittagong district was under 90% for years. On the other hand, one field worker informed the author that about 5–6 defaulters existed in each samity. And the other worker said there were not a small number of groups where over half of the members were defaulters.

to resistance. The samity meetings became confusing when the attendees discussed credit repayment. Many group members demanded CODEC debt cancellation. At times negotiations between the workers and the samity members broke down and never advanced. It has been certainly convinced among the CODEC staff that the facilitation scheme strengthens samity members' sense of agency. But defaulters and debt-cancellation protests symbolically show, CODEC fails to beef up members' spirit of self-reliance among not a small number of the samity.

Why did the samity members request debt cancellation? And why did they angrily protest the payback order from CODEC? As we have seen in the former section, subsistence ethic acts as the social background of these far-agency manners. If so, then, why the samity members resorted to the ethic on the default issue? Because they identified CODEC workers as a new patron. A female member suggested the logic.

Case 4: A Female Samity Member

She lives in a fishery village with her husband and two sons. Her husband's job is net repairing. There are also fishery-related Jordas persons (net repairmen, net craftsmen, and others) who live in fisher communities. She supports her husband's repairing work with her elder son. During an interview, she claimed that COEDC must forgive the members' debt because "workers came and talked to me, they gave me a loan." The other attendant members also agreed with her statement.

Her talk in the interview gives an explanation that CODEC's facilitation led her to view CODEC as her benefactor. CODEC's facilitation induces villagers to adopt the subsistence ethic when they access microcredit. Ironically, the technocrats' approach to people's self-help may hamper it. In the next sections, we would like to examine the logic referring to some arguments.

6   Same Happenings in Another Society

In development studies, the critical discourse called the *Tyranny* critique (Cooke and Kothari eds., 2001) has emerged. The central issue of the arguments is the effect that development agencies evoke for governance inside the community-based organizations (CBOs). Facilitation gives the local power structures the leeway to impact organization management—an impact expressed as "tyranny." The tyranny refers to the fact that participants' social relations within the local community will impact the activities of the CBOs. The typical case is a situation where the community's interests are reflected in the relationships between members within the CBO, and the CBO is led in a direction that will promote the interests of the powerful persons (Cooke and Kothari, 2001: 7–8).

Regarding the paradox of facilitation, one development researcher David Mosse (2001) attempts a unique argument from the perspective of the *Tyranny* critique. Mosse suggests that technocratic facilitation induces the patron-and-client relationship between the development agency and the CBOs. Using a development project implemented with a west Indian tribe known as the Bhil, he shows that residents use facilitation as an opportunity to incorporate the development agency into the relationship.

The project Mosse cites comprised multiple programs such as irrigation improvements and afforestation. The development agency contacted the Bhil tribe with participatory tools, encouraging them to form an organization. And then the agency provided the necessary means, all the while reiterating the significance of the program. However, during this process the agency staff were confronted by an unexpected issue: CBO members had begun to view the development workers as patrons.

The workers demanded the CBO members proceed with the various programs; however, the members did not show the expected performance. In response, the agency workers devised a system whereby the CBO members would receive a reward if they acted and a penalty if they refused. When this was implemented, the members began living up to the agency's expectations. Mosse saw this as evidence of the CBO members viewing the development agency as a patron.

As for the reason for such patronizing, Mosse found out it in the different cases in which the CBO members react to the workers. For the most part, the members address the workers as "Bhai" (in Bengali [their language] this is commonly used as a polite but friendly appellation for males). However, when a reward or penalty is given out, they address workers as "sahib" (the equivalent of "sir," an honorific used with someone in a substantially higher position than oneself) (Mosse, 2001: 26). The CBO members were slow to respond to the call of the development agency "change your circumstances for yourselves," but when rewards and penalties are involved, their attitude underwent an abrupt change. These manners deliver a view that the CBO members became to regard the development agency as a benefactor of their own experiences in the development program. Due to this kind of awareness, they went far away from the sense of proactive initiatives but felt indebtedness and attempted to meet expectations (Mosse, 2001: 26, 29–30). It was no longer an autonomous manner: nothing more than the heteronomous one.

It appears that the paradox of facilitation might be seen in microcredit. Agricultural scientist Kazuo Ando (Ando, 1998a) discusses the same matter as Mosse shows on the microcredit program in a Bangladeshi village. In this village, Grameen Bank and other development agencies were working to organize residents, and residents were joining multiple groups simultaneously, taking out several loans. On the villagers' intensity for microcredit, Ando pointed out the background of such ardor for the loan: it is the effect of development workers' authority. In the Bangladeshi villages, these workers—the majority of them are highly educated young persons—would visit regularly to lend and collect money. The villagers addressed the workers as "sir." They were seen as influential persons coming from outside the village and were therefore accorded respect. The program workers are "significant figures that were accommodating about financing" (Ando, 1998a: 179). So, the borrowers vested workers with authority and worked hard with a sense of awe toward that authority (Ando, 1998a: 184).

Why exactly did the villagers stand in awe of the workers and address them as "sir"? In a separate paper, Ando uses a road improvement project in the same village to illustrate the influence of external influential persons in the village's decision-making process (Ando, 1998b). In Bangladeshi villages, there is a system whereby matters are decided through a discussion centered around the local leader. However, if the discussions become complicated and at last the leader fails to settle down, an external influential person, such as the leader of a neighboring village, may be asked to intervene. Ando acknowledges the role of such "borrowed authority" (Ando, 1998b: 222). He says the villagers grant the same kind of authority to the young workers (Ando, 1998a: 179).

These examples given by Ando enable an empirically based reaffirmation of Mosse's view that technocratic facilitation in and of itself gives rise to an ironical outcome. Based on the arguments of Mosse and Ando, this section considered the theory that facilitation orients the relationship between the development agency and residents into a kind of tyranny via the "paradox of facilitation."

From the above arguments here we arrive at the provisional conclusion that there is potential for the irony of governmentality to manifest when the bottom workers, following a subsistence ethic, become involved in a development opportunity. The issue of microcredit, namely the process of governmentality still-informalizing the bottom people into distress, appears just when the facilitation repeatedly has been performed. We have learned this social engineering aspect in the fisher society around Chittagong city.

7   Nature of Governmentality in Microcredit: What It Delivers and
       What Delivers It

The previous argument showed that the subsistence ethic in Bangladeshi societies works fairly powerfully enough to manifest the antipathy against microcredit. Arguing empirically the irony of the rule system of the microcredit program, this chapter attempted to clarify the issue of the nature of governmentality in microcredit, namely the practical limitation of the present development scheme. From now, investigating some significance the limitation connotes, the remaining paragraphs will pick up arguable points about the governmentality of microcredit program.

This chapter already found that Jordas samity members used several weapons to resist the CODEC's manner on the default issue. The target of their protest was the governmentality accompanying the institutes and rules of the CODEC's microcredit program. The institutes-rules specifically listed are 1) loan interest with minutely designed rate, 2) rigid schedule of loan payback, and 3) group liability for the debt. These are kinds of engineered techniques for the development agencies governing the microcredit program. For the borrowers, however, they can be apparatuses coercing them harshly into a debt inferno.

The level of the interest rate in CODEC's microcredit program is not as high as that of the dadandar. CODEC officers assert confidently the reasonability of the interest rate level they set in the program. But it is so hard for the Jordas fisher folks to return loan money because the amount of fish caught is declining rapidly. (Samity members unanimously say, "I can't catch fish.") The reason for the decline is the capitalization of fish catch and environmental problems (shipyards). Hence the Jordas began to wish to switch livelihood ("I want to be a factory worker."), their desire hardly comes true. Their religion and Jāti block the switch. These matters make the samity members fall into a further predicament. In light of those facts, it is quite natural to say that microcredit is only the machine heightening the destitution of the destitute.

The clocklike weekly repayment schedule is not the same as the preexisting repayment rule the dadandar imposed on the Jordas fisher folks for a long time. Although the manipulation of dadandar in moneylending is a kind of scurvy trick during the fishing season, nevertheless it is hardly possible to claim that microcredit is purely harmless. The repayment system of the credit strikes to impress the fisher people with the discipline to return money date-strictly. Such a schedule-first system pressures a considerable level of stress or frustration on whom were habituated to the local loan culture. And additionally, the field workers repeatedly visit the debtor to collect money. The thoroughness of CODEC workers' supervision raises the stress/frustration level of credit debtors.

By the group liability rule, samity members must expose themselves in the interactive supervising structure. Each member must monitor the other members' microbusiness. So meanwhile s/he must be checked by the others in one's own business. Under these kinds of governing institutes/rules, the Jordas fisher folks have a hard time surviving. The governmentality in microcredit would involve the desperation of the borrowers. It can make poor people live one step before the terminal end up by death. (Fortunately, the researcher never heard the suicidal case among the Jordas samity members like those in Andhra Pradesh.)

Therefore, not a small number of samity members resisted the set of institutes-rules. In Foucault's words there arose "counter conduct" (Foucault, 2007: 389) just when CODEC governed the samity members in microcredit. On the term "counter conduct," Watts (2003) discusses its generation mechanism persisting on the governmentality. Watts examines the development history of the oil industry in the Niger Delta since the 1960s. As an economic geographer, he grasps the images of counter-conduct as topological ones; called "ungovernable spaces." To seize the titles for oil money (that means to be an oil nation), Watts says, Nigerian state efforts to govern local oil basin areas. One skill of governing is to sectionally administrate the local society by local people's ethnicity for the distribution of oil wells. But after that oil workers' anti-government movements occurred. Each workers' group appealed its portion of oil money (Watts, 2003: 16–8).

Incidentally, these antigovernment movements were carried out by ethnically unified groups. Why did the ethnicity-singled groups emerge? Because the governing skills of Nigerian states brought the local people sense of ethnicity. They began to be awakening to their ethnicity. Ethnic leaders emanated around the groups and arranged the movements. In the national oil project, governing the population by ethnically-harnessing local capital control, Nigerian states tried to integrate the population into the nation. But as a result, such operations made ungovernable spaces in the governing place (Watts, 2003: 23–4).

In the national history of Nigerian oil development, Watts clarifies the counter conducts against governability from the topological perspective; that is ungovernable "space." The word *ungovernable* suggests governmentality rarely completes "its panoptical sense of closure and overwhelming aura of domination" (Watts, 2003: 26). Namely it is reasonable to say that governmentality reflexively produces counter-conduct against the governmentality itself. It can be said Watts's text shows this logic from the topological-geographical perspective. And so does this chapter from the communicational-sociological one.

8   Endowment of Capitalocentrism

"Put poverty in the museum." Muhammad Yunus, the founder of Grameen Bank, appealed repeatedly in interviews and speeches. Microcredit has been regarded as a brilliant artifact to salvage the poorest of the poor from the state of destitution. This chapter, however, clarified that microcredit would keep embedding them in the destitution. Exactly, as was seen in the previous sections, the governmentality of credit agencies' management techniques, reproduced the destitution of the destitute. Spivak (1999) worries that microcredit should rush those who are exploited by capitalism into further exploitation in the capitalist world. Spivak criticizes microcredit as one of the development programs inducing the subaltern into the global capitalist world. She says microcredit can be measured as an aspect of "globalization as financialization" (Spivak, 1999: 102) of the world. Namely, according to her text, microcredit is placed as a tool of baiting the subaltern to lure into sweated laborers convenient for the global trade system (Spivak, 1999: 102). Now, along with our discussion here, it would be logically appropriate to say that such "micro-baiting" (Spivak, 1999: 102) be realized under the credit agencies' governmentality.

There have been few reactions in development studies to Spivak's criticism of the exploitative disposition of microcredit. Indeed, development scholars and experts equally have paid much attention to the issues like loan arrearage and default. But these development technocrats (except for some theorists in *Tyranny* critique) all alike attributed the issues to the outcome from technical errors of facilitation (misuse/misfit of participatory tools). That is to say, the technocrats ascribe the reason to a lack or deficit of willingness for self-reliance. It means they have no insights into the working of the agencies' governmentality.

Under such circumstances, Chizu Sato (2008, 2016) describes somewhat concerns about the governmentality of microcredit. Inheriting Spivak's view, Sato stated that the methodology of microcredit is granted by development technocrats' "neoliberal understanding of subjectivity" (Sato, 2016: 155). According to her, development scholars and experts simply convince poor people's potentiality. These scholars and experts unanimously problematize poor people's lack of capacity. For them, the poor only lack opportunities inherently. While obtaining opportunities, they stress, poor people will maximize utilities and climb out of poverty (Sato, 2016: 155). We can find out such thoughts instantly in the text of Yunus. He says:

> Poverty is not created by the poor. It is created by the structures of society and the policies pursued by society. Change the structure as we are doing ... and you will see that the poor change their own lives. Grameen's experience demonstrates that, given the support of *financial capital*, however small, *the poor are fully capable of improving their lives.*
>
> YUNUS, 2008: 205 author's emphasis

These remarks suggest Yunus's strong conviction pertinent to microcredit. He believes firmly that poor people, on the whole, have brilliance for business and they all are eager to show one's entrepreneurship. But is this truly right? He appeals that the flowering of business talent is the true line for poverty alleviation in today's world. Rightfully, however, the life of the bottom people is not the same as that of the capitalists. His appeal portrays his neoliberal way of thinking toward the present world economy far away from the real life of the bottom people.

It is not faulted, as Yunus's words suggest, to say that the development technocrats stake microcredit as one of the beneficial participatory development programs with the neoliberal way of thinking. Such technocrats' devotion is, Sato points out, formed under the dominant influence of capitalism in today's world economy. She phrases this kind of ideological manner as capitalocentrism among the development scholarly (Sato, 2008: 5, 2016: 153). The term "capitalocentrism" was coined by the pair of geographers J. K. Gibson-Graham (1996) to portray a trend of economic essentialism that represents "economy as equal to monolithically conceived capitalism" (Sato, 2008: 27). Gibson-Graham defined it as a way of thinking where

> other forms of economy (not to mention noneconomic aspects of social life) are often understood primarily with reference to capitalism: as being fundamentally the same as (or modeled upon) capitalism: as being deficient or substandard imitations; as being opposite to capitalism; as being the complement of capitalism; as existing in capitalism's space or orbit.
>
> GIBSON-GRAHAM, 1996: 6

About the concept of capitalocentrism, here must be noted that Gibson-Graham questioned the capitalocentric scholars' negative evaluation of the noncapitalist economic forms (for example, found in household domestic labor). These scholars, the pair states, problematize such forms lacking "the fullness and completeness of capitalist 'development'" (Gibson-Graham, 1996: 7).

9   The World of Poverty Capital

It is noticed that, along with the charismatic leader Muhammad Yunus, development technocrats are steeped in capitalocentrism. The technocrats launch and manage the microcredit program all over developing countries. Now more and more bottom people become credit borrowers. It is appropriate to say that such a spectacle embodies the world of "poverty capital."

According to Ananya Roy (2010), microcredit is the development scheme integrating the bottom people into the BOP (Bottom of the Pyramid) market. Poverty capital, Roy indicates, is the capital that absorbs the bottom into the BOP market. Microcredit is a global development scheme that makes the poor enter the global BOP market. Namely, it undergoes a contextual power embedding the bottom workers to access the poverty capital.

Grameen Bank's Village Phone Program (VP) is a very example of the case. VP is a microcredit program that loans the fund for the opening of public mobile phone services. With loan money the borrowers buy a mobile phone and make the telephone call contract with Grameenphone (Bangladesh's leading mobile phone carrier and also an affiliated company of the Grameen Group), then start the public telephone call business. The service operator hands customers the mobile phone. After the call, the service person demands the service charge (it becomes the profit) in addition to the call fee.

It is said VP brings meaningful outcomes in various aspects. Remarkably, it makes 1) the business chance for the poor, 2) the chance to deliver new IT business (tethering PC browsing service ... etc) and 3) the chance for overseas migrant workers to enjoy communication with hometown people. It can be said that VP contributes to stimulating the Bangladeshi's emigration business as well as emigration work. In these manners, VP helps the Bangladeshi bottom workers access the global BOP market. So, microcredit is one of the central axes torrenting poverty capital ceaselessly and globally.

CODEC's microcredit program also integrates the Jordas people into a corner of the global BOP market. But the road of integration is not as simple and clear as the one VP shows. It is a long and hazy one. In the interview, the Jordas samity members who reacted negatively against the system of the CODEC's microcredit program inversely highly applauded the CODEC's nonformal school program.[9] They encourage their children to attend the CODEC school. Why the members encouraged her children to go to school? A female informant (in Case 4) replied to this question. Because she firmly believes that "the educated person can get a good job." Before this Q&A, the researcher asked her if Jordas people can get jobs other than fishing. She answered, "I can't get another job because I am Jordas. I am a lower caste person." From these answers, a common recognition among the Jordas fishers can be known. Namely,

– The entry of mega-capital fishing and water pollution destroyed our livelihood.
– But we can't change our work because we are the Hindu lower caste.
– We must continue fishing with CODEC's support for our children's schooling.
– Because (we think) education gives boys/girls good jobs (other than fishing).

At the interview, some other group members highlighted the importance of education for children. The reason is that education opens the Jordas youths on the road to some kind of salary jobs. A male samity member told the researcher as follows. "Thanks to the CODEC's school, the next generations will be able to become garment factory workers, company workers, and any other salary jobs." Needless to say, the garment industry (fast fashion) is the one embodying the rapid growth of the BOP market. It can be regarded that the school program is a device canalizing the Jordas into the BOP market.

The Jordas people are convinced that school carriers can liberate themselves from job discrimination. Hence, they commit to CODEC's microcredit program as well as its school program. Often encountering scenes of resistance, every time the researcher saw repeatedly those who regularly lent and repay the loan in silence at the samity meetings. Probably, such silent members were also discontent with the credit rules. Anyway, however, they steadily effort to continue their job with loan money. Such labor projects their wish to arrange the children the path into the global labor market. It is not necessarily false that CODEC's microcredit program supports the samity members' subsistence strategy.

As has been seen thus far, however, the program also doesn't necessarily alleviate the "present" pain of the samity members. Paradoxically it possibly enhances their poverty condition. We perceive the case as an irony of

---

9   Child samity members (young family members of adult samity members) attend CODEC's elementary school program. Because of the poor management of the public school system, CODEC opened the program for village children. Tuition is free. Teachers are employed by CODEC. The adult samity members are responsible for preparing the schoolroom (a small hut) before the sessions start.

microcredit. Nevertheless, remarking again, the Jordas people commit the microcredit program. The reason, the author assumes, is that CODEC also offers an educational opportunity for the community children. Education led the samity members to commit to microbusiness.

Microcredit is a financial development scheme. On the other hand, school program is the human development scheme. Referring to Roy's sentences we differentiate the former from the latter on the directional view. Microcredit is delivered from the idea "concerned with entrepreneurialism rather than redistribution, with opportunity rather than equality ... that is simultaneously ... anti-welfare" (Roy, 2010: 24). Oppositely, the school program is the pro-welfare development scheme concerning redistribution and equality. Along with this typology, CODEC adopts a multi-instrument method aiming the human development as well as financial development.

Such a multi-direction project style has popularity among Bangladeshi NGOs. As Roy also described (Roy, 2010: 25), BRAC (Bangladesh Rural Advancement Committee), well-known as the world's largest NGO, is a typical institute proceeding with the style. On the other way, then, Grameen Bank is monolithically concerned with microcredit. Such orientation, Roy likewise suggests (Roy, 2010: 24–5), mirrors the ideology of the founder Muhammad Yunus.

Microcredit is the financial operation accompanying the rigid government system. It makes the borrowers submit to strict discipline. The development technocrats—of course, the top runner is Muhammad Yunus—invent, embody, and operate the system all over the world. From Yunus's remark (Yunus, 2008), it is speculated that the motive power for these technocrats to create the global microcredit world is, capitalocentrism. Thereupon, those who can fit the system should get the capital and be able to succeed in the BOP business. In other words, it is probable that capitalocentric borrowers flawlessly catch the wave of capital flow and surf in the ocean of the BOP market. VP managers are typical ones. If so, then, what becomes of non-capitalocentric borrowers? For the non-capitalocentric, several pathways can appear. We have already seen three corresponding cases. The first is the tragic withdrawal from the microcredit program in India. The second is resistance against the program in Chittagong Jordas communities. The third, also in the Jordas communities, is entry into the sustainable trial transversely committing both financial development and human development.

The Jordas samity members challenge to access the BOP market via two nodes. One is microcredit (financial development) and the other is the school program (human development). As the global development scheme, microcredit advances all over developing countries. In reality, however, CODEC shows us that social development can be accomplished where human development schemes fully run parallelly as financial development schemes do. But unfortunately, it is natural that CODEC's school program little helps the samity members to overcome the "present" poverty. People's destitution is still left.

Just when encountering Yunus' allegation, we can understand that development scholars/practitioners pay little attention to the noncapitalist commitment to social development. In Chittagong coastal areas, microcredit was shaped on the moral economy—namely a noncapitalist economic form—by the Jordas fisher folks. This chapter clarified the bottom workers' access to microcredit along with the subsistence ethic: a notion totally unlike capitalocentrism. In doing so it suggested the probability of the people's destitution enhancing via the ideological clash between capitalism and noncapitalism, in the world poverty capital whirling around.

References

Ando K (1998a) NGO no hatten wo sasaeru zaichisei [Contributory aspects of rural society to NGO's evolution]. In: Chihiro S (ed.) NGO ga kaeru minami asia [NGOs in South Asia]. Tokyo: Commons: 155–191.

Ando K (1998b) Nōson kaihatsu ni okeru zaison leadership to infra seibi jigyō no kanōsei: Bangladesh dokkinchamuria-mura no jirei [The potential background for the nurturing of local leadership and infrastructure maintenance in rural development: a case study of North Chamuria Village in Bangladesh]. In: Hiroshi S (ed.) Kaihatsu enjo to Bangladesh [Developmental Assistance and Bangladesh]. Chiba: Institute of Developing Economies: 203–257.

Bateman M (2010) Why Doesn't Microfinance Work?: The Destructive Rise of Local Neoliberalism. London: Zed Books.

Cernea M (ed.) (1991) Putting People First: Sociological Variables in Rural Development 2nd ed. New York: Oxford University Press.

Chambers R (1983) Rural Development: Putting the Last First. Essex: Longman Scientific and Technical.

Chambers R (1997) Whose Reality Counts? Putting the First Last. London: Intermediate Technology.

Cooke B and Kothari U (2001) The case for participation as tyranny. In: Cooke B and Kothari U (eds) Participation: The New Tyranny?. London: Zed Books: 1–15.

Cooke B and Kothari U (eds) (2001) Participation: The New Tyranny?. London: Zed Books.

Foucault M (Translated by Burchell G) (2007) Security, Territory, Population: Lectures at the Collège de France 1977–1978. New York: Palgrave Macmillan.

Freire P (1972) Cultural Action for Freedom. Harmondsworth, UK: Penguin Education.

Friedmann J (1992) *Empowerment: The Politics of Alternative Development*. Cambridge, Mass: Basil Blackwell.

Gibson-Graham J K (1996) *The End of Capitalism (as We Knew It): A Feminist Critique of Political Economy*. Cambridge, Mass: Blackwell Publishers.

Mosse D (2001) 'People's knowledge', participation and patronage: operation and representation in rural development. In: Cooke B and Kothari U (eds) *Participation: The New Tyranny?*. London: Zed Books, 16–35.

Pieterse J N (2010) *Development Theory: Deconstructions/Reconstructions 2nd ed.* London: Sage.

Roy A (2010) *Poverty Capital: Microfinance and the Making of Development*. New York: Routledge.

Sato C (2008) *Rethinking Women, Development and Empowerment: Toward Transnational Feminist Literacy Practices*. Doctoral Dissertation, Amherst: University of Massachusetts.

Sato C (2016) Two frontiers of development?: a transnational feminist analysis of public-private partnerships for women's empowerment. *International Political Sociology* 10(2): 150–167.

Scott J C (1976) *Moral Economy of the Peasant: Rebellion and Subsistence in South-east Asia*. New Haven and London: Yale University Press.

Scott J C (1985) *Weapons of the Weak: Everyday Forms of Peasant Resistance*. New Haven and London: Yale University Press.

Sinclair H (2012) *Confessions of a Microfinance Heretic: How Microlending Lost Its Way and Betrayed the Poor*. San Francisco: Berrett-Koehler Publishers.

Spivak G C (1999) *A Critique of Postcolonial Reason: Toward a History of the Vanishing Present*. Cambridge, Mass: Harvard University Press.

Watts M (2003) Development and governmentality. *Singapore Journal of Tropical Geography* 24(1): 6–34.

Yunus M and Jolis A (2008) *Banker to the Poor: Micro-lending and the Battle against World Poverty*. New York: Public Affairs.

PART 3

Bottom Workers and Homelessness

∵

CHAPTER 8

The Spatial Distribution of Bottom Workers in Tokyo

Tatsuto Asakawa

Abstract

The purpose of this chapter is to explore where bottom workers live in Tokyo using macro-statistical data. Bottom workers, who, as defined in Chapter 2, are workers under downward pressure that is difficult to define with a single set of macroeconomic data. Therefore, in this chapter, the author first selected regions with a relatively high percentage of poor people as the target regions for analysis, and then attempted to get a closer look at the living conditions of bottom workers by depicting the lives of people living in these regions using the social atlases. The scope of Tokyo is first addressed in Section 1, and the explanation of obtaining the household income data necessary to estimate the location of bottom workers were described in Section 2. Section 3 showed the results of the visualization and classification of bottom workers, and Section 4 then provides a summary and discussion of the findings. This chapter shows that bottom workers living in Tokyo are not scattered throughout the city but are unevenly distributed in certain areas.

The purpose of this chapter is to explore where bottom workers live in Tokyo using macro-statistical data. The word "Tokyo" is not always used by Japanese ordinary people to mean Tokyo Metropolis. For example, Tokyo Disneyland, a famous tourist attraction, is not located in Tokyo but in Chiba Prefecture. Even though it is located in Chiba Prefecture, it is represented as a Tokyo facility. Thus, when the people use the term, they generally refer to the Tokyo metropolitan area, which is about the size of Tokyo and its three prefectures (Kanagawa, Saitama, and Chiba) plus the southern part of Ibaraki Prefecture. Tokyo, as used in this study, is also generally used to refer to the Tokyo Metropolitan Area.

The Chicago School of Urban Sociology is the origin of the research method to visualize the daily life of people living in cities. Where and how do these people from Japan and abroad live, and what kind of social problems do they face, where, and why? One of the methods used in social research to visualize these issues was the depiction of social atlas, such as Thrasher's (1927) depiction of gangs and Zorbaugh's (1929) social atlas of the Gold Coast and slums.

In addition to the research method of drawing the social atlas based on the fieldwork of each researcher, there is another research method of drawing the social atlas using macro-statistical data such as the population census and economic census. In Japan, Susumu Kurasawa was the first sociologist to analyze the 23 wards of Tokyo using the research method and published *Social Atlas of Tokyo* (Kurasawa eds., 1986). The work was followed by the publication of *New Social Atlas of Tokyo 1975–90* (Kurasawa and Asakawa eds., 2004), which extended the analysis to the Tokyo metropolitan area, including Tokyo, Kanagawa, Saitama, and Chiba Prefectures, and the southern part of Ibaraki Prefecture. More recently, *Social Disparity and Urban Space in the Tokyo Metropolitan Area 1990–2010* was published (Hashimoto and Asakawa, eds., 2020), which combines social atlas research and questionnaire surveys to depict the current state of social disparity in the Tokyo Metropolitan Area.

Based on these previous studies, this chapter attempts to explore where bottom workers live in Tokyo using macro-statistical data. The area of Tokyo treated in this chapter is the gray-colored area in Figure 8.1. Bottom workers, who, as defined in Chapter 2, are workers under downward pressure that is difficult to define with a single set of macroeconomic data. Therefore, the author first will select regions with a relatively high percentage of poor people as the target regions for analysis, and then attempt to get a closer look at the living conditions of bottom workers by depicting the lives of people living in these regions using social atlases.

The outline of this chapter is as follows. The author will outline the scope of Tokyo in Section 1, explain how to obtain the household income data necessary to estimate the location of bottom workers in Section 2, visualize bottom workers in Section 3 and then provides a summary and discussion of the findings in the last section.

1   Scope and Origin of Tokyo

1.1   *From Edo to Tokyo*

In this section, the author will present an overview of the spatial extent of Tokyo, the region analyzed in this study, and the process of its establishment as a city. Tokyo can be broadly classified into the inner city and the surrounding suburbs. The inner city of Tokyo roughly corresponds to the 23 wards of Tokyo. The origins of the 23 wards of Tokyo are as follows. The Industrial Revolution began in Japan in 1886, when the country shifted to a silver standard, and the

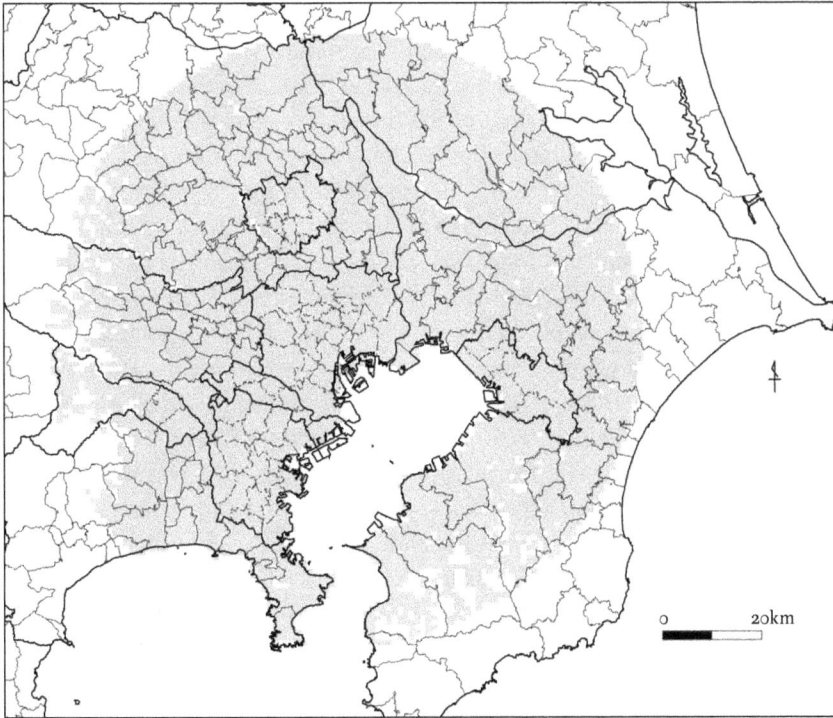

FIGURE 8.1   Tokyo coverage

rise of business centered on spinning and weaving. In 1901, the largest number of factories in Tokyo was located in the east of current Tokyo Station
(Minagawa, 2007: 29). The area to the east of Edo Castle (today's Imperial
Palace) has been home to native engineers such as forge, foundry, and plating
craftsmen since the Edo period, who entered the machine and metal industry
in the Meiji period. In addition, the area to the southwest of Edo Castle was
home to many small factories that became independent from the pioneering
machine shops of the public and private sectors during the Meiji period. These
areas were the Shitamachi (downtown) areas formed in the low-lying areas
located east and south of Edo Castle.

     On the other hand, on the plateau located to the west of Edo Castle, a res-
idential area called Yamanote spread out. One of the reasons why Yamanote
became a residential area was the Great Kanto Earthquake. The population
growth rate every five years for the 15 years from 1905 to 1920, before the earthquake, was high in the area surrounding Edo Castle. However, since the Great
Kanto Earthquake of 1923 damaged those urban areas, the highest five-year

population growth rates during the 15 years from 1925 to 1940 were in the then-suburban area of present-day Yamanote (Isomura 1953). In other words, the Great Kanto Earthquake was one of the triggers that led to the formation of the residential area known as Yamanote on the plateau west of Edo Castle, where the upper middle-class white-collar residents were concentrated.

The second time the 23 wards of Tokyo were scorched to the ground was during the Tokyo Air Raid. In February 1945, just before the air raid, the population of the 23 wards of Tokyo was 4,986,600. Although the exact number of deaths due to air raids is not known, the Economic Stability Headquarters estimates that 95,374 people died as a result of the war in the 23 wards of Tokyo (Hashimoto, 2020a: 90–91). Based on this estimate, the mortality rate is roughly estimated at 1.91%. However, there were extreme differences in mortality rates among regions. While most areas had a mortality rate of less than 1%, the rate in the area east of Edo Castle, i.e., present-day Shitamachi, was much higher than the average. In these areas, "most of the residents were laborers and self-employed workers in town factories, craftsmen and laborers engaged in miscellaneous occupations, and their families" (Hashimoto, 2020a: 91–92). Thus, "the Tokyo Air Raid made the disparity between downtown and uptown areas, which had existed since the prewar period, even more decisive" (Hashimoto, 2020a: 92).

1.2 *Urbanization Era*

The postwar Japanese economy was lifted by special demand from the Korean War, and industrial production recovered to its prewar level in the early 1950s. At that time, agriculture was the core industry of rural communities in Japan, and it was customary for the eldest son of a farm family to inherit the farm solely (Asakawa 2022). Therefore, men below the second son of a farm family and women who did not marry into a farm family flowed into the three major metropolitan areas, which were forming industrial cities, as laborers. Those from rural areas who flowed into Tokyo formed the working class as factory workers and the old middle-class as the urban self-employed (Tamano 1993).

After a period of rapid economic growth, central management functions became concentrated in Tokyo. The workers responsible for central management functions were white-collar workers who preferred to live uptown and commute to the city center by train. Looking at the distribution of the daytime migratory population relating to the city center at that time, it can be seen that the daytime migratory population was higher in the uptown areas and lower in the downtown areas (Isomura 1953).

On the other hand, the machine industry, which mainly produces durable consumer goods, and light industry, which mainly produces daily consumer goods, both developed, and they were functionally combined as follows: parent factory, subcontract factory, cottage industry, wholesaler, manufacturing wholesaler, processor, and domestic worker. These industrial clusters, that functionally combined the parent factory, subcontract factory, cottage industry, wholesaler, manufacturer, wholesaler, processor, domestic worker, were then observed (Itakura et al., 1973). Daily consumer goods produced in Tokyo were shipped to markets throughout Japan for consumption. To this end, it was essential for micro-scale processors responsible for the manufacture of various products and distribution sectors such as wholesalers and manufacturing wholesalers to combine and overlap functionally and spatially to develop. In this way, a fan-shaped arrangement was formed in the northeast direction, with the wholesale complex area on the east side of the Imperial Palace at the center, where various processing industries were folded into one another. This is how the spatial configuration of downtown was formed, with the CBD, wholesale commercial district, and blue-collar residential areas fanning out in a northeasterly direction with the Imperial Palace at the center (Asakawa 2009).

Thus, the relative disparity between Yamanote, where the highly educated white-collar class lives, and downtown, where the working class and formerly middle-class live, was formed by this time and still exists as of 2020 (Asakawa 2022). This is the origin and basic structure of Tokyo's inner city.

1.3   Reuse of Urban Centers (Re-urbanization)

From 1997, the period of the Heisei recession following the collapse of the bubble economy, to the present in 2020, social growth has continued in Tokyo. The number of new residents has remained constant at about 450,000, indicating that the increase in the number of new residents did not cause an increase in the number of total populations in Tokyo. The social increase occurred because the number of people moving out of the city fell below 450,000 to around 350,000.

What kind of people were those who stopped moving out? Asakawa (2022) shows the demographic trends by five-year age group from 1990 to 2010 (Figure 8.2). 0–4-year-olds always show population growth because they are born immediately after birth, while those aged 15–24 years are the most likely to move to Tokyo in search of employment and schooling opportunities. This trend has been consistent from 1990 to 2010. Yearly changes can be observed from the late 20s to the late 40s: from 1990 to 1995, there was a significant decline in the population between the ages of 25 and 49. However, from 1995 to 2000, there was a smaller decline in the population between the ages of 25 and 49. In other words, the number of out-migrants decreased. Matsumoto

(2004) also pointed this out. From 2010 to 2015, the population between the ages of 25 and 34 increased, while the population between the ages of 35 and 49 decreased.

Thus, the number of people moving out to the suburbs began to decline after 1997, the period of the Heisei recession that followed the bursting of the bubble economy. In other words, it became possible to live relatively close to the city center without moving out to the suburbs. During the bubble economy, factories near the city center moved out to the suburbs and overseas. The former sites of these factories were mini-developed to provide relatively inexpensive housing. Thus, the city center came to be reused as a residential area.

As seen in Figure 8.2, there has been almost no change in the situation where people in their late 20s to late 40s have stopped leaving Tokyo since 2000. The socio-spatial structure created by the reuse of central Tokyo areas as residential areas is depicted in the cluster diagram by Asakawa (2020a). In the 1990 cluster diagram drawn by Kurasawa and Asakawa (2004), the downtown area was centered on the Imperial Palace and spread out over the surrounding area. However, in the 2010 cluster diagram, the area southwest of the Imperial Palace was transformed into a white-collar residential area.

Another major change was taking place. It was a change that occurred amid a structural shift from an industrial structure centered on manufacturing to one centered on finance, information, and service industries. The children of the urban self-employed who supported the industrialization of the 23 wards of Tokyo did not become the old middle-class by taking over the family business of self-employment but were absorbed into the new middle-class. The generation at the time of demographic transition and the generation that followed them, who had been responsible for the urban self-employment class, aged out of business, making it difficult for them to continue their businesses. In the inner city of Tokyo after 2000, this kind of social class turnover occurred.

1.4   Changes in Tokyo's Suburbs

In this section, the author will outline changes in the suburban areas surrounding the inner city of Tokyo since 1990, the end of the bubble economy period, based on Asakawa (2020b).

In 1990, although the hollowing out of the manufacturing industry in Tokyo was pointed out by the mass media, the ratio of secondary industry workers was high in southern Ibaraki, Saitama, and Kanagawa Prefectures, and the manufacturing industry was heavily concentrated in the peripheral areas of the Tokyo suburbs. On the other hand, Chiba Prefecture had a relatively high ratio of primary industry workers, and rural areas remained.

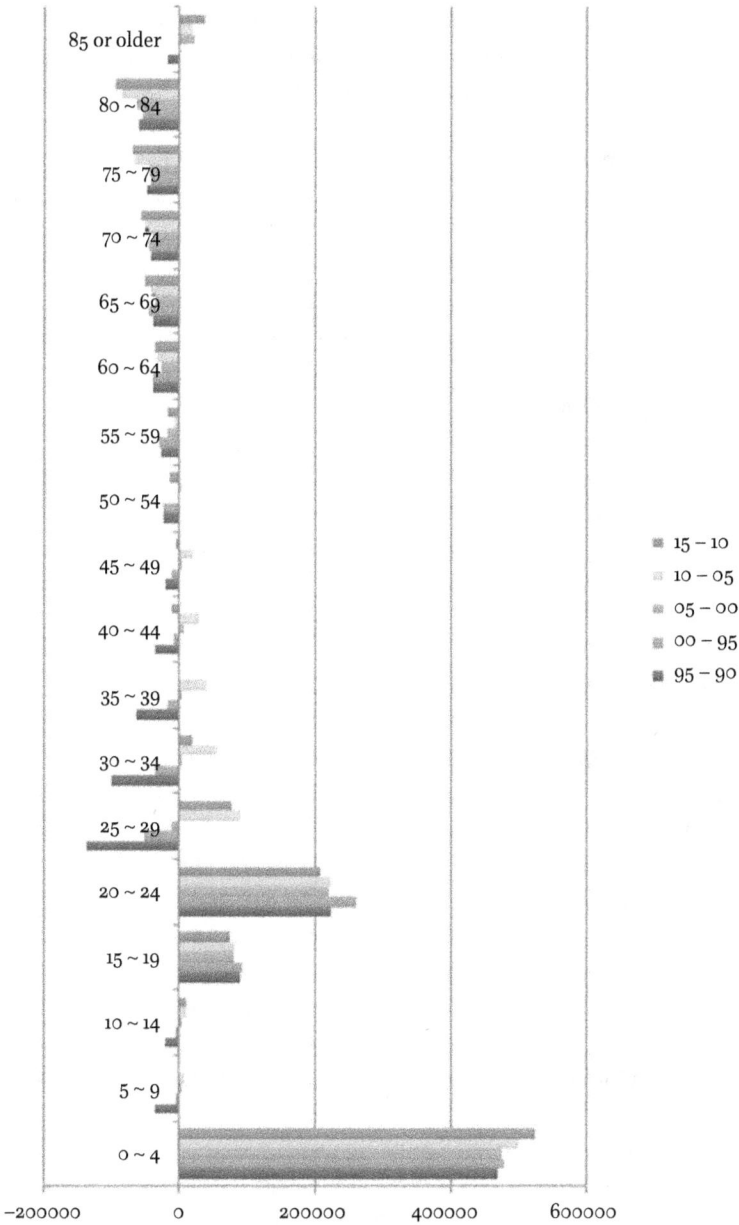

FIGURE 8.2 Population change by cohort (Tokyo)
SOURCE: ASAKAWA, 2022: 161

By 2000, white-collar workers began to encroach on the blue-collar living belt seen in 1990. The inner city of Tokyo is surrounded by social districts with a high ratio of white-collar workers commuting to the inner city, and social districts with a high ratio of secondary industry workers extend beyond the inner city to include not only southern Ibaraki, Saitama, and Kanagawa Prefectures, but also Chiba Prefecture. The remaining rural villages in Chiba Prefecture in 1990 were incorporated into industrial areas.

In 2010, there was no significant change in Tokyo's inner city. On the other hand, there was a marked change in the outer fringes of Tokyo. The social areas with a high ratio of secondary industry workers were concentrated only on the border of Saitama Prefecture in southern Ibaraki Prefecture, and the rest of the city was covered by social areas with a high ratio of commuters to other cities, towns, and villages in the prefecture. In this area, warehouses lined the industrial parks, and logistics-related industries became concentrated. Instead of commuting to Tokyo for long hours, an increasing number of people commuted to logistics facilities established in other cities, towns, and villages in the prefecture. Thus, the suburbs of Tokyo have transformed.

2   Estimation of Household Income

2.1   *Official Data Indication Economic Conditions*
In this chapter, the author operationally will define the poor as those earning less than half of the median household income in Japan. In Japan, the official data on household income and other economic conditions include the *Household Income and Expenditure Survey*, and the *Housing and Land Survey*. The former presents household income and expenditure data. However, the sample size of the household survey is about 9,000 households, which is very small given that the total number of households in Japan as of 2020 is about 59.07 million.

On the other hand, the latter has a sample size of approximately 3.7 million households, which is a larger sample size than the former. In the survey, household income is indicated in units of municipalities such as cities, wards, and towns. Therefore, it becomes difficult to find income disparities among people living in the same municipality in the *Housing and Land Survey* data. For example, Adachi Ward, located in the inner city of Tokyo, is a ward with a large area, where both rich and poor people live. Data from the *Housing and Land Survey* alone cannot provide information on the status of income inequality among Adachi Ward residents.

Therefore, as Hashimoto (2020b, 2021) did, the author will estimate household income for each standard area mesh using data from the *Housing and Land Survey* and the *National Census*, analyzed the areas where the poor live in relatively high proportions, and depicted the lives of people living in these areas using the social atlas.

2.2   *Estimation Method*

According to the *Basic Survey of National Living Standards* released by the Ministry of Health, Labor and Welfare in 2019, the median household income in Japan was 4.37 million yen (31,000US$). Generally, the poor are defined as having less than half of the median household income. Therefore, households with household incomes of less than 2 million yen (14,000US$) can be viewed as the so-called poor. Hashimoto (2020b, 2021) developed a method for estimating the percentage of households with household incomes of less than 2 million yen (hereinafter referred to as "poor households") using the *Housing and Land Survey* and the *National Census*.

Hashimoto (2020b, 2021) first conducted a multiple regression analysis using the *Housing and Land Survey*, which is tabulated on a municipal basis, to obtain a regression equation for estimating the ratio of poor households. This analysis yielded the independent variables and unstandardized partial regression coefficients necessary to estimate the ratio of households in poverty. Next, the regression equation was used to estimate the mesh-by-mesh poverty household ratio for the *National Census* regional mesh statistical data. In other words, independent variables and unstandardized partial regression coefficients obtained from multiple regression analysis of the *Housing and Land Survey* using municipalities as the tabulation unit were applied to the Census regional mesh statistical data to estimate the poverty rate for each mesh unit.

In this study, the estimation method of Hashimoto (2020b, 2021) will be used to estimate the poverty household ratio. However, the author will attempt to increase the predictive accuracy of the regression equation by adding several more independent variables to the independent variables used by Hashimoto (2020b, 2021) in the analysis. The *Housing and Land Survey* used for the estimation is data from 2008. The data set covers Tokyo, Kanagawa, Saitama, Ibaraki, and Chiba Prefectures.

The dependent variable in the multiple regression analysis is the ratio of households in poverty. The independent variables are shown in Table 8.1. In addition to the variables used by Hashimoto (2020b, 2021), variables related to labor, households, and foreigners will be added to the analysis.

The obtained regression equations will be fit to the 2010 census area mesh statistics (tertiary mesh) to estimate the proportion of households in poverty

TABLE 8.1   Independent variables

Category	Variable
Occupation	Managerial worker ratio
	Professional and technical workers ratio
	Office worker ratio
	Sales force ratio
	Service worker ratio
	Ratio of security workers
	Agriculture, forestry and fishery workers ratio
	Production process workers ratio
	Transport and machine driver ratio
	Construction and mining workers ratio
	Ratio of transportation, cleaning, packaging, etc. workers
Employee status	Regular staff ratio
	Self-employed ratio
Employment status	Percentage of temporary workers
	Part-time job ratio
Educational status	University graduate ratio
Age	Young population ratio
	Production age population ratio
	Elderly population ratio
Labor market	Unemployment rate
	Non-labor population ratio
Household	General household ratio
	Institutionalized household ratio
	Single-person household ratio
Foreigner	Foreigner ratio

on a mesh-by-mesh basis. The independent variables shown in Table 8.2 are represented by a mesh with 1 km on a side.

2.3   *Estimation Results*

The data is from the 2008 *Housing and Land Survey*, the dependent variable was the percentage of households in poverty, and the independent variables are shown in Table 8.2. To keep only independent variables with significant explanatory power, variables are imputed using a stepwise method. To avoid the multicollinearity problem, a multicollinearity test will be conducted at the same time, and variables with VIF values greater than 10 will be removed from the multiple regression analysis. The resulting independent variables that are significant (p <.05) are shown in Table 8.2, where B represents the unstandardized partial regression coefficient and β represents the standardized partial regression coefficient. The adjusted R-squared value is 0.743, higher than Hashimoto's (2020b) value of 0.619. The adjusted R-squared value also indicates that equation explains 74.3% of the total variance.

The mesh data are then estimated. The data are 2010 Census regional mesh statistics (tertiary mesh), and Equation are used to estimate the percentage of poor households in each mesh. Some meshes shows negative predicted values, so they are treated as 0%. On the other hand, there are no meshes with predicted values exceeding 100%.

The poverty ratio in the *Housing and Land Survey* is shown in Figure 8.3. The quartiles are used in the mapping process. As shown in the legend, the lower quartile is 6.6%, the median is 10.0%, and the upper quartile is 13.8%. San'ya in

TABLE 8.2   Significant independent variables

Variables	B	β
(Intercept)	7.949	
Office worker ratio	-0.563	-0.434
Single-person household ratio	0.390	0.877
Non-labor population ratio	0.666	0.670
Professional and technical workers ratio	-0.542	-0.486
Managerial worker ratio	-1.086	-0.202
Unemployment rate	-0.350	-0.080
Ratio of security workers	-0.483	-0.096
Transport and machine driver ratio	-0.663	-0.173
Percentage of temporary workers	-0.975	-0.129
	adjusted R-squared	0.743

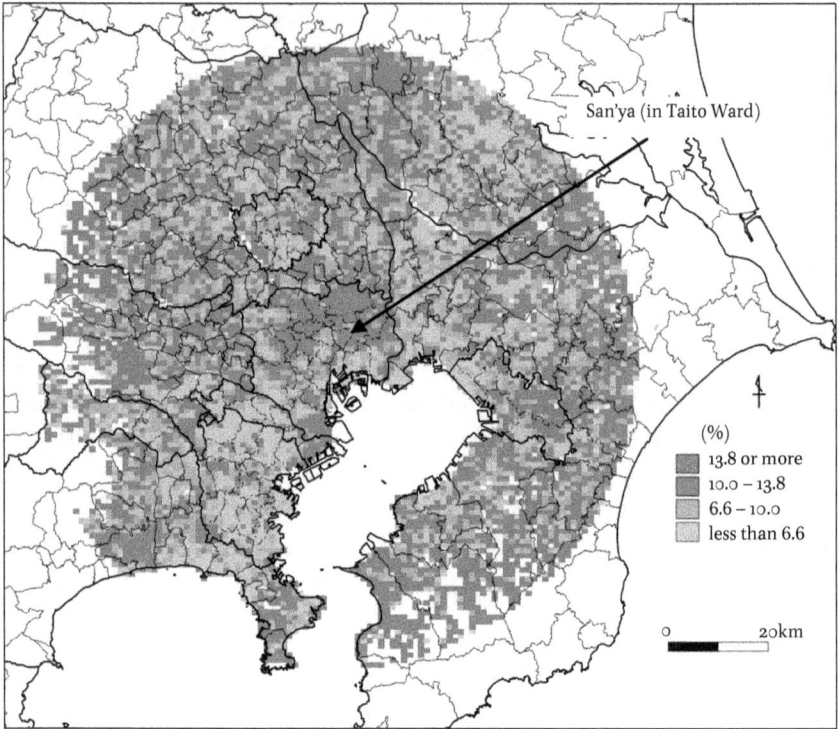

FIGURE 8.3   The ratio of households in poverty (estimated)

Taito Ward which is a well-known town for day laborers (see Chapter 10) shows a high ratio.

To select areas with relatively high ratios of poor households for analysis, only meshes with a median ratio of 10.0% or higher (4,348 meshes) are considered as poor residential areas for the following analysis. Figure 8.4 shows a social atlas of the two classifications based on the median-poverty rate for the poor. In Kanagawa Prefecture, as indicated by the green ellipse A, there are few meshes classified as poor residential areas. This overlaps with the area pointed out as a white-collar belt in Kurasawa and Asakawa (2004). In addition, there are a few meshes classified as poor residential areas along the recently opened Tsukuba Express high-speed rail line (green ellipse B).

The poor residential areas are concentrated in the northern and eastern parts of Tokyo's inner city. They are also concentrated in Hachioji City, which corresponds to the suburban part of Tokyo. As mentioned earlier, there are relatively few poor residential areas in Kanagawa Prefecture. However, Isehara City, Hiratsuka City, Atsugi City, and the Miura Peninsula, which are located in

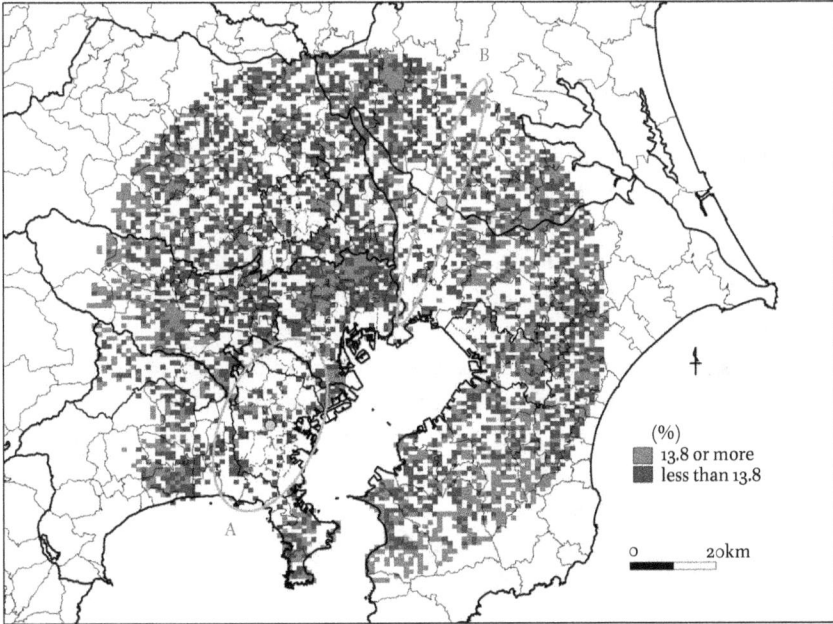

FIGURE 8.4   Percentage of poor households in poor neighborhoods

the central part of Kanagawa Prefecture, had a relatively high concentration of poor households (13.8% or more). In Ibaraki Prefecture, relatively high earned households are concentrated in Yachiyo-Cho and Tsukuba City.

Thus, while Tokyo, Kanagawa, and Ibaraki Prefectures show areas of concentration of the poor, Saitama and Chiba Prefectures represent no specific areas of concentration, and the mesh showing relatively high earned households are distributed evenly throughout the prefectures. In the next section, the author will examine the characteristics of these areas where the poor are concentrated, and attempt to produce a picture of bottom workers.

3   Visualization and Classification of Bottom Workers

3.1   *Visualization of Bottom Workers*
The author will attempt to visualize the lives of bottom workers living in poor areas (4,348 meshes) by using a social atlas to depict how people live in these areas.

Figure 8.5 shows the percentage of the immigrant population. Although some of the immigrants in Japan are wealthy people who are called the "global elite," the majority are workers and their families who are engaged in low-wage, simple labor. Since the distribution is not normal and is significantly skewed, it is mapped by using quartiles and painting four levels. In the northern and eastern parts of Tokyo's inner city and the southern end of the city, the ratio of foreign residents is high, at more than 15.4 per 1,000 population. Yachiyo Town in Ibaraki Prefecture, Hiratsuka City and Atsugi City in Kanagawa Prefecture, and Tomisato City in Chiba Prefecture have a high ratio of more than 15.4 immigrants per 1,000 residents.

Since information on nationality is not available in the census data used for the analysis, it is not possible to show the social atlas by nationality. However, previous studies have reported that the northern and eastern parts of Tokyo's inner city are populated by Korean, and Chinese residents, and that Filipinos, Brazilians and Peruvians of Japanese descent, and others are concentrated in the residential areas found in Kanagawa, Ibaraki, and Chiba Prefectures (Kurasawa and Asakawa 2004).

Figure 8.6 shows the ratio of temporary workers (the percentage of temporary workers among all workers). Since bottom workers are precariously

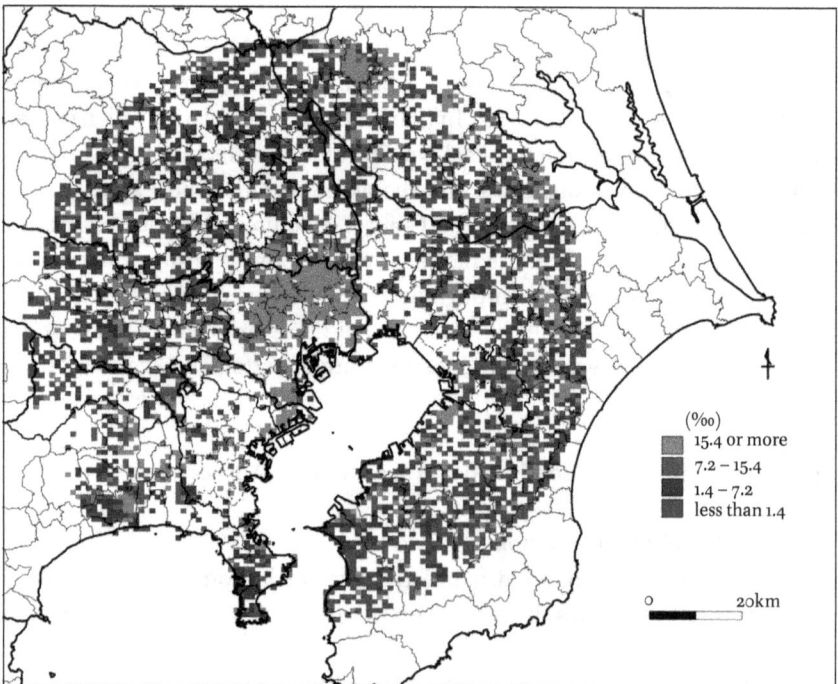

(‰)	
	15.4 or more
	7.2 – 15.4
	1.4 – 7.2
	less than 1.4

0   20km

FIGURE 8.5   The ratio of foreign population in 2010

employed and excluded from the formal job market, it is assumed that areas with a high ratio of temporary workers include bottom workers. Since the distribution is not normal and significantly skewed, it is mapped by using quartiles and painting four levels. The left side shows the ratio of male temporary workers, and the right-hand side shows the ratio of female temporary workers.

The left side shows a slight concentration of male dispatched workers in the inner city, but there are some meshes in the suburban areas of Kanagawa, Saitama, Ibaraki, and Chiba Prefectures that show a high ratio of dispatched workers above the median.

In contrast, when looking at the ratio of female dispatched workers (right side), the eastern part of the inner city and the area from Toshima to Nakano Wards show a concentration of meshes with a higher ratio than the median. On the other hand, unlike the ratio of dispatched workers for men, there were fewer meshes with high ratios in the suburban areas.

Although there is some concentration of male dispatched workers in the inner city, there are areas where the ratio of dispatched workers exceeds the median in almost all areas within a 60-km radius. Thus, it can be seen that there are many cases of men working as temporary workers in the areas where the poor live. In contrast, for women, the areas with a high ratio of temporary workers are concentrated in inner-city areas. This suggests that many women working as temporary workers live in inner-city areas among the poor.

The ratio of part-time jobs, another form of precarious employment, is shown in Figure 8.7 (the left are males, and the right are females). Since the distribution is almost normal, the mean, standard deviation, and one-half standard deviation are used to divide the data into six levels. For both men and women, the areas with high ratios are spread evenly in the suburbs. For the inner city, areas with high ratios are concentrated between Toshima and Nakano Wards for males and between Adachi and Katsushika Wards for females. The area between Toshima and Nakano Wards is home to many young people, including university students, which may explain the high ratio of part-time jobs among males. On the other hand, Adachi to Katsushika Wards are areas where many single, elderly people live, suggesting that female elderly people cover their living expenses through part-time jobs.

Figure 8.8 shows the total unemployment rate. Since the distribution is almost normal, it is divided into six levels using the mean, standard deviation, and one-half standard deviation. The unemployment rate is the ratio of the unemployed to the labor force (employed + unemployed). In the inner city, areas with high ratios are concentrated between Nakano and Toshima Wards, and between Kita and Adachi Wards. As shown in Figure 8.5, these areas have

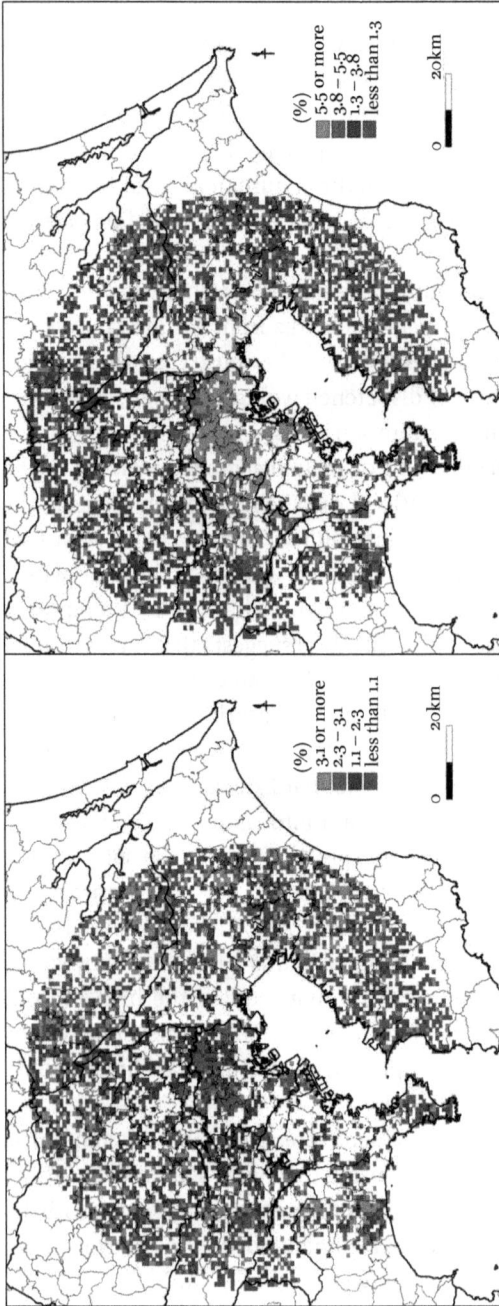

FIGURE 8.6   The ratio of temporary workers in 2010

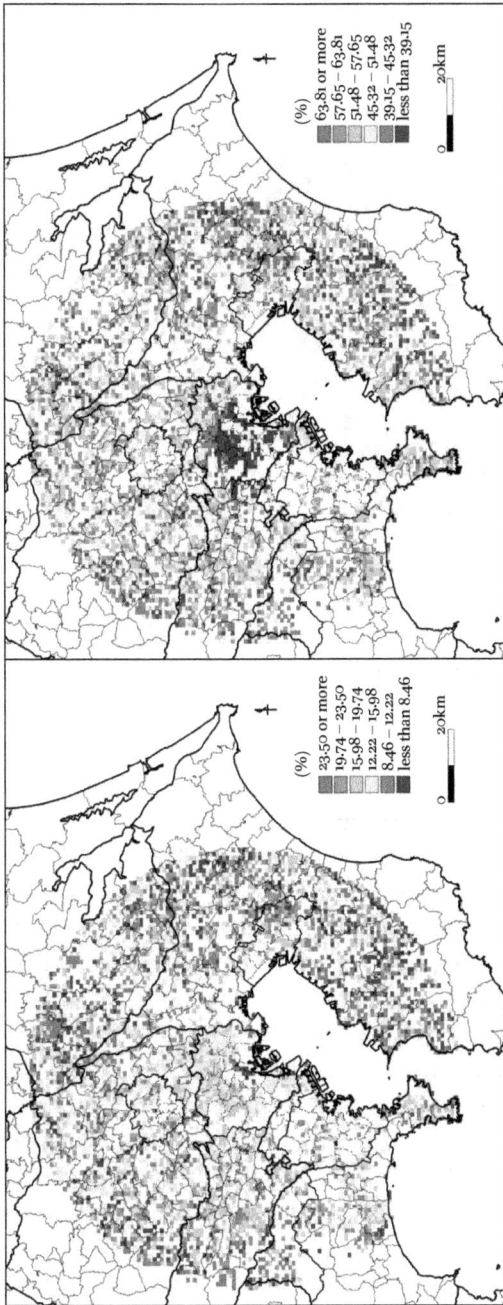

FIGURE 8.7   The ratio of part-time workers in 2010

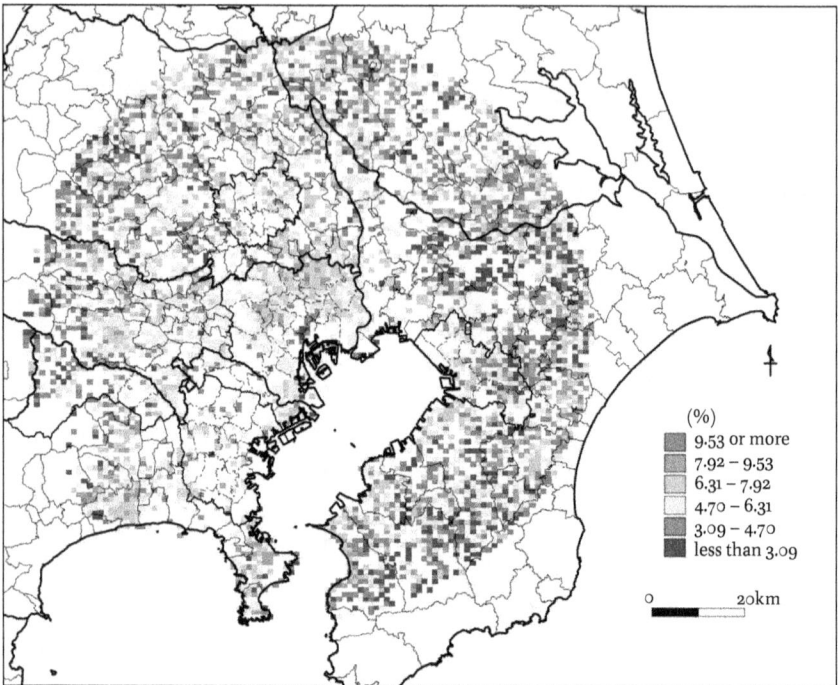

FIGURE 8.8   The complete unemployment rate in 2010

a high ratio of immigrants and dispatched workers, as shown in Figure 8.6, and a high ratio of male part-time workers, as shown in Figure 8.7.

Figure 8.9 shows the ratio of single-person households. The right side of the map shows the ratio of single-person households with the head of household aged 20–29. The ratio of single-person households for all ages is higher in the inner city and the western part of the city. The ratio of single-person households headed by a head of household aged 20–29 approximates the ratio of single-person households for all ages, but there are some catchment areas, such as Tsukuba City, where the ratio was not seen for all ages. We can note that young single-person households, including students attending universities and vocational schools, are concentrated in inner cities and areas with large universities (such as Hiratsuka City in Kanagawa Prefecture, where Tokai University Shonan Campus is located, and Tsukuba City, where Tsukuba University is located).

Figure 8.10 shows the ratio of elderly households, with the left panel showing the ratio of elderly single-person households and the right panel showing the ratio of elderly couple-only households. The distribution of elderly singles

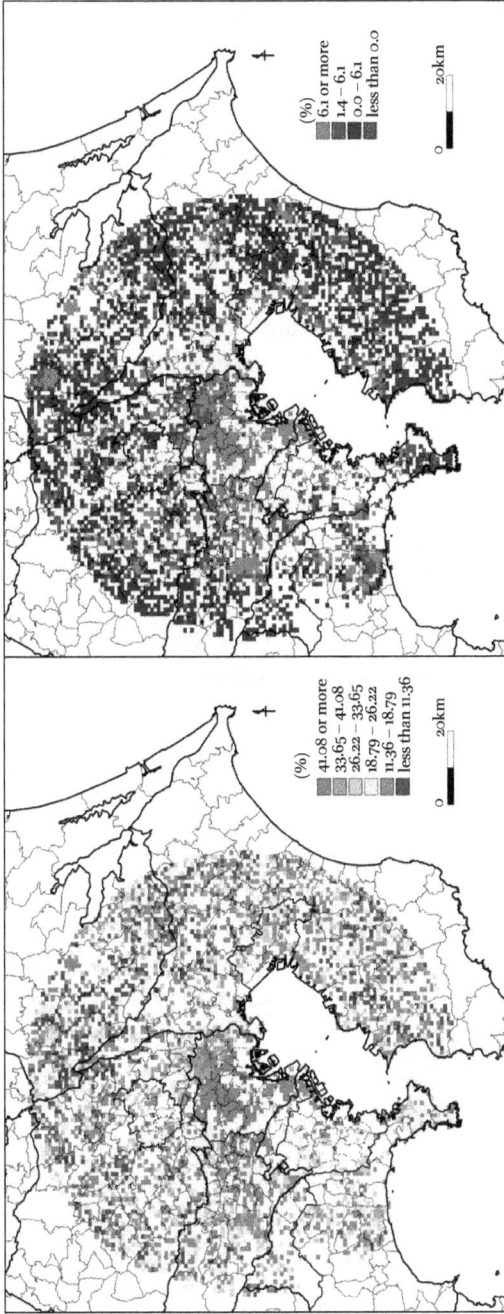

FIGURE 8.9   Single-person household rate in 2010

and elderly married couples living alone includes some wealthy people but also includes many bottom workers, so we draw their distribution for the poor neighborhoods. We can see that elderly single are concentrated in the inner city, while elderly couple-only households are widely distributed in the suburbs. Figure 8.9 shows that two types of single-person households of different ages, young single-person households and elderly single-person households, are concentrated in the inner city among the poor residential areas. On the other hand, elderly couple-only households were found to be widespread in the suburban areas.

Figure 8.11 shows the ratio of high school graduates at the last level of education. In Japan, it is well known that educational attainment is positively correlated with occupational class and income, so it is expected that areas with a high ratio of high school graduates, who have lower educational attainment than college graduates, include bottom workers. The inner city and its surrounding areas have a relatively low ratio of high school graduates, while the ratio is higher in the surrounding areas. With the recent trend toward higher education, the ratio of college graduates tends to be high among the young, while the ratio of high school graduates tends to be high among the elderly. The ratio of high school graduates is relatively low in inner cities, where young and elderly people live together, while the ratio of high school graduates is high in peripheral areas, where there are many elderly people.

3.2   *Classification of Bottom Workers*

We have analyzed poor neighborhoods and depicted the lives of people, including bottom workers, living in poor neighborhoods using multiple social atlases. To organize the characteristics of the residents, the author will organize the communities that making up Tokyo on a coordinate space using two axes: distance from the city center and the age of the residents (Figure 8.12).

The poor residential areas in the inner city are concentrated in the northern region. Kita and Adachi Wards in the eastern part of the inner city were classified as Quadrant 1 in Figure 8.12 because they have a high proportion of elderly people. On the other hand, Nakano and Toshima Wards, which are located in the western part of the inner city, are classified as quadrant 2 in Figure 8.12, because they are close to the city center but have a high proportion of young people.

Most of Tokyo's suburban areas are spread across Saitama, Chiba, and Ibaraki Prefectures. These areas are classified as Quadrant 4 due to their high proportion of elderly people. On the other hand, there are some areas in the suburbs where a relatively large number of young people also live. These include Hachioji City in Tokyo, Hiratsuka City in Kanagawa Prefecture, Yachiyo

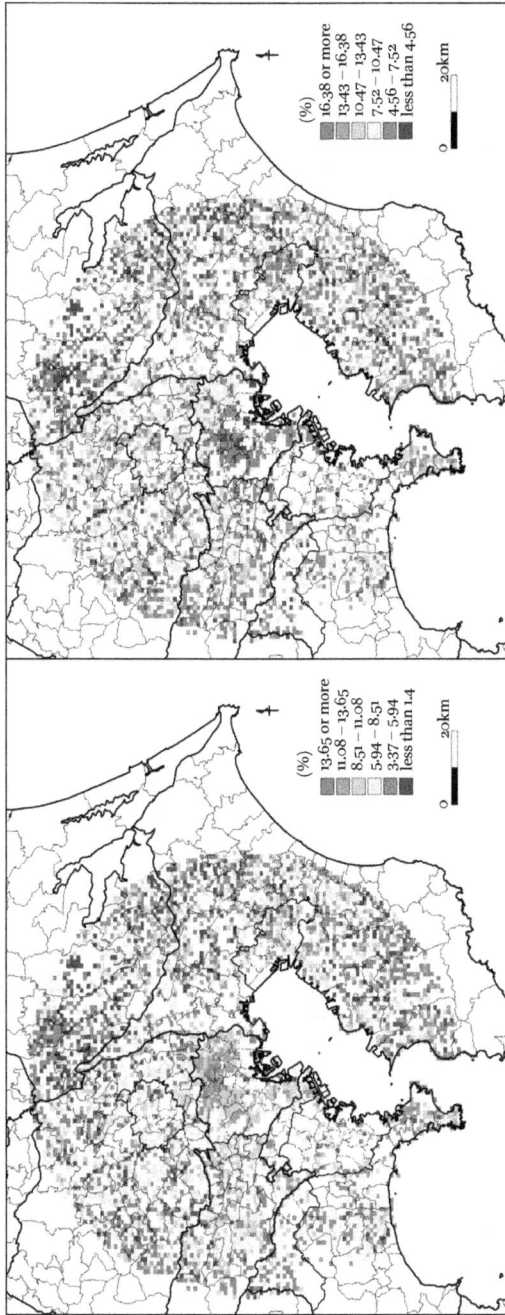

FIGURE 8.10 The ratio of elderly households in 2010

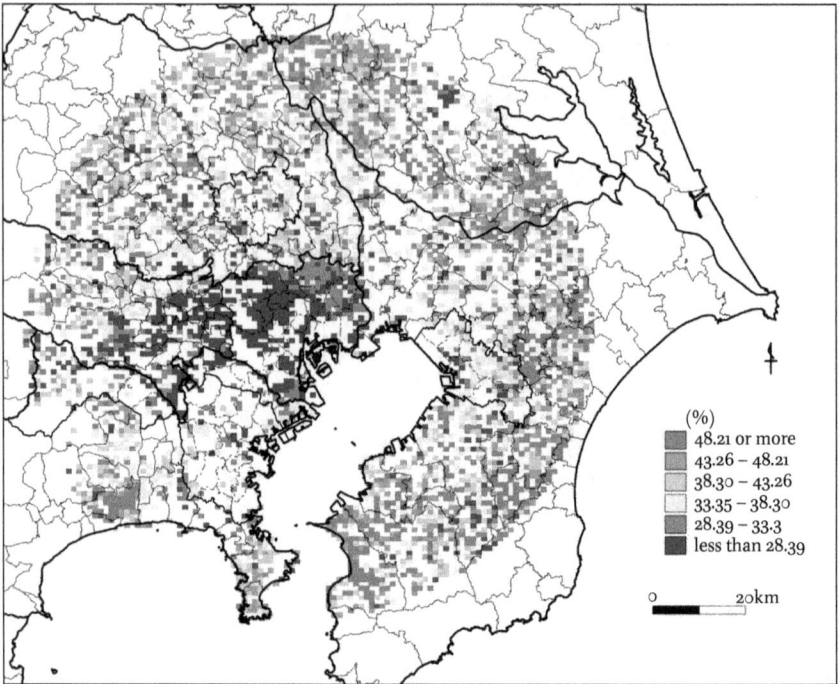

FIGURE 8.11 High school graduates ratio in 2010

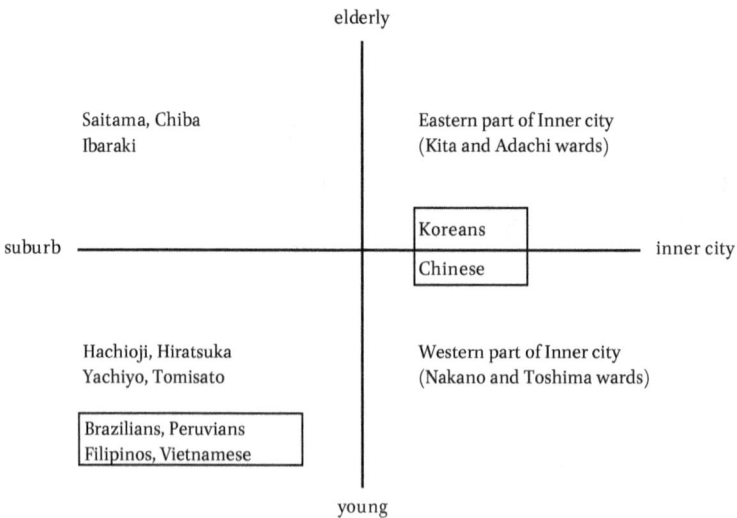

FIGURE 8.12 Typology of bottom workers

Town in Ibaraki Prefecture, and Tomisato City in Chiba Prefecture. These were classified in the third quadrant.

We also add ethnicity as the third axis of analysis. In the inner city, it has been pointed out that many Koreans and Chinese live in the inner city. Although many of these people are young, a relatively large number of them are middle-aged or older. In contrast, in some suburban areas, such as Yachiyo Town in Ibaraki Prefecture and Tomisato City in Chiba Prefecture, there are many Japanese-Brazilians, Japanese-Peruvians, Filipinos, Vietnamese, and others living in agricultural areas and warehouses as laborers. These people are relatively young.

4   Conclusion

The purpose of this chapter was to explore where bottom workers live in Tokyo Metropolitan Area using macro-statistical data. First, to determine where the poor live in Tokyo Metropolitan Area, we estimated the percentage of poor households, or the percentage of households with household incomes of less than 2 million yen, using data from the *Housing and Land Survey* and the *National Census*. The results showed that poor residential areas were concentrated in the northern and eastern parts of Tokyo's inner city. In the suburbs, they were found to be concentrated in Hachioji City in Tokyo, Isehara City, Hiratsuka City, and Atsugi City in Kanagawa Prefecture, as well as in the Miura Peninsula, Yachiyo Town and Tsukuba City in Ibaraki Prefecture. In contrast, no specific areas of concentration were found in Saitama and Chiba Prefectures. Therefore, Tokyo Metropolitan Area has not developed uniformly in all areas, experiencing spatially uneven development.

Next, social atlases were plotted for only the poor residential areas. The results showed that the northern part of the inner city had a higher percentage of immigrants, a higher percentage of temporary workers, and a higher percentage of male part-time workers. In Tokyo, where the industrial structure is centered on the finance, information, and service industries, the upper white-collar class was concentrated in the central and southern parts of the inner city. On the other hand, those who work in the industries that support the daily lives of these workers are concentrated in the northern part of the inner city, which is assumed to include the bottom workers. The poor living in Tokyo's inner city includes immigrants, young people working part-time jobs, and the elderly who have no choice but to work part-time in their old age.

The poor living in the suburbs were mostly elderly people who had no choice but to work part-time in their old age. However, several clusters of poor residential areas with a high percentage of immigrants were found in Ibaraki and Chiba Prefectures. In these areas, many immigrants live as laborers in agricultural areas and warehouses. Thus, it was shown that bottom workers living in Tokyo are not scattered throughout the city but are unevenly distributed in certain areas.

In this chapter, the author attempted to explore where bottom workers live in Tokyo Metropolitan Area using macro-statistical data. As a result, the life of bottom workers emerged. However, the census mesh statistics do not capture, for example, single-mother and single-father households because they do not represent marital status. Finally, the author wants to point out that there are other types of bottom workers that were not captured due to data limitations.

References

Asakawa T (2009) Tokyo daitoshiken no keisei katei [Formation Process of the Tokyo Metropolitan Area]. In: Tamano K and Asakawa T (eds) *Tokyo daitoshiken no kukankeisei to community* [Spatial Formation and Community in the Tokyo Metropolitan Area]. Tokyo: Kokonshoin.

Asakawa T (2020a) Tokyo 23-ku no kukankouzou to sono hendou [Spatial structure of Tokyo's 23 wards and its variations]. In: Hashimoto K and Asakawa T (eds) *Kakusasyakai to toshikuukan Tokyo no syakaichizu 1990–2010* [Social Inequality and Urban Space: The Social Atlas of the Tokyo Region 1990–2010]. Tokyo: Kajimasyuppankai.

Asakawa T (2020b) Tokyoken no kukankouzou no henka [Changes in the spatial structure of the Tokyo area]. In: Hashimoto K and Asakawa T (eds) *Kakusasyakai to Toshikuukan Tokyo no syakaichizu 1990–2010* [Social Inequality and Urban Space: The Social Atlas of the Tokyo Region 1990–2010]. Tokyo: Kajimasyuppankai.

Asakawa T (2022) *Toshi wo miru – social atlas de kashikasita tosisyakai no kouzou* [Watching the City: The Structure of Urban Society Visualized by the Social Atlas]. Kanagawa: Syunpuusya.

Hashimoto K (2020a) *<Kakusa> to <Kaikyu> no sengoshi* [Postwar History of <Disparity> and <Class>]. Tokyo: Kawade Shobo Shinsya.

Hashimoto K (2020b) Tokyoken niokeru keizaikakusa no kuukantekikouzou to sono hensen [Spatial Structure of Economic Inequality in the Tokyo Area and its Evolution] In: Hashimoto Kenji and Asakawa Tatsuto (eds) *Kakusasyakai to toshikuukan Tokyo no syakaichizu 1990–2010* [Social Inequality and Urban Space: The Social Atlas of the Tokyo Region 1990–2010]. Tokyo: Kajimasyuppankai.

Hashimoto K (2021) Time Difference Gentrification as a Bloodless Revolution: Class Structure and Spatial Polarization in the Tokyo Metropolitan Area After the 1980s, *International Journal of Japanese Sociology* 30: 23–63.

Hashimoto K, Asakawa T (eds) (2020) *Kakusasyakai to toshikuukan Tokyo no syaka-ichizu 1990–2010* [Social Inequality and Urban Space: The Social Atlas of the Tokyo Region 1990–2010]. Tokyo: Kajimasyuppankai.

Isomura E (1953) *Toshi syakaigaku* [Urban Sociology]. Tokyo: Yuhikaku.

Itakura K, Ide S and Takeuchi A (1973) *Daitoshi reisaikougyou no kouzou* [Structure of Micro-Industry in Large Cities]. Tokyo: Shin Hyoron.

Kurasawa S (eds) (1986) *Tokyo no syakaichizu* [Social Atlas of Tokyo]. Tokyo: Tokyo University Press.

Kurasawa S, Asakawa T (eds) (2004) *Shinpen tokyoken no syakaichizu 1975–90* [Newly Edited Social Atlas of the Tokyo Area 1975–90]. Tokyo: Tokyo University Press.

Matsumoto Y (2004) *Tokyo de kurasu: toshisyakaikouzou to syakaiishiki* [Living in Tokyo: Urban Social Structure and Social Consciousness]. Tokyo: Tokyo University Press.

Minagawa M (2007) *Tokyo sisei* [Tokyo City Council]. Tokyo: Nihon Keizai Hyouronsya.

Tamano K (1993) *Kindai nihon no toshika to cyonaikai no seiritsu* [Urbanization and the Formation of Neighborhood Associations in Modern Japan]. Tokyo: Kojinsya.

Thrasher F M (1927) *The Gang: A Study of 1,313 Gangs in Chicago*. Chicago: The University of Chicago press.

Zorbaugh H W (1929) *The Gold Coast and the Slum: A Sociological Study of Chicago's Near North Side*. Chicago: The University of Chicago Press.

CHAPTER 9

The Past and Present Homeless Issues in Japan

Keishiro Tsutsumi

Abstract

In Japan, the term "homeless" has been used by national and local governments and citizens to refer exclusively to rough sleepers. This reflects their awareness of them of the problem of the presence of rough sleepers. However, in Japan, as in Europe and the US, homelessness has become a phenomenon that is not limited to rough sleepers. This chapter discusses the developments of the homeless issue in Japan, mainly based on data obtained from a social survey conducted in Osaka City, the city with the largest number of rough sleepers in Japan, from the 1990s to the present. The main arguments are as follows: the people who were forced to become rough sleepers in large numbers at the beginning of Japan's homeless issue were construction day laborers who were mobilized for national land development after the period of rapid economic growth. "The internet cafe refugees" who have since attracted public attention in the 2000s were also created against the backdrop of changes in the industrial structure. Their work and living conditions are similar to those of construction day laborers. In Japan, the number of people forced to live under precarious work and housing conditions, despite legal definitions, has expanded to a wider range of industries than in the past. Through this situation, Japan has only just begun to create a framework for the poverty program.

This chapter discusses the development of the homeless issue in Japan since the 1990s. We want to clarify how the sources that produce homeless people have changed in the past and present with the structural changes in Japanese society. Finally, we would argue that this change has resulted in the need to expand the concept of homelessness in Japan. The data used in this chapter are mainly from social survey projects in which the author participated in Osaka City, with the highest number of rough sleepers in Japan, both past and present.

Comparing the social treatment of homelessness in Japan in the past with the present, some things changed, and others did not. To better understand it, I will proceed with a discussion keeping two perspectives in mind. First, it is about the approach to people living outdoors. In Japan today, both the public and the media mainly refer to people living outdoors as *hōmuresu* (homeless), which are "People Living Rough" in the ETHOS[1] typology. Previously, another term was used to refer to those at the bottom of urban areas. The term homeless was adopted to distance itself from various discriminatory expressions and became widespread around the 1990s (Hirakawa, 2005: 230–1). At the time, the number of people living rough has increased rapidly, especially in large cities. Japanese society came to call this situation "the homeless problem." The law promulgated in 2002 defines a *hōmuresu*(homeless) as "a person who engages in his/her daily life in the park, river, road, station or any other facilities where he/she lives without any notice." (Article 2 of Act on Special Measures concerning Assistance in Self-Support of Homeless (after this, Special Measures Act)). People have used the term homeless in the same sense as people living rough, *nojukusha*, in both administrative measures and daily usage.

In recent years, however, the usage condition has changed. Deregulation has caused a sharp increase in the number of non-regular workers and the expansion of the unstable working and living class working in unstable conditions and living in unstable accommodations such as dormitories, rental rooms, etc. As a typical example, the mass media focused on people sleeping in Internet cafes. The mass media called them "internet cafe refugees," and their existence became widely known. They have often been described as "invisible homeless." The government (Health, Labour and Welfare Ministry) that defined who the homeless are by law also used this word in the 2009 White Paper (MHLW, 2009: 103).[2] Thus, the term homeless initially referred only to rough sleepers have included those who do not live outdoors. The term homeless is used in a complex way. The government's limited definition of the term has significantly impacted society's perception of the homeless issue.

Since the beginning of the 2000s, Japan's term homeless has steadily changed. This has proceeded parallel with a change in Japanese society's perception of homelessness. This is the second one. This social phenomenon appears in the process of "externalization," "objectification" and

---

1   FEANTSA (European Federation of organizations working with the people who are homeless) has developed a typology of homelessness and housing exclusion called ETHOS (European Typology of Homelessness and housing exclusion). "These conceptual categories are divided into 13 operational categories that can be used for different policy purposes such as mapping of the problem of homelessness, developing, monitoring and evaluating policies"(FEANTSA HP, retrieved Nov.29 from https://www.feantsa.org/en/toolkit/2005/04/01/ethos-typology-on-homelessness-and-housing-exclusion.).

2   At this time, the government referred to people sleeping in Internet cafes as "*jūkyo sousitsu fuantei syūgyousha* (unstable workers with loss of housing)," but this term is not widely used today.

"internalization" (Berger and Luckman, 1967). Methods and systems for dealing with homelessness have been built on people's perceptions of homelessness beforehand. This is a case of objectifying people's subjectivity. The process of resolving homelessness involves an epistemological space traditionally shaped by how one interacts or does not interact with those at the bottom of the city.

The changing situation surrounding homelessness, symbolized by the development of homeless support activities by private organizations, has also prompted us to change how we perceive homelessness. The way they exist is objectified as various institutions. Against this background, the issue of impoverishment is becoming increasingly important in Japan.

Second, I will point out that it is significant to use the bottom-worker concept, and define the terms used for those who live outdoors and work and live in unstable conditions. Hideo Aoki examined the various Japanese terms used when people called those sleeping outdoors; *furousha*, *jushofuteisha*, *rojou-seikatsusha*, *hōmuresu*, *nojuku-roudousha*, and *nojukusha* (Aoki, 2000). Living and sleeping outdoors can always be defined only conditionally in the concrete context (Aoki, 2000: 104). So, it is difficult to decide how to refer to them with any one term. Aoki explained that *nojukusha* is a term that is the safest one because it gives the minimum definition of those with diverse backgrounds. I will follow this understanding of homelessness and use rough sleepers instead of *nojukusha*, except for citations to references and materials. Then, homelessness or homeless people will be used when referring to precarious work and precarious residence groups, including rough sleepers, or the Japanese state's use of the term to refer to rough sleepers.

1   What It Means for Day Laborers to Sleep Outdoors

In the process of modernization, commerce and industry developed extremely well in the city center of Osaka. Osaka was called the "Manchester of the East." Along with this, a thick inner city with diverse characteristics has been formed in concentric circles surrounding the city center. The urban spatial structure of Osaka City is like that once found in Chicago by Ernest Burgess. The city center has developed while partially inheriting the legacy of the historical urban spatial structure. The urban center is the node of metropolitan exchange, where people, goods, capital, and information converge along with the development of capitalism. The inner city has provided the labor force to support the development of the city center. In the inner city, people with *Buraku*, Korean, and Okinawan roots and day laborers have lived in a crescent-shaped area surrounding the Osaka Loop Line. And that characteristic remains strong even today (Mizuuchi, 2005). People living in the inner city tended to live in poverty to varying degrees.

Kamagasaki is one of the inner-city areas. Under Fordism,[3] Japan pursued rapid land development to achieve high economic growth. Executing and accomplishing national events such as the Tokyo Olympics (1964) and the Osaka Expo (1970) were driving forces. The largest construction day labor market in Japan, located in Kamagasaki, has served as a base for supplying large numbers of day laborers to these developments. Poverty is most severe among day laborers living in *doya* (a flophouse). Poverty is created under a free and unregulated open labor market that is largely outside the reach of law and politics. They are sent to the work site through a private agency called a *"tehaishi."* It was considered illegal under the labor laws but was effectively tacitly approved as an *exception* in this region (Haraguchi, 2009). Kamagasaki in Osaka, Sanya in Tokyo, Kotobukicho in Yokohama, and Sasajima in Nagoya, representative day labor markets in these industrial cities in Japan, created many rough sleepers in the early years of the homeless issue in Japan. Until the 1990s, 20,000 to 30,000-day laborers lived in Kamagasaki.

At the beginning of the high economic growth, the region first attracted attention from society due to problems such as out-of-school children and prostitution (Haraguchi, 2003). In 1961, a riot broke out among day laborers in the region due to the disregard for their human rights by the police and shopkeepers. This was the most significant cause for the area to be known by the public, with a strong sense of heterogeneity and discrimination.

On the other hand, the riots revealed that the state has failed to do what the Japanese Constitution obliges the state to do for the workers of this area; the government must ensure that all workers are guaranteed a minimum healthy and cultural standard and that their fundamental labor rights are protected. The riots prompted the national, prefectural, and municipal governments to adopt various policies to demonstrate to society that they control the workers in this city. They first gave the area a different name, the *"Airin* district" (Haraguchi, 2003). As a result, this series of interventions created a system in Kamagasaki where workers' job search, livelihood, response to destitution, and death were all handled within the area. This is called the " *Airin* measure."

The poverty of construction day laborers has been discussed while its heterogeneity has been emphasized. However, what makes their heterogeneity

---

3 See Haraguchi (2009) for discussing the relationship between Fordism as an economic form and construction day labor markets in Japan.

stand out is the working environment in which they are placed. The number of daily job openings in the construction day labor market is significantly affected not only by the economy but also by weather and the time of year, such as New Year's. The number of days they can work per month is limited due to the drastically changing number of daily jobs. They are forced to face many challenges in the very act of earning and living everyday life. More workers endure on the streets during short work periods and wait for work. Their rough sleeping was routinely produced by construction capital to satisfy its appetite for accumulation (Shima, 1999).

In addition to the irregular working days, they cannot make their homes since their worksites are located all over the country. They have always slept and woken up in *doya* or *hamba* (accommodation for workers). They have been forced into a state of permanent homelessness.

However, the rough sleepers have been neglected due to regional discrimination against Kamagasaki and the disdain for day laborers. Their situation was rarely recognized as a human rights issue. The system described above has also functioned as a device to conceal the contradiction between pursuing wealth while creating poverty (Shima, 1999; Tsutsumi, 2010). In urban society, rough sleepers have not been considered a social problem to be solved as long as it remains within the confines of the particular zone of Kamagasaki. The day laborers of Kamagasaki have been treated as ambivalent in urban society, as both objects of exclusion and inclusion. Osaka City has been Japan's largest supplier of daily labor, which is essential for national land development. Its presence, however, has been perceived by urban residents as an object to be feared beyond the boundaries.

The modernization of Osaka City was also a process of creating an urban space that could make such a cognitive divide among the city's residents. Under Fordism in Japan, many people were included in an affluent society with higher national incomes, forming families, building their own homes, and becoming more prosperous. On the other hand, Fordism needed an exceptional labor force to support itself and an exceptional space to gather and carefully manage such people (Haraguchi, 2009). Subsequently, the *Airin* measures did not show significant changes for more than 20 years, from 1970 to the 1990s (Mizuuchi, 2005).

2   The Beginning of the Homeless Issue

With the bursting of the bubble economy and the worsening of the construction recession, Osaka City faced homeless issues, which were quite different from what they had been before. Kamgasaki-workers who supported the high economic growth at the bottom have grown old. Constructors began sending young workers from *hamba* and dormitories to the job site. On the other hand, the labor market in Kamagasaki mercilessly regarded old workers as non-labor. They were driven into the street. This meant that the day labor market in Kamagasaki was being dismantled, along with the structural transformation of the construction industry and the expansion of non-regular employment in the general labor market. Many researchers analyzed that this factor was more significant than the recession in driving them into the field (Shima, 1999; Shima, 2001; Fukuhara and Nakayama, 1999; Aoki, 2000). Then, in the 2000s, Japan experienced the longest economic boom period in its history (Izanami Boom). However, the number of job openings in Kamagasaki did not recover during that period (Asahi Shimbun, October 30, 2009). The dramatic increase in the number of rough sleepers in the city was also a sign of the fraying of the archaic system that Osaka city had formed to control the lower class.

Osaka City faced an overwhelming number of people living outdoors, more than the *Airin* measures could ever handle. In May 1998, Osaka City established the "Osaka City Liaison Committee to Study the homeless issues" and commissioned Osaka City University to conduct a general survey of the number of rough sleepers living in the city (1998) and a fact-finding survey (1999).

As of the summer of 1998, the number of rough sleepers in Osaka City, as compiled in a general survey of the number of rough sleepers, was 8,660. This number was far beyond the imagination of those in charge of survey.[4] Figure 9.1 shows the geographic distribution of rough sleepers in the summer of 1998. Of the 24 wards in Osaka City, Nishinari-Ku, where Kamagasaki is located, had the largest number of residents with 1,910 (22.0%). And 1,585 (18.3%) were found in Naniwa-ku, 1,117 (12.9 %) in Chuo, 1,084 (12.5%) in Tennoji, and 1,079 (12.5%) in Kita, all of that have downtown areas and business areas. The CBD and its five neighboring districts accounted for 78.2% of the total.

Focusing on CBDs, in the Chuo ward they have been distributed in downtown areas (Namba and Sennichimae), office and wholesale districts (Midosuji, Shinsaibashisuji, Shimanouchi, and Semba), a little further north, and in Osaka Castle Park. In Kita ward, it exists in all townships, mainly in the vicinity of

---

4   This survey was conducted visually during the summer, at night and during the day. In areas with a high density of dwellings, an all-inclusive survey was conducted by bicycle. On foot and in areas where the density of homeless people was considered relatively low, a base survey was conducted by bicycle and car. In this survey, the entire city of Osaka was examined in considerable detail, although not all streets were covered.

FIGURE 9.1   Geographic distribution of rough sleepers in Osaka City in
             the summer of 1998 (Osaka City University, 2001: 11)

parks and terminals, but also on the banks of the Yodogawa River (Osaka City
University, 2001: 5–6).

These were not the only typical places where rough sleepers were found.
Tennoji Park (430 people), Nagai Park (313 people), Nishinari Park (254 people),
and other large parks, temples, and shrines in the city were filled with tents set
up with blue sheets.[5] The existence of rough sleepers has obviously become

---

5   Almost half of the rough sleepers identified in the same survey were of the "rug" type, a quar-
    ter was of the "tent/hut" type, and around 10% were of the "nothing" or "enclosed cardboard"
    type (Osaka City University, 2001: 6).

more widespread throughout the city. The characteristics of rough sleeping currently in the homeless issue were a quantitative increase, widespread, prolonged, and increase in the number of tent dwellers (Tsumaki, 2001: 126–8).

In the past, many urban residents have adopted an attitude of indifference when passing by rough sleepers sitting on the streets. It was a way to avoid expressing our latent hostility toward them or for us to be able to live in a *wealthy society* (Shima, 1999: 195). However, with the mass of construction day laborers becoming rough sleepers, it is no longer possible to manipulate such notions to make the reality that is problematic in the first place—a reality that should not exist in a *wealthy* or *democratic* society—seem as if it were not a problem at all. In other words, the emergence of the homeless issues, at its beginning, meant the limits of the urban social system that constituted the reality of our *wealth* and the limits of Kamagasaki as a day labor market.

3   Large-Scale Fact-Finding Survey

Around 1998, fact-finding surveys of rough sleepers began to be conducted in municipalities where the number of rough sleepers had increased rapidly. The surveys conducted in the 23 wards of Tokyo and Osaka City were unprecedented. In Tokyo, a questionnaire survey of 710 rough sleepers was conducted mainly in areas with high concentrations (Toshi seikatsu kenkyukai, 2000). In Osaka City, 672 people were interviewed about their life history, including occupation, family, housing, and their current living conditions and needs, mainly among rough sleepers living in tents in parks and riverbeds (Osaka City University, 2001).

These surveys revealed that the current homeless problem today is very different from what it used to be. Age restrictions were noticeably placed on the day labor market ("must be 45 years old or younger"). On the other hand, the illegal operation of the Welfare Law was the norm at welfare offices in many municipalities. The government considered those under 65 years of age as "able to work" and did not accept their applications for public assistance unless they had a severe illness or disability. When it became difficult for the workers to continue "rough sleeping to wait for jobs to appear" in Kamagasaki, they sought hope for survival outside of Kamagasaki. As a result, the places where rough sleepers could be found were diffused. Those who could work were forced to survive by doing miscellaneous jobs in the city, such as collecting aluminum cans. Those who no longer have any hope of working due to old age, illness, or disability are forced to live on the backs of others or wait to die. The average age of the rough sleepers in all surveys was in the mid-50s due to this operation of the system by capital and the state, which folds exclusion into the system.

The fact-finding survey included in-depth interviews with the rough sleepers about their current living conditions. The survey revealed that many of those unable to find day labor in the face of the expected prolonged period of squatting are instead trying to eke out a living by doing miscellaneous jobs. The blue tents they set up tended to symbolize the nuisance of their presence to the neighbors. However, the tents reflect the will to protect oneself from the harsh environment and continue living as humanly as possible. As the period of rough sleeping lengthens without active support measures by government agencies, their lives are arranged as a sedentary "homeless life" (Tsumaki, 2001). Urban rough sleeping proceeded as a qualitative change from "rough sleeping to wait for jobs to appear."

These surveys reveal the demographic characteristics of rough sleepers and the details of the process leading to homelessness (see Table 9.1). The basic demographics of the respondents were mainly "middle-aged, single, and male," and their educational backgrounds were (and still are) skewed significantly toward the less educated. The fact that 20–30% of the respondents were from Hokkaido, Kyushu, and Okinawa and that not a small number of them had moved to industrial cities against the backdrop of labor migration from rural villages to the cities around the period of high economic growth, etc., was also revealed.

There are also differences between Tokyo and Osaka. Both surveys point out that many people continue to change jobs in unstable employment environments and precarious employment such as construction day labor. However, a difference was observed in the percentage of those who had worked in the day labor market: 40% in Tokyo and 60% in Osaka. Differences were also found in the content of miscellaneous jobs in the field. This may be due to differences in the level of development of the service industry between the two cities, differences in the job recruiting function of day labor markets, and differences in the geographical conditions surrounding the rough sleeping environment.

4   Beginning of Measures for Homeless People

As mentioned above, in the day labor market in Kamagasaki and other areas of Japan, an increasing number of workers were noted to be staying outdoors since the early 1990s. Even outside of these areas, people were gradually being seen. However, it must be said that the government was extremely slow to respond to this trend. In a 1997 article, Iwata (1997) points out that the fragility

TABLE 9.1 Results of Tokyo and Osaka surveys (partial)

	Tokyo survey (Research Representative: Iwata, Masami. Conducted in March 2000)	Osaka survey (Research Representative: Morita, Yoji. conducted in August 1999)	Notes
Number of people surveyed	710	672	
Mean age	54.0	55.8	Both of them show the mountain type age distribution with 50 year-old generation as a top.
Sex	men 97.7%, women 2.1%	men 97.0%, women 3.0%	
Hometown	Tokyo metropolitan area 37.5% local area 37.2% remote location 22.5% Osaka area 2.7% (N = 698)	Osaka area 29.6% local area 34.8% remote location 29.0% Tokyo metropolitan area 6.6% (N = 655)	This classification is based on the Tokyo Survey. Tokyo metropolitan area: Tokyo, Kanto. local area: Tohoku, Chubu, Hokuriku, Chugoku, Shikoku. remote location: Hokkaido, Kyushu and Okinawa. Osaka area: Kinki
Educational status	junior high-school graduate 60.2% high-school graduate 28.8% specialized school graduate 2.4%	junior high-school graduate 60.3% high-school graduate 32.2% specialized school graduate 1.5%	

TABLE 9.1   Results of Tokyo and Osaka surveys (partial) (*cont.*)

	Tokyo survey (Research Representative: Iwata, Masami. Conducted in March 2000)	Osaka survey (Research Representative: Morita, Yoji. conducted in August 1999)	Notes
	junior college or technical college graduate 0.6% university or graduate school graduate 5.1% not graduate or non-completion of compulsory education 2.7% others 0.3% (N = 706)	junior college or technical college graduate 0.3% university or graduate school graduate 3.6% not graduate or non-completion of compulsory education 1.7% others 0.5% (N = 665)	
Whether or not he/she has used Yoseba	Yes 39.7%(Sanya 31.1%, Kotobuki-cho 10.0%, others 11.8%) No 60.3%	Yes 57.9% No 42.1%	Tokyo survey used multiple answers,and asked about their experiences using Yoseba. The Osaka survey asked about their experience of using Kamagasaki(Yoseba in Osaka).

TABLE 9.1 Results of Tokyo and Osaka surveys (partial) (cont.)

	Tokyo survey (Research Representative: Iwata, Masami. Conducted in March 2000)	Osaka survey (Research Representative: Morita, Yoji. conducted in August 1999)	Notes
A rough sleeping period	Less than 1 year 33.7% 1–3 years 27.2% 3–5 years 13.4% 5–10 years 14.5% more than a decade 11.1% NA 0.1%	Less than 8 months 23.1% 8 Months to 1 Year and 8 Months 33.9% 1 Year and 8 Months to 3 Years and 8 Months 22.2% more than 3 Years and 8 Months 18.6% NA 2.2%	Tokyo survey asked them how long they felt they spent most of their lives outdoors. Osaka survey asked about the period from when they first slept outdoors.
Do you have a work now?	Yes 49.4%, No 50.6%	Yes 79.9%, No 20.1%, NA 0.1%	
Substance of work	construction day labour 32.6% a part-time work of lining up instead to buy tickets 17.6% collecting and selling books 11.9% collectting and selling waste materials(aluminum cans) 14.6% (The transport day labour 8.4% (The rest is omitted. N = 350)	collectting and selling waste materials(aluminum cans) 87.2% construction day labour 9.1% a cleaning job provided by the Osaka Prefectural Government for homeless people 4.1% others 10.2% (The rest is omitted. N = 537)	Multiple responses were used in both surveys.

This table was created by Tsutsumi based on Osaka City University (2001) and Urban Life Research Association (2000).

of the view of rough sleeping as a poverty problem (strange and falling people) has led to a lack of positive attitude toward making this reality a social problem, especially by the state.

Indeed, the government has been ineffective in addressing this issue, only instructing local governments to encourage using existing measures such as public assistance. Against the backdrop of this difficult situation, in November 1998, Osaka Mayor Takafumi Isomura requested that Prime Minister Keizo Obuchi address the homeless issues by the national government. A "Liaison Conference on Homelessness" was established, consisting of relevant ministries and local governments (five ministries and six local governments), including Osaka City. In February 1999, the conference released a report, "Immediate Measures to Address the Homeless Problem." This report paved the way for subsequent measures to support the self-reliance of the homeless. In other words, it took about ten years from the time the problem was perceived to be serious in the field until a national-level response began to be taken.

The main feature of this report was that it organized the homeless into three categories and presented measures to deal with each of them. Those who are able and willing to work will be supported toward "self-reliance through employment." Elderly persons who cannot work are provided with support for "self-reliance through welfare and other forms of assistance." Those who refuse to receive such support and continue to live outdoors will be corrected or eliminated as "those who refuse to live in society." Many criticisms were made of this category, especially the third category and the measures taken by the government. These categories were to disappear in terms of representation (Tsumaki, 2003). However, the aims of this much-maligned report constituted the blueprint for the nation's subsequent policies to support the self-reliance of the homeless: Japan's first Homeless Law (Special Measures Act) was enacted in 2002, and the National Basic Policy was formulated in 2003.

In municipalities with many homeless people, homeless self-help centers (SHCs) were established. Measures for homelessness based on support for employment and self-reliance were initiated and have continued today. From the outset, however, it has been far from running smoothly. The jobs offered at the centers are basically Hello Work (public employment offices) jobs. It is extremely difficult for middle-aged and older workers who have already experienced exclusion from Hello Work jobs to find a new employment through Hello Work jobs. For example, from 2000 to 2002, 37.9% of those who left one of the SHCs in Osaka City found jobs and lived in apartments after leaving the center. Of these, 56.7% continued to work afterward (Mizuuchi and Keno, 2003). Many people were forced to live in the streets again after leaving the center.

Since then, the average age of the SHCs residents has become younger, in their mid-40s (Asahi Shimbun, February 11, 2010). This is thought to be because the SHCs can hardly function as a route to employment independence for middle-aged and older people, and therefore the target population for admission is narrowed down. For young people, this measure will have a certain effect. However, the role of this measure is limited, as the age structure of rough sleepers remains predominantly middle-aged and older.

One of the factors that contributed to the worsening of the nation's growing problem of homeless people was the operation of the welfare system, which did not accept applications from men under 65 years of age after deeming them capable of operating work. In Osaka City, in addition to this, another factor may be the fact that the city has not allowed people to receive public assistance at *doya*. Against the backdrop of the poor performance of the support for self-reliance through the SHCs, the Ministry of Health, Labor, and Welfare issued a notice dated July 31, 2003, instructing each welfare office to provide a security deposit when a homeless person secures a place to stay in a house. Subsequently, the number of households receiving public assistance in Osaka City increased, accelerating.

At that time, against the background of the inadequacy of the system, there were not a few people who continued to live outdoors without entering an institution, or who left an institution and then reentered the open-air shelter.[6] But, ordinances to regulate urban miscellaneous businesses making homeless living possible were enforced in various places.[7] Surviving in the open became more difficult than ever before.

As the project of inclusion progresses, the pressure of exclusion increases. This is probably because the blueprint of the measures for *homeless* itself is

---

6 Large-scale eviction occurred, according to Act on Subrogation of Administrative Acts, in Shirakawa Park, Nagoya in January 2005, in Utsubo Park and Osaka-jo Castle Park, Osaka in January 2006, and in Nagai Park, Osaka in February 2007. It should not be overlooked that national events are behind these administrative executions, such as "Expo 2005 Aichi, Japan" in Nagoya and "World Rose Convention" "IAAF World Championships" in Osaka. Haraguchi (2008) points out that the concept of "imagineering of cities" which drives the policies of sightseeing and events in cities, has been promoting the elimination of homeless people.

7 Such regulations are developed through interactions among various actors such as government, support groups, and local residents, and are implemented with institutional changes at the formal and informal levels. It is also implemented with institutional changes at both formal and informal levels, and the way it is implemented varies depending on the regional and historical context of the city. Therefore, there is a high degree of arbitrariness in the application of the system, and the homeless recyclers may or may not be subject to crackdowns. For details, see Hayashi (2007). In recent years, more stringent formal regulations have been created in some places.

strongly based on an abilities or achievement ideology. They *cannot uncon-ditionally accept* the opportunity to reintegrate a rough sleeper into society, which tends to be regarded as an object of "discomfort" and "nuisance." The SHCs, based on the value of "self-reliance through work" and institutionalized, make them "compete for effort" and function as a sorting mechanism to iden-tify those who are extremely inclusive or who should be excluded.[8]

Rough sleepers tend to be ambivalent. The positive side image of those who use the measure, *serious* and *trying hard* people becomes fodder for moral con-demnation of those who live on the streets. They are increasingly demonized on the streets.[9] At that time, inclusion projects, based on a typological under-standing of rough sleepers, inevitably reproduced the rough sleeper image as an exclusion category and intensify the pressure on exclusion. However, with the collapse of Lehman Brothers in the late 2000s, new welfare measures devel-oped as the number of people becoming homelessly expanded and became visible in other ways. Against the backdrop of the "dispatch cut-off" after the Lehman Shock, a notice issued on March 18, 2009, ensured that when an appli-cation for public assistance is received from a homeless person, the munic-ipality that received the application is responsible for the protection.[10] The increase in the number of welfare recipients has not only affected the number of people receiving public assistance from the homeless. The increase in the number of elderly households in Japanese society has also been impacted. And after the Lehman Shock, the increase in "other households" (which includes working-age households) in the welfare statistics has had a significant effect. This is against the backdrop of changes in the attributes of people who have become impoverished since the mid-2000s. This has been accompanied by structural changes in Japanese society, which have also forced a transforma-tion in the concept of homelessness in Japanese social policy.

---

8   Kitagawa (2006) described SHCs as "rough sleeper screening device to justify exclusion," which was based on interviews with people who left SHCs in Tokyo. In addition, in this chapter, Kitagawa revealed that rough sleepers had not been given sufficient explana-tions when they entered SHC, and that the Tokyo Metropolitan Government had not been given enough information to make a decision on "self-determination" which is the basis of "self-responsibility" as stated in the objectives of the policy.

9   See Young (1999).

10 Kitagawa (2021) examines a series of homeless measures taken by the government in Tokyo, and discusses how they were influenced and changed by the number of home-less people, the response of homelessness movement groups, and public opinion. The changes can be read as a process of oscillation between punitive and welfare measures.

5   People Sleeping and Waking in Urban Service Facilities

According to the Ministry of Health, Labor, and Welfare, the number of rough sleepers in Osaka City has decreased yearly from 6,603 in 2003 to 4,069 in 2007 and 1,208 in 2017. This is mainly due to the aforementioned *improvements* in how the welfare system is administered and the generous support provided by private support groups. Meanwhile, the streets continued to be filled with poor people who could no longer make ends meet. Around 2006–07, media reports uncovered young people living in extreme poverty, staying in Internet cafes, and engaging in precarious work represented by "the dispatch of temporary workers to daily-paid jobs". They were noted as the "New homelessness." This problem was called the "Internet Cafe Refugee Problem" in reference to the emerging business of the time. Around the same time, the NPO's counseling center in Kamagasaki recognized a gradual increase in the number of consultations not from middle-aged men in the construction industry, who had been the typical clients for some time, but from younger people working in the service industry other than the construction industry.

We conducted a survey in 2007 in Osaka City, interviewing 100 people who were/are staying at Internet cafes, etc.[11] The basic attributes of the survey respondents were as follows. Since this is not a sampling survey, caution should be exercised in interpreting the figures. Gender: 96 males, four females. Age: 1 teenager, 22 in their 20s, 53 in their 30s, 16 in their 40s, 6 in their 50s, one over 60, and 1 unknown. The number of respondents who were born in their home prefecture (place of residence upon graduation) was the largest in Osaka Prefecture (39 respondents), although the number of respondents who were born in Osaka Prefecture was spread across the country. The following prefectures were followed by Hokkaido (6), Nara (5), Aichi, Hyogo, Wakayama, Fukuoka (4), and Tokyo (3). By region, the Kinki region had 54 respondents. There was a slight bias toward western Japan. The survey was conducted in the vicinity of Internet cafes and other service establishments in downtown Osaka City by asking store users at the start and end of the late-night low-priced hours.

Only a few of those surveyed had been using Internet cafes as their residence place for a long time. Many of them were working under poor working conditions, often as day laborers. Their employment careers are roughly summarized below. About 60% of the first jobs were in production processes and labor work

---

11   For details, see NPO Kamagasaki and Osaka City University (2008). All cases cited in this section are extracted from the life histories included in this report. All quotations have been rearranged for this publication by omitting parts in the middle of the text.

in manufacturing, food processing, and other industries (from large companies such as automobile manufacturing to small businesses such as spinning). The construction industry had five workers. Other workers scattered among the workers were transportation assistants and drivers in the transportation industry, pachinko parlor workers, salespeople selling educational materials, newspaper deliverers, and restaurant workers (including nightlife workers).

In terms of their employment status at their first job, 56 were in regular employment, 29 were in irregular work (including four dispatched workers), 3 were family employees, and ten were unknown/other. Although many of them were initially employed regularly, the nature of their work, although regular, was not necessarily stable, as many of them were similar to irregular workers. Some left their hometowns when they took their first jobs, but many found employment where they had lived when they graduated. While there was a scattering of those who could find new work after leaving their first job, some were able to re-enter the workforce with full-time treatment, but many entered the non-regular or temporary labor market at the stage of leaving their first job. Many of them had continued to work in non-regular or temporary employment, but there were a few cases where they repeated non-regular and formal work. Their work careers converge into poorly treated jobs as they change jobs. Most were working directly, but a small number of more recent jobs involved dispatch work (registered or spot dispatch).

Many of the jobs they have held (and are currently holding) involve work in factories, distribution centers, and warehouses. Their work includes assembly, inspection, sorting, packing, and transportation on production lines. Day labor in the construction industry was also common. There were also many day laborers for set-up and take-down work at events, which often take place on Saturdays and Sundays, and temporary heavy lifting work such as moving, which is subject to seasonal fluctuations, and guardsmen. At the time the survey was conducted, a Toyota-affiliated auto parts manufacturing plant in Aichi Prefecture was cutting dispatch workers in large numbers. We met three men who had worked at the same plant. Case 31 describes one of them.

> *Case 31:* "In Hokkaido, it is standard to have no work in winter. The area where I was born is a Self-Defense Forces town, and there are no other jobs available. Everyone goes to Sapporo (in the city center), Tomakomai, or Chitose to work." Since he quit his job in the winter, Mr. M registered with a temporary employment agency. He was introduced to a subcontracting company of a major automobile manufacturer in Aichi Prefecture.
>
> "I had an interview in Hokkaido. I was told that the person in charge in Aichi was waiting for me at Centrair (Central Japan International

Airport), so I flew there." "In winter, all the job offers to come out at once. Most of the jobs are in the Tokai and Kinki regions." He worked on a line specializing in AT/transmissions for cars at this company. He said the working conditions were easy. "I had reasonable breaks, and it was better than a bad construction job," he said. "The pay was fair, and I got two days off a week." Workers worked an extra two hours if they worked the day shift and an extra hour of overtime if they worked the night shift. Social insurance was in place. He was also able to send money home to his parents. But after a year and a half on the job, "We were being restructured; 50 to 60 people were forced to quit altogether." He regrets a bit that, at this time, he was so ticked off about being restructured that he popped out without any formal procedures about social insurance. One year ago (2006), in the spring, he was restructured. Upon being restructured at this company, Mr. M headed for Osaka.

Late 30s, male

The non-regular work they performed was precarious, with both employment and unemployment. The man in Case 42 complained of irregular working hours and, in Case 27, of irregular working days.

Case 42: He worked as a temporary worker for one and a half years. The work schedule is two shifts. At the beginning of the contract, he worked from 8:00 AM to 5:00 PM but had to work overtime for about 2.5 hours every day until 8:00 PM. "When I signed the contract, I was told that I would have two 10-minute breaks, one at 10:00 and the other at 3:00, but I found that I had a 5-minute break when I went in. Of the 10 minutes, take a 5-minute break and use the remaining 5 minutes to prepare to return to the line. In the end, there is only a five-minute break." He was told that he would have one hour for a lunch break, but he was given five minutes to return to the line.

Early 40s, male

Case 27: He works one to three days a week through a temp agency. His job is sorting and shipping at a bakery, and he works the night shift from 8:30 p.m. to 8:30 a.m. He is paid 7,000 to 8,000 yen per day. The daily wage is 7,000 to 8,000 yen, and the number of days of work is three days in most weeks and sometimes only one day in fewer weeks (so his monthly income is far less than 100,000 yen).

Late 30s, male

Many of those engaged in time-limited employment labor for many years are experiencing intense regional migration. Their need to secure permanent housing must diminish. Tired of this kind of life, some people said, "No more dormitories or live-ins. I am tired of being used by others."

> *Case 67:* He had his first temp job in Okinawa. The same temp agency introduced him to his next career. The next job was in Hiroshima Prefecture. The cost of his travel to the next job was deducted from his salary. He registered with several temp-staff agencies. "I don't remember where I went because I was moving from one place to another all over Japan. The only places I remember are Okinawa, Hiroshima, Fukushima, Fukui, and Nagoya. There was no social insurance when I was working as a dispatched worker."
>
> Late 30s, male

Kazuya Sakurada, a member of this study, states that the paradoxical situation is that the poor and precarious work they are doing is causing them to work to rebuild their crumbling livelihoods, which in turn is causing their livelihoods to collapse (Sakurada, 2008). In many cases, workers were forced to bear various necessary expenses or were overcharged for job referrals out of their salaries.

> *Case 48:* He contacts the temp agency by cell phone during the day. If there is work there, he will be got about the next day's meeting place and time. The temp agency seldom contacts him for work. Each time, the workplace is different, often working in a warehouse or sorting packages. He works in Osaka and Kobe. Slightly more work is done in Kobe. The daily wage is around 7,000 yen, but the client doesn't pay transportation expenses. For example, a round trip to Kobe costs about 1,500 yen, plus 250 yen for insurance and 140 yen for taxes. In addition, that tax is doubled, and 280 yen is deducted for overtime work. In the end, only about 5,000 yen remains in his pocket. Work is not always available every day, and "it is still better if I work 3–4 times a week."
>
> Late 20s, male

> *Case 84:* Because he was a live-in worker, dormitory expenses (and food expenses in some places) were deducted from their salaries. However, the worst was temp agency X. Two workers lived together in a 2DK room, and the dormitory fee was 100,000 yen per person. This was just for the room,

and in addition, food, utilities, and other expenses were charged. "Lucky if he had any salary left over," so he was in debt even if he worked, and he had to "pay back the debt with their bodies" by working overtime.

Late 30s, male

Unfavorable situations invite more unfavorable conditions. We met some who ended up in the vice, some who experienced decoys posing as female users of dating sites, and some who were hired managers of illegal sex stores.

Case 35: He worked part-time for a campaign to distribute free broadband modems and as a registered temp (paid daily) for the famous temp agency G. He Also did "vice-type" telemarketing. The salary was paid weekly. He was selling telephones or intercoms to corporations. He made phone calls from every page of the Town Pages. "I did a lot of different jobs and even made some sales that I shouldn't have done four or five years ago. I also did some sales work that I shouldn't have done four or five years ago." The job posting said something that sounded good, like, "Anyone can do it!" And "300,000/month" sounded good, but it was a *pushy* sales pitch for cleaning up plumbing messes, termite extermination, etc. It was a full piecework job, but "I did pretty well." However, "I felt guilty and quit after about two weeks."

Late 20s, male

When they lose their jobs due to poor conditions, their unemployment is often dismissed as their own fault.

Case 84: "When I complained to the company about the different treatment from the job information, I was told, 'Who would believe such a thing? Of course, it's all a lie!' I complained to the job security office and was told, 'We can't know what you're talking about' (inside information). I went to the Labor Standards Bureau and was told, 'If you keep saying that, there will be no more jobs in this world.'"

Late 30s, male

Some had suffered work-related accidents under unfair conditions but could not find work now because their employers did not pay any medical expenses. Others complained of mental exhaustion due to long working hours during their regular employment and stated that they would prefer to work in a non-regular job even if the conditions were not good.

They use capsule hotels, saunas, video screening rooms, etc., depending on their work, money, and other circumstances at the time. The Internet cafes initially highlighted by the media—available for around 1,000 yen per night—are only one of the last-ditch options for barely supporting a life of precarious work, living in unstable housing, and avoiding homelessness. Many have already been camping out, and their lives are often intertwined with camping out. Their lives are very similar to the "rough sleeping waiting for work" of the day laborers in Kamagasaki. On the other hand, many of them expressed avoidance of or unfamiliarity with Kamagasaki and feared staying outdoors. "I know Kamagasaki, but I have never been there because of the image I have had since I was a child. I am from Osaka, so I have a strong 'bad image' of Nishinari (Kamagasaki)" (late 40s, male). "I have never lived rough. I don't want to go that far" (late teens, male). "Even if I could get a job, I don't want a temporary day job. I can't think of any job that doesn't provide a stable income. Especially, I don't want to work as a construction day laborer. I don't want to and won't fit in with the lifestyle of Nishinari workers" (late 30s, male). Etc. In terms of subjective awareness and perception, they may be in a different phase from the rough sleepers. However, they are very close in terms of how their lives are manifested.

This transformation of urban society began with the gradual formation of "small unit labor markets" in various parts of urban society since the 1980s due to the shift to a service economy and changes in the way labor is procured (Shimodaira, 1988: 87). And the spread of cell phones and the Internet has certainly reduced the need for places like Kamagasaki. The figure of people sleeping and waking in downtown urban service facilities or dormitories is similar to that of people who slept and woke in the *doyas* of Kamagasaki. Unlike rough sleepers, their poverty is difficult to see. Invisible homeless people, hiding in their own spaces, have spread throughout urban society (Tsutsumi, 2010: 22).

Not all the people I met were with a residence. During an early morning investigation downtown, I met a woman, estimated to be in her 30s or 40s, coming out of an Internet cafe. She was single and lived alone in an apartment in an area that required a 40+ minute subway ride to downtown. She was working three part-time cleaning jobs in an office building. She said, "That's barely enough to live on." She was scheduled to work at a building near Osaka Station that day. Since she could not make it to the start of that workday from home, she uses a low-cost plan at an Internet cafe every week. Thus, in addition to the homeless people identified in this study, there are also people like her who maintain apartment living but whose working conditions and working environment have eroded their lives, creating unstable workers and unstable residents who *live* by using the downtown area of the city.[12]

6   Inclusion and Exclusion through Social Policy

With the outbreak of the internet cafe refugee problem, the term homeless, which had previously been used only for rough sleepers, was separated from the government definition to include those who cannot work or live stably. In addition, during Lehman Shock in 2008, many temporary workers, mainly in the manufacturing industry, were laid off and forced to sleep outdoors. From the end of December 2008 to early January 2009, NPOs and labor unions in Tokyo set up a shelter in Hibiya Park in front of the Ministry of Health, Labor, and Welfare. This activity attracted public attention and was discussed in the Diet. As a result, poverty became a social issue. Makoto Yuasa of Moyai, a Tokyo-based NPO that supports the needy that was at the center of this movement, says that a combination of education, corporate welfare, family welfare, public welfare, and exclusion from themselves have led people to poverty and homelessness (Yuasa, 2008). This paradigmatic explanation of social exclusion encouraged people to view the homeless issues as an extension of the general poverty problem.

However, people's perceptions of homelessness—rough sleepers have not changed, reflecting how they think about it. The homeless issues are an extension of the non-regular employment problem. And the pain of non-regular employment can be traced back to the history of industries that relied heavily on non-regular employments, such as the coal and construction industries. As the problem has expanded from rough sleepers to homelessness in the broadest sense, homelessness has come to include not only the original rough sleepers but also middle-aged and young adults and even women.

When poverty becomes an open social issue, some active intervention by the state is necessary. Self-support for the needy became law in 2013 and started in 2015. This made it mandatory for local governments to set up consultation services for the poor. Under this system, local governments must support individuals early before receiving public assistance through home visits and other means and create a self-support plan tailored to their circumstances. In addition, communities need "community development," such as strengthening

---

12   Since private rooms are now rare in Internet cafes, it is no longer possible to stay in the same style as in the past.

local networks and developing social resources that can help support them. This project has not yet worked effectively in many municipalities (Sakurai, 2016). However, given that there has been no policy that calls for the inclusion of the needy in the community, it is fair to say that the poverty program in Japan has finally begun.

However, it should be noted that this system, which was established as a new safety net to support the poor in preparation for the implementation of public assistance, was also intended to reduce expenditures under the welfare system. Even when a homeless person can receive public assistance, as Yuki points out in Chapter 10, there are still cases where it is merely hidden away in an institution, ultimately ignoring their right to self-determination.

It should also be noted again that the problems of Japan's industrial structure and labor market, which are the causes of homelessness and other forms of poverty, retreated into the background. In creating this system, the government and private homeless support groups set up a council to develop new measures to address poverty. The insistence that poverty should be viewed not only in terms of economic deprivation, as has been the case in the past, but also focusing on social isolation provided both good and bad suggestions in the formulation of this policy.

7   Conclusion

Construction day labor was the primary source of the city's rough sleepers in the past. By the demands of capital, day laborers traveled around the country by themselves, working and losing their jobs daily. Their lives, characterized by non-family and non-settlement, could have been homelessness in the broad sense of the term. However, the state has not considered that the construction industry is dependent on creating large numbers of people who are forced to live this way as a problem. Therefore, the concept of homelessness in Japan has been limited to those who live and sleep on the streets, whether in urban communities, local governments, or the national government. The limited definition was also reflected in Japan's homeless law.

The sheer determination of what is the social problem itself already suggests the direction that should be taken to solve the problem. These various actors have been concerned with this limited definition because homelessness has been perceived not as a matter of their survival and human rights but primarily based on the nuisance that accompanies the visibility of their presence in public spaces. However, shortly after enacting the homeless law, it has become less meaningful to be concerned with such definitions, at least in understanding the "homeless phenomenon" about the sources from which they are discharged.

In the 1990s and 2000s, the limitations of Japanese Fordism came to be pointed out, and the post-Fordism system began to take over. The expansion of non-regular employment since the 1990s has proceeded in the form of the state responding to the requests of management groups of large corporations (this was most symbolically demonstrated by the gradual revision of the Worker Dispatching Act). As a result, the precarious employment and unstable residence that was once mainly generated by the construction industry has expanded into many occupations, including manufacturing and service industries. They also tend to live in housing with instability, such as company dormitories. If they lose their jobs, they must leave their housing immediately. Although the construction industry is still the main source of the homeless, it has become more diversified than in the past.

It was also apparent that the forms of existence of the precariously employed and precariously housed population thus identified are also diversifying. In addition to those discharged to the streets, the study also produced people who are shuttling between the streets and urban service facilities and those who barely maintain their lives in apartments but whose living arrangements are set in working conditions that could become precarious at any moment.

The precariousness of their employment and living conditions can overlap with the problematic situation of day laborers and homeless people in Kamagasaki, who was once the most despised target of urban society. The concept of bottom-workers is needed because, while the main source of homeless people has been day labor, the working poor, part of the precariat, the underclass, and the urban poor are about to be added to the mix. Here, the homeless issue in Japan has come to resemble the situation experienced in the US in the 1980s. As if to mock the country's still unchanged definition of homelessness, civil society is trying to revamp the concept of homelessness so that it can be taken more broadly.

COVID-19 has brought to the fore the downward pressure on bottom workers that was shown in Chapter 2, especially among female non-regular workers in the service sector. Ren Onishi of NPO Moyai, Tokyo, has been distributing foodstuffs to needy people near the Tokyo Metropolitan Government Office in Shinjuku Ward since the Corona disaster and said that the number of people who gathered there in 2020 was about 100, but by 2022, more than 500 people had gathered. Before the Corona disaster, the consultants were mainly people who were homeless or in internet cafes and whose income did not reach the level of public assistance. However, after the Corona disaster, the number of people who are now increasing are those who have a place to live and whose income is slightly above the welfare level—people who should have been out of the reach of support groups, he said. Many are part-time workers in their 20s to 40s, and women are prominent. Those who now have jobs are considered to be financially independent, and because there are very few government support programs available to them, they are having a hard time finding support (Nishinippon Shimbun, May 3, 2022).

Japanese society has not lost its traditional sense of discrimination against those who are forced to be homeless. Do we see the problems of homeless people as "their problems, different from ours," or as "the problems of members of the same society"? Such a shift in perception is required of us. Here, too, we can see the need for the bottom-worker concept to understand social problems and, by extension, make appropriate social policies.[13]

References

Aoki H (2000) *Gendai nihon no toshi kaso* [Urban Underclass in Modern Japan]. Tokyo: Akashishoten.

Berger P and Luckman T (1967) *The Social Construction of Reality*. New York: Penguin Press.

Fukuhara H and Nakayama T (1999) Hiyatoi-roudousha no koureika nojukuka mondai [Aging and homelessness of day laborers]. *The Journal of Socual Policy and Labor Studies* 1: 21–38.

Haraguchi T (2003) Yoseba no seisan-katei ni okeru basho no kouchiku to seido-teki jissen [Construction of Place and Institutional Practice in the Process of the 'Production' of Yoseba:The Case of Kamagasaki, Osaka City]. *The Human Geographical Society of Japan* 56(2): 121–143.

Haraguchi T (2008) Toshi no imajiniaringu to nojukuseikatsusha no haijo: 1980-nendai ikou no Osaka wo jirei toshite [Imagineering of cities and the exclusion of homeless people: the case of Osaka since the l980's]. *Ryukoku Journal of Economic Studies* 47(5): 29–46.

Haraguchi T (2009) Toshi-shakai no bundan wo yomitoku [Deciphering the fragmentation of urban society]. In: Takenaka et al. (eds) *Jimbun chiri gaku* [Human Geography]. Kyoto: Minerva Shobo.

Hayashi M (2007) Seisei suru chiiki no kyōkai—naibuka shita 'hōmuresu mondai' to seidohenka no rōkarithi [The emerging boundaries of regional society: geographical diffusion of homeless street people and institutional changes at the local level]. *Soshioroji* 52(1): 53–69.

---

13   This chapter is based on Tsutsumi (2010; 2019) with significant additions.

Hirakawa S (2005) "Ishitsu na tasha" tono kakawari [Relationship with 'heterogeneous others']. In: Inoue S and Funatsu M (eds) *Jiko to tasha no shakaigaku* [*The Sociology of Self and Others*]. Tokyo: Yuhikaku: 227–243.

Iwata M (1997) Rojou no hitobito: Shinjuku1995nen-96nen [The homeless in Shinjuku 1995–1996]. *The Journal of Social Sciences and Humanity* 13: 73–99.

Kitagawa Y (2006) Nojukusya no saisenbetsu katei: Tōkyo-to'Jiritsu Shien Center' riyoukeikensya kikitorichosa kara [Reclassification process for homeless people: from interviews with experienced users of the Tokyo Metropolitan Government 'Center for Supporting Independence']. In: Kariya A (ed.), *Furachi na kibo: Hōmuresu/ yoseba wo meguru shakaigaku* [Vicious Hopes: Sociology on Homeless and Yoseba]. Kyoto: Shoraisha: 119–160.

Kitagawa Y (2021) Homeless policy as a policy for controlling poverty in Tokyo: considering the relationship between welfare measures and punitive measures. *Critical Sociology* 47(1):91–110.

Ministry of Health Labor and Welfare (MHLW/Kousei roudou shou) (2009) *Kousei roudou hakusho: kurashi to shakai no antei ni muketa jiritsu shien* [White Paper on Health, Labour and Welfare: Support for self-reliance for the stability of life and society].

Mizuuchi T (2005) Minority/Shuuen kara mita sengo Osaka no kuukan to shakai [Society and Space of the Minority and Marginal People in the Post-War Osaka]. The Anuals of Japan Association for Urban Sociology 23: 32–56.

Mizuuchi T and Keno T (2003) Osaka shinai no jiritsu shien centā: nyushosya taishousya no keikou, tokuchou bunseki [Self-support center in Osaka: analysis of trends and characteristics of residents and retirees]. *Shelter-less* 17: 80–101.

NPO Kamagasaki and Osaka City University (2008) *Jakunen fuantei shurou fuantei jukyosha kikitori chousa houkokusho*[Report on Interview Survey on Young Unstable Workers and People Living in Unstable Housing].

Osaka shiritsu daigaku toshi kankyou mondai kenkyukai (Osaka City University Institute on Urban Environmental Problems) (2001) *Nojuku-seikatsusha (Hōmuresu) ni kansuru sougouteki Chousa kenkyu Houkokusho*[Report on the general survey of rough sleepers (homelessness)].

Sakurada K (2008) Fuantei-roudou ni okeru jikan kuukan seikei no hatan [Time, space, and livelihood disruption in precarious work]. In: NPO Kamagasaki and Osaka City University (2008) *Jakunen fuantei shurou fuantei jukyosha kikitori chousa houkokusho* [Report on Interview Survey on Young Unstable Workers and People Living in Unstable Housing].

Sakurai J (2016) Chihou-jititai niyoru seikatu-konkyusha jiritsu shien seido no jissi niokeru kadai: Osakafu Hirakatashi no jirei ni motozuite [Curent situation and problems with self-reliance support program for needy persons provided by municipalities: case study of Hirakata City in Osaka Prefecture]. *Ritsumeikan Social Sciences Review* 52(3): 19–34.

Shima K (1999) *Gendai nihon no nojuku-seikatsusha* [Homeless People in Contemporary Japan]. Tokyo: Gakubunsya.

Shima K (2001) Roudou-shijou toshite no Kamagasaki no genjou to sono "henyou" [Labour market of today's Kamagasaki and its "transformation"]. *Jimbun Kenkyu* 53(3): 23–49.

Shimodaira H (1988) Koyou-hendouki no naka no yoseba [Yoseba under the change of labor market]. *Yoseba* 1: 74–88.

Toshi seikatsu kenkyukai(Urban Life Study Group) (2000) *Heisei 11-nendo rojou seikatsusha jittai chousa* [Survey on the conditions of the homeless].

Tsumaki S (2001) Ikiru [To Live]. In: Morita Y (eds) *Rakusou: Nojuku ni ikiru* [Dropping: Living as Homelessness]. Osaka: Nikkei Osaka PR: 124–144.

Tsumaki S (2003) Nojuku seikatsu: "shakai seikatsu no kyohi" toiu sentaku [Preference for homelessness categorized as "refusal of a decent civic life"]. *Soshioroji* 48(1): 21–37.

Tsutsumi K (2010) Hōmuresu sutadhīzu heno syoutai [Invitation to homeless studies]. In: Aoki H (eds) *Homeless Studies*. Kyoto: Minerva Shobo: 1–29.

Tsutsumi K (2019) Toshin kaiki suru Osaka no hinkon [Poverty in Osaka, of which population has come back to the center]. In: Ajisaka M et al (eds) *Samayoeru dai-toshi Osaka* [Osaka, a Wandering Metropolis]. Tokyo: Toshindo: 263–278.

Yuasa M (2008) *Han hinkon* [Anti-Poverty]. Tokyo: Iwanami Shoten.

Young J (1999) *The Exclusive Society—Social Exclusion, Crime and Difference in Late Modernity*. New York: SAGE.

CHAPTER 10

Displacement and Entrapment of Bottom People in Tokyo

Urban Regeneration and Slow Violence

Tsubasa Yuki

Abstract

This chapter illustrates displacement/entrapment of the bottom people in Tokyo, especially those experiencing homelessness and taking Public Assistance (PA), in relation to the urban regeneration of Tokyo and the transformation of the welfare system since the 1990s. Drawing on 27 semi-structured interviews and case files of visitors to Moyai, an NGO supporting homeless and other impoverished people in Tokyo, this chapter demonstrates that PA applicants without secure housing are increasingly expelled to suburbanizing shelters where the residents cannot access to basic services and infrastructures, and that San'ya, a former day labor market provides an alternative for those people. Moreover, this chapter also shows that people in suburban shelters and San'ya area are both forced to be immobile due to a decrease in the number of affordable housing and to a restrictive operation of PA system. It has been argued that the urban regeneration since the 1980s in Tokyo has not caused overt conflict such as massive direct displacement of the low-income households. However, the main argument of the chapter is that such a long-term shift in the socio-spatial structure of Tokyo has caused 'slow violence' against the bottom peoples, which curtails their capabilities of mobility.

1 Displacement/Entrapment of the Bottom People in a Regenerating City

This chapter aims to illustrate the displacement/entrapment of the bottom people in Tokyo, especially those who experienced homelessness[1] and taking Public Assistance (PA), the general and comprehensive social welfare system

---

[1] In Japan, the term 'homeless' usually denotes rough sleeper on public space such as park, street, and riverside. However, in relation to the PA system, those who do not have secure housing tenure (e.g., those staying in cyber cafes) are treated differently from those having

in Japan in relation to the urban regeneration of Tokyo and the transformation of the welfare system since the 1990s.

The population recovery, often called the 'back-to-the-city' movement, accompanied by the socio-spatial transformations of Tokyo, has attracted extensive attention from sociologists and geographers in the country, leading to debates on distinctive characteristics of the process compared to gentrifications in other cities (Hashimoto 2021, Machimura 2021, Shimomura 2016, Shimomura and Igarashi 2017, Hashimoto and Asakawa 2019, etc.).

The regeneration process of Tokyo since the 1990s is not identical to classical cases of gentrification in Western cities. In contrast to those cities such as London and New York, Tokyo did not experience a significant counter-urbanization process in the 1970s and 1980s due to a relatively robust economic development and the persistence of small-scale industries in the inner-city area. It should be also noted that the population decline in the 1990s was not only due to the industrial restructuring but also caused by the unusual rise in property prices triggered by financial deregulation, which was followed by new-build gentrification rather than large-scale displacement of existing residents (Lützeler 2008).

Another important feature of urban restructuring in Tokyo is that it has proceeded over a relatively long span. According to Hashimoto (2021: 43), "There was a time difference in the succession of the three processes: the decline of the old middle class since 1980, the decline of small capitalists since 1990, and the increase of the new middle class since 2000. Therefore, this process should be called 'time difference gentrification'" (43). He calls this long-term process the 'bloodless revolution':

> Although some conflicts did appear over land acquisition and redevelopment, on the whole the changes proceeded peacefully and without a tangible class struggle. Change continues today. The old classes are being replaced with new ones, transforming the class and socio-spatial structure of the 23 wards into a formation that is more suitable for a global city. This can be called gentrification, in the form of a bloodless revolution. (47)

To be sure, he is not optimistic about the prospect of the regeneration process as he expresses concern about the disappearance of the 'underclass'—those

---

secure tenure. This chapter adopts the wider definition of homelessness since it has a crucial importance in the operation of PA system.

in precarious employment status—in the Core City could occur in the future. Nevertheless, while his argument on the changes in the class composition in Tokyo since the 1980s seems to be robust and insightful, the argument on the 'bloodless revolution' poses two problems. For one thing, recent arguments on the concept of displacement have been largely absent from his argument. Particularly important here is the idea of indirect displacement.[2] Secondly, in his argument, little attention has been paid to the people excluded even from the 'underclass' such as homeless and unemployed PA recipients.[3] So, it must be questioned that what has happened to the bottom people excluded from his analysis amid the 'bloodless revolution'? Is there any other form of violence than 'disappearance' or physical displacement? To address these questions, this chapter aims to illustrate the experience of bottom people during the regeneration process using an extended idea of displacement and violence.

1.1   *Displacement, Entrapment, and Slow Violence*
The concept of displacement was one of the core elements in Glass' (1964) description of the socio-spatial change in London. While in the 1990s and 2000s gentrification studies tended to focus on characteristics of gentrifiers rather than displacement of residents, the influential papers of Slater (2006, 2009) urged researchers to revisit the now classic study of Marcuse (1986) on the relationships between abandonment, gentrification, and displacement. Marcuse's (1986) idea of indirect displacement (displacement pressure and exclusionary displacement) has been particularly influential in various areas of gentrification studies including retail gentrification (Gonzalez and Dawson 2016 and Hubbard 2017) and new-build gentrification (Boddy 2007, Davidson and Lees 2005, 2010), which spurred academic as well as political debates on the nature of displacement and urban changes.

There are some recent attempts to extend his argument further. The idea of displacement pressure enables us to look at the perception of changing landscape by residents who are not (yet) physically displaced. To fully recognize emotional or psychological attachment to place and dwelling, Atkinson

---

2   It can be said that his argument does not take displacement into account since he does not give any definition of displacement while he defines gentrification as "the replacement of the inhabitants of a particular district in an urban area by superior classes or classes with more modern characteristics of the same rank."(Hashimoto 2021: 37).

3   More recent studies on the restructuring of Tokyo also disregard harmful effects other than direct displacement and ignore the experience of the least well-off (Ueno and Nakano 2017, Kim 2013, and Kohama 2017). A notable exception is Kimura (2019) who argues displacement of homeless people in Shibuya amid a large-scale public-private-partnership redevelopment project orchestrated by the ward office.

(2015) uses the term 'un-homing', "a form of violence that removes the sense of belonging to a particular community or home-space" (Elliot-Cooper et al. 2020: 533). The above formulation of the concept, however, presumes that people have been embedded in their community and/or home in favorable manners before the displacement in question. This is clearly not always the case. For example, highly mobile people including homeless may not have such social relations to attach themselves to in the first place (Kitagawa 2001 and Yamakita 2006). Furthermore, for people caught in illicit relations (e.g., those abused and/or discriminated against in their home and/or community) and/or environments (e.g., precarious housing conditions), moving out of one's place could be a better option. In short, staying put in a certain community or place may not be a preferable option for everyone.

This drives us to extend the idea of 'exclusionary displacement'.[4] The concept concerns the affordability of the residential area, which also implies "that poorer households may become 'trapped' in their current housing as the pool of options available to them in the local area decreases" (Easton et al. 2020: 291). In this light, we should include not only forced mobility (displacement) but forced immobility (entrapment) in socio-spatial injustices (DeVerteuil 2011, 2012). In this chapter, our primary focus is on entrapment, which is almost totally absent from the literature on the recent spatial restructuring of Tokyo, although displacement and entrapment are often interrelated.

Another important insight of Marcuse's (1986) argument is that displacement should be understood as a process rather than a single event disembedded from temporality. This indicates that displacement/entrapment could appear as 'slow violence'. According to Nixon, slow violence is 'a violence that is neither spectacular nor instantaneous, but rather incremental and accretive, its calamitous repercussions playing out across a range of temporal scales' (Nixon, 2011: 2). Thus, while direct displacement might appear as a conflictual event in a particular moment, indirect displacement and entrapment might progress in a slow and less conflictual ('peaceful') manner within the transformation of socio-spatial structures ranging across different regional scales.

1.2   Methods and the Structure of the Chapter

To address this form of violence amid the urban regeneration in Tokyo, we need to look at Tokyo as a whole and a particular place within the region.

---

4   Originally, Marcuse (1986: 206) uses the concept "[w]hen one household vacates a housing unit voluntarily and that unit is then gentrified or abandoned so that another similar household is prevented from moving in, the number of units available to the second household in that housing market is reduced".

Here, we limit our focus on San'ya area located in the inner city of Tokyo, since San'ya, a former "Yoseba"[5] area where single male day laborers were concentrated, has a close relationship to the dramatic increase in the homeless population in Tokyo in the 1990s and a distinctive way the PA system is operated in this region. This chapter uses interview data collected by a group of researchers including the author who are members of a project of comparative studies of six cities across the globe: New York, Paris, Tokyo, Manila, Mexico City, and Nairobi.[6] To date, we have met 27 informants and we conducted 1 to 2 hour(s) long semi-structured interview with each of them. We explained them in advance the aim of this project and how the interview data are used. We recorded our interview when they gave us permission, whose transcripts are anonymized. Among them, 22 persons are male, 4 persons are female, and one person identifies themselves as A-gender.

Additionally, this chapter uses the case files of people who visited Moyai Support Centre for Independent Living[7] (hereafter, Moyai), an NGO supporting the homeless and other impoverished people in Tokyo. These cases include 941 persons who visited Moyai between October 2018 and March 2021 and gave Moyai permission to use the case files for research and advocacy. They are also anonymized and partly modified to protect their privacy and security. The gender composition of visitors excluding the 4 unknown cases is as the following: cisgender male 722 (77.1%); cisgender female 206 (22.0%); nonconforming gender 9 (1.0%).

The next section provides an overview of the urban regeneration process in Tokyo and the reorganization of the PA system which became highly dependent on private shelters. The relationship between the suburbanization of low-cost accommodations and the enduring existence of San'ya for the (male) bottom people will be pointed out in the third section. Section 4 investigates specific aspects of entrapment of the bottom people in relation to the urban

---

5 "Yoseba" can be generally defined as an unregulated day labor market often located in inner city. The three biggest Yoseba areas include San'ya in Tokyo, Kamagasaki in Osaka, and Kotobuki-Cho in Kanagawa which absorbed large amount of intranational migrants in the latter half of the 20th century. They worked primarily as construction workers and/or dockworkers indispensable to the post-war rapid development of Japanese economy.

6 This research project aims to analyze hardships imposed by neoliberalized and globalized contemporary capitalism on the bottom people in different continents with particular focus on their labor, livelihoods, and lifeworlds. The project team is composed of six working groups for respective cities and a general team that overviews the whole process of the project.

7 https://www.npomoyai.or.jp/english/overview.

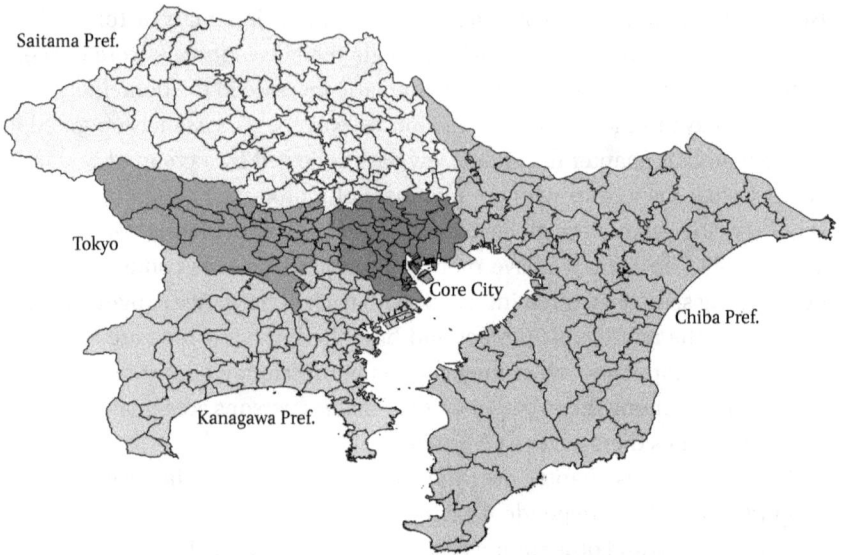

FIGURE 10.1 Tokyo metropolitan region
SOURCE: DIGITAL NATIONAL LAND INFORMATION (CREATED BY THE AUTHOR
USING QGIS 3.6.3)

regeneration and the welfare system, which will be followed by a concluding section.

2   Regeneration of Tokyo and Recomposition of Welfare Systems

The Tokyo Metropolitan Region (TMR) consists of four prefectures of Tokyo, Kanagawa, Saitama, and Chiba, which has more than 36 million inhabitants. The suburban part of the TMR covers the western part of Tokyo (Tama region) and three other prefectures. The 23 autonomous special wards are considered to be the Core City of Tokyo (Figure 10.1). Within the Core City, Chiyoda, Chuo, and Minato Wards are conventionally called the city center. San'ya area, to which we will turn to in the next section, is also located in the inner area of the Core City (Figure 10.2).

2.1   *Regeneration of Tokyo and Decreasing Affordable Housing*
In the post-war Japanese society, the construction, housing, and real estate sectors played a leading role in boosting economic development. "The 'iron triangle' between the Liberal Democratic Party (LDP), government bureaucrats and

Special wards
1. Chiyoda
2. Chuo
3. Minato
4. Shinjuku
5. Bunkyo
6. Taito
7. Sumida
10. Meguro
11. Ota
12. Setagaya
13. Shibuya
14. Nakano
15. Suginami
16. Toshima
17. Kita
18. Arakawa
19. Itabashi
20. Nerima
21. Adsushika
22. Katsushika
23. Edogawa

FIGURE 10.2 Core City and San'ya area
SOURCE: DIGITAL NATIONAL LAND INFORMATION AND NATIONAL CENSUS
(CREATED BY THE AUTHOR USING QGIS 3.6.3)

the construction sector, which constituted the political core of the developmental state system, was devoted to encouraging mass housing construction" (Hirayama and Izuhara 2018: 20). Although the economic crisis in the 1990s drove the central government to neoliberalization of housing policy, the close relationship between the government and construction industry has been not abandoned. Rather, while the government rolled back from direct housing provision, its strategy for economic recovery has been highly dependent on the construction industry, which caused urban regeneration and decreasing housing affordability since the 2000s.

During the asset bubble in the 1980s triggered by financial deregulations and increasing demand for offices in the city center, Tokyo saw a significant loss of its population. As the asset bubble collapsed in the early-1990s, both national and metropolitan governments adopted entrepreneurial urban policies including the deregulation of land planning, public subsidies to private developers, financial liberalization, and the securitization of real estate to promote regeneration of Tokyo (Machimura 2021, Hirayama 2020). Thus, Tokyo was designated as an economic engine to get out of the recession (Takagi 2016, Ueno 2010).

Within this climate, the central part of Tokyo saw its resurgence in population growth since the mid-1990s. As the re-urbanization process goes on, the estimated income distribution has become more centripetal configuration, although the northern part of the inner city still shows the concentration of low-income households working as non-regular workers (see Asakawa 2023 in this book for a more detailed analysis of the distribution of the bottom workers in Tokyo). It must be also noted that while average income has been decreasing, the ratio of low-income households in the TMR has increased from 1990 to 2010 (Hashimoto and Hirahara 2019).

Amid the socio-spatial restructuring of Tokyo, housing affordability has been declining. In the post-bubble era, housing policies have also been reformed into market-oriented ones[8] (Hirayama and Izuhara 2018). While the provision of public housing had been already marginalized in the post-war Japan housing policies, the new construction has almost completely stopped since the mid-2000s, which is reflected in the weak presence of public housing in Tokyo and the Core City (3.9 % and 3.5% of the total occupied dwellings in 2018). Furthermore, for the entrepreneurial city, there is little incentive to invite low-income households that are not supposed to contribute to local finance. Hirayama and Izuhara (2018) argue that the new fiscal system would have led local governments to adopt more competition-oriented strategies and to residualize housing measures for low-income households.

Therefore, for low-income households who cannot access public housing, private rental housing is the almost only option left. More than 80% of rental housing in Tokyo and the Core City are provided by private landlords. As demonstrated in Table 10.1, the number of low-cost housings (whose rent prices are under 60,000[9]) and its rate have decreased between 1993 and 2018 in general. Not surprisingly, this trend is more profound in the city center area (Chiyoda, Chuo and Minato) followed by Koto Ward where waterfront redevelopment has been taking place. The ratio of low-cost housing in 2018 is lower

---

8   The GHLC that had been playing a major role in providing housing loans to the middle-class population in Japan was abolished in 2007, whose role is now taken over by private financial institutions. The Housing and Urban Development Corporation, the successor to Japan Housing Corporation that contributed to the construction of affordable housing complexes in suburban areas, was reorganized. The new Urban Renaissance Agency, established in 2004, focuses on the coordination of housing developments by private enterprises rather than on direct provision of affordable housing.

9   It is a matter of debate whether this threshold is appropriate for 'low-cost housing' or not. Nevertheless, this threshold would be reasonable considering that the upper limit of housing aid provided to single-person household through PA system is 53,700 yen in the Core City of Tokyo and that no finer scale of rent price is available in published dataset of the survey.

in the city center and adjacent areas including Bunkyo, Taito, Meguro, and Shibuya compared to those in the outer areas of the Core City (Kita, Itabashi, Katsushika and Adachi). Understandably, decreasing income and increasing rent prices aggravate the burden of housing expenditure of low-income households (Kawata and Hirayama 2016).

For those who cannot access either of public/private rental housing, informal housing including flophouse (*doya*) provides an alternative space of dwelling. 'Doya' is a type of cheap inn that has a relatively long tradition, whose primitive form can be traced back at least to the Edo period. In Japan, the Act on Land and Building Leases (hereafter ALBL) provides strong protection to residents in private/public rental housings.[10] However, although flophouse is not illegal or unregulated as it is covered by Hotel Business Act (1948), its residents do not have any rights the ALBL enacts. In Tokyo, flophouses are now almost exclusively concentrated in San'ya area. Other informal housings include cyber cafes[11] and trunk rooms (Inaba 2009). Neither of them is designed for residential use but they are utilized by the bottom people population as quasi-housing which is not protected by the ALBL. As formal housing has become less affordable, the bottom people population has little option but precarious and unprotected space.

2.2   San'ya, Homeless, and Welfare Systems

While the entrepreneurial urban policies transformed the socio-spatial structure of Tokyo, welfare systems have also been recomposed since the 1990s when the population of homeless in major cities was swollen, which constitutes another context of the difficulties faced by the bottom people.

The presence of San'ya, a former Yoseba area, is an indispensable factor in the dramatic increase of homeless population in Tokyo in the 1990s. San'ya is an approximately 1.65 m² area stretching over Taito and Arakawa Wards, the northeastern part of the Core City (Figure 10.2). After World War II, San'ya

---

10   However, since the enforcement of the Act on Special Measures concerning Promotion of Supply of Good Rental Housings in 2000, 'fixed-term rental contract' has become legalized. While normal rental contract strictly regulates displacement of existing tenants, the new type of contract enables landlords to terminate the contract when the fixed-term (usually 1 month to 12 months) ends. Thus, this new legislation is often used by landlords to avoid legal obligation imposed by the ALBL.

11   A recent survey by Tokyo Metropolitan Government estimates at least around 4000 people are staying cyber cafes having no other stable housing (Tokyo Metropolitan Government 2018). However, the number of homeless population using informal housing is underestimated as this survey does not cover any other similar spaces such as manga cafés, fast food restaurants, trunk rooms.

TABLE 10.1   The number and ratio of low-cost housing in the Core City

	The number of low-cost housing (under 60,000 yen/ month)			The rate of low-cost housing against all rental housing		
	1993	2018	2018–1993	1993	2018	2018–1993
Core City	7,97,590	5,97,700	-1,99,890	45.6	25.6	-19.9
Chiyoda	3,630	2,790	-840	74.4	13.5	-60.9
Chuo	5,680	5,410	-270	45.9	10.6	-35.3
Minato	15,570	8,290	-7,280	51.4	13.3	-38.1
Shinjuku	31,550	22,160	-9,390	44.3	22.8	-21.5
Bunkyo	14,360	8,050	-6,310	39.5	13.0	-26.4
Taito	11,020	7,340	-3,680	39.9	13.9	-26.0
Sumida	20,710	15,580	-5,130	49.2	21.6	-27.6
Koto	42,750	30,760	-11,990	60.3	25.2	-35.2
Shinagawa	30,290	21,230	-9,060	43.5	19.5	-24.0
Meguro	17,940	10,210	-7,730	33.3	15.8	-17.5
Ota	58,330	43,440	-14,890	43.0	24.7	-18.3
Setagaya	75,690	48,520	-27,170	38.5	24.0	-14.5
Shibuya	15,080	9,190	-5,890	35.7	13.7	-22.1
Nakano	32,390	25,750	-6,640	39.6	23.1	-16.5
Suginami	48,230	38,670	-9,560	37.9	25.8	-12.0
Toshima	32,840	18,790	-14,050	45.9	20.6	-25.3
Kita	48,640	31,940	-16,700	59.7	32.6	-27.1
Arakawa	16,030	10,340	-5,690	54.4	24.9	-29.6
Itabashi	54,640	55,030	390	50.0	35.0	-15.0
Nerima	54,780	49,610	-5,170	39.9	29.2	-10.7
Adachi	77,540	55,680	-21,860	61.1	42.2	-18.9
Katsushika	44,410	35,150	-9,260	56.3	42.5	-13.9
Edogawa	45,540	43,800	-1,740	40.1	31.2	-9.0

SOURCE: THE HOUSING AND LAND SURVEY (CALCULATED BY THE AUTHOR)

became one of the major unregulated (day) labor markets ('Yoseba') in Japan into which many intra-national migrants flew.[12] While San'ya provided a massive amount of flexible labor power during the post-war high-growth period, the area and its residents were regarded as 'pathological' by sociologists and the wider public due to the high poverty rate and other 'social problems' including blood selling and alcohol addiction. Thus, San'ya was 'adversely incorporated' (Hickey and Du Toit 2007) into the post-war Japanese society (Nishizawa 1995).

In the 1990s, San'ya lost its function as a day laborer market and many of those laborers became homeless, which is often called the 'dissolution of Yoseba'. What triggered this change was the collapse of the asset bubble in the early-1990s despite the central government's effort to mitigate the devastating impact on the construction industry. In addition, there were several backgrounds including the increasing automation of construction work, the aging of day laborers in San'ya, and change in recruitment routes from face-to-face negotiation to indirect ones using job advertisements and other methods (Okura 2006, Nakamura 1998, and Yamaguchi 2001). As a result, the number of people staying in flophouses in San'ya significantly decreased from approximately 15,000 in 1965 to 3,783 in 2018.[13]

The dissolution of San'ya, combined with large-scale personnel restructuring in other industries, led to the emergence of a huge number of homeless in cities (25,296 people in total and 6,361 people in Tokyo only in 2003[14]), which posed a serious problem for national and metropolitan governments. In response to the problem, national and local governments took various policies and projects,[15] but here we focus on Public Assistance (PA), the general welfare policy that has played a major role in reducing the homeless population. In Japan, the PA was installed just after WWII as a comprehensive safety net for the whole population of Japan including the homeless. The Public Assistance Law enacted that "[t]he state, using local government's welfare offices, has a

---

12   For the detailed history of San'ya, see Iwata (1995) and Imagawa (1987).

13   This number is based on 'Major Statistics of San'ya Area' issued by the Metropolitan Police and the Survey on the Occupants of Flophouses in San'ya reported by the Bureau of Social Welfare and Public Health, Tokyo Metropolitan Government.

14   These numbers are based on visual observation by government officers in daytime and do not include homeless people other than rough sleepers.

15   Alongside the PA system, there are other two important support systems in Tokyo for homeless people. Self-help Support System started in 2001 prior to the establishment of the Act on Special Measures concerning Assistance in Self-Support of Homeless. Another system temporarily installed during 2004 to 2009 is the Transitional Housing Project which is installed by the TMG aiming for 'rationalization' of public space as well as supporting homeless individuals. See Kitagawa (2021) for details of these systems.

duty to provide low-income households with a combination of seven different types of aid mainly on a cash basis (living aid, housing aid, educational aid, medical aid, maternity aid, funeral aid and vocational aid) according to their circumstances" (Iwata 2003: 176). However, in the 1990s when many people became homeless, most of them were refused to take PA even though they met the legal requirements. By the mid-2000s, after a series of intense and complex struggles between activists and local/national governments, PA became open to homeless people as well, which caused a rapid decrease in the number of homeless people.

In the context of this transformation, what is remarkable in Tokyo is the huge presence of low-cost accommodations. Low-cost accommodation is a welfare facility, whose legal ground is on the Social Welfare Act (1951), which is supposed to provide cheap or free accommodation mostly but not exclusive to PA recipients. The number of low-cost accommodations began to increase in the 2000s to absorb the homeless population applied for the PA (Yamada 2016). It must be noted that in addition to low-cost accommodation, unregistered shelters which have no legal basis have been also used to accommodate homeless people. Most of them are managed by private entities such as non-profit organizations and social welfare service corporations while public shelters have been reduced in its number and capacity (Iwata 1995).[16] In this sense, the PA system, particularly in the TMR, has been dependent on private shelters including informal ones.

The dependence of the PA system on low-cost accommodations has been even more deepened recently while access to affordable secure housing has worsened. The standard of housing aid was revised in 2015, according to which, the upper limit of housing aid is divided by the floor space. When your room is smaller than 15 square meters, the housing aid will be reduced by 10% to 30%, which makes it more difficult to find an apartment in the Core City. The rationale for the revision was to eliminate the facilities that do not provide decent housing conditions by cutting housing aid, but, being faced with opposition from facility providers, eventually low-cost accommodation and flophouse are exempted from the revision under certain conditions. Consequently, finding an apartment became more difficult while temporary accommodations were hardly affected.

---

16   After WWII, Tokyo City Government started to accommodate 'tramps' living on streets and parks inside Tokyo. Until the late 1960s the government had tried to increase the number of publicly managed accommodations for 'tramps'. As the accommodation policy ended, the number of those accommodations have been decreasing, which caused the shortage of accommodation facilities when many people became homeless in the 1990s.

In addition to the housing aid level, there is another problem that hinders access to decent housing. Article 30 of the Public Assistance Law enacts the principle that living aid must be provided to recipients in their dwellings, which means that taking PA in shelters and flophouses is exceptional. Due to this principle, welfare office grants the cost of moving into a secure dwelling (in most cases, an apartment). The MHLW notices for welfare offices show a guideline by which the welfare office decides whether they can grant the cost for moving and another standard by which the welfare office judge whether former homeless recipients can make a steady living in an apartment and thus be eligible for the grant. However, as argued below, this guideline often does not effectively work and thus PA recipients are often entrapped in shelters and flophouses.

Thus, on the one hand, in the post-bubble era, the TMR saw a population recovery accompanied by the establishment of a hierarchical structure in terms of occupation and income, which has also caused decreasing affordability of rental housing in Tokyo. On the other hand, at the same time, we have seen the dissolution of San'ya area and an increase in the homeless population in Tokyo, followed by the reconfiguration of the welfare system heavily relying on the existence of private shelters and being unable to deliver decent housing. Together, these changes in the socio-spatial structure of Tokyo and the PA system compose a context of entrapment of the bottom people described in the following sections.

3 Suburbanization of Low-Cost Accommodation and San'ya as an Alternative Place

3.1 Suburbanization of Temporary Shelters

It is undeniable that low-cost accommodations have significantly contributed to the radical reduction in the number of homeless people in Tokyo. However, it is also reported that some, if not all, of those facilities fail to deliver decent housing conditions to the users. Yamada (2016) reports that in some cases PA recipients staying in low-cost accommodations face disadvantages including: low-quality food; lack of decent space enough to secure their privacy; unclear contract without printed document; and little discretion on their expenditure and time management. In addition, at least 22 out of 164 cases of Moyai who used low-cost accommodation reported that they are/were in trouble with shelter personnel and/or other residents.[17] Furthermore, while

---

17   For example, Ms. Harada, in her 40s, told us that the chief personnel in her facility frequently used abusive words to the residents including her, which caused a flashback of

the Public Assistance Law says that the welfare office cannot force applicants to live in accommodation facilities, it is often the case that applicants with no secure housing have little option.[18]

As the precarious conditions in low-cost accommodations have been revealed, the Ministry of Health, Labour and Welfare (MHLW) has embarked on a nationwide survey on the management of low-cost accommodations on a regular basis since 2009, although the details are not publicly available. According to the latest survey, in 2018, 424 out of 570 low-cost accommodations are concentrated in the TMR: 163 in Tokyo; 60 in Saitama; 73 in Chiba; and 128 in Kanagawa (MHLW 2018). Although Tokyo still has a considerable number of accommodations, it is not unusual that those who applied for PA in Tokyo to be transferred to shelters outside Tokyo or even outside the TMR. Besides, it is indicated from the cases of Moyai that staffs of low-cost accommodations located in the outer fringe of TMR regularly come to the city center and surrounding area to bring homeless people to their accommodations and make them apply for PA at the area.

As we can see in Table 10.2, while the number of facility and occupants have been increasing in the TMR, those figures for Tokyo have been decreasing since 2015 where access to affordable housing has been undermined.[19] According to the estimation provided to the Committee on Social Welfare Accommodation and Daily Life Support of Public Assistance Recipients, labor cost and rent account for 32% and 21% of management cost per unit while living cost (foods

---

emotional and psychological abuse she experienced when she was in her parents' home. Mr. Minegishi, a young man in his 20's, was transferred to a different shelter as he was threatened with a knife by his roommate.

18   In response to a growing concern about living conditions of these shelters, national and local governments took off a regulatory measure by creating a guideline for low-costs accommodations. In 2003, the Ministry of Health, Labour and Welfare issued a notice to local governments concerning the guideline for management of low-cost accommodation in terms of its condition of living space and cost, although this notice did not authorize local offices with any coercive measure against those facilities that fail to meet the criteria. To be sure, the Social Welfare Service Act entitles local governments with the authority to conduct administrative guidance including limitation or suspension of business. This point was made clear in the revision of the guideline in 2015.

19   We should consider the possibility that non-registered accommodations have become registered as low-cost accommodation in order to get approved as 'Residential Facility Providing Daily Life Support' (Nitijou-Seikatsu Shien Jukyo Shisetsu) which could receive financial subsidies from the government. However, this system was just installed in 2019 and only a minor proportion of low-cost accommodations have been approved so far, and even if this system has affected the number of facilities in TMR, it cannot explain its decrease in Tokyo.

TABLE 10.2   The number of low-cost accommodations and their occupants in the TMR

		2006	2007	2008	2009	2015	2018
Saitama	Facility	30	31	33	34	53	60
	Occupants	1,642	1,740	1,821	2,006	2,264	2,566
Chiba	Facility	40	45	46	49	53	73
	Occupants	1,952	2,130	2,110	2,351	2,407	3,704
Tokyo	Facility	167	167	169	170	165	163
	Occupants	4,228	4,180	4,367	4,684	4,241	3,991
Kanagawa	Facility	91	93	100	103	131	128
	Occupants	2,804	2,839	2,997	3,096	3,391	3,208

SOURCE: MHLW (2018)

and infrastructures) compose just over 30%.[20] Thus, it is presumed that, from the perspective of facility providers, suppression of labor costs and rent prices would be important for sustainable management, which (at least partially) explains the suburbanization of shelters.

What is remarkable about low-cost accommodations, especially for those located in the suburban part of the TMR, is that those accommodated often face difficulties in getting secure access to medical care and employment opportunity. Mr. Fuji, a man in his 60s, was sleeping on the street in Akihabara close to the city center after he left a shelter in Setagaya Ward because his belongings were robbed in the shelter and had trouble with other residents. He was then picked up by staff from another shelter located in the eastern part of Chiba Prefecture and brought there. Although he is suffering from diabetes, the shelter is distant from his designated hospital[21] so he could not easily get there on his own. Similarly, for those people willing to find or continue their job in Tokyo, being accommodated in suburban shelters robs them of employment opportunities.

---

20   The Committee on Social Welfare Accommodation and Daily Life Support of Public Assistance Recipients (https://www.mhlw.go.jp/stf/shingi2/0000167016_00003.html).

21   PA recipients have to choose their hospital from lists of hospitals registered as "designated medical care providers" based on the Public Assistance Law.

3.2   San'ya as an Alternative Space

It is not only low-cost accommodations that absorb the ex-homeless population. Flophouses, once home to day laborers are now dominated by PA recipients, most of whom are ex-homeless. In 2018, more than 90% of residents
living in flophouses in San'ya are PA recipients and thus the area, once called
'the City of Day Laborers', is now called 'the City of Welfare' (Goto 2013, and
Yuki 2019). A similar trajectory can be observed in other former Yoseba areas
such as Kamagasaki in Osaka and Kotobuki-Cho in Yokohama (Shirahase 2017
and Yamamoto 2010, 2013).

People in homelessness often seek better options than low-cost accommodations, one of which is staying in flophouses in San'ya. It is frequently observed
in cases of Moyai that those experienced shelters want to get into flophouse to
secure individual rooms and to avoid troublesome regulations of shelters. For
example, Mr. Narasaki, a 62-year-old man, once used a temporary shelter in a
suburb of Tokyo but left there because he was harassed and sponged on by his
roommates. After he visited Moyai, he found a flophouse with help from his
friend and successfully applied for PA.

The proximity of San'ya to the city center is also attractive to some people.
Mr. Nishiyama, in his 40s, has been working as a dispatched laborer and living
in cyber cafes. As his income had been decreasing, he decided to take PA but
was not willing to quit his job since he believed that once he quit, it will be
even harder for him to find another job. Although he was not familiar with
San'ya area, he wanted to stay in the flophouse because he knew that he may
not be able to continue his job if he was accommodated in a shelter.

Another distinct feature of San'ya is that flophouses and local supporting
networks are concentrated in the area due to its history as Yoseba. Mr. Toyama,
an interviewee in his 80s was born in Tokyo and grew up in an orphanage
and foster families. He had been working as a day laborer in San'ya for more
than three decades until he lost his job due to an age limit and became homeless. In the mid-2000s, after he was hospitalized due to pancreatitis, an NGO
in San'ya helped him to find a flophouse in San'ya. Another interviewee, Mr.
Okita was born in Tochigi prefecture and has been doing various jobs including Self Defense Forces, automobile manufacturing, and security officer. While
he was living in Adachi Ward, close to San'ya area, he was laid off and fell into
arrearage with his rent.[22] Immediately after that, he received repayment from

---

22   Even though the Act on Land and Building Leases forbid landlords to forcefully evict
      renters unless there is some illicit behavior that seriously damage their credibility such
      as long-term and repeated arrearage, he was kicked out by the guaranteed company for
      one-month delinquency.

a private financial agency to which he had made an overpayment. While he could not rent any apartment due to a lack of joint guarantee, he could find a flophouse in San'ya. Now he is living in an apartment near San'ya area with help from a local supporting group he met in a soup kitchen. These cases indicate that flophouses in San'ya provide an immediate shelter for the homeless and local supporting groups, which are often absent in low-cost accommodations in the suburban area, help them to stabilize and secure their livelihood without being dislocated from their former place of living.

Thus, San'ya area could work as an alternative to low-cost accommodations for people in homelessness, where they can avoid unnecessary troubles, keep their job opportunities, and get support from civil organizations (although this is mostly limited to male homeless since most flophouses do not accept women). The shift from 'the city of day laborers' to 'the city of welfare' is another aspect of the establishment of the current welfare system in Tokyo that heavily depends on low-cost accommodations. As the suburbanization of shelters proceeds, the importance of San'ya for PA applicants in homelessness would also increase.

4   Difficulty in Moving Out: Housing Provision and PA System

4.1   *Unsuccessful Principle of the PA*

This section demonstrates how and why PA recipients are entrapped in temporary accommodations. One of the major reasons why PA recipients in temporary shelters are entrapped is that the welfare offices do not grant the moving cost for unjustifiable reasons. For example, Mr. Deguchi, in his 20s, applied for PA in a ward within the Core City of Tokyo and was accommodated in a shelter in another ward. He repeatedly told his caseworker that he wants to move into an apartment. Nevertheless, the caseworker always said that the grant will not be provided until he found a job during his stay in the shelter, even though the standard issued by the MHLW does not require the recipient to find work beforehand the provision of grant. Mr. Kanai, in his 50s, also takes PA in one of the special wards and has been staying in a shelter for 6 months. As he requested the caseworker to provide the moving grant, he was told that he cannot move into an apartment until he stayed in the shelter for a year, which is not following the guidelines of the MHLW.

Why is this the case? In some cases, welfare officers simply do not understand the guideline provided by the MHLW. In other cases, the excessive burden on welfare officers may make it difficult to immediately respond to recipients' demands. However, Yamada (2016) argues that the lengthening of the stay in temporary shelters may be caused by the welfare office's intention to save their expenditure.[23]

It must be noted that the problem of grant approval can be also found in the cases of PA recipients staying in flophouses. According to *The Survey on Occupants of Lodging Houses in San'ya Area* (TMG 2018), a complete count survey on people staying in flophouses in San'ya conducted every three years by the TMG, of 1,739 valid responses 18.1% claim that they cannot get out of flophouses because "The welfare office has not told me to move". However, the problem seems to be more serious in low-cost accommodations in suburban areas. It is assumed that the continuing suburbanization of temporary shelters would have made it difficult for caseworkers to make the decision on the grant approval correctly and justly. Interestingly, in some cases, the grant request was rejected because shelter personnel told the caseworker that the recipient does not conform to rules decided by the manager, which implies the responsibility of casework is blurred. Although this cannot be immediately generalized, the suburbanization of shelters would lead to the normalization of this case.

4.2   *Detained by the Facility Manager*

PA recipients do not have to take the moving grant from the welfare office as long as they can find jobs and dwellings by themselves. However, the case of Mr. Sakai, one of our interviewees, demonstrates a different problem. He was born in the Kyusyu region and left his home when he was 25 years old for a certain reason. Then he worked as a dispatch worker in some automobile manufacturing factories in Aichi prefecture until he was laid off during the economic recession triggered by the global financial crisis in 2008/2009. It brought him to Tokyo, but he could not find any job or shelter and became homeless. 5 or 6 years before the interview, he was picked up by an NGO staff patrolling around the Shinjuku area and was brought to a low-cost accommodation located in Ibaraki Prefecture, far from Shinjuku, where he stayed for six months. During his stay in the shelter, he could not find any job:

> [Sakai told the interviewer that less than 20,000 yen remained in his hand after paying the accommodation fee but he could earn some by doing assistant to the manager]

---

23   Basically, respective city/ward office is responsible for part of expenditure on PA recipients. But in some prefectures including Tokyo, the cost for PA recipients staying in temporary shelters are supplemented by prefectural office.

SAKAI: I began to feel it annoying, so I kick myself out [from the shelter].

YUKI: Annoying, ... You mean the job or relationships ...

SAKAI: Relationships. And, yes, I didn't want to use it [work of vice-manager] as an excuse for not finding other jobs, though it was him [the manager] who forced it on me.

YUKI: Oh, so you didn't want to do that, but he made you ...

SAKAI: I did it cause he said there's no one he can rely on. But [on the other hand] he told me that I'm using it as an excuse. So, I threw it up.

So, he left the accommodation and came back to Tokyo to find a job and is not willing to take PA again as long as he can work. In the last section, it is implied that the recent suburbanization of shelters may have been an outcome of cutting down the management cost. Letting some residents work as vice-manager can be considered as another tactic to save the expenditure. Thus, PA recipients without secure tenure are, not always but often, detained in temporary shelters by both welfare offices and facility managers under the circumstances of re-urbanization and fiscal pressure.

4.3   Increasing Housing Unaffordability: Exclusionary Displacement and Entrapment

As noted in Section 2 above, the presence of public housing in the TMR is fairly limited and most PA recipients seeking secure dwellings must find one from the private rental market. As briefly noted above, there is a limit on the amount of housing aid of PA, which is 53,700 yen for a single occupant in the Core City. However, in these 25 years, the number and ratio of low-cost housing (under 60,000 yen/month) have been decreasing all over the Core City (see Table. 10.2).

When you applied for PA in a certain municipality, regardless of the location of the shelter or flophouse you are designated, you need to find an apartment in the municipality.[24] For example, Mr. Akagi applied PA in Chiyoda Ward in the city center and was designated for a low-cost accommodation in the outer fringe of Tokyo Metropolis. He must find an apartment in Chiyoda Ward where

---

24   Technically, you can move into apartment whenever you want and can get grant since there is no legal obligation to find apartment in the municipality you are taking PA from. However, at least in Tokyo, you are always asked to do so by your caseworker. This is because of the financial system of PA. When you move from city A to city B, the welfare office of A must consult and negotiate with that of B since the movement of PA recipient also means transferring financial burden to B.

you can find little affordable housing and thus cannot get out of the temporary shelter.[25]

As the number of low-cost housings has been also decreasing in Taito and Arakawa Wards, the same thing can be said for those using flophouses instead of low-cost accommodation. According to TMG (2018) cited above, not a small portion of people in San'ya do not want to stay living there or in flophouses. The survey asks welfare recipients the reason they stay living in flophouses. Over half of the respondents (1,155/1,739) answered that they are satisfied with the current room and 15.2% keep staying because they have attachment to the place. However, 13.7% claimed that they are staying in flophouses because they "cannot find an apartment" even though they want to move.

Moreover, this number could be underestimated since some respondents who were willing to get out might have given up. Mr. Seto, in his 70s, has been living in a flophouse in San'ya for nearly a decade. During the interview, he referred to the survey noted above and told us that he was asked to write down whether he wants to continue living in the flophouse or to live elsewhere, but, for him, "the question is meaningless, cause there's no place I can get in". He came to San'ya because he could not afford a private apartment in the first place.

This is partly due to the poor standard of housing aid in the PA system. Mr. Midorikawa, in his 60s has been staying in a flophouse in San'ya. He found an apartment whose rent is slightly over 60,000 yen/month. Although he was willing to supplement the rest of the rent that exceeds the limit with his living aid, his caseworker insisted that he should find a cheaper apartment, and thus he was entrapped in the flophouse. Thus, increasing rent prices, combined with the low level of housing aid, render them entrapped in temporary shelters.

4.4   *Exclusion from Social Housing and Private Rental Housing Market*

As mentioned, the stock of social housing in Tokyo is fairly limited. Moreover, in Tokyo single-person household is not entitled to apply for social housing except for those over 60 years old or handicapped. According to the Ministry of Land, Infrastructure and Transport,[26] the application rate for social housing in Tokyo in 2014 was 22.8 per room and the rate for rooms designated to single-person households was even higher. It is usually the case that relatively

---

25   In three wards that compose the city center, the limit of the housing aid is often raised up to 69,800 yen. But still, it is quite hard to find apartment in these areas. Less frequently, one can move to other areas in Tokyo despite the convention noted above. While this may be helpful for individual recipients, but it also means that the bottom people (PA recipient in homelessness) are expelled from the city center.

26   https://www.mlit.go.jp/common/001139782.pdf.

available room is located on the fringe of Tokyo, which would not be a realistic option for elderly and handicapped applicants. As gentrification in the Core City and surrounding area proceeds, private rental housing would be less and less affordable, which reinforces the exclusionary displacement of the PA recipients.

Even though one can find decent and affordable housing, there is another problem for PA recipients who wish to leave temporary shelter or flophouse. When you rent an apartment, you will be required to have a joint guarantee or need someone provided as an emergency contact in case you use any guaranteeing company. Either way, it would not be easy for people in poverty and/or homelessness to prepare such a guarantee. To make matters worse, owners and/or estate management companies are often not willing to let low-income people and minorities (homeless, the elderly, handicapped, ethnic minorities, PA recipients and single-parent households, etc.) live in their properties, which make secure housing less accessible for them (Japan Property Management Association 2018). Combined with the rent increase in general, discriminatory practices in the housing market undermine the motility (Flamm and Kaufmann 2004) of the bottom people.

5   Conclusion

Since the 1990s, the socio-spatial restructuring of Tokyo and market-oriented housing provision has reinforced the centripetal class structure which has produced increased housing unaffordability for the urban poor on the one hand. On the other hand, the PA system in Tokyo has been reformed to one that is heavily dependent on low-cost accommodations provided by private entities, which seems to be increasingly suburbanized due to the urban restructuring despite its exemption from housing aid reform in 2015. While San'ya can be an alternative to suburbanizing shelters, the soaring rent prices combined with the low-level housing aid has led to increasing housing unaffordability in the central part of Tokyo, by which homeless and PA recipients are entrapped in indecent housing environments.

While each experience of entrapment might be a short-term phenomenon in one's life story, the current conditions that expel and entrap the urban poor have been formed incrementally since the 1990s or even earlier. Thus, behind the 'bloodless revolution', the capability of the bottom people to choose the space/place of their living has been curtailed. Under the guise of a seemingly 'peaceful' process of gentrification, violence against the bottom people population is already evident, even though it might not be overtly conflictual.

In this chapter, the concept of entrapment as a form of slow violence is elaborated by extending the idea of exclusionary displacement. Although it needs further sophistication, the advantage of using the concept would be that violation of both 'the right to stay put' and 'the right to move out' can be understood in relation to socio-spatial restructuring including but not limited to gentrification. Difficulties faced by those entrapped in temporary shelters in suburban areas and flophouses in Yoseba cannot be detected by formulating the problem of gentrification as mere displacement. By focusing on the problem of entrapment, we can better understand the consequence of gentrification that extend beyond a short-term event such as direct displacement.

At the same time, this chapter has also demonstrated the merit of the concept of the bottom worker by supplementing the arguments by Asakawa and Tsutsumi in this volume. In Chapter 8, Asakawa provides a macro picture of the bottom workers based on population census and other statistics. PA recipients, a major target of this chapter, are usually not in the labor force and are often less visible on official statistics. Thus, the displacement and entrapment of PA recipients described in this chapter supplement the overall distribution of the bottom people population illustrated by Asakawa. Also, the cases in this chapter tell us that such experience cannot be understood by examining urban spatial restructuring alone. Rather, those cases urge us to see the restrictive operation and unreasonable aid level of the PA system. This indicates that to better understand the experiences of a particular group of the bottom people, we need to take relevant social, economic, and policy contexts into account. The comprehensiveness and heterogeneity of the concept of the bottom people encourage us to analyze the complexity of the urban reality and to develop analytical tools that capture the reality.

In Chapter 9, Tsutsumi points out that the 'homelessness issue' in Japan has been usually limited to that of rough sleepers. The PA recipients who appeared in this chapter are mostly the ex-homeless population. More importantly, as the case of Sakai shows, they often drift between different kinds of homelessness (street, shelter, flophouse, bunkhouse, etc.). The comprehensive conception of the bottom people thus drives us to reconsider existing analytical categories and poses questions about their (dis)continuity and mobile nature.

Finally, I would like to note some of the limitations of this study. First, the material used in this study is based on interviews or case files of the urban poor themselves except for some statistical data. To deepen our understanding of the conditions described in this chapter, it would be necessary to collect more information on the management of shelters and flophouses, which is usually invisible and hardly accessible. Second, as the bottom people population has been disregarded in the literature on the urban restructuring of Tokyo, this chapter focused on PA applicants/recipients in homelessness. However, they do not represent the whole population of the poor in Tokyo. In this regard, it should also be noted that the cases cited in the study are mostly male Japanese, which require further study on the gendered and/or racialized experience of displacement/entrapment.

References

Asakawa T (2023) "The Spatial Distribution of Bottom Workers in Tokyo" Aoki H and Ishioka T eds., *The Bottom Worker in East Asia: Compositon and Transformation under Neoliberal Globalization,* Boston: Brill Publisher, pp. 205–229.

Atkinson R (2015) Losing one's place: narratives of neighbourhood change, market injustice and symbolic displacement. *Housing, Theory and Society* 32(4): 373–388.

Boddy M (2007) Designer neighbourhoods: new-build residential development in nonmetropolitan UK cities: the case of Bristol. *Environment and Planning A: Economy and Space* 39(1): 86–105.

Davidson M and Lees L (2005) New-build 'gentrification' and London's riverside renaissance. *Environment and Planning A: Economy and Space* 37(7): 1165–1190.

Davidson M and Lees L (2010) New-build gentrification: its histories, trajectories, and critical geographies. *Population, Space and Place* 16(5): 395–411.

De Verteuil G (2011) Evidence of gentrification-induced displacement among social services in London and Los Angeles. *Urban Studies* 48(8): 1563–1580.

De Verteuil G (2012) Resisting gentrification-induced displacement: advantages and disadvantages to 'staying put' among non-profit social services in London and Los Angeles. *Area* 44(2): 208–216.

Easton S, Lees L, Hubbard P and Tate N. (2020) Measuring and mapping displacement: the problem of quantification in the battle against gentrification. *Urban Studies,* 57(2): 286–306.

Elliott-Cooper A, Hubbard P, and Lees L (2020) Moving beyond Marcuse: gentrification, displacement and the violence of un-homing. *Progress in Human Geography,* 44(3): 492–509.

Flamm M. and Kaufmann V. (2004). Operationalising the concept of motility: a qualitative exploration. *Discussion Paper at 'Mobility and Social Differentiation' of the 32. Kongress der Deutshen Gesellschaft für Soziologie.*

Freeman L and Braconi F (2004) Gentrification and displacement New York City in the 1990s. *Journal of the American Planning Association,* 70(1): 39–52.

Glass R (1964) Introduction: aspects of change. In Centre for Urban Studies (ed.) *London: Aspects of Change.* London: MacKibbon and Kee.

Gonzalez S and Dawson G (2016) Resisting retail gentrification in traditional public markets in London. In: Working Paper Series Contested Cities.

Goto H (2013) *Homuresu joutai karano 'Dakkyaku' ni muketa shien: ningen-kankei, jison-kanjou, 'Ba' no hosyou* [Supporting for 'Escape' from Homelessness: Social Relations, Self Esteem, and Guarantee of Place]. Tokyo: Akashi Syoten.

Hashimoto K (2021) Time difference gentrification as a bloodless revolution: class structure and spatial polarization in the Tokyo Metropolitan Area after the 1980s. *International Journal of Japanese Sociology* 30(1): 23–63.

Hashimoto K and Asakawa T (eds) (2019) *Kakusa-shakai to toshi-kukan: Toukyouken no shakai-chizu 1990–2010* [Unequal Society and Urban Space: Social Map of Tokyo Metropolitan Region 1990–2010]. Tokyo: Kashima Shuppankai.

Hashimoto K and Hirahara Y (2019) Toukyouken ni okeru keizai-kakusa no kukanteki-kouzou to sono hensen [Structure and transformation of economic disparity in Tokyo Metropolitan Region]. In: Hashimoto and Asakawa T (eds) *Kakusa-shakai to toshi-kukan: Toukyouken no shakai-chizu 1990–2010* [Unequal Society and Urban Space: Social Map of Tokyo Metropolitan Region 1990–2010]. Tokyo: Kashima Shuppankai: 111–139.

Hickey S and Toit du A (2007) Adverse incorporation, social exclusion and chronic poverty *CPRC Working Paper* No. 81. Chronic Poverty Research Centre, Institute of Development Policy and Management. Manchester: University of Manchester: 1–31.

Hirayama Y (2020) *'Karizumai' to sengo-Nihon: jiIkkazumai, chintaizumai, kasetsuzu-mai* ['Temporary Residence' and Post-War Japan: Parental Home Dwelling, Rental Housing, Provisional Housing]. Tokyo: Seitosha.

Hirayama Y and Izuhara M (2018) *Housing in post-growth society : Japan on the edge of social transition.* London: Routledge.

Hubbard P (2017) *The Battle for The High Street: Retail Gentrification, Class and Disgust.* London: Macmillan.

Imagawa I (1987) *Gendai-kiminkou:'San'ya' ha ikanisite keisei saretaka* [Thought on Contemporary Abandoned People: How "San'ya" has been Formed]. Tokyo: Tabata Syoten.

Inaba T (2009) *Hauzing Pua: "Sumai no Hinkon" to Mukiau* [The Housing Poor: under-standing housing poverty]. Tokyo: Yamabuki Shoten.

Iwata M (1995) *Sengo-shakai-fukushi no tenkai to daitoshi-teihensou* [Development of Post-War Social Welfare and the Bottom of Metropolitan Tokyo]. Tokyo: Minerva Shobo.

Iwata M (2003) Commonality of social policy on homelessness: beyond the different appearances of Japanese and English policies. *European Journal of Housing Policy* 3(2): 173–191.

Japan Property Management Association (2018) Survey Report on Registration System of Rent Liability Guarantee Companies. In: Kaufmann V, Bergman M and Joye D (2004) Motility: mobility as capital. *International Journal of Urban and Regional Research* 28 (4): 745–756.

Kawata N and Hirayama Y (2016) Housing expenditure, income inequality and poverty in Japan: focusing on the after-housing income approach. *Journal of The Housing Research Foundation (Jusoken)* 42: 215–225.

Kim S (2013) [The role of art in revitalizing Tokyo's inner-city: between gentrification and diversification of local culture]. *The Annals of Japan Association for Urban Sociology* (30): 43–58.

Kimura M (2019) Privatization and protest of commons: on the gentrification and homeless movement in Shibuya. *Space, Society and Geographical Thought* (22): 139–156.

Kitagawa Y (2001) Nojukusya no shudan-keisei to iji no katei: sinjukueki-shuhenbu wo jirei tosite [Processes of formation and maintenance of homeless community: from the case of Shinjuku station area]. *The Liberation of Humankind: A Sociological Review* (15): 54–74.

Kitagawa Y (2021) Homeless policy as a policy for controlling poverty in Tokyo: considering the relationship between welfare measures and punitive measures. *Critical Sociology* 47(1): 91–110.

Kohama F (2017) Gentrification and the spatial polarization in Tokyo: the restructuring of the Kyojima area in Sumida Ward. *Bulletin of the Graduate School of Humanities and Sociology* (33): 15–42.

Lützeler R (2008) Population increase and 'new-build gentrification' in Central Tokyo: *Erdkunde* 62 (4): 287–299.

Machimura T (2021) Gentrification without gentry in a declining global city?: vertical expansion of Tokyo and its urban meaning. *International Journal of Japanese Sociology* 30(1): 6–22.

Marcuse P (1986) Abandonment, gentrification, and displacement: the linkages in New York City. In: Smith N and Williams P (eds) *Gentrification of the City*. Boston: Allen and Unwin 121–152.

Ministry of Health, Labour and Welfare (2018) Muryou-teigaku-shukuhaku-jigyou wo okonau shisetsu no joukyou ni kansuru chousa-kekka nit suite [Report: Survey on the situations of low-cost accommodations].

Nakamura M (1998) Yoseba to hanba no 10 nen: San'ya wo chushin ni [A decade of Yoseba and bunkhouses: with particular focus on San'ya]. *Yoseba* (11): 168–75.

Nishizawa A (1995) Inpei sareta gaibu: toshi-kasou no esunogurafi [Hidden Outside World: ethnography of the urban poor]. Tokyo: Sairyusya.

Nixon R (2011) *Slow Violence and the Environmentalism of the Poor*. New York: Harvard University Press.

Okura Y (2006) *Toshi-Kasou ni okeru shyugyou-kouzou no henyou to 90-nendaini okeru nojuku-seikatsusya no kyuzou* [Transformation of the Employment Structure of the Urban Poor and the Rapid Increase of Homeless Population in the 1990s]. Doctoral thesis. Osaka City University.

Shimomura Y (2016) [Gentrification and the restructuring of urban space]. *The Annals of Japan Association for Urban Sociology* (34): 40–43.

Shimomura Y and Igarashi Y (2017) [Urban problems and discourses of gentrification in the age of bubble economy: why weren't the 'Jiage' phenomena described as 'gentrification'?]. *The Annals of Japan Association for Urban Sociology* (35): 1–4.

Shirahase T (2017) *Hinkon to chiki: Airin chiku kara miru koureika to koritsushi* [Poverty and Region: Ageing and Isolated Death Viewed from Airin-Area]. Tokyo: Chuo Kouron Shinsya.

Slater T (2006) The eviction of critical perspectives from gentrification research. *International Journal of Urban and Regional Research* 30(4): 737–57.

Slater T (2009) Missing Marcuse: on gentrification and displacement. *City* 13(2–3): 292–311.

Takagi K (2016) [Gentrification and the urban policy: a case study of the transformation of the socio-spatial structure of Tokyo Metropolitan Area]. *The Annals of Japan Association for Urban Sociology* (34): 59–73.

Tokyo Metropolitan Government Department of Welfare and Health (2018) San'ya-chiki: shukuhakusya to sono seikatsu [San'ya area: dwellers and their livelihood].

Ueno J (2010) ['Global city' strategies of Tokyo and political reform: how could a developmental state be neoliberalized?] *The Annals of Japan Association for Urban Sociology* (28): 201–217.

Ueno J and Nakano Y (2017) Build-environment and local community in urban core districts of Tokyo. *St. Andrew's University Sociological Review* 51 (1): 73–142.

Yamada S (2016) *Muryou-teigaku-shukuhakusyo no kenkyu: hinkon-bijinesu kara Ssyakai-fukushi-jigyou* [The Study on Low-cost Accommodations: From Poverty Business to Social Welfare Enterprise]. Tokyo: Akashi Syoten.

Yamaguchi K (2001) Toukyou San'ya ni miru housetsu to haijo no kouzou: nojukusya no zouka to yoseba no henyou nituite [Structure of inclusion and exclusion in San'ya, Tokyo: on the increasing homelessness and the transformation of Yoseba]. *The Liberation of Humankind: A Sociological Review* (15): 26–53.

Yamakita T (2006) Comradeship within communities of homeless people. *Japanese Sociological Review* 57(3): 582–99.

Yamamoto K (2010) The changes in the social structure and social activism in the urban underclass area: a case of Yokohama, Japan. *Toshi-Kagaku-Kenkyu* (3): 83–93.

Yamamoto K (2013) Changes and restructuring of social issues of the urban underclass area with increasing welfare needs in Kotobuki, Yokohama. *The Annals of Japan Association for Urban Sociology* (31): 95–110.

Yuki T (2019) San'ya district after the 'dissolution of Yoseba': an attempt to analyse San'ya through the lens of gentrification. *Social Theory and Dynamics* (12): 59–77.

Epilogue

Tomonori Ishioka and Hideo Aoki

This book analyzed bottom workers in East Asia, with particular reference to Japan, where bottom workers are continuously produced through a complex interplay among women's labor, migrant labor, and informal labor. As noted in the Introduction, "bottom worker" is a *sociological* concept. This category does not simply indicate those who are subject to the same severe economic condition of precarity or poverty. It illuminates the nature of the social being produced in concert with institutional arrangements and social processes, including dormitory labor, selective gender, and racial placement in the formal and informal labor market, and forced (im)mobility and mobilization. By examining East Asian societies by means of this concept, the authors in the volume have lifted the veil of "the narrative of class and racial homogeneity" (Gottfried and Fasenfest, 2020: 150), which, as a conventional and misunderstood representation of Japan and East Asian society, has dominated understanding of this region, and we have captured "knowledge born in the struggle" (Santos and Meneses, 2022) in the age of neoliberal globalization.

In this epilogue, we make two arguments. First, we summarize how the study of bottom workers intersects with current sociological debates. We present the junction points related to earlier chapters together with topics such as the cycle of poverty and intersectionality. Second, the analysis in the earlier chapters is reorganized with reference to the three themes of migration policy, uneven development, and transforming the meaning of labor. Bottom workers are not residuals, leftover from East Asian economic development, but are instead emergent in the ongoing process of neoliberal globalization. We also provide a rationale for the book's contributors adopting the research method of intensive ethnography and in-depth interviews.

1 Bottom Worker: Three Issues

1.1 *Bottom Worker*

The key word in this book is the bottom worker. In Chapters 1 and 2 of Part 1, the bottom worker was defined, and we explained the need for the concept of the bottom worker for analyzing contemporary working people. The bottom worker is a concept that captures the increasing impoverishment of those working at the bottom of society under the downward pressure of neoliberal globalization, which has affected most working people: casual workers, self-employed, unemployed, homeless, part of lumpenproletariats, and even economically inactive persons. The bottom worker is also a concept that encompasses the whole of people's lifeworlds and actions, the whole of urban and rural workers, both in the North and the South.

Holding this understanding of the bottom worker, this volume proceeds in two more parts. Part 2, Chapters 3 through 7, offers a series of international comparisons on the nature of the bottom worker in different countries by analyzing the jobs, residences, lives, and lifeworlds of bottom workers in five cities and suburbs in four Asian countries. Through these five case studies, it was revealed that they are suffering from the hierarchically downward pressure caused by neoliberal globalization, and it demonstrated that the bottom worker is a useful concept for analyzing their circumstances. Part 3, Chapters 8 to 10, takes a closer look at homelessness among the bottom workers in Tokyo through a description of where they are located, how homelessness has changed over time, and the persistence of how displacement and entrapment keep bottom workers suffering from slow violence in the face of urban regeneration and development.

Diverse bottom workers appeared in this book: domestic and foreign migrant women, married migrant women, Japanese Brazilians, slum dwellers, fishery workers, the destitute, and the former/present homeless. These chapters analyzed bottom workers' jobs, residences, lives, and lifeworld, the processes in which they became trapped in harsh living conditions, the way they confronted and overcame those conditions, and how they organized their communities. Eight chapters were a collection of stories in which job, residence, poverty, migration, ethnicity, and gender complexity overlapped and intersected. And they suggested many important theoretical ideas and empirical data, providing clues for further theoretical development. This part of the Epilogue supplements three theoretical issues that eight case studies raised: the cycle of poverty, dormitory labor, and intersectionality.

1.2   *Cycle of Poverty*

Poverty underlies all issues that bottom workers face in this book. Downward pressure brings impoverishment to bottom workers. Once impoverished, it is almost impossible for them to escape the trap of poverty. Chapter 4 analyzed the situation of married migrant women who were caught in a circuit of precarious jobs: factory work, informal side jobs, and English teaching (the cycle of bottom jobs). Chapter 7 analyzed the impoverishment of poor fishery workers caught in the debt trap of microcredit (the cycle of debt). Chapter 8 analyzed the spatial structures where diverse destitute are enclosed in Tokyo's peripheral zones (the cycle of bottom space). Chapter 9 analyzed the impoverishment in which people from diverse backgrounds lose jobs and housing and become homeless (the cycle of bottom life). And Chapter 10 analyzed a circuit of exclusion and entrapment in which the formerly homeless move into low-rent housing in the suburbs and return to flophouses in the city center (the cycle of bottom housing). These are stories of people becoming bottom workers, and of people finding it almost impossible to escape the bottom of society. We must not miss these cycles in which the vulnerable are trapped.

In a word, this is a story of the cycle of poverty or poverty trap. Cycles of the bottom of jobs, debt, life, and housing are reduced to the cycle of poverty. Downward pressure has driven the vulnerable to the bottom of society. Moreover, capitalist society has a closed structure that keeps them at the bottom of society. According to the surveys of homeless' life histories in Japan, most homeless were born into poor families, itinerated through the bottom jobs, and became street dwellers. They did not know the world outside the bottom. Those born into poor families are unable to receive an adequate education. Those who cannot receive enough education cannot get decent jobs. Those who cannot get decent jobs cannot earn a good income. Those who cannot earn a good income are forced to live in poverty. Thus, poverty is reproduced and cycled. Downward pressure has trapped more and more people into the cycle of poverty, making it harder for more and more for people to escape it. Countless reserves are waiting behind them.

The study of the cycle of poverty has a long history. In the United States, starting with Lewis's culture of poverty (Lewis, 1959; 1965), there has been a debate over whether poverty is caused by insufficient social opportunities such as unemployment (Gans, 1982; Wilson, 1987; Goode and Eames, 1996) or the culture of poverty due to insufficient education (Moynihan, 1965), of personal failures. And the causes of the cycle of poverty have been explained in two aspects. First is situational poverty which means the cumulative effect of various social factors (job, education, family income, etc.) on poverty (Tsumaki, 2012). Poverty is repeatedly reproduced in the lives of people. Second is generational poverty which means the historical effect of the economic and social structure in which poverty is embedded. Poverty is transmitted from one generation to the next. These are the self-reinforcing mechanisms that reproduce poverty and its status. In other words, social power drives the vulnerable to the bottom of society and keeps them there for their lives intergenerationally.

1.3   *Dormitory Labor*

Bottom workers, especially migrant workers, often live in workplaces and houses or facilities provided by employers: dormitory labor. This working style is convenient for itinerant and migrant workers who cannot easily find houses. However, they lose their houses when being laid off from their jobs. And dormitory labor causes long working hours and whole-day-management of workers by employers. Chapter 3 analyzed the dormitory labor of domestic and foreign migrant women working at the hotel which caused long working hours with virtually no clear distinction between work and out-of-work. In this case, employees work during the contractual period of work, and when the contract expires, they have to return to their hometowns and countries. Japanese Brazilians in Chapter 5 lost their houses provided by companies after being laid off from their jobs but moved into public housing arranged by the local government. This is a lucky case. Because, if they cannot find the next jobs and houses, they have to return to their home country or may be pushed out onto the streets. Chapter 9 includes many Japanese who followed such a course.

Dormitory labor is not only housing for migrant workers as a tool of workers' management by employers (Campbell, 2016; Ngai, 2007; Ngai and Chan, 2013), but also has a historical background of family-oriented labor management in East Asia. In Japan, for example, there have been three types of dormitory labor: 1) sumikomi (live-in) where a single person or a couple lives in a room at a workplace. This is more like a temporary shelter for people with urgent problems—perhaps when someone is living on the second floor of the employer's house as in the case of a pinball parlor. 2) hanba (bunkhouse), where all single male workers are housed in bunkhouses in the cities or construction sites (Watanabe, 2017). Many are prefabricated houses. There are two types of bunkhouses: the first type in which the recruitment agencies rent rooms or build houses from which they dispatch workers to the workplaces, and the second type in which the employers themselves build bunkhouses and move workers there. In the former case, bunkhouses are located in the city and are managed by the agencies. In the latter case, bunkhouses are built on spatially isolated workplaces and managed by employers. 3) ryō or shataku (company's room and house), where employees live in rooms or houses that companies or recruitment agencies rent or build from which workers commute to the workplaces. This sometimes involves large companies building many houses, in which case the whole of the housing complex and the employees' families are managed by the employers.

There is a long history of dormitory labor in Japan. Typically coal miners worked in mines living in bunkhouses near mines in slave-like conditions in the primitive accumulation period of Japanese capitalism of the Meiji era. On the other hand, Japanese companies have managed workers in a family-oriented way in which workers and their families have been housed, and the whole families have been managed by companies. It has been part of the corporate welfare of workers, which, together with lifetime employment, ena-bled employers to increase workers' loyalty to the companies. The dormitory labor of migrant workers is the extension of historical family-oriented worker management in Japan, as in the case of Toyota, which created Toyota City, where many workers employed by Toyota live, and also in other East Asia countries, where family-oriented employment practice has been strong.

1.4   *Intersectionality*

Bottom workers are those who work in precarious jobs but comprise a diverse group of people bracketed by categories such as gender, ethnicity, nationality, etc. Bottom workers are usually subjected to multiple categories that give rise to serious disadvantages in society. In Chapter 3, Yamaguchi analyzed people who work in precarious jobs influenced by gender and ethnicity (and age), tar-geting Japanese and foreign women working in Japanese hotels. In Chapter 4, Kim and Koo analyzed Filipino women who migrated to Korea by marriage, and who work in precarious jobs influenced by gender and ethnicity (and nationality). Both emphasized the need to take the viewpoint of intersection-ality, which explains the structure that gender and ethnicity drive people into precarious work. How, then, do gender and ethnicity influence each other and drive those people into the trap of precarious work?

There are many studies of the seriously disadvantaged (bottom work-ers), which use the word intersectionality (Kimberlé, 1989; Collins, 2019). "Intersectionality as an analytic tool gives people better access to the com-plexity of the world and themselves." (Collins and Bilge, 2016: 2). However, not many studies have fully explained the mutual intersection between those factors. Yet, 'Intersecting' multiple factors that cause serious disadvantages to bottom people is not the same as 'overlapping' multiple factors. Most studies, while using the word intersectionality, only describe that multiple factors over-lap and cause serious disadvantages for people.

The interest of intersectionality is the interrelatedness of social categories. Let us take an example from Chapter 4, of gender and ethnicity. There are three points for understanding intersectionality. First, a category (Filipinos) is embed-ded in an interwoven political situation with other categories (for example, women). Each category does not exist independently or in a closed form, but with other categories. A minority's disadvantage always occurs in a set category i.e., "an amalgamation of multiple categories" (Kumamoto, 2020: 388). 'Filipino women' is a social category. They face the unique disadvantage different from Korean women and Filipino men in the Korean labor market. Second, the sit-uation continually reorganizes the relationship between multiple categories. Filipino women's wage is less than Korean women's in terms of ethnicity. At this time, Filipino women are 'Filipino – women.' And Filipino women's wage is less than Filipino men's in terms of gender. At this time, Filipino women are 'female –- Filipinos.' Third, by identifying the disadvantage of minorities as a set category (Filipino women), we can subjectivize those who have marginal status in both ethnicities (Korean and Filipino) and gender (men and women) and give them a voice to problematize and prosecute their unique disadvantage. Sharing one category ('Filipino' or 'women') does not mean sharing disadvantages with a set category (Filipino women). Thus, intersectionality is a critical social theory that reveals the unique disadvantages faced by groups marginalized from main categories (ethnicity, gender, etc.).

2   Clarification of the Chapters' Discussions

First, we described the connection between the concept of the bottom worker and existing sociological accounts. We turn now to a systematic explanation of the contents of each chapter of this book. We consider the chapters along the following three dimensions: migration policy and the production of the bottom people, uneven development, and transforming the meaning of labor and production. Finally, we provide a rationale for the book's contributors adopting the research method of intensive ethnography and in-depth interviews.

2.1   *Migration Policy and the Production of Bottom Workers*
Chapter 5 examined the intergenerational disadvantages of Japanese Latin Americans. In intergenerational exploitation in certain categories, neoliberal globalization produces those who are "stuck in bottom work" (Chapter 4), where they are restricted in their chances to upward social mobility. This is an ambiguous process. In a special issue of *Critical Sociology* on Japanese capitalism, Ogaya (2020) argued that children born to a Japanese and Filipina couple are "born out of place" (Ogaya, 2020: 59). Japan's strict immigration control policy officially bars unskilled migrant workers. Filipino women living in Japan on an entertainment visa, engaging in night work, who then marry Japanese men, constitute a stigmatized category of immigrants, not the skilled professionals sought by the Japanese government. Here, it is critical that, in reality, a large influx of migrant workers is engaged in menial labor in Japan. This extends beyond the South Americans of Japanese descent that are described in Chapter 5 to the Vietnamese and Chinese people who have been arriving in Japan under the technical internship system (Yoshida, 2020), behaving as migrant workers engaged in menial labor. The intergenerational exploitation of this population can easily reproduce bottom workers. This group is not

regarded as workers but as interns or Nikkei people, occupying a particular stigmatized category. This raises the following question: *How is denying that Japan is hosting migrant workers engaged in menial labor linked to the actual production of bottom workers?*

The official narrative that migrant workers in Japan are all highly specialized workers simultaneously assigns to an immigrant engaging in menial labor an illegitimate status. These workers are officially denied as social beings and are thus open to exploitation across generations. Chapter 4 describes the similar system of marriage migration in South Korea. In labor markets in East Asia, including both Japan and South Korea, bottom workers are racialized, and menial workers from countries like the Philippines and Vietnam are effectively set at the bottom of society, at the same time as they are officially denied recognition as workers. This discrepancy and the contradiction between the symbolic denial and the actual existence of migrant menial workers operate as a mechanism that produces bottom workers.

Immigration policy forms also a vital point of reference in domestic labor migration. As indicated in Chapter 3 regarding hotel labor, Japan's rapid economic growth in the twentieth century has mobilized migrants from rural areas to metropolitan areas to perform cheap labor. However, a system is currently in place to mobilize workers from further abroad than the domestic periphery, although it is officially denied, which calls for clarification.

2.2 Uneven Development and the Production of Bottom Workers

Chapter 8 presented the spatial arrangement of bottom workers in Tokyo, and Chapter 10 analyzed elderly welfare recipients and former day laborers who have become trapped in Tokyo's inner city. The spatial arrangement of bottom workers is a crucial research topic. This, along with the ongoing financialization has created concentrations of poverty not only in the inner city but also in peripheral zones. Seen through Ananya Roy's famous concept of the *territory of poverty*, financialization leads to soaring land prices in urban centers in a social process known as gentrification (Roy and Crane, 2015). In this way, bottom workers become relegated to the suburbs and to the urban-rural fringes. The suburbanization of poverty (Roy and Crane, 2015: 1) is associated with the fact that the suburbs, known as *desakota*, have become the frontline of research in Southeast Asian urban studies (McGee, 1991). This book critically shows that the concept of suburbanization of poverty coincides with the production of bottom workers, who are entrapped in the inner city. The survey presented in Chapter 8 indicates how Tokyo does not take on a complete or monolithic form but rather continues to exist while maintaining uneven development within the larger metropolis.

Further, as argued in Chapter 5, studies of bottom workers have generally examined metropolises (Sassen, 1991), but in reality, bottom workers reside in deindustrialized and declining industrial cities as well. Chapter 5 describes how the "formation of such relationships occurs in regional cities where the manufacturing industries are concentrated, rather than in metropolitan areas where the financial sectors that have shown growth under globalization are located." While studies of bottom workers have hitherto centered on metropolises, post-industrial regional cities located outside of these mega-cities are where new bottom worker pools are being formed.

The focus of this book on post-industrial regional cities is linked to two other aspects that recently have become more apparent in Japanese migration studies. First, the migrant so-called trainees who have been appearing in labor-intensive industries are concentrated in regional cities. Yoshida reports (Yoshida, 2020) all assaults on employers by Chinese technical interns have been seen in regional cities, like Hiroshima, Chiba, and Kumamoto. In Japan's regional cities, in labor-intensive industries, such as the seafood-processing industry, interns do much of the work. While the metropolises are being restructured through financial capital, the traditionally labor-intensive sectors of regional cities have been restructured as new concentration zones for bottom workers, especially at sites of microenterprise *rondos*, which are subcontractors and sub-subcontractors for larger industries. Most microenterprises employ dormitory labor. Second, care workers who tend to enter Japan as migrant workers from countries like the Philippines and Indonesia, are often dispatched to regional cities. Unlike in the metropolises, the aging populations of the regional cities are more serious, making it impossible to obtain labor from young people in the cities for caregiving tasks. The small number of native caregivers explains why migrant caregivers are sent to rural care homes.

These points demonstrate the following argument. Post-industrial regional cities and metropolises reflect *uneven development* and its consequences. Economic transformation instantiates different conditions while producing bottom workers and problems of reproduction in regional cities and larger metropolises.

2.3   Transforming the Meaning of Labor and Production of the Bottom Worker

Chapter 3 critically examines the integration of attitudes toward hospitality into labor. This point relates to what Hochschild (1983) referred to as emotional labor. More importantly, the connection between hospitality and emotional labor is becoming ubiquitous in the work situation of the bottom worker, which, taking dormitory labor into account, not only operates in the workplace but also in the dormitory.

To commodify the labor power is to sell workers' time, say 8 hours a day, to capitalists. Hence, in traditional factory labor, a worker works on the assembly line for the time that the worker has sold and is then paid for it. Workers are expected to be obedient laborers, but labor measured in hours is bought by capitalists. Emotions like hospitality and docility are indeed considered a form of labor, but they are not overtly acknowledged or compensated accordingly.

Today's bottom workers, however, have been subjected to all-encompassing emotional labor. Yoshida describes this emotional labor of technical interns, attributing it to a sense of ingratitude in Japanese culture (Yoshida, 2020). This discussion argument needs to be reframed not as a theory of the uniqueness of Japanese culture but as a theory of capitalism in the neo-liberalization of workplaces. As dormitory labor becomes restructured, bottom workers are expected to work flexibly in their free time, outside of their working hours, in response to their employers' requirements, and to carry this out generously and in a hospitable manner, without reluctance. In hotel work, for example, workers' labor is not sold to the employer for given working hours as occurs with the assembly line. Workers instead leave their entire time flexibly up to the capitalist; namely, they are selling their routine time availability as a commodity. The worker may need to work at night, in the morning, even while asleep, if the customer demands something from them. The boundary between work and free time is vanishing, with more of the worker's time being controlled by their capitalist employer. This commodification of routine life is the actual point of dormitory labor.

Moreover, bottom workers cannot easily escape, as they work and live together and, if they leave their jobs, they also lose their housing. Because in these situations, capitalists control houses and households, workers are subject to engage in 24-hour emotional labor for their customers and their capitalist bosses. Bottom workers do not sell their working hours but *all of their time* as a commodity. This point is a crucial issue to consider regarding the downgraded quality in terms of the crisis of the workers' means of existence, such as domicile.

This sale of emotional labor is closely related to the interpretive labor outlined in Chapter 1. Both frequently appear in care work (Chapter 3) and bottom work (Chapters 5 and 7), which are two sources of hospitality work. The difference between the two is that interpretative labor requires the worker to take anticipatory action; the bottom worker always looks to the boss to anticipate what will happen and must observe the situation to avoid violence. The boss in the bottom labor workplace could use violence against workers, such as yelling, hitting, and firing them if he does not like something about them. He does not need to interpret what the worker feels or thinks. Violence is an easy way to resolve undesirable situations for him. That is why the worker takes excellent care through anticipatory interpretive labor to ensure that violence is not exercised against him. The constant anticipation and observation is the key to interpretive labor, which results in workers becoming exhausted and eroded by slow violence (Chapter 10). To "interpret" (Geertz, 1973) a culture or situation is not the privileged act of the researcher; the bottom worker must also interpret his or her surroundings to survive.

2.4   Why Ethnography?

Meanwhile, interpretative labor is linked to the kernel of the method of ethnography, a research style emphasized by the sociologists at ISTAD. As discussed in Chapter 1, most interpretive labor is connected to behaviors of self-effacement. This means that when describing a scene, it must be reconstructed by the ethnographer in a way that makes perceptible those who tend to self-efface. This entails an approach that focuses not on those who occupy the center of the scene, but those who hide from that center. Those who tend to self-efface are the same as those who pay attention to what the majority see but do not notice. This explains why ethnography values the perspective of the excluded. Those who self-efface and move into the margins also, through their interpretive labor, train themselves to be aware of their situation. Ethnographers need to emulate the perspective of these people.

Bottom workers are forced to consider things that the majority does not need to think about. Their interpretive labor is thus an offshoot of critical sociological thinking. ISTAD focuses on bottom workers because the interpretive labor that they practice provides a strategic basis for research that highlights the power structure deeply embedded in our everyday lives. For members of ISTAD, like us, bottom workers are therefore not merely objects of social salvation but are vehicles for the forging of critical sociological reasoning. The lifeworlds of bottom workers are a source for critical theory.

In short, ISTAD focuses on bottom workers for two reasons. First, they are the most vulnerable category of people, and they are the soonest to be harmed in a crisis. Nevertheless, and second, they can serve to shed light on the dominant doxa. The study on bottom workers provides a starting point for reflecting the modern world radically.

References

Campbell S (2016) Everyday recomposition: precarity and socialization in Thailand's migrant workforce. *American Ethnologist* 43(2): 258–269.

Collins P and Bilge S (2016) *Intersectionality.* Cambridge: Polity Press.

Collins P and Bilge S (2019) *Intersectionality as Critical Social Theory.* Durham, NC: Duke University Press.

Gans H G (1982) *The Urban Villagers: Group and Class in the Life of Italian-Americans.* New York City: Free Press of Glencoe.

Geertz C (1973) *The Interpretation of Cultures.* New York: Basic Books.

Goode J and Eames E (1996) *An Anthropological Critique of the Culture of Poverty.* In: Gmelch G and Zennerm W (eds) *Urban Life,* Long Grove: Waveland Press.

Gottfried H and Fasenfest D (2020) Understanding the trajectory of Japanese capitalism, *Critical Sociology* 47(1): 149–161

Hochschild A (1983) *The Managed Heart: Commercialization of Human Feeling.* Oakland, CA: University of California Press.

Kimberlé C (1989) Demarginalizing the intersection of race and sex: a Black feminist critique of antidiscrimination doctrine, feminist theory and antiracist politics. Chicago, IL: University of Chicago Legal Forum 140: 139–168.

Kumamoto R (2020) A Study on Formation of Subjectivity of Discriminated Buraku Women [Hisabetuburaku zhosei no Shutaisei Keisei ni kansuru Kenkyü], Osaka: Kaihō Shuppansha.

Lewis O (1959). *Five Families: Mexican Case Studies in the Culture of Poverty.* New York: Basic Books.

Lewis O (1965) *La Vida: A Puerto Rican Family in the Culture of Poverty,* New York: Random House.

McGee T G (1991) The emergence of Desakota regions in Asia: expanding a hypothesis. In: Ginsburg N, Koppel B and McGee T G (eds) *The Extended Metropolis: Settlement Transition in Asia.* Honolulu, HI: University of Hawaii Press: 3–26.

Moynihan D (1965) *The Negro Family: The Case for National Action,* Washington, D.C., Office of Policy Planning and Research, US Department of Labor.

Ngai P (2007) Gendering the dormitory labor system: production, reproduction, and migrant labor in South China, *Feminist Economics* 13(3 4): 239–258.

Ngai P and Chan J (2013) The spatial politics of labor in China: life, labor, and a new generation of migrant workers, *South Atlantic Quarterly* 112(1): 179–190.

Ogaya C (2020) Intergenerational exploitation of Filipino women and their Japanese Filipino children: "born out of place" babies as new cheap labor in Japan. *Critical Sociology* 47(1): 59–71.

Roy A and Crane E S (2015) *Territories of Poverty: Rethinking North and South.* Athens, GA: University of Georgia Press.

Santos B d S and Meneses M P (2022) *Knowledge Born in the Struggle*. New York, NY: Routledge.

Sassen S (1991) *The Global City: New York, London. Tokyo*. Princeton, NJ: Princeton University Press.

Tsumaki S (2012) "Regional manifestations of poverty and social exclusion" [Hinkon to shakaiteki haijo no tiikiteki kengen]. *Japanese Sociological Review* 62(4): 489–503.

Watanabe T (2017) *To the Bunkhouse: Momorize Life and Work* [*Hanba* he: kurashi to shigoto wo kiorokusuru]. Kyoto: Rakuhoku Syuppan.

Wilson J (1987). *The Truly Disadvantaged: The Inner City, the Underclass, and Public Policy*. Chicago, IL: University of Chicago Press.

Yoshida M (2020) The indebted and silent worker: paternalistic labor management in foreign labor policy in Japan. *Critical Sociology* 47(1): 73–89.

Index

www.ingramcontent.com/pod-product-compliance
Lightning Source LLC
Chambersburg PA
CBHW070056030426
42335CB00016B/1908